WE THE PEOPLE

1

FOUNDATIONS

WE THE PEOPLE

1

FOUNDATIONS

Bruce Ackerman

THE BELKNAP PRESS OF
HARVARD UNIVERSITY PRESS
CAMBRIDGE, MASSACHUSETTS
LONDON, ENGLAND · 1991

This book is printed on acid-free paper, and its binding materials
have been chosen for strength and durability.

Designed by Marianne Perlak and typeset in Simoncini Garamond.

Library of Congress cataloging information is on page 370.

For Sybil and John —
and their world

Contents

Acknowledgments

We the People has been my principal preoccupation during the 1980's. Looking back, I am most conscious of the many friends who have shared it with me. I split the decade between two schools, Columbia and Yale. At both, I was very lucky to find people whose understanding and support meant—and mean—so much. At Columbia: Vince Blasi, Meir Dan-Cohen, George Fletcher, Eric Foner, Charles Larmore, Henry Monaghan, Subha Narasimhan, Tom Pogge, Andrzej Rapaczynski. At Yale: Akhil Amar, Bo Burt, Guido Calabresi, Mirjan Damaska, Owen Fiss, Paul Kahn, Tony Kronman, Jerry Mashaw, David Mayhew, Rogers Smith. I have also profited greatly from ongoing discussions with my friends in the Society for Ethical and Legal Philosophy. At a greater distance, Jim Fishkin and Cass Sunstein provided me with immensely useful commentaries on the manuscript.

Institutions have also helped. Dean Guido Calabresi at Yale and my deans at Columbia—Al Rosenthal, Benno Schmidt, Barbara Black—were unstinting in their support. Most important, they encouraged me to design somewhat unorthodox courses to test the themes developed here. The skepticisms and enthusiasms of my students at Columbia and Yale have made countless marks upon the final outcome. The two law schools also generously provided me with research leaves, to which the Guggenheim Foundation added a Fellowship in 1985–86.

I have, throughout these years, steadfastly tried to reserve every morning for uninterrupted reading and writing. I could not have succeeded without the constant aid of the people who served as my administrative assistants: Yvonne Tenney, Mary Nuñez, Theresa Cerillo, and Joan Paquette. Without their thoughtful help on countless matters of daily academic life, this book would never have been written. Many thanks to Gene Coakley, of the Yale Law Library, whose research assistance has been a priceless aid to me and many other members of the Yale faculty; thanks too to Andrew Coppel, who helped me out with the footnotes to Chapters 2 through 5 during the summer of 1990.

Finally, there is my wife, Susan. She has, for a quarter-century now, been my best friend. Her intellectual contribution is even more evident to me here than in my previous work. Quite simply, I would not have hit upon the central ideas presented in this book without the spur of my constant conversations with her.

Chapter 1 and parts of Chapters 4 and 6 derive from my essay "Constitutional Politics/Constitutional Law," 99 *Yale Law Journal* 453 (1989); parts of Chapters 7 and 9 derive from "The Storrs Lectures: Discovering the Constitution," 93 *Yale Law Journal* 1013 (1984). Passages which have been unchanged are reprinted here by permission of the Yale Law Journal and Fred B. Rothman & Co.

I also wish to note Professor Forrest McDonald's fine book, *We the People: The Economic Origins of the Constitution* (1958). I paused over the question whether another book with the same title would cause undue confusion. My conclusion: this title is special; it is enough for different authors from different generations to use different subtitles.

PART ONE

Discovering the Constitution

Dualist Democracy

LOOKING INWARD?

A MERICA is a world power, but does it have the strength to understand itself? Is it content, even now, to remain an intellectual colony, borrowing European categories to decode the meaning of its national identity?

This was not always a question posed by the American Constitution. When America was a military and economic weakling on the European fringe, it was at the forefront of constitutional thought; as it transformed itself into the powerhouse of the West, its leading constitutionalists became increasingly derivative. Two centuries onward, the study of the American Constitution is dominated by categories that owe more to European than to American experience.

The result has been a peculiarly ahistorical kind of understanding. Because dominant theories have not been designed with American constitutional history in mind, they do not reveal its most distinctive features. Many of the most remarkable parts of the story are entirely ignored—since they would only embarrass European notions never designed to take them into account.

To discover the Constitution, we must approach it without the assistance of guides imported from another time and place. Neither Aristotle nor Cicero, Montesquieu nor Locke, Harrington nor Hume, Kant nor Weber will provide the key. Americans have borrowed much from such thinkers, but they have also built a genuinely distinctive pattern of constitutional thought and practice. Once we have reconstructed this pattern, we shall find that it bears comparison with the deepest reflections on the nature of politics offered up by the Greeks or Romans, Germans or English.

My interest in this reconstructive enterprise is not purely intellectual. The Constitution presupposes a citizenry with a sound grasp of the distinctive ideals that inspire its political practice. As we lose sight of these ideals, the organizing patterns of our political life unravel. If "sophisticated" constitutionalists blind themselves to the distinctively American aspects of the American Constitution, this must be a cause for more general concern. Of course, most people don't require lots of instruction before the basic rhythms of American constitutional life become part of second nature—the two-, four-, six-year electoral cycles, the distinctive interchanges between Congress and President, President and Court, Court and Congress, nation and state, politics and law. Along with these rhythms come a rough-and-ready grasp of the animating constitutional ideals of American democracy.

Nonetheless, the intellectual alienation of opinion leaders takes its toll. Sophisticated talk gets around that political practices having a deep constitutional point are "really" mystifying rituals that distort the character of American politics. Generations of such talk help loosen the popular grasp on the democratic ideals animating our constitutional life, increasing the vulnerability of these ideals during future moments of crisis.

The costs of intellectual alienation are even more evident when we turn to the caste of American lawyers and judges who sustain the Constitution's operation on a day-to-day basis. As we shall see, these men and women have done a better job than academics have in keeping faith with the distinctive principles of American democracy. Nonetheless, they have been unable to escape the predictable consequences of the Europeanization of constitutional theory. Although practitioners are certainly as smart as scholars, they lack one precious resource: time—time to think beyond the particular case at hand and consider the patterns of constitutional law that emerge over decades and generations. Without giving the matter much thought, they have built something I will call a professional narrative, a story describing how the American people got from the Founding in 1787 to the Bicentennial of yesterday. This narrative colors the constitutional meanings lawyers and judges give to the particular problems presented to them for decision. It contains, moreover, insights that purveyors of constitutional sophistication would do well to ponder. Precisely because this pondering hasn't been going on, the existing professional narrative expresses these insights in ways that fail to capture their historical reality or constitutional complexity. If, however, constitutional theorists turned their attention from Locke to Lincoln, from Rousseau to Roosevelt, they might contribute positively to the construction of a better professional narrative—one that is truer to the historical facts and to the constitutional ideals that animate our ongoing experiment in self-government.

Behold, then, a pretty picture: an America in which a rediscovered Constitution is the subject of an ongoing dialogue amongst scholars, professionals, and the people at large; an America in which this dialogue between theory and practice allows the citizenry, and its political representatives, a deepening sense of its historical identity as it faces the transforming challenges of the future. Lest I be mistaken too quickly for Pangloss, let me say that, even if this project succeeded beyond my wildest hopes, it does not lead straightaway to Utopia. As we discover the distinctive features of the Constitution, we will find much that is imperfect, mistaken, evil in its basic premises and historical development. Never forget that James Madison was a slaveholder as well as a great political thinker. And who can imagine that our Constitution's peaceful coexistence with injustice came to an end with Emancipation? We cannot remain comfortable with the status quo; the challenge is to build a constitutional order that is more just and free than the one we inherited.

But we cannot build a better future by cutting ourselves off from the past, especially when Americans routinely treat the constitutional past as if it contained valuable clues for decoding the meaning of our political present. My aim here will be to persuade you that our present patterns of constitutional talk and practice have a deeper order than one might suppose, an order that is best rediscovered by reflecting on the course of its historical development over the past two centuries.

Before plunging into this complex history, it will be best to clear away some underbrush. If I am right, the present moment is characterized by a remarkable breach between constitutional theory and constitutional practice. While our civic practice remains rooted in the distinctive patterns of the American past, sophisticated constitutional thought has increasingly elaborated the genius of American institutions with theories fabricated elsewhere—to the point where these rivals are more familiar than the framework I shall be developing. It seems wise, then, to begin by comparing these familiar academic competitors to a model that is better designed to capture the distinctive spirit of the American Constitution. I shall call this the model of *dualist democracy*.

THE BASIC IDEA

Above all else, a dualist Constitution seeks to distinguish between two different decisions that may be made in a democracy. The first is a decision by the American people; the second, by their government.

Decisions by the People occur rarely, and under special constitutional conditions. Before gaining the authority to make supreme law in the name of the People, a movement's political partisans must, first, convince an extraordinary number of their fellow citizens to take their proposed initiative with a seriousness that they do not normally accord to politics; second, they must allow their opponents a fair opportunity to organize their own forces; third, they must convince a majority of their fellow Americans to support their initiative as its merits are discussed, time and again, in the deliberative fora provided for "higher lawmaking." It is only then that a political movement earns the enhanced legitimacy the dualist Constitution accords to decisions made by the People.

Decisions made by the government occur daily, and also under special conditions. Most importantly, key officials must be held accountable regularly at the ballot box. In addition, they must be given incentives to take a broad view of the public interest without the undue influence of narrow interest groups. Even when this system of "normal lawmaking" is operating well, however, the dualist Constitution prevents elected politicians from exaggerating their authority. They are not to assert that a normal electoral victory has given them a mandate to enact an ordinary statute that overturns the considered judgments previously reached by the People. If they wish to claim this higher form of democratic legitimacy, they must take to the specially onerous obstacle course provided by a dualist Constitution for purposes of higher lawmaking. Only if they succeed in mobilizing their fellow citizens and gaining their repeated support in response to their opponents' counterattacks may they finally earn the authority to proclaim that *the People* have changed their mind and have given their government new marching orders.

Such a brief statement raises many more questions than answers. One set involves issues of institutional design. First, we must consider the design of a good higher lawmaking system: How to organize a process that will reliably mark out the rare occasions when a political movement rightly earns the special recognition accorded the outcomes of mobilized deliberation made in the name of We the People? Second, there is the question of normal lawmaking: How to create incentives for regularly elected officials to engage in public-spirited deliberation despite the pressures of special interests? Third, there is the design of preservation mechanisms: How to preserve the considered judgments of the mobilized People from illegitimate erosion by the statutory decisions of normal government?

And then there are the ultimate issues that transcend institutional mechanics: Is dualist democracy a good form of government for America? The best? If not, what's better?

This chapter does not aim for final answers. It simply describes how the very questions provoked by dualist democracy suggest inquiries different from those now dominant in the academy. Although each academic competitor differs from dualism in a different way, it may help to begin with the one thing they have in common. For all their luxuriant variety, they ignore the special importance dualists place upon *constitutional politics:* the series of political movements that have, from the Founding onward, called upon their fellow Americans to engage in acts of citizenship that, when successful, culminates in the proclamation of higher law in the name of We the People.

But let me be more specific.

MONISTIC DEMOCRACY

Of the modern schools, the monistic democrats have the most impressive pedigree: Woodrow Wilson,[1] James Thayer,[2] Charles Beard,[3] Oliver Wendell Holmes,[4] Robert Jackson,[5] Alexander Bickel,[6] John Ely.[7] These, and many other distinguished thinkers and doers, have made monism dominant amongst serious constitutionalists over the course of the last century. As with all received opinions, complexities abound.[8] But, at its root, monism is very simple: Democracy requires the grant of plenary lawmaking authority to the winners of the last general election—so long, at least, as the election was conducted under free and fair ground rules and the winners don't try to prevent the next scheduled round of electoral challenges.

This idea motivates, in turn, a critical institutional conclusion: during the period between elections, all institutional checks upon the electoral victors are presumptively antidemocratic. For sophisticated monists, this is only a presumption. Perhaps certain constitutional checks may prevent the victors from abrogating the next scheduled election; perhaps others might be justified once one considers the deeper ways normal elections fail to satisfy our ideals of electoral fairness. While these exceptions may have great practical importance, monists refuse to let them obscure the main point: when the Supreme Court, or anybody else, invalidates a statute, it suffers from a "countermajoritarian difficulty"[9] which must be overcome before a good democrat can profess satisfaction with this extraordinary action.

In the work of this school, the brooding omnipresence is (an idealized version of) British parliamentary practice. For more than a century now, the Prime Minister has won her office after a relatively fair and square election, and except in truly exceptional circumstances the House of Commons has given its unswerving support to the proposals of Her Majesty's Government. If the people of Great Britain don't like what's going on, they will return the Opposition at the next election. Until that time, neither the House of Lords, nor the Queen, nor the courts seriously undermine the legislative decisions made by a majority of the Commons.

So far as the monist is concerned, the British design captures the essence of democracy. The problem posed by America is its failure to follow the trans-Atlantic model. Rather than granting a power monopoly to a single, popularly elected House of Representatives, Americans tolerate a great deal of insubordination from branches whose electoral connection is suspect or nonexistent. While the Senate gets its share of the lumps, the principal object is the Supreme Court. Whoever gave Nine Old Lawyers authority to overrule the judgments of democratically elected politicians?

There are monistic answers to this question—which try to reconcile judicial review with the fundamental premises of monistic democracy. Thus, constitutional conservatives like Alexander Bickel,[10] centrists like John Ely,[11] and progressives like Richard Parker[12] have proposed roles for the Supreme Court that operate within monistic premises. For present purposes, it is the monistic question, not the proliferating number of answers, that needs critical scrutiny.

The monist begs a big question when he asserts that the winner of a fair and open election is entitled to rule with the full authority of We the People. It is much better, of course, for electoral winners to take office rather than suffer an authoritarian putsch by the losers. But it does not follow that all statutes gaining the support of a legislative majority in Washington, D.C., represent the considered judgment of a mobilized majority of American citizens. Instead, the dualist sees a profoundly democratic point to many of the distinctive practices that baffle the monist. For her, they express our Constitution's effort to require elected politicians to operate within a two-track system. If politicians hope to win normal democratic legitimacy for an initiative, they are directed down the normal lawmaking path and told to gain the assent of the House, Senate, and President in the usual ways. If they hope for higher lawmaking authority, they are directed down a specially onerous lawmaking path—whose character and historical development will be the subject of the next chapter. Only if a political movement successfully negotiates the special challenges of the higher lawmaking system can it rightfully claim that its initiative represents the constitutional judgment of We the People.

Once the two-track character of the system is recognized, the Supreme Court appears in a different light. Consider that all the time and effort required to push an initiative down the higher lawmaking track would be wasted unless the Constitution prevented future normal politicians from enacting statutes that ignored the movement's higher law achievement. If future politicians could so easily ignore established higher law, why would any mass movement take the trouble to overcome the special hurdles placed on the higher lawmaking track?

To maintain the integrity of higher lawmaking, all dualist constitutions must provide for one or more institutions to discharge a preservationist function. These institutions must effectively block efforts to repeal established constitutional principles by the simple expedient of passing a normal statute and force the reigning group of elected politicians to move onto the higher lawmaking track if they wish to question the judgments previously made by We the People. Only after negotiating this more arduous obstacle course can a political elite earn the authority to say that We the People have changed our mind.

It follows, then, that the dualist will view the Supreme Court from a very different perspective than the monist. The monist treats every act of judicial review as presumptively antidemocratic and strains to save the Supreme Court from the "countermajoritarian difficulty" by one or another ingenious argument. In contrast, the dualist sees the discharge of the preservationist function by the courts as an essential part of a well-ordered democratic regime. Rather than threatening democracy by frustrating the statutory demands of the political elite in Washington, the courts serve democracy by protecting the hard-won principles of a mobilized citizenry against erosion by political elites who have failed to gain broad and deep popular support for their innovations.

This is not to say that any particular decision by the modern Supreme Court can be justified in preservationist terms. The key point is that dualists cannot dismiss a good-faith effort by the Court to interpret the Constitution as "antidemocratic" simply because it leads to the invalidation of normal statutes; this ongoing judicial effort to look backward and interpret the meaning of the great achievements of the past is an indispensable part of the larger project of distinguishing the will of We the People from the acts of We the Politicians.

Rights Foundationalists

In confronting monism, the dualist's main object is to break the tight link monists construct between two distinct ideas: "democracy" on the one hand and "parliamentary sovereignty" on the other. Like monists, dualists are democrats—they believe that the People are the ultimate authority in America. They disagree only about the easy way in which normally elected politicians claim to legislate with the full authority of the People.

In contrast, the primacy of popular sovereignty is challenged by a second modern school. While none of these theorists completely denies a place for democratic principles, their populist enthusiasms are constrained by deeper commitments to fundamental rights. Unsurprisingly, members of this school differ when it comes to identifying the rights that are fundamental. Conservatives like Richard Epstein emphasize the foundational role of property rights;[13] liberals like Ronald Dworkin emphasize the right to equal concern and respect;[14] collectivists like Owen Fiss, the rights of disadvantaged groups.[15] These transparent differences should not blind us to the idea that binds them together. Whatever rights are Right, all agree that the American constitution is concerned, first and foremost, with their protection. Indeed, the whole point of having rights is to trump decisions rendered by democratic institutions that may otherwise legislate for the collective welfare. To emphasize this common thread, I shall group these thinkers together by calling them *rights foundationalists*.

As with the monists, this school is hardly a trendy creation of yesterday. There is, however, an interesting difference in the intellectual lineage they construct for themselves. While monists refer to a series of Americans from Wilson and Thayer to Frankfurter and Bickel, foundationalists favor philosophical writers further removed in time and space—with Kant (via Rawls)[16] and Locke (via Nozick)[17] presently serving as the most important sources of inspiration. Right now, I am not interested in these internal debates. My aim is to describe how foundationalists as a group differ from more democratic schools.

Begin with the monists. It is fair to say that they are hostile to rights, at least as foundationalists understand them. Indeed, it is just when the Supreme Court begins to invalidate statutes in the name of fundamental rights that the monist begins to worry about the "countermajoritarian difficulty" that renders judicial review presumptively illegitimate.[18]

This "difficulty" does not seem so formidable to the foundationalist. Instead, she is more impressed by the fact that a democratic legislature might endorse any number of oppressive actions—establish a religion, or authorize torture, or . . . When such violations occur, the foundationalist demands judicial intervention despite the breach of democratic principle. Rights trump democracy—provided, of course, that they're the Right rights.

And there's the rub. Indeed, it is their anxiety over the arbitrary definition of rights that induces thoughtful foundationalists to recur to great philosophers like Kant and Locke in an effort to understand the Constitution. If judges are to avoid arbitrariness in defining fundamental rights, shouldn't they take advantage of the most profound reflections on the subject available in the Western tradition?

For the monist, this turn to the Great Books is yet another symptom of the foundationalist's antidemocratic disease. Whatever its philosophical merits, the foundationalist's discourse is invariably esoteric—involving encounters with authors and doctrines that most college-educated people successfully avoided during their most academic moments. This exalted talk of Kant and Locke only emphasizes the elitism involved in removing fundamental questions from the democratic process.

These objections hardly convince the foundationalist. They serve only to generate further anxieties about the ease with which monistic democracy can be swept by demagogic irrationality. And so the debate proceeds, with the two sides talking past one another: democracy versus rights versus democracy versus—point and counterpoint, with all the talk changing few minds.

How does the introduction of dualism change the shape of this familiar conversational field? By offering a framework which allows both sides to accommodate some—if not all—of their concerns. The basic mediating device is the dualist's two-track system of democratic lawmaking. It allows an important place for the foundationalist's view of "rights as trumps" without violating the monist's deeper commitment to the primacy of democracy. To grasp the logic of accommodation, suppose that a rights-oriented movement took to the higher lawmaking track and successfully mobilized the People to endorse one or another Bill of Rights. Given this achievement, the dualist can readily endorse the judicial invalidation of later statutes that undermine these rights, even when they concern matters, like the protection of personal freedom or privacy, that have nothing much to do with the integrity of the electoral process so central to monistic democrats. As we have seen, the dualist believes that the Court furthers the cause of democracy when it preserves constitutional rights against erosion by politically ascendant elites who have yet to mobilize the People to support the repeal of previous higher lawmaking principles. Thus, unlike the monist, she will have no trouble supporting the idea that rights can properly trump the conclusions of normal democratic politics. She can do so, moreover, without the need for non-democratic principles of the kinds proffered by the rights foundationalist. Thus, the dualist can offer a deeper reconciliation of democracy and rights to those who find a certain amount of truth in both sides of the debate.

This reconciliation will not, of course, prove satisfactory to all members of the previously contending schools. The problem for the committed foundationalist, unsurprisingly, is the insufficiently deep foundations the dualist has built for the protection of rights.[19] Granted, concedes the foundationalist, the dualist will applaud the judicial protection of rights if a warrant can be found in prior higher lawmaking activity. But that is an awfully big "if." What if the People have not adopted the right Bill of Rights? Should the Constitution then be construed in ways that allow the statutory perpetration of injustice?

It is their different answers to this question that continue to distinguish dualist from committed foundationalist. For the dualist, judicial protection of rights does depend on a prior democratic affirmation on the higher lawmaking track. In this sense, the dualist's Constitution is democratic first, rights-protecting second. The committed foundationalist reverses this priority: the Constitution is first concerned with protecting rights; only then does it authorize the People to work their will on other matters. Having isolated this disagreement, we must next see whether it can be resolved. Are there very general arguments that indicate whether the American Constitution has been built on dualist or foundationalist lines?

My answer is yes. Once again, the decisive consideration is drawn from the distinctive character of two-track lawmaking. My argument against foundationalism focuses on the fact that our Constitution has never (with two exceptions I will consider shortly) explicitly entrenched existing higher law against subsequent revision by the People. While the original Constitution gave higher law protection to slavery, at least it did not try to make it unconstitutional for Americans of later generations to reconsider the question; similarly, when Americans of the early twentieth century enacted Prohibition into higher law, they did not seek to make the amendment unamendable. In these two cases, of course, the People have exercised their right to change their mind. And few among us would say that we were the worse for repeal. Foundationalists, however, must acknowledge the general availability of repeal with embarrassment. For this open-ended practice allows constitutional amendments of a kind that most modern foundationalists would consider morally disastrous.

A hypothetical case: Suppose that the religious revival now prominent in the Islamic world is the first wave of a Great Awakening that envelops the Christian West. A general revulsion against godless materialism yields mass political mobilization that finally results in a successful campaign for partial repeal of the First Amendment. With the dawn of the new millennium, Amendment XXVII is proclaimed throughout the land:

> Christianity is established as the state religion of the American people, and the public worship of other gods is hereby forbidden.

This enactment would inaugurate a deep transformation of our higher law heritage—on more or less the same order, though of a very different kind, as those achieved by Reconstruction Republicans and New Deal Democrats in earlier generations. Moreover, such an amendment would deeply offend my own commitment to freedom of conscience. Nonetheless, if I were then so unlucky to be a Justice of the Supreme Court (serving as a holdover from the last secular Administration), I would have no doubt about my judicial responsibility. While I hope that I would stick to my conviction that this Christianity amendment was terribly wrong, I would uphold it as a fundamental part of the American Constitution: if some diehard brought a lawsuit in 2001 seeking to convince the Supreme Court to declare the Christianity amendment unconstitutional, I would join my colleagues in summarily rejecting the petition—or resign my office and join in a campaign to convince the American people to change their mind.

But I wouldn't take the course suggested by foundationalism: stay on the bench and write a dissent denying that the First Amendment had been validly amended. I doubt, moreover, that one may find many American lawyers who seriously disagree—even among those who presently wrap themselves up in foundationalist rhetoric.*

Judicial dissent would not be preposterous in other countries, most notably modern Germany. In the aftermath of Nazism, the new West German constitution explicitly declared that a long list of fundamental human rights *cannot* constitutionally be revised, regardless of the extent to which a majority of Germans support repeal. Given this self-conscious act of entrenchment, it would be absolutely right for the German constitutional court to issue an opinion, absurd in the American context, striking down an amendment blatantly violating freedom of conscience. Under this foundationalist constitution, judges would be within their rights to continue resisting: if the dominant political majority insisted on repeal, it would be obliged to replace the entire constitution with a new one in its grim determination to destroy fundamental rights.[20]

But this only makes it clear how far dualist America is from foundationalist Germany at the present time. Insofar as America has had constitutional experience with German-style entrenchment, the lessons have been very negative. The Founders were perfectly aware of entrenchment in 1787, but they did not use the device to serve the cause of human freedom. They used it to entrench the African slave trade—explicitly forbidding the American people from enacting an amendment barring the practice before the year 1808.[21] This history suggests that the foundationalist interpretation is inconsistent with the existing premises of the American higher lawmaking system. In America, in contrast to Germany, it is the People who are the source of rights; the Constitution does not spell out rights that the People must accept (or settle for).†

---

*The recent flap over President Bush's proposed flag-burning amendment illustrates this point. No serious opponent suggested that the First Amendment could not be validly revised, even though the Bush initiative went to the very heart of the amendment's concerns with free political expression. Instead, opponents trusted to the good sense of the American people and successfully persuaded them to reject this flag-waving assault on their heritage of freedom.

†My hypothetical Christianity amendment involves a right that most foundationalists would consider fundamental but that almost all lawyers—and all dualists—would immediately recognize as repealable. While this example suffices to distinguish dualism from foundationalism, the hypothetical does not allow us to consider whether dualist theory allows any conceptual room at all for entrenchment.

To test this question, imagine that a religious movement managed to ratify a second

Speaking as a citizen, I don't take much joy from this discovery. I myself think it would be a good idea to entrench the Bill of Rights against subsequent revision by some future American majority caught up in some awful neo-Nazi paroxysm.[22] But this, in a way, only makes my point—which is to clarify the spirit of the Constitution as it is, not as it may (or may not) become. Unless and until a political movement does succeed in entrenching a modern Bill of Rights, dualism describes the ambition of the American enterprise better than any foundationalist interpretation. The Constitution puts democracy first, though not in the simple way that monists suppose.

HISTORICISM

The clash between monists and foundationalists dominates the present field of constitutional debate and has moved beyond the classroom to the courtroom. The sharp split between the two schools mimics the split between plaintiff and defendant in the typical lawsuit—the plaintiff insisting that a statute has violated her fundamental rights, the defendant responding that courts should defer to the democratic authority of Congress. Little wonder that thoughtful judges and citizens are drawn to reflections about democracy and

---

amendment along with the one hypothesized in the text: "Any American advocating the repeal of Amendment XXVII is hereby declared guilty of treason and subject to capital punishment upon conviction." This amendment, in contrast to the first, aims to make it impossible for the People to reconsider its commitment to Christianity, and so amounts to the repeal of dualist democracy itself. Would it therefore be constitutionally appropriate for judges to invalidate it? Or would it simply be best for all decent people to quit the regime and struggle to overthrow it?

Such questions are best left to the dark day they arise. For now, it is enough to beware easy answers. In particular, I do not believe that judges would be justified in asserting a general authority to protect the fundamental principles of dualist democracy against repudiation by the People. Suppose, for example, that the next round of our constitutional politics were dominated by a mobilized coalition of liberals who sought to entrench a modernized version of the Bill of Rights, guaranteeing a right to a minimum income along with other new rights unknown to our eighteenth-century Founders. *This* act of entrenchment, no less than the second Christianity amendment, would be inconsistent with the principles of dualist democracy, since it makes it impossible for the People to change their mind about certain constitutional values. Yet would the judges have the constitutional authority to force the People to keep *these* possibilities open?

rights—creating an audience for the work of the two competing schools.

Dualism expresses a more hopeful possibility. Perhaps the conflict between plaintiff and defendant is not a sign of unremitting conflict between the democratic and rights-oriented aspects of our tradition. Instead, both the enactment of normal statutes *and* the judicial protection of constitutional rights are part of a larger practice of dualist democracy. This abstract synthesis, of course, is hardly enough to decide concrete cases. But it points in a particular direction—toward a reflective study of the past to determine when the People have spoken and what they have said during their historic moments of successful constitutional politics.

The Paradoxes of American "Burkeanism"

This historicizing tendency allows the dualist to make contact with a third strand of constitutional thought. I will call it Burkean, since it has yet to find its modern spokesman who is Burke's equal.[23] While one can isolate Burkean aspects of recent theoretical work,[24] this tendency is far more pronounced amongst practicing lawyers and judges.

These professionals do not require brilliant theorists to convince them to cultivate Burkean sensibilities. They are already deeply immersed in a common law tradition that demands the very skills and sensitivities that self-conscious Burkeans commend. What counts for the common lawyer is not some fancy theory but the patterns of concrete decision built up by courts and other practical decision-makers over decades, generations, centuries. Slowly, often in a half-conscious and circuitous fashion, these decisions build upon one another to yield the constitutional rights that modern Americans take for granted, just as they slowly generate precedents that the President and Congress may use to claim new grants of constitutional authority. The task of the Burkean lawyer or judge is to master these precedents, thereby gaining a sense of their hidden potentials for growth and decay.

This basic conception can be elaborated in conservative or reformist directions. Reformist incrementalists will try to keep the precedents abreast with the "evolving moral sense of the country"; more

conservative types may be more open to the incremental development of new Presidential powers than new constitutional rights. As
always, it is more important to focus upon the point that all these
common lawyers have in common—which is an emphasis on the
ongoing cultivation of a concrete historical tradition that is sorely
missing from the talk of the "high theorists" of either the monistic
or the foundationalist persuasion.

So far as these Burkeans are concerned, there is more wisdom in
the gradual accretion of concrete decisions than in the abstract
speculations of our most brilliant academics. The only "theory" with
any real value is found in the opinions of judges responding to the
facts of particular cases. And even these theories should not be taken
too seriously. They will take on different meanings as they are tested
over the generations by different judges confronting different cases.
The Constitution simply cannot be understood by speculative theorists who have failed to immerse themselves in the historical practice
of concrete decision, and hence have been unable to cultivate the
prudent sense of statecraft necessary for wise constitutional development.

Such sentiments contain important insights—but they should not
be confused with the whole truth. To put the Burkean sensibility in
its place, I begin with the aspect of dualist constitutionalism it
entirely ignores. Only then will it be possible to isolate important
points of convergence.

The common lawyers' blind side can be summarized in two words:
constitutional politics. Indeed, on those occasions that Burkeanism
reaches self-consciousness—as in the work of the later Bickel[25]—
constitutional politics is aggressively disparaged. All that Burkeans
see in popular political movements are the charismatic, but unscru-
pulous, leaders; the loud, but hopelessly ambiguous, pronunciamentos; the excited, but ignorant, masses. They recoil from the scene of
mass mobilization in disgust. At best, eruptions of collective irrationality will quickly disintegrate amid clouds of factional recrimi-
nation. Otherwise, a government seized by utopian rhetoric can
degenerate into unspeakable tyranny with bewildering speed. Given
this nightmare, could anyone of sound mind support any regime in
which the sober and sensible Burkean did not have the final say?

The dualist responds by rejecting the Burkean's self-congratulatory statement of the alternatives. While only a fool fails to recognize the dangers of mass demagogy, the dualist refuses to forget a very different possibility. Here a political leadership challenges the traditional wisdom on behalf of principles which, though inevitably open-ended, do have rational content. While these transformative initiatives inspire mass involvement, passionate commitment, great sacrifice, the result is not some unspeakable tyranny but a deepening dialogue between leaders and masses within a democratic structure that finally succeeds in generating broad popular consent for a sharp break with the status quo. Finally, the dualist challenges the Burkeans' suggestion to constitutional lawyers that they forget, as quickly as possible, the results of these nightmarish popular eruptions. To the contrary: most Americans identify our great popular struggles as culminating in the nation's greatest constitutional achievements. Thus, the original Constitution codified the Revolutionary generation's defeat of monarchy on behalf of republican self-government; the Civil War amendments codified the struggle of an entire generation to repudiate slavery on behalf of a new constitutional ideal of equality; and so forth. Rather than forgetting such popular achievements, *our* Constitution seeks to protect them against erosion during more normal times, when the People are less involved in affairs of state.

This dualist conclusion challenges the standard Burkean sensibility in four ways. First, it undermines its commitment to incrementalism. Although gradual adaptation is an important part of the story,[26] the Constitution cannot be understood without recognizing that Americans have, time and again, successfully repudiated large chunks of their past and transformed their higher law to express deep changes in their political identities. Perhaps these changes do not seem radical to those who long for a total revolution that (vainly) seeks to obliterate every trace of the old regime. But, when judged by any other standard, they were hardly incremental. If a label will clarify matters, American history has been punctuated by successful exercises in *revolutionary reform*—in which protagonists struggled over basic questions of principle that had ramifying implications for the conduct of large areas of American life.

Which leads to a second challenge from the dualist. The Burkean is suspicious not only of big breaks but of the self-conscious appeals to abstract principles that accompany them. He prides himself in avoiding loose talk of Freedom, Equality, or Democracy. Even more modest theories dealing with "free speech" or "equal protection" seem impossibly vague to him. The dualist, in contrast, finds an encounter with abstract ideals an inescapable part of the American past. Whatever else may be said about the Founders, they were hardly content with the Burkean arts of muddling through crises. They were children of the Enlightenment, eager to use the best political science of their time to prove to a doubting world that republican self-government was no utopian dream.[27] Otherwise they would never have tried to write a Constitution whose few thousand words contained a host of untried ideas and institutions. If abstract ideals were important to the Founders and their successors in constitutional politics, how can we pretend to understand our legacy without confronting them?

But there is a particular abstraction that gives the Burkean special trouble. And that is rule by the People. The People rule best, the Burkean says with a broad wink, when they leave the business of government to a well-trained elite immersed in the nation's concrete constitutional tradition. Slowly but surely, this elite will sense the drift of popular sentiment and take the countless small steps needed to keep the tradition responsive to the present's half-articulate sense of its special needs. For the Burkean, however, the public dialogue accompanying such ongoing adaptation is best kept to relatively small elites—judges talking to one another about the relationship of past decisions to present problems, statesmen telling one another that their constituents haven't given them a mandate to accomplish particular goals but have selected them for their prudent capacity to make sensible public policy.

Once again, it is not necessary for the dualist to belittle the importance of this ongoing enterprise in normal political adaptation. She refuses, however, to allow this elite conversation to obscure the even greater importance of a different dialogue—one through which mobilized masses of ordinary citizens may finally organize their political will with sufficient clarity to lay down the law to those who speak in their name on a daily basis in Washington, D.C. While competing elites play a critical role in this higher lawmaking dialectic, the process typically involves a conflictual kind of ideological politics that Burkeans disdain. This disdain is all the more unfortunate because successful higher lawmaking also requires prudence and statesmanship—to which Burkeans might otherwise make important contributions.

To sum up the dualist critique in a fourth point that presupposes the first three: the Burkean fails to recognize that he can easily become part of the problem, rather than its solution. The problem is how to prevent normal government from departing from the great principles of higher law validated by the People during their relatively rare successes in constitutional politics. Burkeans threaten to make this problem worse by taking advantage of the citizenry's weak involvement in normal politics to embrace "statesmanly" solutions that undercut fundamental principles previously affirmed by the People. In these cases, Burkean "prudence" degenerates, in dualist eyes, into obscurantist elitism that prides itself on ignoring the greatest constitutional achievements of the American people.

Burke himself understood this. While he is principally remembered today for his famous contrast between the abstract and excited politics of the French Revolution and the concrete and incremental development of the British constitution, Burke himself recognized that the American Revolutionaries eluded this easy dichotomy—and tried, as best he could, to appreciate the distinctive character of the Americans' experiment in revolutionary reform.[28] Perhaps he would have been the first to protest the effort by self-proclaimed Burkeans to ignore the popular mobilizations that punctuate American history.

Maybe modern English history does conform to the incremental model embraced by modern Burkeans—though I'm not convinced. But Burkeans must keep their Anglophilism in check when confronting the American past. If they are to put their historicizing genius to good use, they must recognize that American history reveals the ongoing popular development of a politics of principle that results, when successful, in revolutionary reform—whose principled meaning must be deeply understood if the tradition is to renew itself.

Once this essential point is recognized, the dualist and Burkean can discover common ground. First, the Burkean's emphasis on the demagogic pathologies of an excited mass politics cautions us to exercise the greatest care in understanding our higher lawmaking system—both as it was originally conceived and as it has developed in response to the concrete challenges of American history. Not that this study can guarantee us against outbursts of collective irrationality in the future. There can be no such guarantee. Demagogy is an endemic risk in any democratic system that places real decision-making authority in the hands of a mass public with limited time and energy for the great issues of politics. Nonetheless, these risks can be controlled—first by the popular cultivation of the arts of citizenship in a wide variety of daily contexts, from the union hall to the school board to the Little League; and second, through studying ways in which constitutional structures may encourage transformative movements to channel their energies into a productive dialogue with the larger body of the American people.

This second task defines one of my central concerns. In reexamining two centuries of higher lawmaking experience, I will be on the lookout for the concrete historical processes that allowed Americans to transform moments of passionate sacrifice and excited mobilization into lasting legal achievements—ones that might continue to inspire us today as we confront the challenges of the future. I hope that much of this study will remind the common lawyer of his own effort to learn from the historical precedents of the past, with one important caveat. We will not be concentrating on the decisions of judges, but on those made by lawmakers. The critical higher lawmaking precedents were established during moments of crisis by leaders like Madison, Lincoln, and Roosevelt—who, in a complex interaction with other institutions and the people at large, finally gain democratic authority to make fundamental changes in our higher law. While courts played a secondary role in the evolving higher lawmaking process, we cannot narrowly focus on judges if we hope to describe, and reflect upon, the constitutional practice of popular sovereignty in American history.

A first link with the Burkean sensibility, then, will be a concern with the concrete historical process through which practical statesmen have confronted and resolved the distinctive dilemmas of constitutional politics. This will lead us to glimpse a second point of commonality. Here the dualist joins the Burkean in insisting that the Constitution is best understood as a historically rooted tradition of theory and practice—an evolving language of politics, as it were, through which Americans have learned to talk to one another in the course of their centuries-long struggle over their national identity.

This sense of an ongoing tradition of discourse eluded the first two schools we have considered. The monistic democrat worships at the altar of the Present—he supposes that he knows all he needs to know about democratic rule if he simply consults the last statutory word approved by Congress. The foundationalist seeks to escape the limits of time altogether—he hopes to define some ahistorical State of Nature or Original Position to serve as a constitutional platform from which to pass judgment on history's passing show. In elaborating the constitutional will of the People, the dualist begins neither with the will of the present legislature nor the reason of some utopian assembly. Her aim is the kind of situated understanding one might reach after a good conversation. Only this time, the conversation is not between friends—or even enemies—who share the same moment of time and so can observe each other's tone of voice and gestures, continue tomorrow what is left unsaid today.

The challenge, instead, is to locate ourselves in a conversation between generations. As we come to our political maturity, today's Americans do not encounter one another as if they were explorers setting up a new colony on some previously uninhabited new world. They enter upon a political stage already set with a complex symbolic practice charged with meaning by the thought and action of prior generations. There is, of course, no need for us to seek to understand these symbols. We may try, if we choose, to sweep them away in a grand gesture of disdain, or let them die a lingering death by refusing to hear the voices of those who came before us.

There is, however, wisdom in these voices, if we but try to hear them. They can teach us how prior generations have managed, on occasion, to engage in great democratic achievements on a continental scale; how they managed to sustain democratic politics during those periods when citizen involvement was less constitutionally creative. In seeking to engage these voices in conversation, my aim is hardly to prostrate myself before their superior wisdom. A conversation with the past is only a part of the process through which the present gains its own voice and thereby makes its own lasting contribution to the constitutional tradition. Surely the American People have not yet pronounced the last word on their constitutional identity? How best to continue the practice of dualist democracy into the third American century? How best to revise our higher law legacy so that it will be equal to the demands of the future?

I have my own answers—and so, I am sure, do you. Yet none of us can expect to win popular consent without passionate struggle and bitter disagreement. Do we not owe it to ourselves to understand, as best we can, how Americans have tested one another's answers in the past? For all its historical contingency and moral imperfection, our constitutional language has set the terms within which previous generations have disagreed with one another, and sometimes has allowed them to move beyond disagreement to a transformed understanding of their political commitments. Is it wrong to suppose that it remains a crucial resource in our own struggles over national identity?

The Republican Revival

I have begun with Burke not because he is the world's greatest philosopher of history, but because he expressed a powerful current of opinion amongst the community of lawyers and judges who interpret the Constitution on a daily basis. It seemed important to warn them that the constitutional tradition of revolutionary reform is quite distinct from common law adaptation; and that, if they are to preserve a Burkean sense of the distinctive texture of American history, they will have to move beyond the narrow incrementalism so often associated with the name of Burke.[29] Yet it would be a mistake to end our discussion of historicism with the prevailing professional wisdom. Just as American law has, in the past, shown a remarkable capacity to assimilate a host of popular and academic critiques, there is every reason to hope for similar revision in the future.

Indeed, if a recent wave of legal scholarship proves a reliable guide, this process of historical reorientation has already begun. Over the past few years, the law journals have been full of efforts to join a larger critical project already undertaken by many political scientists and historians. The object of this rising generation's critique, unsurprisingly enough, has been its parents—historians like Richard Hofstadter,[30] political scientists like Robert Dahl,[31] sociologists like Daniel Bell[32]—whose work bulked large on the academic horizon of the 1960's. This work, in the eyes of many, endowed American liberalism with a social solidity and pervasiveness it did not in fact possess—provoking complex responses in both the social and historical sciences intended to set the record straight.

The critical effort most relevant here tries to revitalize the republican aspect of the American political tradition. The pathbreaking work of Bernard Bailyn[33] and Gordon Wood[34] has not only set an agenda for many historians, but has increasingly loomed large in legal scholarship as well—with Frank Michelman,[35] Suzanna Sherry,[36] Cass Sunstein,[37] and Mark Tushnet[38] making notable contributions. These initial explorations suggest that the "republican revival" is no monopoly of any single political viewpoint.[39] Their diversity should not blind us to the common invitation implicit in all of them: wouldn't it be foolish for lawyers to ignore the "republican revival" amongst American historians?

I will record my own debt by engaging two modern classics: Louis Hartz's *Liberal Tradition in America*[40] and John Pocock's *The Machiavellian Moment*.[41] These works are rightly seen as the most philosophically self-aware statements of the older "liberal" thesis and its more recent "republican" antithesis. Rather than joining one side of this debate, I propose to use both in a larger synthesis—one that allows us to glimpse the roots of dualist constitutionalism in the deeper patterns of American political history.

The Liberalism of Hartz   I share with Louis Hartz an abiding skepticism about the power of European models to enlighten American politics without fundamental conceptual reorganization. The particular model that concerned Hartz was the familiar Marxist view condemning all modern societies to a compulsory three-step march to utopia: first feudalism, then capitalism, then (but only then) socialism. For Hartz, this model was a non-starter for one basic reason: Americans had never experienced anything like European feudalism. Since the first term in the three-stage sequence was lacking, America lacked the social ingredients necessary to spark the later movement from the second capitalist stage to the third socialist stage. America was a case of arrested development, permanently frozen at stage two. It was a land locked in the grip of a "Lockean consensus" which trivialized politics and glorified the natural rights of isolated individuals to life, liberty, and the pursuit of property (or is it happiness?). Since Americans never were obliged to use state power to liberate themselves from feudalism, they were "born equal" and could afford to look upon the state as an unmitigated threat to natural liberty. The government that governs best governs least. Let the Europeans say otherwise.

While there is some truth in Hartz's account, it also serves as a cautionary tale for those, like myself, who see something distinctive in the American political experience. While Hartz was obsessed with the inadequacies of a Euro-centered Marxism, his critique implicitly accepted far more of this theory than he appreciated. This is, at least, the way I diagnose the great *non sequitur* at the heart of Hartz's theory. I agree with Hartz that the American Revolutionaries were not in a life-and-death struggle with feudalism (whatever that term may mean when applied to the eighteenth, rather than the thirteenth, century).[42] But it hardly follows that Americans found nothing important to struggle about in politics. It is easy to see how an old-fashioned* Marxist might reach this erroneous conclusion. Since, by hypothesis, he believes that the only "really important" use of state power is to serve as a revolutionary mechanism for the long march from feudalism to capitalism to socialism, the fact that the Americans didn't "need" a revolution to push them to the capitalist stage meant that the American Revolution couldn't be about anything "really important." If, however, there is more to political life than a struggle over the timing of a compulsive three-stage sequence, the mere fact† that Americans had escaped Old World feudalism hardly implies that they could afford to relax and embrace a comfortable Lockean-ism that denied any creative role for the state in social life. By embracing this *non sequitur,* Hartz remained in the thrall of the Marxist theory he sought to reject.

To put my criticism more affirmatively, Hartz's mistake resided in his interpretation of Tocqueville's dictum that Americans were "born equal."[43] I am happy to adopt this slogan—so long as it emphasizes

---

*"Old-fashioned" because, since Lenin, lots of Marxists have been trying to leap from feudalism to socialism; and lots more have been trying to liberate themselves from the deterministic economism that old-fashioned Marxism, especially as interpreted by Engels, represented.

†If it is a fact. After all, there were feudalistic as well as capitalistic aspects of the Southern plantation system. But it is not necessary to quibble with Hartz's facts to make the points that really matter.

the rich cultural, material, and geopolitical resources that enabled Americans to build a regime which, over time, has protected the liberties of an increasing proportion of its population. If, however, Hartz meant that this "equality" could be sustained without ongoing political struggle over its meaning and its scope, or that Americans believed that they could "do without" a serious politics that required great acts of creativity, he was simply wrong. Rather than supposing that Americans were "born equal," the Founding Federalists believed that the New World would become Balkanized into a host of petty tyrannies. They urged their fellow Americans to join in unprecedented acts of constitutional construction and to ignore their opponents' warnings that the new Union would lead only to a resurgent monarchy. Rather than supposing that Americans were "born equal," Reconstruction Republicans were painfully aware of the disgrace of slavery. They urged their fellow citizens to use national power to guarantee freedom for all Americans and to ignore their opponents' warnings that Reconstruction would lead only to a military despotism. Rather than supposing that Americans were "born equal," New Deal Democrats were convinced that modern economic conditions had transformed "natural rights" of property and contract into symbols of mass oppression. They urged their fellow citizens to empower the national government to regulate free markets for the general welfare and to ignore their opponents' warnings that the New Deal would lead only to a totalitarian dictatorship. It is only as a result of these, and many other, political struggles that Americans enjoy whatever equality they have today; and there is every reason to believe that the nature and scope of American equality will be open to similar debate and redefinition in the future.

Americans have not been "born equal" through some miraculous act of immaculate conception. To the extent that we have gained equality, we have won it through energetic debate, popular decision, and constitutional creativity. Once the American people lose this remarkable political capacity, it is only a matter of time before they lose whatever equality they possess—and much else besides.

The Republicanism of Pocock   Which leads me to John Pocock. Over the past generation, his work has led to a deeper appreciation of the republican dimension of the American experience that Hartz trivialized. Pocock refused to allow the liberal individualist's struggle against feudalism to dominate his understanding of the modern predicament. Deemphasizing Locke, he placed the Founding against a different intellectual background—one that ultimately gained its inspiration from the classical Greek polis. Within this classical republican tradition, the fundamental challenge of human life is not to lose oneself in the Lockean pursuit of life, liberty, and property but to join with fellow citizens in the ongoing project of political self-government. Pocock's magisterial study, *The Machiavellian Moment,* traces the way this classical ideal was revived and transformed during the Italian Renaissance, before it was taken up by radical Commonwealthmen during the English Revolution of the seventeenth century. Defeated by the Restoration of 1660, the English Commonwealthmen gained a belated victory over the Crown during the American Revolution—providing the fundamental categories for the Revolutionary generation's diagnosis of the Crown's corruption and its republican cure. When set against this intellectual background, the Founding Federalists seem something more than a bunch of Lockean social engineers working out the implications of the "natural" equality miraculously enjoyed by Americans. Pocock invites us to view them as self-consciously confronting the classical ideal of republican self-government and seeking to redefine its place in the modern world.[44]

I mean to take this invitation seriously. It will lead us to discover in the American Constitution a fund of dualistic theory and practice that contributes to humanity's enduring quest for self-government. Before pressing forward, though, it is best to explain why Pocock's work has not generally been read to invite a sustained inquiry into America's effort to reshape the republican tradition.

The problem is that it is impossible completely to deny Hartz's basic point about the importance of liberalism, especially as the country evolves through the nineteenth and twentieth centuries. On the historiographic level, this concession to Hartz takes the form of a dismal kind of dating game—in which the debate concerns the precise moment that the (Neo-)Classical Republican Ideal was conquered by the increasingly aggressive forces of Liberalism: Perhaps it was the Founding Fathers themselves who killed the republican spirit with their new Constitution? Perhaps the Spirit staggered

onward in a variety of nineteenth- and twentieth-century devia-
tions?[45] Whatever remains obscure about the precise location(s) of
the *corpus delicti,* one thing seems clear enough: the ghost of Republicanism has long since deserted the center of American life,
where Liberalism is now Hegemonic.

This historical diagnosis leads in one of two directions when it
becomes self-consciously normative. Some writers despair at the very
thought of reviving republicanism and use it simply as a platform
for proclaiming one's estrangement from the dominant "liberalism";*
others, more hopeful, seek to use republicanism as a tool for moving
beyond "liberalism."[46]

Liberal Republicanism   I choose to do neither. I mean to question
the dichotomy between liberalism and republicanism, Hartz and
Pocock, which makes the choice seem necessary.[47] This will require,
among other things, clear definition of the relevant terms. No synthesis will be possible so long as we allow two very different currents
of thought to masquerade under the liberal label. The first is better
called libertarianism—which has recently enjoyed a revival, amongst
philosophers at least, through the work of Robert Nozick and David
Gauthier.[48] Such writers do express views close to those that some
republicans caricature under the name of liberalism. Nozick and
Gauthier outdo Locke in reasoning from a "state of nature" inhabited by isolated individuals who claim natural rights to property and
contract and deny the authority of the state to disturb the enjoyment
of the hard-earned fruits of their possessive individualism. Indeed,
if these libertarian views exhausted the liberal tradition, I would
agree that my effort to transcend the Hartz/Pocock dichotomy is
foolish; and that the rise of "libertarianism" in nineteenth- and
twentieth-century America necessarily meant the death of republicanism.

---

*This seems to be Pocock's view. See, for example, his poorly concealed outrage at
a Marxist critic's confusing him for a "neoliberal," or even for an American. J. G. A.
Pocock, "Between Gog and Magog: The Republican Thesis and the Ideologica Ameri-
cana," 48 *J. Hist. Ideas* 325 (1987). Within the law, this tack is taken, by and large, in
Mark Tushnet, *Red, White, and Blue: A Critical Analysis of Constitutional Law* (1988).
See the perceptive review essay by Richard Fallon, "What Is Republicanism, and Is It
Worth Reviving?," 102 *Harv. L. Rev.* 1695, 1703–15 (1989).

We should not allow the polemical use of L-words, however, to divert attention from a second strand of liberal thought. This kind of liberalism does not look upon people as abstract individuals, divorced from their social contexts, nor does it embrace the notion of "natural rights" to property and contract, nor does it treat politics as if it were beneath the contempt of all but knaves and fools.* It insists that the foundation of personal liberty is a certain kind of political life—one requiring the ongoing exertions of a special kind of citizenry. Rather than grounding personal freedom on some putatively prepolitical "state of nature," this kind of liberalism makes the cultivation of *liberal citizenship* central to its enterprise. Since this is the view of people like John Stuart Mill and John Dewey and John Rawls,[49] it seems odd to define liberalism in a way that makes the very possibility of liberal republicanism seem a contradiction in terms.

I am greatly encouraged, then, by evidence that others are increasingly dissatisfied with the sharp dichotomy between liberalism and republicanism that has become a banality of trendy constitutional scholarship.[50] As I hope to show in Part Two of this book, the origins of liberal republicanism go back to the Founding itself. We will search the *Federalist Papers* in vain for an elaborate description of a "state of nature" or a penetrating analysis of our "natural rights," Lockean or otherwise. These matters simply do not gain the sustained attention of Madison, Hamilton, and Jay as they try to convince their fellow Americans to support the proposed constitution. What does bulk large in the *Federalist* is a profound diagnosis of the prospects and pathologies of citizenship in the modern world.

This is not because the Founders thought that citizenship was everything and private rights were nothing. It was because they believed that the fate of private freedom in America, and much else besides, depended upon a realistic appreciation of what could, and could not, be expected of American citizens. The liberal idea of citizenship is not only central to my interpretation of the Founding;[51] it will also be crucial to my view of the subsequent course of American history. The basic pattern of constitutional development pre-

*Or "rent-seekers," as they are called in the technocratic jargon now fashionable in academic libertarian circles.

sented here challenges the paradigms of both Hartz and Pocock. Against Hartz, I deny that America has been living in some Lockean time warp, lacking serious politics or significant ideological transformation. American history cannot be understood without confronting the revolutionary reforms that have, time and again, reworked the nation's constitutional identity. Against Pocock,* I deny that this centuries-long development can be best described as a decline from eighteenth-century republicanism to twentieth-century liberalism. American history has a cyclical pattern which we will learn to identify as the characteristic product of a liberal citizenry. One part of the cycle is characterized by normal politics, during which most citizens keep a relatively disengaged eye on the to-and-fro in Washington while they attend to more personal concerns. Although this relative passivity meets the predictable disapproval of political activists who hope to transform the status quo, they find that their appeals to the People for a transformative politics are regularly rebuffed at the polls in favor of politics-as-usual. Then, for a wide variety of reasons, one or another transformative appeal begins to engage the attention of a wider audience. Often it requires a generation or more of preparatory work before a constitutional critique gains the mobilized support of enough citizens to push it onto the center of the political stage. Even then, it is hardly guaranteed success. Long years of mobilization may serve only to reveal that a majority of American citizens reject a fundamental reworking of the status quo.

But there have been times when political movements generated mobilized popular consent to new constitutional solutions—and it will be the aim of the next chapter to examine the story constitutional lawyers tell about these recurring successes of the past two centuries.

---

*Perhaps I am being unfair to Pocock here, since he has been more alert than most to the survival of republican forms and ideals in twentieth-century life. Nonetheless, it is plain that he numbers himself "among the intellectuals . . . [whose] mood is and has long been Tocquevillean; they accept the primacy of liberalism but proceed at once to turn that thesis against itself, asking pressingly whether a society which is liberal *et praetera nihil* can satisfy the deeper demands of the human (or the Western) spirit." J. G. A. Pocock, "Between Gog and Magog: The Republican Thesis and the Ideologica Americana," 48 *J. Hist. Ideas* 325 (1987). Rather than inviting us to synthesize liberalism and republicanism into a holistic understanding of American political identity (as, *pace* Pocock, did Tocqueville), Pocock continues to insist that "the republican thesis is not part of a hypostatized liberalism but has been treated as an attack upon it." Id.

The important point here is to see how the recurring cycle of normal, then constitutional, then normal politics invites us to rethink competing paradigms of American history. Perhaps we have been premature in announcing the disintegration of the civic republican tradition in America? Perhaps the distinctive cycle of American constitutional development lives on to the present day? Perhaps liberal citizens have not yet abandoned their intermittent involvement with American politics, which has sometimes led in the past to such great constitutional achievements?

Which is not to deny that the spirit of dualist democracy *will* die if the present generation of American citizens fails to discover in their Constitution a living language for self-government.

CONCLUSION

In conclusion, let me emphasize that this is only an introduction. I have not tried to answer, or even ask, all the important questions—either philosophical or historical—suggested by my claim that *America is a dualist democracy*. I have simply tried to establish this hypothesis as worthy of serious investigation.

My strategy has been to suggest dualism's distinctiveness by contrasting it with a series of competing political conceptions. Each of these is a serious competitor in at least three senses. First, reasonable people might conclude that one of these rivals offers a political ideal that is more attractive than dualism. Second, if we consider the constitutions of other countries, these rivals may provide interpretive insights that are superior to those generated by the dualist ideal. Once we cross the Atlantic, both the monistic democrat and the Burkean historicist may have more to contribute in defining the genius of the English constitution; if we go to the Federal Republic of Germany, the foundationalist may be a more insightful guide to a constitution that places fundamental rights completely beyond the reach of democratic politics; and so on. Third, each of the rivals does illuminate some important aspects of the American Constitution. The monist is right to insist that our government is, first and foremost, based on democratic principles; the foundationalist is right to emphasize its protection of fundamental rights against normal political change; the Burkean is right to point out the historically rooted character of our constitutional tradition; and the partisans of Hartz and Pocock are right to see that America is distinctive in its embrace of a special sort of liberalism and republicanism.

But it is only dualism that incorporates all these insights into a larger whole—a whole that invites deepening reflection upon the distinctive strengths and weaknesses of the American Constitution, as it has come down to us over two centuries of debate and decision. Hence my opening jeremiad against the Europeanization of American constitutional thought. Although our evolving constitutional practice has been enriched by all of the influences surveyed in this chapter (and many more), the trick is to see how Americans have managed to combine them into a whole that is more than the sum of its parts. To do this sensitively, we must look inward, not outward, and trace the efforts of generations of American citizens and statesmen to fashion a dualistic constitutional language adequate to the ongoing crises of democratic self-government in the life of a liberal republic.

CHAPTER TWO

The Bicentennial
Myth

FROM PHILOSOPHY TO HISTORY

THE FIRST CHAPTER presented the dualistic idea of democracy that motivates our constitutional arrangements. But the Constitution is more than an idea. It is an evolving historical practice, constituted by generations of Americans as they mobilized, argued, resolved their ongoing disputes over the nation's identity and destiny. As we confront the same task today, we do not look upon this history as if it were merely an obstacle to a better future. Our public discourse constantly treats the great constitutional achievements of the past as if they contained valuable clues for decoding the meaning of the political present.

This American habit is by no means a universal feature of political society. Public discourse in Russia today does not look back to the nineteenth century in the same respectful way we recall the Civil War amendments; nor do today's Germans allow themselves to recall the 1930's as positively as Americans do when they describe the New Deal's response to the challenges of the Great Depression. For many Europeans, the past two centuries are full of dramatic breaks and false starts. While we have had our share of bitter conflict and profound transformation, modern Americans tell themselves stories that assert the deep continuity of two centuries of constitutional practice, narratives that thoroughly enmesh today's events in a web of constitutional reference stretching back two hundred years to the Founding. While the French have run through five republics since 1789, we have lived in only one.

Or so we tell ourselves in countless ways every day. Yet do we really believe this Bicentennial Myth? Do we really have much in common with the generation who wrote the Civil War amendments?

And what of the "miracle" of Philadelphia? When Madison and the rest drafted the Constitution in the name of the People, they spoke for a million white male planters and merchants, farmers and mechanics, who were just beginning to assert the independence of the Eastern Seaboard. What can these people really tell us today about the challenges of political life in the world's most powerful military and economic system? If we are to ransack the past for insights, wouldn't it be better to study late republican Rome than early republican America? Indeed, cruel paradox, why not study the constitutional development of the early Americans' great enemy, imperial Britain?

At least since Woodrow Wilson published his great book on *Congressional Government* a century ago, modernist questions like these have dominated the agenda of constitutional thought. Modernists do not deny the existence of institutional forms inherited from the deep past: Congress, Presidency, Court, the written Constitution on permanent display in Washington, D.C. For them, this panoply merely represents our ceremonial Constitution. If we are to do justice to American realities, we must see that effective power is organized on very different lines, that it has a very different genealogy from the one set out by our paper Constitution.[1] Rather than take the Bicentennial Myth seriously, intellectually serious people should describe the radically different government that Americans have made for themselves, and then try to adapt the ceremonial Constitution to promote a better form of political community than the Myth contemplates.

This modernist impulse has driven American constitutional theory further and further afield in its search for enlightenment. Woodrow Wilson sired the most enduring line of modern thought when he approached the Constitution as if it were a botched version of English parliamentary democracy and tried to adapt our antiquated machine to conform to his monistic ideal of modern English democracy. Wilson's effort to displace American dualism with British monism has succeeded only in provoking a host of competing efforts. Many others have also looked to England but have found the spirit of the American constitution more in the thought of Locke or Harrington, Hume or Burke, than in the evolving practice of Westminster.

Competing with the Anglophiles have been the Germanophiles,

with the influence of different Germans waxing and waning over time. Before the Second World War, Marx was the brooding omnipresence; since then, Kant has become an increasingly influential guide to the mysteries of American constitutional arrangements. As Chapter 1 suggested, these different sources of inspiration imply different diagnoses of the American constitutional predicament. But they all begin in the same place: each treats the Bicentennial Myth as a mystification, each denies that the key to understanding the American Constitution is to reflect as deeply as we can on the Founding achievement and what Americans have made of it over the past two centuries.*

But must all myths be mystifications? The Greek *mythos* points in a different direction: the narrative we tell ourselves about our Constitution's roots is a deeply significant act of collective self-definition; its continual re-telling plays a critical role in the ongoing construction of national identity. While this is true for all mature nations, it is especially true for Americans. History shows that it is possible for the French or the Poles, the Germans or the Jews, to survive as a people for centuries, even millennia, despite ceaseless change in their political arrangements. The defining narratives these national communities tell themselves have more to do with deep continuities in culture and religion than constitutional law. For us, matters stand differently. If, as in the case of postwar Germany, the United States were fractured into pieces, each with a different constitutional arrangement, how long would it take before the citizens of New England thought of themselves as more similar to the Canadians of the North than their erstwhile compatriots of the Southwest? Three generations? Four? Five?

In part because Americans differ so radically in other respects, our constitutional narrative constitutes us a people. If you and I did not try to discover meaning in our constitutional history, we would be cutting ourselves off from each other in a way that could not be readily replaced by television talk shows or even Melville, Twain,

---

*Not that modernist commentators disdain the use of selective quotations from the *Federalist Papers* and other canonical sources. They simply do not use these sources to elaborate the distinctive political ideas that they contain. Instead, they cast the Founders as derivative social engineers, the makers of a better mousetrap from plans prepared elsewhere.

and Faulkner. To discover the Constitution is to discover an important part of oneself—insofar as one recognizes oneself as an American. The story you and I tell each other about the nature and history of our constitutional past will, in turn, shape the meanings we are prepared to give to our country's present and future.

Hence the present exercise. Rather than looking *through* the Bicentenial Myth in search of some deeper reality manufactured in England or on the Continent, I mean to look *at* it. How precisely do Americans construct the story that links their constitutional present to their past two centuries? There are many possible stories. Which ones do we tell each other? Are any given a privileged position? Should we tell different stories, ones that give a deeper sense to the constitutional achievements of the American people? How does, how *should,* the story we tell about our past relate to the dualistic democratic principles that organize our present constitutional arrangements?

THE DEEP PAST

These questions may seem unmanageably ambitious. Every day, millions of Americans tell each other countless stories which, in one way or another, use the constitutional past to place their present predicaments in meaningful perspective. These exercises in collective recollection are bewilderingly diverse, in substance and style, in depth and clarity. The very notion that they have much in common seems doubtful. But if we ask some simple questions about their narrative construction, perhaps a certain order will appear to view.

Begin by noticing that modern Americans do not suppose that every year of our past contributes equally to today's Constitution. The significance of 1787 is recalled every time somebody refers to one of the institutions—Congress, Presidency, Court—created at the Founding. Very few Americans feel the need to recall what happened in 1887, although it is a century closer to us in chronological time. People constantly refer to the Reconstruction amendments, while nobody talks much about the constitutional significance of the Spanish–American War; and so forth.

More generally, the constitutional stories Americans tell about themselves have a two-part structure. First, there are lots of references to current events—things that have been decided, mostly by courts, over the past generation or so: *Brown v. Board of Education, Miranda v. Arizona, Roe v. Wade,* the Nixon tapes case, the Bork nomination. Second, there is a far more selective pattern of reference to a more distant past, one that preceded the days before living Americans walked the political stage. By reason of mortality, the line between lived experience and deep past shifts over time. As I write these words in 1988, darkness is beginning to set over the interwar period. While there are still lots of politically active people who were young adults during the war against Hitler, those who were politically conscious during the Great Depression are moving off the stage. The constitutional meaning of the New Deal, like that of the Civil War or the Founding itself, will soon enough be determined exclusively by Americans whose first acquaintance with the facts was gained indirectly—in half-remembered conversations with elders, in tenth-grade civics, in books of law, history, and political science.

It is this deep past—the first hundred fifty years from 1787 to 1937—that will serve as our focus here. While it has many interpreters—from professional historians to T.V. actors—I believe that the ongoing constitutional narrative constructed by lawyers and judges is entitled to a central place. This professional narrative has the most direct impact upon the ordinary lives led by all of us. Day in and day out, judges check our most powerful officials by searching the deep past: they speak as if it were self-evident that decisions made a century or two ago in the name of the People trump the exercises of power by the most powerful elected officials of today. Whatever we may say in the end about such claims, the way judges construct the American relationship to the deep past is not a matter that any of us can take lightly: the things that they allow themselves to see control, sometimes dramatically, what all of us can do in the here and now.

This professional narrative does not have a fixed and unchanging structure. Time and again, it has responded both to popular and scholarly critique. I hope this book will play a part in another such change. Nonetheless, given its profound and pervasive importance to all citizens, it doesn't seem especially controversial to give its study a central place in our civic life. What is controversial, of course, is that we will find very much worth knowing if we hunt for such an illusive entity as *the* professional narrative. Many thoughtful people suspect that the stories modern constitutional lawyers tell are infinitely malleable, best treated as transparent covers for more pressing political convictions. For skeptics, there is no such thing as *the* professional narrative—just stories that liberals or conservatives, reactionaries or radicals, tell one another when wearing black robes. Or if there is anything that distinguishes all legal stories, it can only be described in such vague generalities as to be without practical bite.

I disagree. I believe that American law in general, and constitutional law in particular, is a relatively autonomous part of our culture. It is *relatively* autonomous in that what counts as a plausible legal argument does indeed change, and change profoundly, over time. But it is relatively *autonomous* in that, at any moment of time, even the most powerful of our lawyers and judges are profoundly constrained by the patterns of argument built up by the legal community over the past two centuries of disputation—more powerfully than the judges themselves recognize, for they do not consciously interrogate many of the core elements of their legal culture. They simply take them for granted as they go about their business deciding cases. And yet these cultural constructions are hardly innocuous; the challenge is to make their presuppositions self-conscious objects of reflection. Only then can we begin to appreciate how profoundly they have shaped the development of the modern Constitution, and consider whether we should allow them to block our constitutional vision.

This is, at least, my project here. The bare-bones narrative we shall be scrutinizing is shared by all participants in the legal debate— by Justice Scalia no less than Justice Brennan, Ronald Dworkin no less than Raoul Berger, Robert Bork no less than William Kunstler. It is a mistake to look upon the narrative as if it had been consciously chosen by any individual lawyer or judge after a serious confrontation with alternatives. The story line simply presents itself as an unassailable part of the conventional legal wisdom, presupposed in countless legal arguments by all sides of the endless constitutional debate about other, seemingly more controversial, matters.

And yet this narrative cannot withstand an encounter with the facts of American history.

THE SHAPE OF THE CONSTITUTIONAL PAST

When modern lawyers and judges look to the deep past, they tell themselves a story that has a distinctive structure. Though special problems may lead them to appreciate the relevance of one or another aspect of America's constitutional history, three historical periods stand out from the rest. These eras have a pervasive significance: the lessons a judge draws from each of them organizes her entire approach to concrete cases. The first of these jurisgenerative[2] eras is the Founding itself—the framing of the original Constitution and the Bill of Rights, the Supreme Court's initial assertion of judicial review in *Marbury v. Madison*. A second great period occurs two generations later, with the bloody struggles that ultimately yield the Reconstruction amendments. Then there is another pause of two generations before a third great turning point. This one centers on the 1930's and the dramatic confrontation between the New Deal and the Old Court that ends in the constitutional triumph of the activist welfare state.

This three-part story defines the legal meaning of modernity: All of us live in the modern era that begins with the Supreme Court's "switch in time" in 1937, in which an activist, regulatory state is finally accepted as an unchallengeable constitutional reality. For a modern judge, one of the worst insults is that she is reenacting the sin originally committed by the pre–New Deal Court in cases like *Lochner v. New York*. Of course, different moderns define the nature of original sin differently. What is important is not the competing diagnoses but the universal recognition that the constitutional world before the Roosevelt era was profoundly different from our own.

In contrast, today's lawyers and judges experience no similar estrangement in dealing with more recent history: the New Deal Court that digs itself out of the wreckage of laissez-faire jurisprudence in the late 1930's is recognizably *our* Court. Just as it struggled to define a new conception of individual rights in a burgeoning bureaucratic state, so do modern constitutionalists. While the New Deal Court's early confrontations with these questions differ from more recent encounters, we still think we can learn from these early cases in very positive ways.[3] Rather than functioning as negative precedents like *Lochner,* these early decisions of the New Deal Court mark the very dawning of the modern world.

So much, I think, is shared by all competent constitutional lawyers, regardless of their more particular political or philosophical convictions. I believe, moreover, that the profession's selective concentration upon these three historical turning points is fundamentally sound. Though other periods have contributed a lot to the modern practice of American government, lawyers and judges are right to look upon the Founding, Reconstruction, and the New Deal as decisive moments at which deep changes in popular opinion gained authoritative constitutional recognition. The problem comes only when we consider the way the profession has transformed this selective chronology into a meaningful narrative that roots the modern age in the deep past.

The Existing Narrative

The problem is this: the stories lawyers tell about each of the three turning points do not invite them to reflect upon the common features of these great transformative exercises. Instead, each of these three jurisgenerative events is cabined by a set of lawyerly categories that emphasize how different one episode is from the next.

Of the three, the Founding is treated as if it were the most radical break with the past. Modern lawyers are perfectly prepared to admit that the Constitutional Convention was acting illegally in proposing its new document in the name of We the People. The Founding Federalists, after all, were not prepared to follow the ratification procedures set out in the Articles of Confederation that had been solemnly accepted by all thirteen states only a few years before. The Articles required the unanimous consent of all thirteen state legislatures before any new amendment could come into effect. In contrast, the Federalists blandly excluded state legislatures from *any* role in ratification, and went on to assert that the approval of special constitutional conventions meeting in only nine of the thirteen states would suffice to validate the Convention's effort to speak for the People.

Illegalities like these may not be among the first things that surface in the legal mind, but modern lawyers show no great resistance coming to terms with them.[4] Indeed, there is a conceptual sense in which our very identification of the Founding as a Founding presupposes that the Philadelphia Convention acted without legal warrant under the preexisting Articles. If this were not the case, the *real* Founders of our Republic were the folks who wrote and ratified the Articles of Confederation; the Philadelphia Convention simply gained the ratification of some sweeping "amendments" to the Founding document. Since modern lawyers do not trace the origin of the Republic to the Articles of Confederation but to *the* Constitution of 1787, the discovery of some Founding illegalities confirms, rather than denies, their sense of the overall shape of our constitutional past.

Things are different when the subject turns to the constitutional amendments enacted after the Civil War. Here modern law-talk exhibits a sharp dichotomy between substance and procedure. Substantively, everybody recognizes that these three amendments profoundly transformed preexisting constitutional principles. But if we turn to the process by which they became part of our higher law, a remarkable silence descends on the legal community. While it has no trouble admitting the dubious legality of the Founding, professional talk contains no hint that Reconstruction might be similarly tainted. If asked to explain why the Civil War amendments are part of the Constitution, the modern American lawyer or judge would almost certainly point to the rules for constitutional amendment contained in Article Five of the 1787 Constitution. According to received opinion, the Civil War amendments are just that: ordinary amendments which, like all the others, owe their legality to their conformity with the formal rules for constitutional revision established by the Federalists in the 1787 Constitution. To put this point in a formula: while the professional narrative insists that Reconstruction was *substantively creative,* it supposes that it was *procedurally unoriginal.*

Even this much originality is denied the New Deal. While all lawyers recognize that the 1930's mark the definitive constitutional triumph of activist national government, they tell themselves a story which denies that anything deeply creative was going on. This view of the 1930's is obtained by imagining a Golden Age in which Chief Justice Marshall got things right for all time by propounding a broad construction of the national government's lawmaking authority. The period between Reconstruction and the New Deal can then be viewed as a (complex) story about the fall from grace—wherein most of the Justices strayed from the path of righteousness and imposed their laissez-faire philosophy on the nation through the pretext of constitutional interpretation. Predictably, these acts of judicial usurpation increasingly set the judges at odds with more democratic institutions, which acutely perceived the failure of laissez-faire to do justice to an increasingly interdependent world.

The confrontation between the New Deal and the Old Court climaxes this traditional morality play of decline, fall, and resurrection. Only Justice Roberts's "switch in time," and the departure of the worst judicial offenders, permitted the Court to expiate its countermajoritarian sins without permanent institutional damage. If only the Justices had not strayed from Marshall's original path, perhaps all this unpleasantness could have been avoided!

As always, this basic story line invites countless disagreements about the precise character of the Marshallian vision, the precise scope of the latter-day aberrations during the *Lochner* period of laissez-faire. For present purposes, the critical point is simple enough: in contrast to the first two turning points, modern lawyers do not describe either the substantive or the procedural aspects of the New Deal by telling themselves a tale of constitutional creation. The triumph of activist national government is mediated by a myth of rediscovery—as if the Founding Federalists had foreseen the works of Franklin Delano Roosevelt and would have been surprised to learn that the great struggles of the 1930's were necessary to gain the welfare state's constitutional legitimation.

Founding Federalists → Illegal Constitution; Reconstruction Republicans → Formal Amendments; New Deal Democrats → Judicial Rediscovery of Ancient Truths: this schema suggests a subtle but unmistakable decline in the constitutionally generative capacities of the American people. Apparently, We the People have never again engaged in the sweeping kind of critique and creation attempted by the Founding Federalists. We have made substantive revisions in the original structure of the Constitution, but we have never gone so far as to revise the very process of constitutional revision. A similar loss is implied by a comparison between the nineteenth and twentieth centuries: while the Reconstruction Republicans gained the consent of the American people to fundamental changes in governing principles, the sweeping transformations won by the New Deal Democrats represent nothing more than a return to the wisdom of the early Founders.

A Revisionary Narrative

I mean to question the prevailing interpretive schema. Despite its familiarity, it is built on sand. If we return to our sources, they tell a very different story. They reveal both Reconstruction Republicans and New Deal Democrats engaging in self-conscious acts of constitutional creation that rivaled the Founding Federalists' in their scope and depth. In each case, the new spokesmen for the People refused to follow the path for constitutional revision set out by their predecessors; like the Federalists before them, they transformed existing systems of higher lawmaking in the process of changing the fundamental direction of political development. Rather than meekly following the marching orders of the Federalists, both Republicans and Democrats were constitutionally creative procedurally no less than substantively—and they knew it.

Now there is only one way to establish this claim—and that is to return to the sources, and follow both nineteenth-century Republicans and twentieth-century Democrats step-by-step in their transformative exercises. Only then can we gain an adequate sense of their remarkable creativity in defining new roles for the Presidency, the Congress, the Court, and the voters in the higher lawmaking process. Only then will we come to understand how they finally *earned* the constitutional authority to speak in the name of the People.

This is a pretty big job. The story is full of fascinating examples of creative statesmanship, but there is a danger of losing sight of the forest by moving too quickly into the description of particularly striking trees. Since this part aims to present an overview of my entire project, I will only summarize the most important constitutional innovations won by the Republicans and Democrats. The second volume in this series, *Transformations,* will be entirely devoted to redeeming the promissory notes offered below.[5]

RECONSTRUCTION

Reconstruction was just that—rebuilding the Union from the ground up. The Reconstruction amendments—especially the Fourteenth—

would never have been ratified if the Republicans had followed the rules laid down by Article Five of the original Constitution. The Republicans were entirely aware of this fact, as were their conservative antagonists. The amendments gained recognition only because the Reconstruction Congress successfully challenged, with remarkable self-consciousness, two basic premises of the system for constitutional revision handed down by the Founding Federalists.

First, and most fundamental, was the federalist principle itself— the idea that a constitutional amendment must obtain the support of both the national government and the states, acting independently of one another, before it could be recognized as a legitimate addition to our higher law. Although the first breach of federalist premises occurred during ratification of the Thirteenth Amendment, the great crisis was provoked by the Fourteenth Amendment. To prevent the South from using the Federalist rules of Article Five to defeat the proposal and ratification of the amendment, the Reconstruction Republicans elaborated a new, and more nationalistic, system of constitutional decisionmaking—one in which the states played only a secondary role. It was this revised process, and not the one designed by the Founding Federalists, that determined the legitimacy of the constitutional solution we now identify as the Fourteenth Amendment.

The nationalization of the amendment process led the Republicans, in turn, to challenge a second Founding premise. Writing against the background of the English Whig experience, the Founders supposed that only popularly elected assemblies, analogous to the English House of Commons, had the authority to change the Constitution in the name of the People. While Presidents and courts might play important roles in other matters, the fate of constitutional revisions would be determined by a dialogue monopolized by elected assemblies on the national and state levels. As the Republicans gave more responsibilities to the nation, however, new national institutions began to gain expanded powers. Most important, Presidents Lincoln and Johnson discharged a whole series of critical functions in the process through which the Thirteenth and Fourteenth Amendments were proposed, debated, legitimated. At certain points, the Supreme Court also played an important part.

To put these two nineteenth-century innovations together in a single line: the Reconstruction Republicans transformed the national *separation of powers* into an alternative to the Federalist system of constitutional revision that had been based exclusively on the *division of powers* between state and nation. Our study of the Thirteenth and Fourteenth Amendments will also allow us to define two important variations on this new nationalistic theme. The Thirteenth Amendment introduces *the model of Presidential leadership* that will bulk large in our subsequent analysis of the New Deal transformation. In this model, President and Congress cooperate with one another to secure the validation of a constitutional amendment, despite the amendment's questionable legality under the rules and principles laid down by the Federalist Constitution. Within the context of Reconstruction, however, a second model, generated by the struggle over the Fourteenth Amendment, will require more elaborate analysis. As a result of the defection of President Andrew Johnson to the side of the constitutional conservatives, it fell to the Republicans to develop *a model of Congressional leadership* if they hoped to win higher law validation of their proposed Fourteenth Amendment.

I will be tracing the way a reformist Congress and a conservative President interacted during the critical years of Reconstruction to elaborate this new model—permitting the general citizenry first to understand and then to participate decisively in the resolution of the critical issues of constitutional identity raised in the aftermath of Civil War. If I am successful, this analysis will require a revision of the basic categories modern lawyers use to interpret the Republican constitutional achievement. After immersing yourself in the historical context, the received view of the Civil War amendments as normal amendments will simply dissolve. The Republican Reconstruction of the Union was an act of constitutional creation no less profound than the Founding itself: not only did the Republicans introduce new substantive principles into our higher law, but they reworked the very process of higher lawmaking itself.

Not that this Republican exercise was entirely alien to the Federalist spirit. The Federalists too were relatively nationalistic for their time; they too confronted, in the Articles of Confederation, a pre-existing system for constitutional revision that gave too much power to the states by insisting on unanimous consent for any amendment; and they too responded by restricting the power of the states to veto their more nationalistic conception of the Union. When we investigate the facts more deeply, we will discover many more parallels between Federalist principles of higher lawmaking and Republican innovations. I have said enough, though, to motivate the next phase of the argument.

THE NEW DEAL

The next stage uses our new perspective on the Republican achievement to win a new view of the next great turning point in constitutional history: the successful struggle by the New Deal Democrats to place activist national government on solid constitutional foundation. The reigning narrative trivializes this New Deal victory even more emphatically than the Republican achievement. According to the modern myth of rediscovery, the New Dealers did not even contribute new substantive principles to our higher law, let alone rework the very process of higher lawmaking. Instead, their redefinition of American government involved little more than the recollection of some forgotten bits of Founding Wisdom.

My counterthesis: Like the Reconstruction Republicans, the New Deal Democrats relied on the national separation of powers between Congress, President, and Court to create a new institutional framework through which the American People might define, debate, and finally decide their constitutional future. The key institutional difference between the two periods involves the Presidency. Franklin Roosevelt remained at the helm of the reformist coalition throughout the Democrats' period of constitutional transformation, whereas Lincoln's assassination deprived Republican reformers of Presidential support during the critical struggle over the Fourteenth Amendment. Roosevelt's long tenure had fundamental, if unsurprising, implications for the Presidency's role in the process of higher lawmaking. While the Republicans successfully experimented with Presidential leadership in the process of legitimating the Thirteenth Amendment, they could not build on this experience once Andrew Johnson declared war on the Fourteenth Amendment. In contrast, the Democrats were in a position to develop the power of the Presidency in a far more incisive fashion.

When due allowances are made for the defection of President Johnson from the Republican coalition, however, it will be possible to identify remarkable similarities in the way in which the separation of powers tested, and finally legitimated, the constitutional revisions proposed by nineteenth-century Republicans and twentieth-century Democrats. Each higher lawmaking exercise began with the reformers in control of only part of the national government—in the case of the Republicans, it was Congress that took on the mantle of reform leadership with Johnson's defection; in the case of the Democrats, the Presidency was the leading reform branch. In both cases, the constitutional reformers' proposals were exposed to an initial period of incisive critique by conservative branches, which publicly appealed to the People to decisively reject the dangerous innovations proposed by the reformers. In the case of the Republicans, the leading conservative branch was the Presidency; for the Democrats, it was the Supreme Court.

These institutional differences were important, of course, in explaining the different dynamics of constitutional debate and decision. But it is even more important to see the deeper similarities. In both cases, the institutional deadlock in Washington forced both sides to mobilize their supporters in the country at large. These remarkable efforts at popular mobilization, in turn, gave extraordinary constitutional meaning to the next regularly scheduled election. If one or another side could win a decisive victory at the polls, it would try to use its popular support to break the institutional impasse.

This process of interbranch struggle and popular mobilization made the elections of 1866 and 1936 decisive events in constitutional history. On both occasions, the reformers returned to Washington with a clear victory at the polls. They proceeded to proclaim that the election results gave them a "mandate from the People," and that the time had come for the conservative branches to end their constitutional resistance.

This demand by the electorally victorious reformers inaugurated the period of ratification—in which the conservative branches considered whether to continue their resistance or to recognize that the People had indeed given their fixed support to the reformist movement. In both cases, this decision was not made in silent contemplation but in response to a challenge by the reformist branches to the conservatives' continued legitimacy. During Reconstruction, the reformist Congress finally threatened President Johnson with impeachment if he continued to use his office to sabotage ratification of the Fourteenth Amendment. During the New Deal, it was the reformist President's threat of packing the Court that provoked the conservative Justices to consider the wisdom of continued resistance. In both cases, however, the question was very much the same: Should the conservatives in the dissenting branches finally recognize that *the People had spoken?*

In both cases, the conservatives' answer was the same. Rather than escalating the constitutional crisis further, they decided, with evident reluctance, that further resistance would endanger too many of the very values they held fundamental. They made the "switch in time": Johnson called off his effort to prevent the formal ratification of the Fourteenth Amendment; the Supreme Court repudiated its doctrinal defense of laissez-faire capitalism and began to build new constitutional foundations for activist national government.

In turn, the victorious reformers responded in the same way. The Republicans refused to convict the President, allowing Johnson to remain in office to proclaim the validity of the Fourteenth Amendment; the Democrats called off the threat of court-packing, allowing the Old Court to proclaim that activist New Deal government was constitutionally legitimate.

As a consequence of these "switches in time," all three branches emerge from the period of democratic testing once again united, and the separation of powers remains intact for use by the next constitutional regime. But it is now in the service of the new constitutional solution that had previously been so controversial.

Interbranch Impasse → Decisive Election → Reformist Challenge to Conservative Branches → Switch in Time: This separation of powers schema will require lots of elaboration before it can gain legal credibility. There is no way to avoid the hard historical work required to appreciate the functional similarities between President Johnson's veto of Congress's Civil Rights Act and the Supreme Court's veto of the NIRA; between the critical election of 1866 and the critical election of 1936; between the Republican effort to impeach the President and the Democratic effort to pack the Court; between the final ratification of the Fourteenth Amendment by Johnson's Secretary of State and the final ratification of the welfare state by the New Deal Court; and so forth. Fortunately, many of these

fascinating events have attracted the sustained attention of generations of historians; and I will try to make use of their insights as best
I can. An even more formidable challenge will be to set each particular episode into the larger context of higher lawmaking—and
thereby grasp the evolving constitutional process through which the
separation of powers first forced the contending parties to refine
their constitutional vision and counter-vision, then presented the key
issues in dramatic form to a mobilized electorate, and then provided
a further period during which thoughtful conservatives could consider whether the time had not come to recognize that the People
had indeed spoken.

In elaborating these striking parallels between Reconstruction and
the New Deal, I shall be building upon the insights of the protagonists of the 1930's. Time and again, the New Dealers invoked Reconstruction precedents in their efforts to build a modern model of
Presidential leadership in the higher lawmaking process. The challenge is to *listen* to these voices, not insist upon viewing the New
Deal reformers as if they were exhausted epigones, capable only of
returning to the forgotten wisdom of the Founders.

Only after we define what is really new about the New Deal can
we begin to confront the deep problems they left for us. Should the
New Deal model of Presidential leadership once again be revised to
better confront the higher lawmaking challenges of the next century?

FROM PAST TO PRESENT

The events of the last decade make this question of pressing practical
importance. The 1980's saw a serious effort to lead the American
people to repudiate the New Deal's affirmation of activist national
government. The upshot—thus far, at least—has been paradoxical.
Rather than winning the struggle to revise the foundations of the
welfare state, the Reagan Republicans only succeeded in confirming
the vitality of the higher lawmaking precedents created by the Roosevelt Democrats.

As in the 1930's, the Republicans did not attempt to repeal the
New Deal by a vigorous campaign for formal constitutional amendments of the kind envisioned by the Federalists in the original Constitution. Instead, like the New Deal Democrats, the Reagan Repub-

licans used the Presidency as the institutional focus for their effort to lead the American people to revise their constitutional identity; as in the 1930's, the critical question was the extent to which the President could succeed in convincing the other branches of the national government to take seriously his demand for fundamental change—a demand that reached its climax in a struggle in the Senate over the President's effort to appoint new Justices to the Supreme Court who would give hard doctrinal shape to the new constitutional ideals so insistently proclaimed from the Oval Office.

At this point, a big difference between the two periods emerges. Roosevelt was ultimately successful in gaining Congressional consent to a series of transformative Supreme Court appointments; by the beginning of his third term, a unanimous Court had joined the other branches in ratifying the constitutional legitimacy of activist national government. In contrast, Reagan transparently failed to convince a decisive majority of Americans to support his radical critique of the welfare state premises inherited from the New Deal; rather than gaining the consent of the Senate to a series of transformative Supreme Court appointments, the President saw his constitutional ambitions rejected in the battle precipitated by his nomination of Robert Bork.

For present purposes, however, a study of the institutional dynamics of Reagan's failed constitutional moment can be no less revealing than Roosevelt's successful transformation. It will provide us with a new perspective upon one of the most striking constitutional innovations of the 1930's. This involves the legal process through which the New Dealers successfully memorialized their new constitutional solution. While the Reconstruction Republicans broke new ground in their use of the separation of powers as the principal engine of constitutional revision, they nonetheless managed to codify their reforms in legal instruments that bore the surface appearance of "constitutional amendments." These Reconstruction texts are only amendment-simulacra, since they were not generated in accordance with the principles laid down by the Federalist Constitution. Nonetheless, at least the Republicans managed to pour their new constitutional wine into old legal bottles.

In contrast, the New Dealers rejected the traditional form of an amendment; instead they relied on the New Deal Court to elaborate their new activist vision through a series of transformative opinions. It is worth emphasizing that this decision was entirely self-conscious and public. We will hear President Roosevelt and leading spokesmen of his Administration explaining why it was wrong to codify the New Deal transformation through forms sanctioned by Article Five; why we should rely instead on the appointment of new judges to give new meaning to the Constitution. After 1937, moreover, Roosevelt and Congress used this technique of transformative judicial appointment with unprecedented success. By the early 1940's, a reconstituted Court had not contented itself with rejecting a few offending decisions of a bygone era. It revolutionized reigning constitutional doctrine in a thoroughgoing way—to the point where the Court was now unanimously rejecting fundamental doctrines that shaped the entire body of constitutional law only a decade before.[6]

This Rooseveltian precedent haunted Ronald Reagan when, despite his failure to emulate Roosevelt's success in sweeping Congress, he nominated Robert Bork to the Supreme Court. Bork's very achievements as a lawyer and thinker symbolized the President's transformative constitutional ambitions. Here was a distinguished law professor, like Frankfurter and Douglas in the Roosevelt Administration, who obviously had the skills to write transformative opinions that would set constitutional law in a new direction. Although his appointment alone would not suffice to generate the kind of 9-to-0 decisions that came out of the New Deal Court by the early 1940's, he could supply the intellectual firepower necessary to write judicial texts that would shape the law as fundamentally as had the great New Deal opinions.

Only by setting the Bork nomination against the New Deal precedent can we appreciate the anxiety and energy with which both sides prosecuted the struggle over his appointment. Rather than reviewing the particulars of this struggle, it is far more important to see in the Bork affair a larger problem we confront in grappling with the Rooseveltian precedent: Is this New Deal tendency to transform the Constitution through judicial appointments, rather than formal amendments, a good thing? If not, what can be done about it?

I think this emphasis on transformative appointments threatens core dualist values, for three reasons. First, the debate over the constitutional principles involved in the confirmation of a particular

Supreme Court nominee is, almost inevitably, poorly focused. These vital questions will often be deflected by the personal style, charisma, and frailties of the individual nominee. They may be obscured by the strategic manipulation of rhetoric by both the nominee's friends and foes, to the point where it is no longer clear in what direction the nominee is seeking to lead the Court. Contrast the potential for confusion with the classical system of Article Five amendment. Here the partisans of constitutional change must formulate a formal amendment before they can expect a serious debate to begin. While textual statement of principle hardly eliminates all ambiguity and confusion, it does provide a focus for democratic discussion that can be entirely lost in the swirl of bobbing and weaving characteristic of a Senate confirmation hearing.

Second, although the classical system is deficient in failing to provide the President with any role in the process of constitutional change, the evolving system of transformative appointment gives him far too weighty a role. Most Presidents do not come into office with a mandate for fundamental change of the kind that Franklin Delano Roosevelt plausibly claimed in the aftermath of the elections of 1936.[7] After all, Roosevelt had done far more during his first term than simply prepare the way for reelection. He had gained Congressional support for an activist program that sharply broke with traditional constitutional principles, and he won massive popular support despite the Old Court's eloquent constitutional critique of the New Deal's interventionist premises. If the American people were ever endorsing a break with their constitutional past, they were doing so in the 1930's.[8]

The constitutional precedents established during Roosevelt's second term, however, may easily be abused by future Presidents with far more equivocal mandates for fundamental change. So long as they can convince a bare majority of the Senate to consent to a series of transformative appointments to the Court, constitutional law may be jolted onto a new course without persuasive institutional evidence that a mobilized majority of the American people endorse the change. Once again, compare the requirement that a bare majority of Senators consent to a transformative appointment with the kinds of institutional assent demanded by the classical system of constitutional revision. Under Article Five, no amendment can even be proposed

by the Congress in the name of the People unless two-thirds of both
Houses agree, not just a bare majority of the Senate. Even such a
weighty showing of institutional support suffices only to put the
proposal on the constitutional agenda; a second, institutionally
weighty, round of debate and decision is then necessary before the
classical system allows a new constitutional vision to be enacted into
law. In short, the modern practice seems far too flimsy to give
credible evidence of the deep and broad popular support classically
required for a sharp constitutional break with the past.

But the emerging system of transformative appointment not only
lacks *institutional weight* and *legal focus* remotely comparable to the
classical system. It also raises a third threat: unacceptable elitism.
Think again about Article Five's stipulation that our representatives
in Washington, D.C., may only propose amendments, and that a
much more open-ended debate is required in the several states before
an amendment can be ratified. While we may no longer believe that
the states should always have a veto over national political change,
it is still possible to design a national mechanism requiring our
political elite in Washington to go to the country and make a special
effort to gain general public acceptance for their constitutional proposals.

The device I have in mind—the referendum—is already familiar
in the constitutional practice of our states, as well as many foreign
nations. Properly structured, it can serve as a catalyst for the broad-
ranging popular debate essential for the democratic legitimation of
proposed constitutional initiatives. While President and Congress,
acting together, should be able to propose an amendment, they
should not be able to ratify an amendment without first going to the
People and gaining the specially focused and considered consent
permitted by the use of the referendum device.

Legal focus, institutional weight, popular responsiveness—perhaps
these ideals can be made more concrete by proposing a constitutional
amendment which captures them better than the current practice of
transformative judicial appointments:

> During his or her second term in office, a President may propose con-
> stitutional amendments to the Congress of the United States; if two-
> thirds of both Houses approve a proposal, it shall be listed on the ballot

at the next two succeeding Presidential elections in each of the several states; if three-fifths of the voters participating in each of these elections should approve a proposed amendment, it shall be ratified in the name of the People of the United States.

I have no vested interest in the details of this particular proposal. I advance it to invite you to begin your own critical examination of higher lawmaking: If you think that my proposal is mistaken, why? Because you disagree with the criteria I propose to test a movement's claim to speak for "the People"? Because you think my proposal can be manipulated too easily by politicians who lack the requisite kind of citizen support? Because you think it will not successfully channel Presidential ambitions and that the White House will still try to push transformative judicial appointments whenever it gets the chance?[9]

What fundamental criteria should be used to judge a movement's claim to speak for "the People"? How *should* a higher lawmaking system be designed that can reliably distinguish between the rare occasions upon which a mobilized majority of American citizens hammer out a considered judgment on a fundamental matter of principle, and the countless decisions of normal politics?

We shall be revisiting these questions before we are done.[10] But it is never too early to start. Above all, don't make the mistake of supposing that our present constitutional version of dualistic democracy is in perfect running order. To the contrary, the constitutional machine will run down unless we make an ongoing effort to reflect on our own dualistic experience and use the opportunities given to us in the future to enact needed reforms.*

Such reformist hopes, however, should not blind us to existing realities. The attempts by Presidents to transform the Constitution through transformative judicial appointments is an entrenched part of modern practice. Not only do Americans owe modern activist government to Roosevelt's success in developing this technique. Roosevelt's success has colored the way the public interprets exercises in Presidential leadership. There is absolutely no reason to believe

---

*In calling for the revision of Article Five, I am taking up a theme that was at the center of Progressive thought during the early part of the century. See, e.g., Herbert Croly, *Progressive Democracy* 229–36 (1914).

that Robert Bork's nomination will be the last one to provoke constitutional countermobilization in a Senate dominated by the President's political opponents. Everybody knows that we owe the modern Constitution to a series of successful transformative appointments. And what can happen once can happen twice.

For all its institutional frailties, moreover, the debate over the Bork nomination did provide an important forum through which the constitutional standing of the Reagan Presidency was tested. The American people showed they were not yet prepared to mobilize themselves in support of a Presidential effort to revolutionize constitutional doctrine through a series of transformative appointments. The Reagan "Revolution" was a failed constitutional moment.

Which is not to say that another President will not succeed in the future. My problem is that, until constitutionalists liberate themselves from the myth of rediscovery with which they cover up the New Deal, they cannot even articulate the relationship between Reagan and Roosevelt that haunted the recent Presidential exercise. Blinded by their trivializing views of the American constitutional past, they cannot recognize that there was something really new about the New Deal. Yet it is this recognition that must precede our own efforts to reshape the New Deal precedents so as better to conform to our own evolving understanding of dualist democracy.

CONCLUSION

The first chapter dealt with constitutional theory; this one with constitutional history. Both are sketches, which depend critically upon details yet to be supplied. But it is not too soon to see how the two chapters build upon one another in a cumulating effort to rediscover the distinctive character of our Constitution.

Begin by observing that both critiques derive from the same diagnosis of the modern situation: "sophisticated" wisdom is losing touch with the Constitution's dualistic roots. On the level of theory, this loss is expressed by the modernist effort to displace dualism with one or another constitutional ideal of foreign manufacture: be it monistic democracy, rights foundationalism, Burkean incrementalism, or something else. On the level of history, this loss is expressed by the construction of a professional narrative that gives only grudging recognition to the most distinctive aspect of the dualist enterprise: the higher lawmaking process by which political movements ultimately gain the constitutional authority to make new law in the name of We the People of the United States. While modern lawyers and judges still recognize that the Founders themselves were constitutionally creative in establishing their authority to speak for the People, they consign even the most creative constitutional movements of later times to a lesser role—to the extent that the transformative character of twentieth-century constitutional politics is completely disguised by a myth of rediscovery.

We cannot allow ourselves to be cast as rootless epigones of bygone eras of constitutional creativity. By confronting the original documents left to us by the Founding Federalists, Reconstruction Republicans, and New Deal Democrats, we will gain the resources to tell ourselves a different story—one in which the dualist project in higher lawmaking begun at the Founding was creatively adapted, time and time again, by Americans of later generations as they struggled over, and sometimes won, the constitutional authority to speak in the name of We the People.

On this view of our constitutional history, dualist theory becomes something more than an academic exercise. It is only by talking together about the deepest values of dualist democracy that we can reflect on the best ways to continue the ongoing American engagement with higher lawmaking. A refusal to engage in this conversation is itself a choice; a choice to stand by silently as the distinctive aspirations of the American Republic become lost in the fog of ancient history.

CHAPTER THREE

One Constitution,
Three Regimes

Toward a Regime Perspective

THE LAST CHAPTER challenged the basic terms within which modern lawyers and judges understand the three great turning points of constitutional history: the Founding, Reconstruction, and the New Deal. The professional wisdom arrays these periods in descending order of constitutional creativity: the Founding was creative both in process and substance; Reconstruction was creative only substantively; the New Deal was not creative at all. To fix ideas, call this a two-solution narrative, since it recognizes only the Founding and Reconstruction as sources of new constitutional solutions. In contrast, I shall be proposing a three-solution narrative—in which both Reconstruction Republicans and New Deal Democrats appear as the equals of the Founding Federalists in creating new higher lawmaking processes and substantive solutions in the name of We the People of the United States.

A re-vision along these lines will have large practical consequences, for it will change the way judges decide a host of concrete cases. I am not suggesting that future judges should abandon customary modes of thought simply out of restless academic trendiness. Modern lawyers should revise their existing professional narrative only if, after immersing themselves in the historical sources, they come to see how much of the constitutional past they have suppressed by telling themselves the familiar two-solution narrative; they must be convinced how much more a three-solution analysis does justice to both the distinctive facts and democratic aspirations of the Founding, Reconstruction, and the New Deal. This single task will require a lot of work with the original sources.

Nonetheless, it can serve only as the first stage in a larger process of narrative revision. By reinterpreting the three decisive turning points, we can open up a new view of our entire constitutional past. I introduce this larger enterprise in the remainder of this part, by describing the distinctive constitutional regimes inaugurated by each of the three great transformations. After some orienting remarks, this chapter begins with a constitutional sketch of the early republic—marking out the distinctive matrix of governing institutions and fundamental values that organized political life from 1787 through 1860. The next chapter continues with a sketch of the middle republic—born in Reconstruction and enduring through the Great Depression. Part One of this book concludes with two chapters that confront the modern regime in which we live today.

I have three aims in presenting this overview. The first is to move beyond the court-centered view that afflicts the modern professional narrative. Lawyers and judges must resist the temptation to make the Supreme Court the alpha as well as the omega. The basic unit of analysis should be the *constitutional regime,* the matrix of institutional relationships and fundamental values that are usually taken as the constitutional baseline in normal political life.[1] The challenge is to grasp the distinctive ways the important institutions—House, Senate, President, the states, voters, political parties—interacted with one another in each of the constitutional regimes. Only then can we assess the Supreme Court's role within each particular epoch.

This holistic approach builds bridges to the political scientists, historians, and philosophers with whom lawyers should be collaborating in winning a deeper understanding of the American past. So long as constitutional history is conceived as the study of judicial opinions, the legal terrain will seem arcane and forbidding to those with more general interests in American political life.* Once the professional narrative becomes more self-conscious about the relationship between Supreme Court decisions and the changing character of the constitutional regime, it will become easier for students

*Speaking broadly, this is the principal deficiency of the most important project in constitutional history of our time: the monumental history of the Supreme Court edited by Paul Freund on behalf of The Holmes Devise. As my endnotes suggest, I am much indebted to these volumes. Nonetheless, their narrow focus on Supreme Court opinions condemns them to too narrow an audience.

of the Presidency or Congress or political parties or political philosophy to see more clearly how their concerns might intersect with those of judges and lawyers. Rather than generating an endless series of narrow monographs, people from different disciplines might see themselves as contributors to a more general field of constitutional studies, exploring the way that the American experience with constitutional politics has changed—and failed to change—the institutional context and fundamental values of dualist democracy.

While I will be gesturing in these interdisciplinary directions, my second aim will be to convince lawyers and judges to adopt the regime perspective—by showing concretely how it provides new resources for the resolution of classic problems of legal doctrine. This work builds on the conception of the Supreme Court introduced in the first chapter. Against the monists, I denied that judicial review is presumptively antidemocratic merely because it deprives Congress of plenary authority to make any statute it likes. Against the foundationalists, I denied that the Court is properly in the business of using the methods of philosophy to elaborate fundamental human rights valid for all times and all places. Instead, its job is to preserve the higher law solutions reached by the People against their erosion during periods of normal politics.

The isolation of the Court's *preservationist function* transparently raised many more questions than it answered: How is the Court to go about its business interpreting the constitutional solutions of the past? Does it even make sense to think of "constitutional interpretation" as a disciplined activity with its own criteria of good and bad arguments, its own claim to integrity? Or is it just a mystifying shell game that conceals each participant's ordinary political commitments?

These questions are absolutely critical to your assessment of the dualist enterprise: if "constitutional interpretation" is the name of a political con game, then you can just as well stop reading this book. Dualism presupposes the possibility of interpretation. Ought implies can: if interpretation is impossible, the dualist shouldn't demand that present politicians defer to (nonexistent) "interpretations" of the past constitutional achievements of the American people. Instead, we would all be well advised to give up on dualism and return to the conventional categories of constitutional debate: either the monist is right in condemning the Court as an antidemocratic institution, or the foundationalist is right in insisting that Justices had better become good philosophers if they are to elaborate the nature of fundamental human rights, or the Burkean is right to suggest . . .[2]

The dualist can only rejoice, then, in finding that lots of people are taking the idea of interpretation more seriously these days.[3] My own contribution will be less abstract than most recent efforts. These have been largely concerned with foundational questions raised by the very idea of interpretation—does it make sense at all? what does it look like? why is it valuable? My concerns will be more concrete. I mean to examine our two centuries of practice in constitutional interpretation. Even if "interpretation" makes sense as an abstract enterprise, perhaps American lawyers have done an especially bad job of it—such a bad job as to lead to a corrosive skepticism about the capacity of courts to discharge the preservationist function assigned to them by dualist theory?

If, to the contrary, courts have done a pretty good job at constitutional interpretation, this puts the case for dualism in a different light. The theory's complex two-track design will no longer seem an unworkable Rube Goldberg contraption. Despite the difficulties, courts have in fact devised a rough-and-ready way to sustain the values of constitutional politics against erosion by normal politics. This conclusion will be of special importance to the professionals charged with keeping the machine in good working order. If the Court has been making a good-faith effort at constitutional interpretation over the past two centuries, don't the Justices have a lot to learn from this experience as they continue their preservationist mission into the next century?

This question motivates a third reason for advancing a regime perspective, one more critical than constructive. I mean to expose how the dominant professional narrative blocks our historical understanding of the interpretive efforts of past generations. This two-solution story explicitly recognizes the tripartite division I shall be making between the early, middle, and modern regimes. Only it anachronistically subordinates its understanding of the early periods so as to satisfy the modern need to legitimate the New Deal through a myth of rediscovery. Like all anachronisms, this blinds us to the genuinely distinctive features of earlier interpretive practices which might be relevant to us today, despite the very different features of our own constitutional regime.

Consider, for example, how the modern professional narrative focuses on a few relatively nationalistic opinions by Marshall and Story in its account of the law of the early republic.[4] This allows the profession to pretend that the New Deal had merely rediscovered the Founding Wisdom about activist national government. But it grievously distorts the character of the early republic. The Founders created the least, not the most, nationalistic regime in our history; the longer the early republic survived, the less nationalistic it became.[5] The Marshall Court was fighting a rearguard action to preserve the Founding Federalists' cautious nationalism against the decentralizing tendencies of the first constitutional regime. This reinterpretation not only discredits the myth of rediscovery through which we veil the constitutional creativity of the New Deal—by making it clear that the Founding Federalists would have flatly repudiated many of the New Dealers' constitutional innovations. It also allows us to ask new questions about the Marshall Court: why and how did it manage to preserve a certain degree of nationalism in the face of the decentralizing tendencies of the early regime? Perhaps we can learn something from this Marshallian effort at preservation that remains relevant today? Can we state, clearly and incisively, the respects in which the interpretive conception advanced by John Marshall in the early republic is different from, but related to, the problem of interpretation modern courts confront in the post–New Deal world?

I shall be pursuing a similar approach to the constitutional law of the middle republic. The present professional narrative mystifies this era even more thoroughly than it obscures the period before the Civil War. Modern lawyers are taught to dismiss as essentially worthless the interpretive effort of the Supreme Court during the long period of Republican ascendancy between 1869 and 1932. The anachronistic impulse is obvious. Only by stigmatizing the middle republic as a dark age can lawyers look upon the 1930's in the way required by the myth of rediscovery. Only if the Old Court of the 1930's was completely wrong can the Rooseveltian Revolution be presented as merely requiring the Justices to rediscover the ancient wisdom of the Marshall Court.

This dismissive view of the middle republic cuts modern lawyers off from one-third of our entire legal history as a people. The period is even more important in the development of the Supreme Court. During the early republic, the Court invalidated only two national statutes, a minor jurisdictional provision in *Marbury v. Madison* and the historic effort by Congress to compromise the status of black Americans in *Dred Scott v. Sandford*. Only during the middle republic did the Court begin to review the constitutionality of national legislation on a regular basis; the scope and intensity of its scrutiny of state legislation also dramatically increased. Though the constitutional doctrines of the middle period were very different from the modern ones, it was during this era that judicial review begins to look like the current practice. Surely, then, it is unfortunate to cut ourselves off from such a potentially rewarding source of insight into our own interpretive predicaments?

I do not mean to argue for a return to the "bad old days" of laissez-faire constitutionalism.[6] I am searching more for suggestive analogies than for straightforward authorities. From lots of points of view, the Nine Old Men in Black of the Republican era look awfully similar to their more recent counterparts. Don't they have something important to teach them (and the rest of us)—other than how stupid and wrong judges can be?

And yet, until we reject the New Deal myth of rediscovery and embrace a three-moment theory of constitutional creation, modern judges will be unable to take this question seriously. To test this hypothesis, compare the way modern lawyers are taught to view famous constitutional cases of the early and modern republics. For present purposes, the most notorious decisions will prove the most instructive: contrast the modern understanding of the pre–Civil War Court's decision, in 1857, to deny blacks citizenship in *Dred Scott v. Sandford*[7] to the Republican Court's decision, in 1905, to repudiate legislation limiting working hours in *Lochner v. New York*.[8]

From a moral point of view, *Dred Scott* is the single darkest stain upon the Court's checkered history. The very idea that the Court could declare that *free* black people were *forever* barred from American citizenship remains, after 130 years, an awful rebuke to our Constitution. Compared to this, even *Lochner v. New York* seems a more modest moral mistake. Yet, when judged by most other standards, *Lochner* ranks way up there on the scale of moral obtuseness. For the overwhelming majority of today's Americans, *Lochner*'s constitutional denunciation of a maximum-hours law, limiting bakers to a sixty (!) hour workweek, speaks in an alien voice. We still place a very high value on each American's right to make basic occupational choices. Fifty years after the New Deal, however, we believe there are some things workers shouldn't be forced to bargain about—like an employer's demand that he or she endure racial or sexual subordination, let alone the grinding indecencies of the sweatshop. Most of us don't think that employers should be allowed to put such humiliating demands on the bargaining table. We support legal guarantees to workers of certain basic rights before they can bargain in a self-respecting way on other conditions of employment. While the proper scope of these guaranteed rights remains an endless subject for democratic debate, the *Lochner* effort to take the issue off the agenda of normal politics seems an ideologically extreme solution to a multifaceted problem. Though some libertarians may believe that laissez-faire remains the best approach to labor relations, very few fail to recognize that others may reasonably and responsibly come to different views. This is what I have in mind in saying that, by present standards, *Lochner* is morally obtuse while *Dred Scott* is morally wrong.

And yet, when a modern judge looks at these cases from a legal, as opposed to a moral, point of view, she will characteristically display a subtle, but revealing, shift in her criteria of professional appraisal. While recognizing *Dred Scott* for the moral evil that it is, the modern judge is perfectly capable of considering that Chief Justice Taney might have had a legally plausible case for his morally notorious decision. Perhaps, on investigating the legal sources, the serious lawyer might conclude that Taney was legally wrong as well as morally outrageous; but perhaps not. Perhaps Americans really did have to fight a Civil War before blacks could become citizens of the United States?

One thing is clear. When I take up such questions with law students or mature judges, I find no deep resistance to exploring them. In contrast, modern judges do resist the very suggestion that *Lochner* might have been a legally plausible decision in 1905, even if they hold the view that the decision is morally obtuse rather than paradigmatically evil. The reason is not hard to uncover. As practical folk, my lawyer-interlocutors are perfectly aware that the status of *Lochner* has vastly different implications for today's constitutional law than does *Dred Scott*. So far as the latter is concerned, absolutely nothing of present legal significance hangs on whether Chief Justice Taney was right about the status of blacks in 1857. Even if Taney's opinion had been legally plausible before the Civil War, it ceased to be good law in 1868, when the Fourteenth Amendment declared: "All persons born or naturalized in the United States, and subject to the jurisdiction thereof, are citizens of the United States and of the State wherein they reside."

By recognizing the creative aspect of the Republicans' achievement, the modern lawyer can gain critical detachment from the decisions of the pre–Civil War judiciary. Once she determines that, thanks to the Reconstruction Republicans, *Dred Scott* is no longer valid law, she is no longer obliged to disparage the Taney Court of 1857 to satisfy herself that blacks are indeed citizens in the modern republic. Instead, she may look upon the pre–Civil War judiciary in a very different spirit. After all, Taney and his fellow Justices were not so different from the judges who succeeded them. Rather than casting them as moral misfits, perhaps we can see them as *judges* trying to do their job as best they could, in ways not altogether dissimilar from modern judges?

A book like Robert Cover's *Justice Accused*[9] suggests how rewarding such an inquiry might turn out to be. And yet, when we turn to Justice Peckham's majority opinion in *Lochner v. New York,* our official theory of the past bars us from a similar effort at critical detachment. If a modern lawyer seriously entertained the possibility that *Lochner* was legally plausible when it was decided in 1905, the prevailing myth about the New Deal prevents her from treating its holding in the legally detached way she deals with *Dred Scott*. Since the New Deal myth of rediscovery tells her that nothing fundamentally new was created in the 1930's, she cannot rid today's Americans of the ghost of *Lochner* in the same way she deals with *Dred Scott*— by pointing to a subsequent period of constitutional creativity that repudiated the old case's justifying principles. Instead, when it comes to *Lochner,* the official theory of our past leads us to narrow our choice to two extreme alternatives:* either *Lochner* was wrong in

*So long as we respect *stare decisis*—which I do.

1905 and the modern activist state is constitutionally legitimate or it was right and the modern activist state is unconstitutional!

So long as modern lawyers restrict themselves to these stark alternatives, there is little wonder they unhesitatingly choose to uphold the modern activist state at the price of unsympathetically casting the Justices of the middle republic as blunderers or worse. As practical people, modern lawyers recognize that Americans *do* recognize the activist state as constitutionally legitimate and that the Supreme Court would commit institutional suicide by taking up once more the Lochnerian struggle against the modern welfare state. If, in order to express this truth, they have to villify most of the Justices of the Republican era, this seems a regrettable—but altogether affordable—intellectual price to pay for a solid constitutional foundation for modern activist government.

Only when we question the myth of rediscovery may we seriously entertain a third interpretive option. Once we recognize that the Democrats of the 1930's successfully led the American people to accept new activist principles and practices into their higher law, we can deal with *Lochner* in the same legally detached way we deal with *Dred Scott.* No longer need we disparage middle republican jurisprudence to affirm the modern activist state. *Lochner* might have been constitutionally plausible in 1905; it was only in the 1930's that the American people decisively repudiated the principles of laissez-faire. This said, we may begin to reinterpret the path of the law from 1868 to 1937 in a new spirit. Granted, the substantive principles articulated during the Republican era no longer bind us during the modern period; nonetheless, may not modern lawyers learn a great deal methodologically from the effort by the Republican Court to discharge its interpretive responsibilities?

We can begin to look upon the Republican judges as judges, not pariahs, whose decisions differ from modern case law largely because *the Constitution they were interpreting was importantly different from the transformed Constitution left to us by the New Deal.* This conclusion prepares the way for an initial confrontation with the law of the modern republic. If I am right, the fresh view of the early and middle republics will provide us with valuable insights into the modern Supreme Court. To make my case, I invite you, in the final chapter in this part, to reread the opinions for the Court in *Brown v. Board of Education* and *Griswold v. Connecticut* from the perspective offered by a revised three-solution narrative.

THE FEDERALIST REGIME OF THE EARLY REPUBLIC

The Founding Scheme

An initial glance at the institutions of the early republic suggests an easy familiarity: House, Senate, President, Court—these labels remain with us today. And yet we cannot be taken in by names. The Founding generation had a radically different understanding of each of these institutions. Only by guarding against anachronism at each point can we grasp the distinctive character of the early republican regime; only then can we begin to glimpse the complex sense in which our constitutional project continues over two hundred years.

Begin with the Presidency. For us, the selection of the President is the occasion for the most focused debate on our future as a nation. Unlike candidates for other offices, each Presidential nominee feels obliged to elaborate a programmatic vision for the next four years, even when he doesn't have much of one. The electoral campaign proceeds through a series of debates—first among would-be candidates of each major party, then through a culminating series of debates between the Democratic and Republican candidates. No wonder that the victor invariably claims a "mandate" from the People on behalf of the leading ideas he developed in the campaign. The Presidency has become a plebiscitarian office, the platform from which the victor seeks to persuade Congress to support his "mandate" from the voters by enacting appropriate legislation.[10]

Whatever else is obscure about this modern system, one thing should be clear: it exists despite the contrary intentions of the Philadelphia Convention. The Founders were perfectly aware that Americans were suspicious of strong executives after their experience with George III. Their study of ancient history emphasized the danger that a demagogic President might destabilize the Republic and attempt to become King. Rather than looking upon the struggle for the Presidency as an occasion to mobilize mass support for programmatic ideals, the Founders designed the system of selection for very different purposes. Today we look at the Electoral College as an embarrassing anachronism at best, a dangerous time bomb at worst—one that may explode by awarding the White House to the candidate who has lost the popular vote. For the Framers, the College was a clever device to avoid the plebiscitarian Presidency. It aimed to encourage the selection of the man with the most distinguished past service to the Republic. Republican virtue, not populist demagogy, was to be the principal qualification.[11]

Doubtless, George Washington's presence at the Convention helped both the delegates, and the people more generally, to think of the office in this way. Washington was the obvious choice for President, but not because George, in collaboration with his media advisors, designed a set of campaign promises that the populace would find irresistible. Washington would gain the support of the Electors because his past service to the Republic had marked him out as the greatest republican character of his time. His past service to the country assured his fellow Americans that he would use the formidable powers of the Presidency to support the republic, not destabilize it.[12]

The changing view of the Presidency is expressed more concretely in terms of the constitutional tool that gives him influence on the future course of legislation: the veto. Today's Presidents use their veto power to further their programmatic ambitions. Whenever they think that the House and Senate have made bad policy, they have no compunction about using the veto to force reconsideration. This freewheeling use of the veto makes the Presidency into the functional equivalent of a third house of the legislature.

This was not the way the veto functioned in the early republic. The first six Presidents together vetoed nine bills—John Adams, Thomas Jefferson, James Monroe, and John Quincy Adams vetoed none at all. Speaking broadly,[13] these rare exercises fell into two categories, both of a defensive kind. Sometimes, the President used it to defend his office, particularly his role as Commander in Chief, by vetoing laws on military grounds. Most of the time, he defended the Constitution, writing veto messages that look rather similar to judicial opinions. This restrictive use of the veto fit comfortably into the Founding view of the office: since the President was supposed to gain the White House on the basis of his past service, it was unthinkable for him to claim that his (nonexistent) "mandate" allowed him to transform his office into a functional equivalent of a third house of the legislature.[14]

If, then, the Presidency was not to serve as a principal forum for future-looking appeals to the People, which institutions *were* intended to serve this function? The House and Senate, of course. But, once again, it was a different House and Senate from the ones we know today. For us, the House is the most parochial of national bodies: we expect each Representative to emphasize the narrower concerns of his or her particular district,[15] while the President tries to persuade the House to take a broader view of the national interest. In contrast, the Founders looked upon the Representatives with different expectations. The House resembled the English Commons, which had traditionally served as a spokesman for the country in opposition to the court. It was then the only part of the American government directly elected by citizens of the United States. Thus, this body was expected to express the more nationalistic side of early republican life. In contrast, the Senate was elected by each state's legislature. While their six-year terms would allow Senators more deliberative independence than their colleagues from the House enjoyed, their mode of appointment made them more like ambassadors from the states, checking the nationalistic tendencies of the House.[16]

All this had been reversed by the twentieth century. We expect Senators to take a broader, more nationalistic, perspective than the typical Representative—although each Senator's partiality to his own state still makes him seem relatively provincial compared to the plebiscitarian President who constantly explains that he is the only official elected by all Americans (even though this is not technically true, since the Electoral College has not been abolished).

We may consolidate these conclusions by comparing them with the previous chapter's discussion of the Founding system of constitutional amendment.[17] We saw there that the Founding scheme had three basic features. First, and most important, was federalism: the national government could not by itself amend the Constitution, regardless of how urgently it might desire a revision; only if three-fourths of the states gave their independent consent could an amendment earn the authority of We the People of the United States.

Second was the monopoly awarded to legislative assemblies in the process of constitutional deliberation: neither executives nor courts could claim a role in the process by which the People changed higher law. Third, and derivatively, was its expectation that neither Presidential proclamations nor court opinions would play a central part in the codification of new higher law. Instead, codifications would look like "amendments" tacked on to the original body of the text.

Once we strip away the anachronisms, these three premises can also be seen as guiding the Founding system of normal lawmaking. Normal statutes would not, of course, require the direct assent of state assemblies, in the manner of constitutional amendments. But they would have to pass muster before a body of Senatorial ambassadors from the states. Similarly, the existence of a Presidential veto power undeniably deprived legislative assemblies of the monopoly they had over higher lawmaking. Nonetheless, given the restricted understanding of the veto, legislative assemblies retained the dominant role in normal, as well as higher, lawmaking. Both higher and normal lawmaking were federalistic and assembly-driven processes. A success on the higher track would be codified in a legislative-looking document called an "amendment"; a success on the normal track would be codified in one called a "statute."

Jefferson, Jackson, and the Rise of Judicial Review

This neat system did not survive the Founding generation. The challengers: Thomas Jefferson and his fellow Democratic Republicans of the 1790's. These famously found Washington and Adams pursuing policies that betrayed the ideals of the American Revolution. Hamilton's domestic program seemed to them a transparent effort to buy support for the national government from mercantile elites, an attempt inspired by the success of the eighteenth-century English crown in corrupting the body politic. This tendency toward centralizing despotism was only confirmed by the Federalist's tilt to the English monarchy in the great war precipitated by the French Revolution. Rather than reciprocating France's crucial support of our own Revolution, the Federalists seemed bent on aping the English monarchy both at home and abroad. In a word much favored by Jeffersonians, the central government was dominated by *mono-*

crats who were dangerously undermining the constitutional foundations of republican liberty.[18]

In presenting this diagnosis, the Jeffersonians were revitalizing—and not for the last time—the dualistic spirit of American constitutionalism: casting the governing party as a bunch of normal politicians corrupting the American system, casting themselves as leaders of a popular movement of aroused citizens determined to renew and redefine constitutional values in the name of We the People. For present purposes, the crucial point is not what the Jeffersonians said, but how they proposed to carry forward their constitutional movement. The Founding scheme offered at least two options. On the one hand, the Jeffersonians could seek to win the ratification of constitutional amendments that repudiated key elements of the Hamiltonian program (such as the Bank of the United States); on the other hand, they could campaign hard in state and national elections with the aim of gaining a majority in the Senate and the House. This would block further elaboration of the monocrats' dangerous program.

One thing the Jeffersonians were discouraged from doing was to transform the Presidential election of 1800 into a referendum on their constitutional movement. Yet this is precisely the course Jefferson took. Unsurprisingly, the effort to transform the Presidency into a plebiscitarian office encountered all sorts of structural difficulties and constitutional crises. The most important point is this: Jefferson was successful (to some degree at least) in gaining public acceptance of his view that his Presidential victory was a "mandate" for the Republican constitutional vision. This transformation of the Presidency, in turn, had two major structural consequences on the regime.

The first concerned the selection of the President.[19] Jefferson's success in transforming the process into a battle between two conflicting political ideals and popular movements was inconsistent with the original design of the Electoral College. Thus, Jefferson's "Revolution of 1800" precipitated the enactment of the Twelfth Amendment in 1804 to accommodate (imperfectly) the Founding constitutional regime with the emerging Presidential reality.

The second had to do with the assertion by the Supreme Court, in 1803, of its powers of judicial review in *Marbury v. Madison*.[20]

The present court-centered narrative views this great decision in one of two ways. Either the court-watcher searches the earlier case law to find earlier English and American precedents for *Marbury*-like judicial behavior. Or he invites us to view the case as testimony to Marshall's political savvy and inventiveness (or he mixes these two approaches into one or another combination).[21] While there is, of course, something to be learned from these traditional approaches, the regime perspective adds a lot more.

Begin by taking Marshall's opinion in *Marbury* seriously. It is an elaborately self-conscious effort to ground the exercise of judicial review in dualistic democratic theory, marking out the preservationist function that I have been emphasizing. Thus, Marshall does not accept the monist's claim that the Court suffers from a "counter-majoritarian" difficulty when it exercises its power of judicial review. Nor does he try, with the foundationalist, to invoke the Court's asserted capacity to understand the eternal laws of nature or reason or justice. He asserts that the Constitution has a superior status as higher law by virtue of its enactment by the People. Until a consti-tutional movement successfully amends our higher law, the Court's task is to preserve the People's judgments against their erosion by normal lawmaking.

But there is more to *Marbury* than Marshall's self-conscious affir-mation of the dualist theory of judicial review. In a second (and longer) part of the opinion, Marshall confronts the Presidency and tries to put Jefferson in his proper constitutional place. The result is a remarkable encounter with some of the constitutional implica-tions of Jefferson's transformation of the Presidency into the spear-head of his "Revolution of 1800." This relatively neglected part of *Marbury* raises one of the main questions we shall be exploring in this book: how should the American constitution respond to the rise of the plebiscitarian Presidency, given the fact that it played no part in the original Founding design?

But Marshall was hardly the only one grappling with this question. Jefferson was no less an interested party. Unsurprisingly, his answer was radically different. So far as the President was concerned, the Marshall Court was trying to sabotage the People's decision to re-pudiate the Federalists' constitutional vision by electing Jefferson over Adams in 1800. He rejected the idea that his Administration should be subordinated to Marshall's interpretation of the Federalist Constitution of 1787. He proposed to subordinate the Court to the Republicans' understanding of their "Revolution of 1800." To accomplish this aim, Jefferson embarked on a multipronged assault on the Federalist judiciary—including a campaign to impeach Federalist judges and replace them with Republicans who would codify the meaning of the Revolution of 1800 in an appropriate set of judicial opinions.[22]

This fierce early struggle marked the beginning of a very different constitutional dynamic from the assembly-driven mechanisms that the Founders had placed at the center of the Republic. Under this schema of Presidential leadership, a plebiscitarian President claims a mandate from the People for a revised understanding of the Constitution; rather than seeking to codify this vision in a series of formal amendments, he aims to gain Congressional support for measures that would transform the personnel of the Court, with the intent of codifying the ascendant Presidential vision in landmark opinions redefining the parameters of constitutional doctrine.

I do not want to read too much into this Jeffersonian exercise. Especially when we compare him to future plebiscitarian Presidents, Jefferson did not trumpet his role as popular tribune very loudly. He worked behind the scenes, using Republicans in Congress as mouthpieces. While this tactic constantly led his opponents to declaim against Jeffersonian duplicity, it gave continuing credibility to the Founding conception of a legislative process in which the President played a secondary role.[23] Moreover, Jefferson failed to win his campaign to purge the Federalist Supreme Court through impeachment; worse yet, he watched with bitter disappointment as his own judicial nominees failed to launch a sustained challenge to Marshall's leadership of the Court.

With Madison and Monroe, moreover, the system returned more closely to Founding expectations. Neither of these men gained the Presidency by mobilizing their countrymen's support in a fierce struggle against ideological opponents. They gained office in the Founding way, by virtue of their distinguished service to the Republic stretching back to the Revolution. All in all, the plebiscitarian Presidency is not a central theme during the first generation of the Republic. The center of the regime remained the federalistic, assembly-driven processes of normal and higher lawmaking described at the Founding. Having survived the Jeffersonian crisis, moreover, the Marshall Court used the Madison and Monroe Presidencies to elaborate a preservationist understanding of its mission. So far as Marshall was concerned, the Jeffersonians' strict constructionist, states' rights vision of the Constitution should not bind the judiciary. Instead, the job of the Court was to elaborate upon the Federalist values that We the People had established in 1787.

To summarize brutally, the Court pursued its preservationist activities along two fronts. I shall call one the power strategy; the other, the rights strategy. The first, exemplified in *McCulloch v. Maryland*,[24] defended a nationalistic approach to the unenumerated powers granted Congress by the original Constitution, and cast the Court as an aggressive warrior against state efforts to undermine the Congressional exercise of these powers. The second, exemplified by *Dartmouth College v. Woodward*,[25] insisted that the original Constitution granted fundamental rights to citizens against violation by the states no less than the national government. The paradigmatic example of these protected rights, however, was very different from those enshrined in the law of the modern republic. At a time when slavery and religious establishment were accepted features of state government, the early Court did not single out values like equality or freedom of conscience for protection against state intrusion. *Dartmouth College* focused on the value of contract as a central example of fundamental rights.

McCulloch and *Dartmouth College* were decided in 1819, during the Presidency of Monroe, the last Revolutionary hero who gained the White House. As the Founding generation died out, the problem of the Presidency once again began to afflict the Republic: Were there members of the next generation whose past service so distinguished them that the Electoral College might reliably reward their service by selecting them for the White House? Would the gap be filled by new plebiscitarian Presidents?

As in 1800, the election of 1824 generated a crisis in the Electoral College that reflected this larger dilemma; no candidate gained the requisite majority, and the election was thrown into the House of Representatives. The resulting victory of John Quincy Adams over Andrew Jackson suggested a possible solution to the problem of

Presidential selection. Adams was not only a distinguished public servant but a scion of the Revolutionary tradition by blood and upbringing. If the Presidency were to remain faithful to the Founders' conception, it would be hard to find a more appropriate candidate.

But Adams's initial victory proved a false start. Jackson's subsequent triumphs were more instructive over the long run. Although his claim to fame was based initially on his victory over the British in the Battle of New Orleans, Jackson's success in Presidential politics was accompanied by a host of new plebiscitarian themes. The rise of Presidential nominating conventions and the triumph of universal white male suffrage was making the Electoral College into an empty gesture: each state's Electors would go to the party that got the most votes.[26] With the help of Martin Van Buren,[27] Jackson constructed a new political party system—one that allowed him to deepen the plebiscitarian precedent left by the Jeffersonian presidency.[28] Once again, the Presidency served as the institutional center of an effort to push American government in the direction of more democracy and more states' rights—pushing the process further than Jefferson had managed to do.[29]

But not without resistance from preservationist institutions like the Supreme Court. Against the Jacksonians' moves toward further decentralization, the later Marshall Court continued to uphold the Federalists' more nationalistic conception of the Union. Jackson's veto message denouncing the constitutionality of the Bank of the United States is meaningful only when set against the Supreme Court's earlier decisions upholding an expansive reading of the enumerated powers.[30] Jackson's refusal to prevent Georgia's mass expulsion of Native Americans took on its awful meaning only in opposition to the Supreme Court's reassertion of the federal interest in the protection of Indian treaty rights.[31] For good or ill, the Marshall Court and the Jacksonian Presidency were locked in a larger dialectical process[32] through which the American people might hear both sides of the constitutional argument as they proceeded to revise their political identity.

As the Jacksonians continued to gain electoral support for their state-centered vision of white male democracy, their relationship to the Court entered a new phase. No longer were they content to use their control over the Presidency and the Congress to project a constitutional vision at odds with the Marshall Court. Like the Jeffersonians before them, Jackson and Van Buren tried to alter the personnel of the Court to make it a platform for the elaboration of the Jacksonian vision of the Republic. In this they were more successful than their predecessors. Jefferson's impeachment scheme failed, and his three Court appointments showed a disappointing tendency to support Marshall's effort to preserve Federalist constitutional values. In contrast, Jackson and Van Buren managed to fill five Supreme Court seats between 1835 and 1837, which had opened up both as a result of death and the Jacksonians' success in expanding the bench from seven to nine Justices.

The Jacksonians' transformative ambitions were aptly symbolized when John Marshall's death allowed them to appoint Roger Taney the next Chief Justice in 1836.[33] Taney's appointment was a reward for his yeoman service in destroying the Second Bank of the United States—that great legacy of the Federalist past whose existence was renewed during Madison's Administration. Fresh from his struggle against the bank, Taney and his fellow Jacksonians lost no time in revising the constitutional structure of the Republic. During the 1837 Term, the Taney Court decisively modified the two-pronged effort by the Marshall Court to limit state power in the name of both national authority and individual rights. Over ringing dissents of Marshall's collaborator Joseph Story, the new Jacksonian majority turned away from the Marshall Court's great precedents of 1819. In contrast to *McCulloch, New York v. Miln*[34] allowed each state new leeways in pursuing its domestic policies at the expense of national authority over interstate commerce; in contrast to *Dartmouth College, Charles River Bridge v. Warren Bridge*[35] gave the rising Jacksonian democracies a similar leeway in promoting economic development at the expense of vested contractual rights. For those who lived through these events, 1837 was experienced as a decisive turning point, marking the success of the Jacksonian Presidency in impressing a new, more decentralized, and populist vision of the Republic into the higher law of the land.[36]

We will have to wait a century before this precise sequence plays itself out again at the center of the constitutional stage. In 1937, as in 1837, the Supreme Court would execute a similar "switch in time," swinging from opposition to support of a new constitutional vision proclaimed from the White House. Yet it is important to avoid anachronism: though the victory of the Jacksonians over the Marshall Court is one of the great precedents for the Roosevelt transformation of the 1930's, there remain crucial differences. Most fundamentally, the Jacksonian Presidency did not inaugurate the *sweeping* transformation I associate with the great regime changes in American history. Indeed, 1837 marked the high point of the Court's revisionary activities. As the years passed, the Taney Court increasingly revealed the extent to which it too was bent on preserving much of the Federalist legacy of the Marshall Court—even supporting Joseph Story in elaborating new nationalistic forms of judicial intervention in state affairs.[37]

In contrast, 1937 was but the beginning of a root-and-branch repudiation of the leading precedents of the "*Lochner* era." Given the radical character of this ongoing judicial enterprise, the New Deal Justices never collaborated with judicial holdovers from the Republican regime in the same way that the Jacksonians found common ground with Joseph Story. By the early 1940's, the Court led by Harlan Fiske Stone was treating the preceding jurisprudential era as if it had been decisively repudiated by the American people. The Court led by Roger Taney never supposed that the constitutional re-vision articulated by the Jacksonians went that deep.

To understand why the Jacksonian Presidency proved less transformative, we must move beyond the courts and take a broader regime perspective. The key here is the very different constitutional visions embraced by the Jacksonian and Rooseveltian Presidencies. In a single line: the Jacksonians were decentralizers, the Rooseveltians were centralizers. This difference in constitutional philosophy shaped the extent to which the two movements would use the Presidency as the cockpit for a decisive regime change.

Consider that the Presidency is our most nationalistic office when it is used for plebiscitarian purposes: given the disintegration of the original Electoral College, the President is the only person who is selected by *all* the People of the United States and hence may claim a "mandate" from the nation as a whole. The nationalistic form of the Presidential mandate, however, sits uncomfortably with the decentralizing content of the mandate advanced by the Jacksonians (and the Jeffersonians before them). The more these decentralizers succeeded in shifting our higher law in the direction of states' rights, the less appropriate it seemed for the most nationalistic official of the national government to take a leading role in further exercises in higher lawmaking. The Jeffersonian and Jacksonian experiments with the plebiscitarian Presidency, in short, tended to undermine their continued legitimacy, reinforcing instead the Founding vision of an assembly-dominated and federalistic lawmaking process.

In contrast, Roosevelt's use of the Presidency to lead Congress, the voters, and ultimately the Court to a new vision of activist national government generated a very different constitutional dynamic. While the Court's response to Presidential leadership in 1837 made future exercises of leadership seem less appropriate, the Court's response in 1937 made Presidential leadership seem more central: given the pervasive character of activist national government after 1937, was it not right that our only nationally elected official take a more central leadership role? Moreover, given the broad range of national powers legitimated in 1937, the President would have many more resources at his command in achieving political effectiveness. In contrast, the decentralizing programs of Jefferson and Jackson stripped the national government of key institutions (like the Bank of the United States) that would otherwise have given the President resources of patronage and power to effectuate his programmatic vision.

Thus, it is no surprise that Jackson's triumphant use of the Presidency did not inaugurate an era of Presidential leadership. Rather than playing the central role in the next great constitutional crisis— the struggle over slavery in the aftermath of the Mexican War—the Presidency took a back seat to the Congress, and especially the federalistic Senate, in searching for a compromise that would sustain the Union. It would be Senators Clay, Webster, and Calhoun who would win the Great Compromise of 1850; Senator Douglas who would undo the Compromise in the Kansas–Nebraska Act.

As every high school student knows, the ensuing struggle over Bleeding Kansas catalyzed the formation of the Republican Party, which served as the leading organization of the fourth great constitutional movement in our history. Like the Founding Federalists, but unlike the Jeffersonian and Jacksonian Democrats, the Republicans sought to push the system in a nationalistic and rights-oriented direction. It is at this point, however, that we encounter one of constitutional history's many paradoxes: As the Republican movement gathered momentum through the 1850's, it could take advantage of the transformation of the Presidency won by Jeffersonians and Jacksonians who would have looked with horror upon the Republicans' nationalistic assertions. Nonetheless, these earlier generations had sown the seeds for the plebiscitarian Presidency; and it was only natural for the Republicans to use the office in the service of radically different substantive objectives.

The Republicans' success in electing Lincoln in 1860 marked the end of the early republic and a bloody battle over the regime(s) that would succeed it—but not before a desperate effort by Roger Taney to preserve the Jacksonian vision of the Republic, a vision that insisted on the supremacy of the white man over the black and red races.[38] For a view, like my own, that emphasizes the Court's preservationist function, Taney's attempt to re-present this racist vision in *Dred Scott* cannot but be a sobering experience, forcing us to recognize the ultimate moral limitations of the kind of judicial review proposed by the theory of dualistic democracy. But this, transparently, is too complex a subject to be confronted in this introductory sketch.[39]

Whatever one's final judgment on Taney, *Dred Scott* discharged constitutional functions very different from those Taney had aimed for. The opinion was intended to rally the country in defense of the old Jacksonian vision of decentralized democracy by white men. Instead, *Dred Scott* emphasized the dark side of the Jacksonian vision to the rising generation of Americans: Was the Jacksonian vision of decentralized slaveholding democracy good enough?

Dred Scott forced protagonists on all sides to confront this question with a deep seriousness. The Taney Court's dialectical challenge can best be explored through the Lincoln–Douglas debates of 1858, occurring shortly afterward. Neither Lincoln nor Douglas accepted *Dred Scott* as if it were the last word.[40] The case spurred both men to elaborate their own constitutional counter-visions. The paradoxical result of Taney's effort was that the Republican Lincoln emerged as a compelling figure. Douglas's effort to deal with *Dred Scott* only made it harder for him to gain the support of a united Democratic

Party in the forthcoming Presidential election. Rather than revitalizing faith in the Jacksonian vision, Taney had contributed to the disintegration of the party of Jefferson and Jackson. With the Democrats split between Northern and Southern candidates in 1860, the Republican Abraham Lincoln gained the White House with less than 40 percent of the popular vote. Unlike the earlier victories of Jefferson and Jackson, this plebiscitarian use of the Presidency did indeed signal the beginning of the end of the early republic.

CHAPTER FOUR

The Middle Republic

CONSTITUTIONAL IDEALS, INSTITUTIONAL REALITIES

THE NEW REPUBLICAN REGIME was more nationalistic than its Federalist predecessor. The Republicans' Fourteenth Amendment opens by proclaiming, for the first time in our history, that national citizenship is primary, state citizenship secondary in each American's political identity.

The very process by which these words became part of the Constitution emphasized the Republic's new nationalistic foundation. As Chapter 2 explained, the Republicans' opponents sought to defeat the Fourteenth Amendment by invoking the veto granted one-fourth of the states by the original Constitution. But the Republicans refused to allow this veto to stand. Rather than follow the Federalist rules for constitutional amendment, they ratified the Fourteenth Amendment in a new way—one that expressed the new importance Americans gave to national institutions. In the aftermath of the Civil War, We the People of the *United* States reconstructed the very process of higher lawmaking to make it plain that the will of the nation was independent of, and superior to, the will of the states.[1]

This new nationalism was tied to a resurgent emphasis on individual freedom. This concern was evident at the Founding—most obviously in the Bill of Rights adopted to constrain the national government. So far as the states were concerned, however, the Federalists were more cautious—while denying the national government authority to establish a religion, they did not challenge the authority of the religious establishments in the states to abridge fundamental rights of conscience; even this concession to authoritarianism paled when compared to the Founders' peaceful coexistence with chattel slavery. Apart from certain minimal guarantees against the abuse of the criminal law, the Founding text only marked out one area of individual freedom against arbitrary state interference. Section Ten of Article One forbids the states from "impairing the obligation of Contracts." Marshall used this text as the foundation of a rights-oriented jurisprudence in the *Dartmouth College* case, but this relatively cautious effort to constrain the states was weakened in the Jacksonian shift from the Marshall to the Taney Court.[2]

Only against this background can we fully appreciate the extent of the Republican transformation. The new amendments abolishing slavery, guaranteeing the "privileges or immunities of citizens of the United States," assuring "equal protection" and "due process of law," safeguarding voting rights against racial discrimination—our modern disagreements about the precise meaning of these provisions should not blind us to the quantum leap the Republicans had made in nationalizing the protection of individual rights against state abridgment.

To put this transformation into perspective, think of it as constraining the ways the middle republic put together three of the basic terms that constantly reemerged in constitutional discourse: nation, state, individual. Before the Civil War, the relative value the Constitution placed on state autonomy vis-à-vis the other two fundamental terms was a matter open to fair dispute: was state citizenship more important than national? was state sovereignty more important than the protection of individual rights? While participants disagreed on the right answers to these questions, all agreed that they were open to fair dispute. After the Civil War, the Republicans had led the People to resolve these issues decisively, replacing them with new problems. The question was no longer whether state sovereignty was more important than individual rights, but which individual rights were sufficiently fundamental to warrant national protection. As always, this question generated different answers, but the Republicans had decisively changed the *constitutional problematic* in ways that shifted the balance of constitutional discourse—requiring even those devoted to states' rights to recognize that something profoundly important had happened during Reconstruction. This shift in problematic rapidly legitimated an unprecedented penetration of the federal courts into areas where the states had previously been free to decide on their own authority. From early on, this involved not only protection of individual liberty, but also judicial review of crucial state decisions on economic development.[3]

The impact of Republican nationalism on the basic character of the House, Senate, and Presidency was less straightforward. Building on earlier plebiscitarian achievements of Jefferson and Jackson, the Republicans had catapulted themselves to the center of the political stage by electing Abraham Lincoln to the Presidency in 1860. The Presidency's constitutional centrality was enhanced not only by the exigencies of war, but also by Lincoln's remarkable capacity to personify the Union and its evolving moral significance. The martyrdom of Lincoln further heightened the symbolic centrality of his office, setting the stage for the epoch-making effort by Andrew Johnson to take the plebiscitarian Presidency to then-unprecedented heights. After intervening decisively in support of the Thirteenth Amendment, Johnson reversed field and used the Presidency as the leading edge of a vast popular movement against the Fourteenth. Johnson's exercise in Presidential leadership played a crucial role in nationalizing the higher lawmaking process—forcing the Republicans to develop a model of Congressional leadership that I have already sketched.[4]

For now, the most important thing to say about Johnson's effort is that it failed. Rather than leading the People to reject the Fourteenth Amendment, Johnson's activities finally provoked his impeachment in 1868 and cast a pall over similar exercises in Presidential leadership for a long time to come. The plebiscitarian potential of the Presidency was undermined further by the constitutional crisis generated by the Hayes-Tilden election of 1876— where the Democrat Tilden won the popular vote and the Republican Hayes kept control over the White House only by abandoning Republican commitments to the black Republicans of the South. Thereafter, the principal forum for the normal politics of the middle republic would be Congress, not the Presidency. Not until the Republican Reconstructers begin to leave the scene would the plebiscitarian Presidency begin to reassert itself as an important constitutional reality.[5]

The election of 1896 was the watershed: as with Jefferson, Jackson, and Lincoln, William Jennings Bryan presented himself as the leader of a populist movement that had impressed new political meaning onto one of America's great political parties. The only difference was that Bryan lost, and lost decisively, to McKinley—leading to a reorganization of the party system that greatly increased the Republican advantage.[6] This *failed constitutional moment* might have further undermined the plebiscitarian Presidency but for another assassin's bullet—which allowed Theodore Roosevelt, a Republican from a very different region and ideological persuasion, to gain the White House.[7] Facing strong opposition from the Republican Congress, Roosevelt sought to exploit the Presidency as a "bully pulpit"—with rather meager success so far as Congressional legislation was concerned. Nonetheless, his Presidency marks a turning point: after serving as the site of a generation's failed plebiscitarian politics, the White House was once again inhabited by a person whose efforts to lead the American people to a "Square Deal" did not lead to outright repudiation (although it hardly led to significant transformation either).[8]

Roosevelt's constitutional contributions did not end with the end of his term in 1908. His effort to regain the Presidency in 1912 indirectly led to a further revitalization of the plebiscitarian Presidency—if only by splitting the dominant Republican majority and allowing Woodrow Wilson to win the White House. Wilson had spent much of his life studying the pathologies of the middle republic's Congressionally centered regime. One of America's first graduate students of political science, Wilson used his doctoral thesis, *Congressional Government,*[9] to condemn the system that had emerged in the aftermath of Reconstruction. According to Wilson, "Congress" governed in name only. National policy was made by parochial committee chairmen. The result was markedly inferior to the British system of parliamentary government. While the British system encouraged the Prime Minister and the leader of the Opposition to lead an ongoing debate on the basic alternatives facing the nation, American policy was made behind closed committee doors by Senators and Representatives more responsive to parochial interests than the good of the nation. To put Wilson's point more broadly: there was a fundamental tension between constitutional ideals and institutional realities in the regime created by the Reconstruction Republicans. Though the middle republic was far more nationalistic in its constitutional ideals than its predecessor, the normal operation of Congressional government did not reward efforts to elaborate a compelling conception of the national interest. If the nationalistic aspirations of the middle republic were to be redeemed in practice, Wilson believed that some further institutional revisions would be required.[10]

Once he gained the White House, Wilson wasted no time putting these beliefs into practice. Though he had won only a plurality of the popular vote, Wilson immediately used the White House as a platform for elaborating his vision of the country's future.[11] He was more successful in gaining Congressional support for his initiatives than any previous President of the middle republic: the Federal Reserve Act and the Clayton Act owed their existence, at least in part, to Wilson's programmatic leadership.[12]

Nonetheless, by the end of his term in office, Wilson had overreached himself: in forwarding the Versailles Treaty to the Senate, Wilson was hoping to culminate his vision of the Presidency. This time, he was not trying merely to speak to Congress in the name of We the People of the United States; he presented the treaty as leader of We the People of Western Civilization, determined to create a new world order out of the tragedy of war. Not only was Wilson denied confirmation of this heroic vision, but Senate resistance led to the greatest failure in plebiscitarian leadership since Andrew Johnson. As in Johnson's case, the President sought to take his case to the People by leaving Washington, D.C., whistle-stopping his way across the country. As with Johnson, the result was a resounding failure—this time leading to the President's physical and mental breakdown.[13]

As the country "returned to normalcy" with the election of Warren Harding in 1920, Wilson's challenge to Congressional domination of politics in the middle republic remained just that—a challenge that had failed to gain popular support at the critical moment. This failure in Presidential leadership contrasts with the vibrancy of the Congressionally led modes of constitutional transformation during the period. Between 1909 and 1920, four important amendments were proposed and adopted under the rules of Article Five—authorizing an income tax (XVI), requiring the popular election of Senators (XVII), imposing prohibition (XVIII), and guaranteeing women's suffrage (XIX). All of them attest to the ability of broad-based citizen movements[14] to use the federalistic, assembly-based forms of Article Five to express constitutional changes that were deeply important to their fellow Americans.

This contrasts sharply with the higher lawmaking balance of the modern republic. On the one hand, Franklin Delano Roosevelt would make Wilson's dream a constitutional reality—gaining the sustained popular support for Presidential leadership that would transform the very foundations of the middle republic. On the other hand, modern constitutional movements on the right (for example, "right to life," "balanced budget") and the left (the equal rights amendment) have regularly failed in their efforts to invoke the federalistic assembly-led forms of Article Five. These repeated failures would only increase the tendency of transformative movements to divert most of their energies from the Article Five procedure to the Presidency—in the hope that a President would show his debt to the movement by repeating the Rooseveltian precedent of constitutional transformation through judicial appointment.

All of this, however, could hardly be foreseen in 1920. With Harding in the White House, and the Prohibition Amendment on the books, the assembly-dominated processes of the middle republic seemed in vibrant good health.

THE SUPREME COURT: THE PROBLEM OF SYNTHESIS

Like the Presidency, the Supreme Court emerged from Reconstruction at a low point in its history. Not only had the Republicans' Fourteenth Amendment repudiated the vision of the Union elaborated by the Taney Court in *Dred Scott*. Reconstruction had also forced the Court into a series of highly visible, and deeply embarrassing, judicial retreats before Republican initiatives.[15] Nonetheless, the Court found it easier than the Presidency to define an independent role in the normal life of the middle republic.

This mission is best understood in preservationist terms. As in the early republic, the passage of time saw new political interests and agendas move to the center of the national stage, pushing to the periphery the fundamental issues of political identity that served as the focus of constitutional politics in the 1860's. As these great popular achievements receded into the background, the Republican

Court—like its Marshallian predecessor—confronted the task of pre-serving the constitutional solutions against undue erosion by the ebb and flow of normal political life. In historical terms, the critical turning point came with the economic depression of 1873 and the political compromise reached in the aftermath of the Hayes-Tilden election of 1876. These two events—the first economic, the second political—pushed the Reconstruction agenda to the periphery of national politics.[16] Though politicians accepted the Reconstruction amendments as legally binding, the concrete concerns that had mo-tivated the Republican struggle for their enactment no longer were pivotal for politicians living out their daily lives in Washington, D.C. Insofar as late-nineteenth-century politics seriously confronted mat-ters of principle, these were raised by civil service reformers and, more profoundly, the Populists. Both these movements had different agendas from the one which had so energized Republicans and Democrats of the previous generation. If Reconstruction values were to be represented forcefully on the national scene, the task would fall to the Supreme Court. How, then, did the Court discharge this preservationist function?

This is a question that modern lawyers and judges fail to take seriously—since the modern myth of rediscovery requires them to look upon the long period of Republican jurisprudence between Reconstruction and the New Deal as some Dark Age obscuring the nationalistic truth revealed by the Marshall Court. It will take a lot of work to gain a more balanced view—both of the character of the Court's preservationist achievement and the nature of its compro-mises with evolving political reality. For the present, I have no choice but to be extremely selective—emphasizing only a few features cen-tral to the overall argument.

Most important is the Court's self-conscious recognition, from the very beginning, that the Republican achievement of the 1860's had fundamentally altered the terms of the interpretive problem as it had first been set out by John Marshall. When John Marshall looked at his copy of the Constitution, he could suppose that "We the People of the United States" referred to a relatively concrete group of historical actors—the generation of Americans who fought the War of Independence and codified its political meaning in the 1787 text and the first wave of constitutional amendments. Even at this early stage, interpreting the Constitution as the deliberative product of a collectivity as vast as "We the People" was a tricky business. The Americans who supported the Federalist experiment notoriously disagreed on important matters; any effort to elaborate the constitutional principles that animated the Founding generation's political practice—the intent of the Framers, if you will*—necessarily involved a great deal of insight and judgment. Nonetheless, the fact that only a single generation of Americans had contributed to the proposal and ratification of the Constitution and its early amendments simplified the interpretive problem. However tricky the task of interpreting the constitutional text, at least the early Federalist Justices could locate it against the background of a relatively concrete political culture—a culture, moreover, within which they themselves were born and reached political maturity.

This focus on the higher lawmaking achievement of a single generation was shattered, once and for all, by the Reconstruction Republicans. From the Court's very first effort to make sense of the Civil War amendments,[17] the Justices are self-consciously confronting an issue that simply had not occurred to John Marshall. I shall call it the problem of multigenerational synthesis: Since the Republicans had repudiated some, but not all, of the Founders' Constitution, the Republican Justices could no longer rest content with the Marshallian task of elaborating the constitutional vision of the Americans who had fought and won the War of Independence. They would first have to identify which aspects of the earlier Constitution had survived Republican reconstruction. Having isolated the surviving frag-

---

*I am willing to use this much-abused slogan so long as we are very clear that it is the intentions of the People that count, not those of the small number of "Framers" who proposed the Constitution or its early amendments. This emphasis on the People will importantly affect our later investigation of Federalist thought. For example, I shall not be concentrating upon the fragmentary reports about the Convention's secret deliberations (see Max Farrand, *The Records of the Federal Convention* [1911]) that have been preserved by history. I shall focus on the most sustained contribution by Federalist leaders to the public debate—the *Federalist Papers*—as well as on the efforts by serious historians to capture the relationship between Federalist leaders and the broader public. See Chapters 7 and 8. It is only in this way that we may begin the process of understanding the intentions that really matter: Why did it seem sensible to a mobilized majority of *American citizens* to give their considered support to the Federalist effort to speak for the People?

ments, they would have to synthesize them into a new doctrinal whole that gave expression to the new ideals affirmed by the Republicans in the name of the People.

This, transparently, would be no easy matter. The Republican world of the nineteenth century was very different from the Federalist world of the eighteenth, both in its legal premises and social life. How to put together a constitutional whole out of such discordant parts?

The problem haunts us still. Like Americans of the middle republic, we too must make sense of a Constitution that has been radically reshaped by generations of constitutional politics. Indeed, the modern problem is more complex than the middle republic's. The earlier era had only to confront the revolutionary reforms of Reconstruction. We must confront the fact that the Constitution was revolutionized yet again in the cauldron of the Great Depression. It will not be enough for us to synthesize the great contributions of two generations of constitutional politics; we must take into account the work of three (as well as the important contributions of other generations). The way modern courts go about this task will, I believe, shape the future of constitutional law.

For this reason, my introductory remarks will focus on the middle republic's struggle with this synthetic aspect of their interpretive problem. This inquiry is especially rewarding because, from the very first, the Republican Justices rejected two easy answers that trivialize the distinctive challenges of multigenerational synthesis. Since these easy answers continue to attract powerful partisans today, I shall locate the distinctive contribution of the middle republic by situating it against these ongoing efforts to trivialize the problem.

My larger aim is to suggest how much modern lawyers have to learn from the middle republic once they discard the myth of rediscovery that treats it as a sixty-eight-year nightmare of the judicial spirit. By isolating a common problem—intergenerational synthesis—we share with these predecessors, perhaps we can find something positive to learn from them about constitutional interpretation? Not that we can mechanically apply their solutions to our problems— these have been transformed by the revolutionary reforms of the New Deal period, which most middle republican Justices did not anticipate. Nonetheless, by engaging the Justices in serious legal conversation about synthesis, may we not put our own interpretive predicaments into useful perspective?

Two Easy Answers

Begin by stating the synthetic problem in bare-bones form. At Time One, the Founding generation announced X as higher law; at Time Two, the Reconstructers Y—where Y is partly, but not entirely, inconsistent with X. How then to put X and Y together into a meaningful whole?

There are two easy ways. Though both seem different on the surface, they share a reductionist ambition. Both try to solve the problem of intergenerational synthesis by focusing attention on either Time One or Time Two, but not both.

The first reductionism solves the problem by exaggerating what was decided at Time Two. It would have us believe that the Reconstructers themselves seriously considered the question of synthesis and led the American people self-consciously to embrace a particular answer to the question. This, most famously, is Hugo Black's position on the relationship between the Republicans' Fourteenth Amendment (Y) and the Federalists' Bill of Rights (X). On Black's view, the Republicans did not merely amend the Constitution (Y) in ways inconsistent with the original understanding of the Bill of Rights (X). They also led the People self-consciously to endorse something I will call a synthetic rule—an S that explained precisely how the new Republican Y should be harmonized with the old Federalist X. According to Black, the Republicans' S said that the Fourteenth Amendment "incorporated" all of the terms of the Federalist Bill of Rights and made them applicable to the states.[18] Once this is conceded, the way has been cleared for the first easy answer to the problem of synthesis. Since the People had considered the problem and answered it authoritatively during Reconstruction, shouldn't the courts simply follow the synthetic rule laid down in 1868?

But there is another way to reach an easy—if radically different—answer. This involves an equal and opposite move from Hugo Black's: while Black looks upon the Fourteenth Amendment as if it were a *comprehensive synthesis* of the constitutional commitments made during the Founding and Reconstruction, the second reductionism treats the amendment as if it were a relatively minor change in constitutional course—something I shall call a *superstatute.* Superstatutes do not try to revise any of the deeper principles organizing our higher law; they content themselves with changing one or more rules without challenging anything more basic. Consider, for example, our last successful effort on the Article Five track: the Twenty-sixth Amendment, enacted in 1971, commands that the voting rights of citizens who are "eighteen years of age or older . . . shall not be denied or abridged by the United States or any state on account of age." This amendment did not serve as the organizing focus of the turbulent constitutional politics of the late 1960's. It was treated as a side issue, engendered by the Supreme Court's decision in *Oregon v. Mitchell* in 1970.[19] A majority of the *Mitchell* Court interpreted the Constitution to invalidate an effort by Congress to require states to allow eighteen-year-olds to vote. Within a year, this interpretation was overruled by the Twenty-sixth Amendment. The speed of this response was a tribute to its proponents' success in explaining that they had a very narrow object: the problem was simply to guarantee eighteen-year-olds the vote that Congress had sought to assure by its original statute. This kind of amendment is rightly interpreted as a superstatute. All it did was change the voting age from twenty-one to eighteen. Nobody looked upon it as something more.

It is, however, quite another thing to treat the Fourteenth Amendment in the same spirit. Nonetheless, many modern interpreters have trivialized the amendment in just this way—the most influential being Raoul Berger.[20] On his view, the Fourteenth Amendment, like the Twenty-sixth, had a very narrow aim: to constitutionalize the rules contained in a single statute, the Civil Rights Act of 1866, that the Reconstruction Congress had enacted into law a few months earlier. Unfortunately for Berger, the text of the amendment does not even mention this act; nor does it, like the Twenty-sixth, affirmatively state, in relatively clear and operational terms, the rules that it wishes to constitutionalize. Its first paragraph speaks the language of fundamental principle. For the moment, however, my concern is not with Berger's bad history,[21] but with his abstract constitutional logic.

On this level, Berger, like Black, does have an easy answer to the problem of synthesis. Once he has trivialized Time Two by characterizing its constitutional amendments as superstatutes, he has cleared a path to insist that the constitutional vision enunciated by the Founders survived Reconstruction essentially intact. This narrow view naturally leads him to take very different substantive positions from Black. On the level of method, however, both men are reductionists. Both assert that the Reconstruction Republicans adopted a particular set of S rules that once and for all resolved the tensions between Time One and Time Two. They differ only on the substance of the S rule: Black believes that the People authoritatively adopted a rule that incorporated all the guarantees of the Bill of Rights, while Berger believes that the People enacted a superstatute that changed the Constitution only in the precise ways enumerated in the Civil Rights Act of 1866.

Transformative Amendments—And How to Synthesize Them

Now I have absolutely nothing against easy answers. Life and law are complicated enough without needlessly complexifying them. My problem with both Black and Berger is that their competing answers, though easy enough, are false to the historical character of Republican Reconstruction. The Republican amendments were popularly understood as much more than a series of superstatutes; but they represented a good deal less than a comprehensive synthesis of the Founding and Reconstruction. What is required, transparently, is a richer set of interpretive categories that allow us to express the kind of constitutional transformation envisioned by the nineteenth-century Americans who supported the Reconstruction proposals.

This is my aim in characterizing them as transformative amendments. In contrast to superstatutes, such amendments do not merely contemplate a change in a few higher law rules. They are the culminating expression of a generation's critique of the status quo—a critique that finally gains the considered support of a mobilized majority of the American people. In working out its critique, however, the constitutional movement has not aimed for something so ambitious as a fully comprehensive synthesis. Though the movement obviously aims to repudiate some of the fundamental principles of the older constitutional order, the impact of its new ideals on a host of other traditional principles has not yet been worked out in a thoroughgoing and considered way. Thus, while popular adoption of the amendments certainly signifies mobilized support for the transformative principles they express, it cannot be said to suggest decisive support for any particular synthetic rule.

A thought experiment might illuminate this distinctive feature of the transformative amendment. Imagine that the Reconstruction Republicans had not contented themselves with the proposal and ratification of their three great amendments. Suppose they had taken a leaf from the Federalist book and used their majority in the first Reconstruction Congress to propose an entirely new text: "We the People of the United States, in order to form a more perfect Union after the terrible ordeal of Civil War, do ordain this Constitution . . ."

To new-model the Constitution, it would not have been necessary for the Republicans to break with all Federalist ideas and terminology. Just as the Federalists borrowed significantly from the Articles of Confederation, so too the Republicans could have borrowed from the Constitution of the early republic (the 1787 text plus the first twelve amendments) in making their own proposal. Nonetheless, if the Republicans had successfully gained the ratification of their 1866 constitution, I would be more sympathetic to Black's proposal to treat the Republican contribution as a comprehensive synthesis. In hammering out a new constitution, the Republican Congress would have been obliged to work out with great seriousness the relationship between the new and the old in their constitutional initiative; even more importantly, when they offered their new constitution to the People for democratic ratification, their comprehensive vision would have been refined in countless public debates, giving decisive higher law meaning to the proposed synthesis if it finally won popular approval.

The problem, of course, is that this is not what happened. Rather than starting anew, the Republicans called their proposals amendments, identifying them as fragments of an evolving whole that began in 1787, not 1866. This did not logically prevent them from synthesizing new and old in the clear rule-like fashion hypothesized by Hugo Black. However, like most other students of the period,[22] I do not believe that Black has made out his case on the facts. While there were undoubtedly some people, including some important politicians, who expressed Blackian views, there were many others who disagreed; and the text itself was not popularly understood to resolve the synthetic issues decisively.[23]

All very well and good, I hear you say, but where does this leave the problem of synthesis? If easy answers, of the Black or Berger type, require courts to mischaracterize Reconstruction, how are courts to integrate Time One and Time Two into a coherent doctrinal whole?

THE PATH OF THE LAW

By self-consciously confronting the tensions between Founding and Reconstruction, and elaborating doctrinal principles which harmonize the conflict in a way that does justice to the deepest aspirations of each. Fancy talk? An impossible dream?

Perhaps. But consider how the process of constitutional litigation invites the judges to take seriously this ideal of principled synthesis. When rules are clear, few have the incentive to bear the costs of litigation; cases go to the Supreme Court principally when good lawyers find it impossible to settle disputes without its guidance. This means that the Court will be fed a steady diet of problems in one-two synthesis. Cases raising these problems will seem peculiarly unsettleable. By hypothesis, lawyers on both sides will find a rich lode of principle to support their arguments: one side, call it the plaintiffs, will predictably assert that Reconstruction principles should be read in an expansive way—that's the way they'll win their lawsuit; for the same reason, the other side will call for an expansive reading of the Founding principles. Since the doctrinal relationship between Reconstruction and the Founding has so many facets, it would be a foolish judge who tried to resolve the problem in a single opinion. What we can expect is an ongoing dialogue over time, where early efforts at judicial synthesis serve as precedents in a continuing legal conversation seeking a principled reconciliation of the tension-full relationship between Times One and Two.

This, at any rate, will be the key to my effort at a sympathetic understanding of the constitutional law of the middle republic. In emphasizing the problem of synthesis, I am not imposing new categories on the Republican Justices themselves. The very first Court opinion construing the Reconstruction amendments, the *Slaughter-*

house Cases,[24] begins with a cogent statement of the problem. The case involved an effort by white butchers in Louisiana to convince the Court that a new state law monopolizing the slaughterhouse business violated the new Fourteenth Amendment. Before the Civil War amendments, the white butchers would never have tried to get their complaint before the Court—under the strong federalist premises of the early republic,[25] the wisdom of a regulated monopoly was up to each individual state to determine. After the amendments, however, the butchers could now suppose that the Louisiana monopoly raised a "hard" case. They argued that the new amendments decisively changed the balance between state sovereignty and the national interest in protecting the fundamental freedoms of each American citizen. By forcing butchers to deal with a monopoly if they hoped to carry on their trade, Louisiana was merely devising a new and subtler form of slavery—only slaves could be required by law to obtain the permission of a single monopolist in order to do business; free men were free precisely because they could *not* be compelled to contract with a single master-monopolist when they found it in their interest to carry on their business in a different way. Before the war, each American's freedom of contract was subordinated to the state's authority to legitimate slavery. But now, argued the butchers, it was every American's fundamental right to demand protection from such unjustifiable restrictions on economic freedom.

In rejecting this argument by a vote of 5 to 4, the Court initiated one of the two fundamental approaches to synthesis that defined middle republican jurisprudence. This involved *particularizing* the constitutional principles announced at Time Two in a way that restricted their impact upon the older principles of Time One, which were conceived in a much more general and abstract way. On the Court's view, the Republican amendments had "one pervading purpose . . . we mean the freedom of the slave race."[26] Though the Court recognized that the amendments revolutionized traditional principles of federalism so far as blacks were concerned, it was entirely unwilling to concede that the amendments required a similar judicial reassessment of traditional principles of federalism more generally. It refused to allow non-blacks to take advantage of the new principles of Time Two when doing so "radically changes the whole theory of the relations of the State and Federal governments

to each other and of both these governments to the people. . . ."[27]
The majority's way of relating Time One and Time Two is easily
represented in pictorial terms (see Figure 1). The big rectangle
represents all the possible cases that could come up for adjudication.
A particularizer, however, does not try to conceptualize the principles of Reconstruction in the same abstract and general way he
conceives those of the Founding. Instead, he divides the rectangle
into two distinct parts. Within the particular domain having to do
with blacks (and groups somehow analogous to blacks), he allows
the principles of Time Two to trump his understanding of the
Federalist principles of Time One; outside this domain, he insulates
Federalist principles from the impact of the new ideas announced
by the Republicans.

   This form of synthesis proved unstable over the life of the middle
republic. Nor should we find this surprising—for particularized synthesis is, I think, especially attractive to judges during the early period
of a constitutional regime. To see why, consider that early republican
judges were first socialized into the law during the latter days of the
preceding regime. It was only after learning their Federalist Constitution from Marshall, Story, and the other great expositors of the
early republic that they proceeded to gain access to the meaning of
the Reconstruction texts in a very different way—through lived experience of the greatest political events of their time. In the words
of the *Slaughterhouse* majority, the Reconstruction amendments were
part of a chain of "events almost too recent to be called history, but

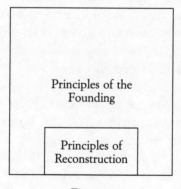

Figure 1

which are familiar to us all."[28] Little wonder, then, that many of them experienced great difficulty in thinking about Time One and Time Two at the same level of generality: to them, Reconstruction was the culmination of something concrete and particular—the struggle against slavery. While this struggle, of course, was motivated by principles of human freedom fully as general as those that motivated the Founders' concerns with federalism, these ideas did not come prepackaged by mainstream constitutional lawyers over generations. Thus, it would seem "natural" for many[29] early judges to marry an abstract understanding of the Founding with a particularistic understanding of Reconstruction in the way described by my picture: Reconstruction principles governed only so far as blacks (and similar groups) were concerned; Founding principles governed everything else.

Over time, two things happen which tend to destabilize this picture. First, Reconstruction begins to fade from lived experience. New people come to the law who increasingly approach the meaning of the Reconstruction amendments in the same manner they approach the Founding: through law books rather than newspapers, through courtroom argument rather than searing political struggle. The legal texts announced in the 1860's no longer seem so very different from the legal texts further removed in time: "Congress shall make no law . . . No State shall . . ." What difference does it make that the first four words were enacted in 1791 and the last three in 1868? Aren't they all part of the same Constitution? Shouldn't they be interpreted in the same spirit, without unduly particularizing one amendment more than another?

But more than the simple passage of time undermines particularistic syntheses. No less important is the continuing process of constitutional litigation. Since the legal relationship between Reconstruction and the Founding is an immensely multifaceted affair, the need for synthesis arises time and time again in the cases—leading to one or another decision, one or another judicial reflection on the best way of resolving the tension between the two constitutionally creative moments. These early decisions in turn prompt critical commentary and further reflection, which generate new insights into the way the diverse principles interact with one another.

The fading of lived experience and the rise of legal dialectic

conspire, then, to erode the particularistic synthesis of the first judicial generation and replace it with something very different. I shall
call it a comprehensive synthesis: rather than the principles of Time
Two being confined to the historical context in which they first
arose, Reconstruction is now understood as a source of legal principles that are no less capable of generalized application than are
those derived from the Founding. The task instead is to develop the
entire set of constitutional principles in a comprehensive way that
harmonizes their deeper aspirations. To return to our rectangle (see
Figure 2), both Reconstruction and Founding principles are conceived on the same level of abstraction and generality. The courts
do not give a particularizing spin to one or another historical epoch.
Instead, they regulate all cases by seeking the harmonious development of all principles, regardless of the particular epoch from which
they originated. To put this transformation in a single line, the path
of the law is from particularistic to comprehensive synthesis.

There is, of course, a lot more happening in the law of the middle
republic than this movement. Nonetheless, I think the shift expresses
a central tendency. Perhaps a metaphor will clarify. Think of the
American Republic as a railroad train, with the judges of the middle
republic sitting in the caboose, looking backward. What they see are
the mountains and valleys of dualistic constitutional experience, most
notably the peaks of constitutional meaning elaborated during the
Founding and Reconstruction. As the train moves forward in history,
it is harder for the judges to see the traces of volcanic ash that

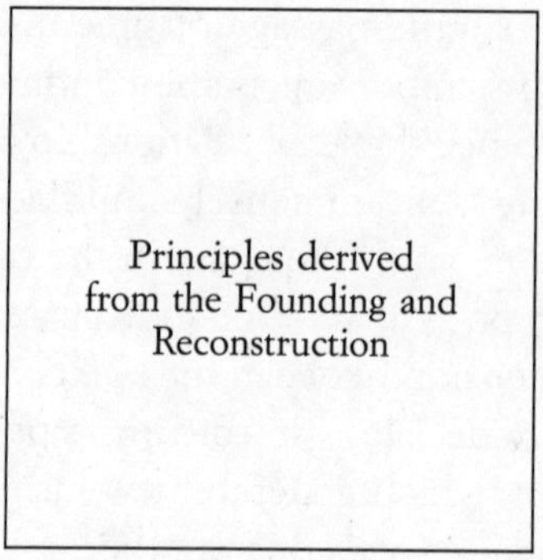

Principles derived
from the Founding and
Reconstruction

Figure 2

marked each mountain's political emergence onto the legal land-scape. At the same time, a different perspective becomes more avail-able: as the second mountain moves into the background, it becomes easier to see that there is now a mountain range out there that can be described in a comprehensive way.

This changing perspective over time is the engine driving the shift from particularistic to comprehensive synthesis. As this shift is oc-curring, lots of other things are happening. Old judges die, and new ones are sent to the caboose by the engineers who happen then to be in the locomotive. These new judges' views of the landscape are shaped by their own experiences of life and law—as well as the new vistas constantly opened up on the mountains by the path that the train takes into the future. The distinctive thing about the judges of the middle republic is that they remained in the caboose, looking backward—not in the locomotive arguing over the direction the train should be taking at the next crossroads, or anxiously observing the passing scene from one of the passenger cars. Doubtless, the rela-tionship between the mountains in the mountain range will be seen differently over time. The crucial question is whether it is fair to view the judges of the middle republic as engaged in this process of retrospective synthesis.

This is precisely what the regnant professional narrative seeks to deny and what I seek to affirm (without, of course, denying the existence of occasions on which judicial performance fell short—sometimes egregiously*—of interpretive possibility). The third vol-ume in this series, *Interpretations,* will make out my case by reinter-preting some of the great cases of the middle republic. Within the limits of the present sketch, I cannot do more than suggest the general character of my proposed reinterpretation.

REINTERPRETING THE MIDDLE REPUBLIC

Look backward with me, then, on the two great achievements that dominate the first American century: on the one side, the Federalist

---

*Most notably in the way the Court peripheralized the Republican concern with racial equality during this period. This will be an important concern of the third volume, *Interpretations.*

ideal of a decentralized republic—in which American citizens could expect only limited assistance from the national government in protecting their personal freedoms against state politics; on the other, the Republican assertion of a more nationalistic Union that would no longer tolerate the enslavement of any American by a dominant state majority but insisted on the equal protection of the laws. How to synthesize these two visions into a comprehensive whole?

By moving beyond the very limited protection of fundamental rights offered by courts during the early republic. Given Reconstruction, it was perfectly appropriate for courts to insist that the nation was now committed to the guarantee of fundamental rights in a deeper way. Surely, it is hard to fault the courts of the *Lochner* era for taking this step; indeed, it is hard to see how any serious effort at synthesis could have moved to a different conclusion.

If, then, something was fundamentally wrong with *Lochner,* it has to do with the particular way middle republican courts conceptualized the nature of fundamental rights. It is here, however, where anachronism distorts modern vision in condemning the middle republic's emphasis on private property and freedom of contract. Given the popular repudiation of laissez-faire during the New Deal, it is no longer right for modern courts to interpret constitutional liberty in free market terms. But before the 1930's, things looked very different. Even during the early republic, the courts had marked out contract as a domain of freedom peculiarly appropriate for national protection.[30] This constitutional understanding was reinforced by the Reconstruction amendments. The Emancipation Amendment, for example, was understood, first and foremost, in legal terms that relied on the language of property and contract. At a minimum, it meant that blacks could not be treated as chattels; no less than whites, they could henceforth freely contract for their labor and own the fruits of their productive work as private property.[31] But if freedom of contract and the right to own private property distinguished the black slave from the black freedman, did they not also serve more generally to distinguish slaves from freedmen of all races? If, for example, whites were deprived of their right to contract over their labor, was this not a kind of slavery? Shouldn't the new nationalistic concern with freedom of contract and the right to private property expressed in the Thirteenth and Fourteenth Amendments trump the old Federalist concern with states' rights?

As we have seen, a narrow majority of the Justices refused to generalize the principles of Reconstruction so broadly in the *Slaughterhouse Cases*. So comprehensive a synthesis threatened to unsettle too much of the received Federalist legal wisdom they had learned during the early republic; it seemed too removed from the concrete struggle over black slavery that served as the testing experience of their political maturation. As time moved on, however, more Justices began taking such generalizing questions more seriously. To put the synthetic point in a single line: if the early republic gave *limited* protection to the fundamental right of *white men* to exercise their freedom through *property and contract,* shouldn't the Reconstruction amendments be interpreted to require *equal* protection to the fundamental rights of *all* Americans to exercise their freedom though *property and contract?*

As we shall see, by the end of the middle republic, the courts had reached just this point: blacks no less than whites, women no less than men, had been granted equal rights of property and contract.[32] This movement toward comprehensive synthesis was, of course, decisively repudiated by the New Deal Democracy that brought the middle republic to an end. But it is a large mistake to look upon 1905—the year that *Lochner* was decided—as if it were 1937. In 1905, the Justices were not confronting a New Deal Congress and a President who had just won decisive popular majorities in support of a decisive break with constitutional laissez-faire. To the contrary: the Justices had just lived through the failed Populist effort to mobilize the American people against the evils of laissez-faire capitalism—a movement that climaxed with the nomination of William Jennings Bryan as the Democratic candidate for the Presidency in 1896. Rather than leading to a Rooseveltian transformation, Bryan's nomination served only to catalyze a decisive popular counterreaction on behalf of William McKinley and the Republican Party.

It is anachronistic for the modern myth of rediscovery to portray the *Lochner* Court as if it were abusing the idea of constitutional interpretation by imposing its idiosyncratic and reactionary views on a polity yearning for the New Deal. Like the courts of the early republic, the *Lochner* Court was exercising a preservationist function, trying to develop a comprehensive synthesis of the meaning of the Founding and Reconstruction out of the available legal materials.[33]

The modern myth serves only to blind us to the extent to which

the synthetic problem confronted by the middle republicans continues to haunt us. After all, modern constitutional lawyers do not deny
that the Constitution prohibits slavery or that this guarantee comes
into play if an American citizen were denied the freedom to control
her body or make fundamental life choices. But moderns express
this point in ways that no longer place great weight on the language
of free contract and private property discredited by the People
during the New Deal. What constitutional concepts have taken their
place? How does the modern effort at multigenerational synthesis
compare with the effort of the middle republic? Once the shattering
consequences of the New Deal are taken into account, can we still
learn something from the synthetic efforts of the middle republic?

I will take up these questions in the next two chapters. Before
doing so, we should glance at a second element in the middle
republican synthesis. While the *Lochner* idea committed the nation
and its courts to the comprehensive protection of fundamental freedoms against the states, this second principle governed national
interventions in state affairs where fundamental rights were not
threatened. The Federalist Constitution had refused to grant plenary
power to the national government, doling out only a limited set of
enumerated powers—a localist bias reinforced by the constitutional
politics of the Jacksonian era.[34] Once again, then, the courts of the
middle republic confronted a fundamental synthetic question: How,
if at all, did the new nationalism of Reconstruction transform the
older notion of limited national power?

Modern lawyers have trouble taking the middle republican struggle with this question seriously. But this is only because the great
opinions of the middle republic seem to undermine national powers
essential to post–New Deal government: powers of taxation and
powers of regulation. Given the crucial importance of these powers
in the modern republic, we have refused to see that it was *reasonable*
for the middle republican Justices to deny that Reconstruction had
radically displaced the Federalist-Jacksonian law on these matters.
Moderns look with disbelief at the *Income Tax Cases*,[35] in which
middle republican Justices declared unconstitutional an early effort
by the national government to assume a power that serves as the
fiscal lifeblood of today's government. Yet before the Sixteenth
Amendment was enacted in 1913, the Constitution *explicitly* denied

unlimited powers of taxation to the federal government.[36] Similarly, moderns dismiss the middle republican effort to impose principled limits on the reach of national regulatory power under the "commerce clause." Yet the original Constitution did not grant plenary lawmaking authority to the national government, but doled out power in a series of enumerated grants. This textual strategy would have been pointless if one of the enumerated powers—over interstate commerce—was read so expansively as to embrace the whole.

Although the enumerated power strategy was finally repudiated by the American people, this happened in the twentieth century, not in the eighteenth or nineteenth, and we are wrong to condemn the Republican Justices for failing to use the right crystal ball. Though we may properly quibble with the precise way the Justices drew their lines around interstate commerce, they were not wrong on the main point: before the New Deal, the People had never self-consciously reallocated plenary power over the economy from the the states to the national government.

Rethinking the New Deal

Must we blind ourselves so thoroughly to the interpretive predicaments of an earlier age? What prevents us from recognizing that the Justices of the middle republic had moved down the path from particularistic to comprehensive synthesis, weaving together the disparate elements of the Founding and Reconstruction into a doctrinal pattern that made sense within the context of their own time? On the one hand, the national government emerged as the guarantor of the right of all citizens to own their labor and property, and to contract freely for their use without being enslaved by a state majority. On the other hand, the national government remained one of limited powers, without plenary authority to oust the states as the primary regulators of economic life. Though our own answers are different, why should we deny that these answers were once reasonable interpretations of the Constitution?

There is a better way to make sense of the New Deal, one that finds a deeper meaning in the struggle between the Roosevelt Presidency and the Supreme Court during the Great Depression. Within the mythic framework of rediscovery, the Old Court's challenge to the New Deal from 1932 to 1937 only revealed the arbitrary character of the interpretive exercise the Justices had attempted over the preceding sixty years. Apparently, it would have been better for the Constitution and the country if the Court had made it plain, from 1933 on, that Franklin Roosevelt and the Democratic Congress were not engaged in normal politics in demanding a New Deal for the American people, but were instead speaking in the authentic higher lawmaking accents of We the People of the United States.

My reinterpretation of the law of the middle republic challenges this view. The Old Court's defense of its comprehensive synthesis helped, not hurt, the democratic process through which the People gave new marching orders to their government in the 1930's. By dramatizing the fundamental constitutional principles raised by the New Deal, the Old Court contributed to a more focused, and democratic, transformation of constitutional identity than might otherwise have occurred. By holding up a mirror to the American people that re-presented the fundamental principles of the middle republic, the Old Court made it easier, not harder, for the citizenry of the 1930's to clarify what they found wanting in the traditional structure—and finally give constitutional legitimacy to a new vision of activist national government that did not have deep popular roots in our previous constitutional experience.

CHAPTER FIVE

The Modern Republic

CONSTITUTIONAL IDEALS, INSTITUTIONAL REALITIES

NEW DEAL DEMOCRACY marked another great leap along the arc of nationalistic self-definition initiated by the American Revolution. Although the Founders broke with the state-centered Articles of Confederation, they did not clearly establish the priority of national over state citizenship; although the Reconstructers resolved this fundamental question in favor of the Union, they did not frontally challenge the Founding notion that the national government had limited powers over economic and social development; with the New Deal, this Founding principle was decisively repudiated. Henceforth, the federal government would operate as a truly national government, speaking for the People on all matters that sufficiently attracted the interest of lawmakers in Washington, D.C.

Not that the states were deprived of their general lawmaking jurisdiction. They too could legislate on any subject they found in the public interest—subject to preemption by national lawmakers and judicial scrutiny for prejudicial impact upon out-of-staters. A commitment to federalism, however, was no longer thought to require a constitutional strategy that restrained the national government to a limited number of enumerated powers over economic and social life.

At the same time the New Deal was transforming the scope of national government, it was also reorganizing its internal structure. The key was Roosevelt's transformation of the Presidency. The history of the middle republic had been marked by a series of dramatic failures to exploit the plebiscitarian potential of the Presidency— Andrew Johnson, William Jennings Bryan, Woodrow Wilson each devising a new way to fail as Popular Tribune. This series of failures in popular mobilization reinforced the centrality of Congress in the nation's normal political life. Rather than successfully confronting Congress with a "mandate" from the American people, middle republican Presidents sometimes seemed less important than the Speaker of the House or the leaders of the Senate.

Franklin Roosevelt changed this. His success in leading Congress and the Supreme Court to affirm the legitimacy of activist national government, reinforced by the wartime experience of national solidarity, established a new paradigm of Presidential leadership. This shift, in turn, encouraged a change in the system of Presidential selection. Nominating conventions of the middle republic gave Congressional leaders a key role in selecting Presidential candidates. The modern system increasingly awarded the Democratic and Republican nominations to the winner of a series of primary elections—giving increased substance to the President's claim to speak for the People independently of Congress.[1]

Over time, it became standard practice for the President to appeal over the heads of Congress for the support of the People in his struggle to enact his program into law.[2] The Founders' principled hostility to the plebiscitarian Presidency became a thing of the past. Congressional leaders, as well as the American people, expected their agenda to be filled mostly by Presidential initiatives; Presidents would use their veto power as if it allowed them to function as a third branch of the legislature, equal in authority to House and Senate. No less important, the new activist state provided the Presidency with an enormous increase in the material resources he might use in his ongoing dealings with Congressional barons: dams, roads, hospitals, military bases in unprecedented numbers were available to the executive branch as means of obtaining Congressional support for Presidential programs.

This is not to say that the modern Presidency reduced Congress to the American equivalent of the Houses of Parliament—which normally can be relied upon to ratify the Prime Minister's legislative initiatives after a decent period of public debate. Even the New Deal Congresses beat back Presidential efforts to consolidate control over the judiciary and the burgeoning bureaucracy—rejecting the President's "court-packing" bill in 1937 and his sweeping executive reorganization proposal in the following year.[3] Moreover, Roosevelt's example inspired the enactment of the most important formal constitutional amendment of the modern republic: the Twenty-second, ratified in 1951, forbade any future President from repeating Roosevelt's decision to break with Washington's self-limitation to two terms in office. The President would not be allowed to assert that he was an indispensable spokesman for the People, who might properly live out his life in the White House on the basis of a series of (often close) popular victories. Though these efforts to restrict the aggrandizing implications of the Roosevelt precedent are important, they should not obscure the fundamental shift in power relationships between Congress and the executive that had occurred. Presidential leadership had now become a normal part of the lawmaking process.[4]

At the same time, the nature of administration was changing. Vast new bureaucracies had come into existence to make good on the domestic and foreign responsibilities of the activist national government. Since massive bureaucratic and military establishments were not a normal part of the early or middle republics, Congress and the President made episodic efforts to consider the systemic implications of these new realities—enacting "framework statutes" like the Administrative Procedure Act and the National Security Act to give constitutional structure to these new institutional presences.*

Speaking broadly, however, it is in the area of governmental structure that the modern republic has paid the heaviest price for the informality which accompanied its birth in the 1930's. As we have seen, Roosevelt and Congress left it to the Supreme Court to codify

---

*Other framework statutes of the early modern period include the Executive Reorganization Act, the Hatch Act, the Legislative Reorganization Act, and the Full Employment Act. We should begin to consider these statutes as part of a "New Deal Constitution" that, together with the Twenty-second Amendment, sought to establish crucial institutional arrangements emerging from the popular embrace of activist national government at home and abroad.

These early modern statutes set a precedent for later efforts to structure the ongoing struggle between the Presidency and Congress over the control of activist national government. For example, Congress passed the War Powers Resolution of 1973 in response to President Johnson's conduct of the Vietnam War and the Budget Control Act of 1985 in response to the fiscal crisis generated by President Reagan's tax-cutting initiatives. I cannot, alas, give these framework statutes the attention they deserve in this introductory sketch.

the constitutional meaning of New Deal democracy in a series of transformative judicial opinions. Unfortunately, the Court has done a much less creditable job on these structural matters than it has done in elaborating a post–New Deal conception of fundamental rights. In any event, the struggle between the Presidency and Congress over the bureaucracy and the military has been one of the great unresolved questions for the modern republic—and one unlikely to be decisively resolved anytime soon.[5]

PRESIDENTIAL LEADERSHIP IN HIGHER LAWMAKING

As during previous eras, the ongoing struggles for advantage by well-organized interests and elites have been punctuated by more populist efforts at mass mobilization and national self-definition. These have come from different parts of the political spectrum. Joseph McCarthy made the Senate the leading voice of the first important postwar effort to mobilize the citizenry—this time, for a national crusade against communism at home and abroad. He failed, however, to gain the public support necessary to overcome the increasing resistance of the other branches (most notably, the executive)[6] to his pretensions to speak for the People. By 1954, he found himself incapable of sustaining his Senatorial support. Though McCarthyism certainly had pervasive and long-lasting effects, it represents the first of the modern republic's failed constitutional moments. Rather than leading the nation to revise its legitimating principles in the manner of Madison, Lincoln, and Roosevelt, McCarthy would go down in the annals of the Republic as a failed demagogue whose loud appeals to the People, when tested, proved incapable of engaging the deep and sustained popular commitment required for a legitimate transformation in fundamental values.

Not so, the leaders of the next important exercise in constitutional politics. The civil rights movement of the 1950's and 1960's was the most successful act of popular transformation in recent history. I can only remark here upon the most obvious ways this transformation diverged from the pattern initiated by Franklin Roosevelt—while reinforcing many other higher lawmaking themes established in the 1930's.[7] First, for the big difference: It was the Supreme Court, not the Presidency, that took the lead in forcing the question of racial equality to the center of the constitutional agenda. Once the Court handed down its *Brown* decision in 1954, however, the central role of Presidential leadership once again became clear. Until the struggling civil rights movement gained the decisive support of the Presidency, the ultimate status of *Brown* remained in doubt. For the next decade, *Brown* energized massive racist resistance no less than civil rights activism—and it was hardly obvious which side of the struggle would gain the support of the majority of the American people. While President Eisenhower did use federal troops in Little Rock to override local resistance to school desegregation, this was about the limit of his support for *Brown;* and the Congress was hardly more supportive.[8]

The Presidential election of 1960 began to mark a change. At least when compared with Eisenhower's position, both Nixon and Kennedy seemed far less equivocal in their support of *Brown*. Since Kennedy was somewhat more aggressive in expressing sympathy for the rising civil rights movement, the victory of the Democratic ticket suggested public support for the continued elaboration of the principle of racial equality.

But much more than this single election was required before *Brown* became an unquestionable part of our higher law. Between 1954 and 1960, the Court had failed to make *Brown* a living reality in the South or elsewhere. It would take much more popular mobilization, much more self-sacrifice and inspired political leadership before the American people would make a considered judgment on this fundamental matter. As civil rights activity accelerated in the early 1960's—boycotts, sit-ins, freedom rides—the Kennedy Administration made a series of choices that defined its relationship to the rising movement: Should it allow mob violence and police brutality in the South to crush the movement? The more the Administration intervened in the South, the more it became committed to making the legal promise of equality into a social reality. The civil rights movement, in turn, was blessed with a great leader in Martin Luther King, who appreciated the importance of constructing a broad-based citizen coalition against racism. It is only against this background that the Kennedy Administration could finally, in 1963, propose a Civil Rights Act that began to place the national government decisively behind the antidiscrimination effort in education, employment, and public accommodations.

The passage of this act in July 1964 set the stage, in turn, for the

Presidential election campaign. The Johnson-Goldwater contest raised the issues of principle starkly: on the one hand, a Southern liberal with a long and emphatic commitment to the national protection of civil rights; on the other, a conservative Republican who had just voted against the Civil Rights Act because it offended traditional values of states' rights, private property, and freedom of contract. If Goldwater had emerged from the election victorious, there would have been another period of institutional indecision about the depth of the nation's commitment to egalitarian values—another period in which the Presidency would resist the civil rights movement's call to redefine and deepen the People's commitment to equality. Johnson's landslide victory, accompanied by decisive Democratic majorities in Congress, established a new institutional pattern. All three branches were now mutually supporting one another in asserting that the People of the United States had made a considered judgment about civil rights. The passage of landmark legislation, like the Voting Rights Act of 1965 and the Civil Rights Act of 1968, moved this commitment far beyond the point where the courts could have taken it by themselves. Without this decisive support from the President and Congress, *Brown* would have remained the embattled and problematic symbol it seemed in the late 1950's.

This brief sketch suggests how much this great constitutional transformation owes to the patterns of Presidential leadership elaborated by Roosevelt in the establishment of the modern republic. While the role of the courts in the 1930's and the 1960's was certainly very different, other elements of the New Deal model, presented in Chapter 2, were very much present. As in 1932, the Democratic victory in 1960 signaled the rise of a new political agenda which proposed to project national power into new domains of social life; then, after a period of further political debate and legal experimentation, the value of the new national principles was decisively affirmed in the next Presidential election, in which the President's party gained decisive majorities in the Congress. After this decisive popular mandate, the tensions between President, Congress, and Court that had characterized the earlier periods of mobilized debate came to an end with the recognition by all three branches that *the People had spoken.* By the end of the second term of the Democratic

Presidency in the 1960's, as in the 1930's, all three branches had placed their institutional weight solidly behind national initiatives of a kind that would have seemed scarcely possible eight years before.

But, of course, there was a lot more happening in the 1960's besides the civil rights revolution. As the decade moved on, a host of new movements sought to use the models of political mobilization developed in the civil rights struggle to gain a similar kind of deep and widespread popular support on behalf of an escalating set of goals—ending the Vietnam War, protecting the environment, redistributing social and economic power to the oppressed at home and abroad. As in the preceding cases, these New Left movements did not devote much time or energy advocating constitutional amendments of the kind contemplated by Article Five of the Federalist Constitution. They showed themselves to be children of the modern republic by focusing their energies on Presidential politics, seeking to make the Democratic Party into the expressive vehicle for their transformative agenda.

Only this time the result was more like the Bryan-McKinley election of 1896 than the Roosevelt landslide of 1936. The Democrats' nomination of George McGovern in 1972, no less than the selection of William Jennings Bryan in 1896, showed the power of movement insurgents to gain control of a major political party. The resulting election, however, dramatized the extent to which the insurgents had alienated the majority of the American people. The McGovern campaign precipitated a broad ideological backlash that gave Richard Nixon an overwhelming reelection victory.

Like the Populists before them, the New Left was unable to recover from this resounding popular defeat.[9] Not that the movement vanished without a legislative trace. Just as the Populist spirit gained many legislative victories before and after the Bryan debacle, the Democrats in Congress gained many noteworthy statutory victories for one or another aspect of the New Left agenda.[10] What is missing from these enactments is the distinctive constitutional symbolism that marks out the legal expression of popular movements that *decisively* carry the day in our national politics. A good example is the War Powers Resolution of 1973, passed over President Nixon's veto, that sought to restrict the power of the President to commit the country unilaterally to future Vietnam Wars. Since Nixon, Pres-

idents have typically refused to recognize that the resolution constrains their constitutional authority, as Commander in Chief, to
commit troops overseas; when faced with this conflict between President and Congress, the courts have stayed on the sidelines, allowing
the matter to drift with the tides of normal politics.[11]

All this makes sense, given the decisive defeat of McGovern in
1972. Consider how differently the constitutional system would have
treated the War Powers Resolution if the McGovern-Nixon election
had gone the other way and the New Left had gained the popular
mandate it sought. Under this scenario, the statute might have been
emphatically endorsed by the President as a paradigmatic product
of the triumphant new movement; rather than staying on the sidelines, a McGovernite Supreme Court would have seized the first
opportunity to announce that the statute would henceforth provide
the fundamental framework for future judicial enforcement of limits
on the warmaking power. As in the case of the Presidentially led
processes of the 1930's and 1960's, the result would have been the
creation of new higher law norms expressing the will of We the
People in a way that decisively bound normal political actors in
Washington, D.C..

But constitutional politics moved in a very different direction:
from the New Left to the New Right. A symbol was the failure of
the women's movement to gain the formal ratification of an equal
rights amendment during the 1970's—surely one of the least controversial of the New Left's objectives.[12] In contrast, the same period
saw increasing support for the constitutional initiatives of the New
Right—most notably, its campaigns for formal amendments that
might guarantee the fetus's "right to life" and require the national
government to operate on a "balanced budget." Significantly, the
election of Ronald Reagan as President in 1980 did not propel these
formal amendments to the center of the political agenda. Instead,
the New Right sought to achieve its constitutional ambitions through
the model of Presidential leadership more characteristic of the modern republic.

We have already reviewed this effort by the Reagan Republicans to
retrace the steps of the Roosevelt Democrats.[13] The upshot was
another failed constitutional moment: Reagan's "Revolution" only
revealed how difficult it would be to mobilize a majority of the

People to repudiate the activist egalitarian vision of government affirmed in the 1930's and 1960's. The 1988 Presidential election was indicative. Candidates who wished to revitalize the transformative ambitions of either the New Right (Kemp or Robertson) or the New Left (Jackson) failed to win either the Republican or the Democratic nominations. Candidates George Bush and Michael Dukakis were closer to one another than they were to the New Right and New Left opponents they had defeated in the primaries. Neither Bush nor Dukakis offered grand new constitutional principles to the American people; both were intelligent and decent men who promised competence and prudent adjustment of preexisting values (though Bush would make the trade-offs in a somewhat more "conservative" way than would Dukakis). The Bush victory meant that a President representing the afterglow of the Old/New Right would confront a Congress in which the Old/New Left still lingered. Neither side has reason to expect that the People will rally to its support if it refuses to cooperate with its antagonist. Normal politics, always important, is now ascendant: politicians trying to reach reasonable compromises in the absence of decisive direction from a mobilized majority of their fellow citizens.

This too will change. But, for the moment, it is even more important than usual to consider how the modern Supreme Court has discharged the preservationist role that dualist theory marks out as its distinctive mission during normal politics.

THE SUPREME COURT

In this introductory survey, I focus on the basic interpretive issue modern courts share with their predecessors in the middle republic: the problem of intergenerational synthesis.[14] Since the Civil War, Justices have no longer looked upon the Constitution as the culminating expression of the revolutionary achievements of a single generation of Americans. They struggled instead with the interpretive questions raised by a Constitution that has been profoundly transformed, but not altogether rejected, through the constitutional politics of a series of generations.

This post–Civil War project took a new turn after 1937. As in Reconstruction, the New Deal Justices witnessed the popular repudiation of some of the central principles of the preceding constitutional regime. Before their very eyes, Supreme Court decisions that served to summarize the judicial understanding of the Constitution—*Dred Scott, Lochner*—were now, after a sustained and bitter struggle, decisively rejected in the name of the People by the victorious Republicans/Democrats. A critical task of both the early middle and the early modern Court was to take the measure of the constitutional revolution that the Justices had witnessed: Did it amount to a total repudiation of the preexisting constitutional tradition and its replacement, in the manner of the original Constitution of 1787, with a new comprehensive synthesis? Did it amount to a minor change of a few rules, in the manner of a constitutional superstatute, leaving the previous synthesis intact?

This parallel between the courts of the middle and modern Republics is obliterated by the modern professional narrative. Since this narrative does not recognize the New Deal as creating a new constitutional regime, it cannot begin to identify common features in the interpretive predicament confronting the courts of the two historical eras. This makes it impossible for moderns to learn from their predecessors as they try to confront their own dilemmas of multigenerational synthesis. Once we strip away the myth of rediscovery, a new historical perspective opens up: We can systematically compare the way middle republican Justices confronted their problem of synthesis over the seventy years between Reconstruction and the Great Depression with the modern judicial confrontation over the last half century.

The Path of the Law

The result is especially rewarding because we shall find some striking similarities in interpretive response. Like its Reconstruction predecessor, the New Deal Court rejected simplistic solutions to the problem of synthesis. It refused to find that popular support for the New Deal amounted either to a comprehensive reworking of the entire Constitution or to the enactment of a few superstatutes that changed nothing fundamental. Instead, the Court treated the popular repudiation of *Lochner*'s property-oriented jurisprudence as a transformative amendment expressing a profound, but not total, change in

American constitutional identity. As it had in the aftermath of Reconstruction, the Court responded to this diagnosis by picking up fragments of the older tradition that had not been repudiated by the recent transformation, reworking them in the light of more recent achievements, integrating them into larger doctrinal wholes. Indeed, if we compare the path of synthesis over the seventy years of the middle republic with the path taken by modern courts over the last half-century, a common dynamic emerges: in both cases, there was a movement from particularistic to more comprehensive efforts at synthesis.

As our sketch of the middle republic suggested, this movement is propelled in part by the simple passage of time. During the early part of the regime, the Justices are acutely aware of the shattering consequences of the last successful movement of constitutional politics. Not only did they live through the agonies of constitutional creation, they often participated as leading protagonists—otherwise, they would never have gained appointments to the Supreme Court. In contrast to their lived experience of the last constitutional solution, the early Justices could approach the achievements of earlier generations only through books. Moreover, these law books were generally written by people of the last generation, who had not lived through the most recent great events.

It is this disparity between lived experience and book learning that, I argued, contributed to the particularistic character of the early synthesis reached by the Justices of the middle republic. They tried to preserve as much of their book learning about the Founding as they could by narrowly interpreting their lived experience of Reconstruction. So far as they were concerned, the Civil War amendments only transformed the status of *blacks;* when, as in the *Slaughterhouse Cases,* white men wished to avail themselves of the amendments, a majority of the Justices refused to generalize the Civil War amendments' new nationalism, libertarianism, and egalitarianism beyond the context of race relations. This particularistic definition of lived experience allowed them, in turn, to interpret their book learning about the Founding in a very different spirit—as the source of general principles that should be followed generally except in the special contexts regulated by Reconstruction.

Over time, this approach gave way to a more comprehensive

approach to synthesis. As the lived experience of Reconstruction faded, it no longer seemed sensible to treat the principles of 1868 as if they were of a different, and more limited, kind than the principles of 1787. Rather than limiting the new Republican principles to their originating context in race relations, the courts increasingly synthesized them with older Federalist ideas in a wholistic way that gave them equal status in the emerging doctrinal synthesis.[15]

My thesis is that a similar movement from particularism to comprehensiveness has marked the synthetic work of the courts of the modern republic.

Triangulating the Problem

To grasp this interpretive movement, we must first define a basic difference between the middle and modern courts. Although both confronted the dilemmas of intergenerational synthesis, the problem took on a new level of complexity for the modern judiciary. Like the middle Court, modern judges would confront the doctrinal relationship between the constitutional achievements of the Founding and Reconstruction generations as they set about deciding concrete cases. But now the New Deal's sweeping legitimation of activist government added two new dimensions to the interpretive problem. Time and again, litigation would force the Justices to define the relationship between New Deal principles and those inherited from both the Founding and Reconstruction.

To appreciate these new challenges, reflect first on the New Deal's impact upon the received legal understanding of the Founding. For the first 150 years, few doubted that the Founding Federalists placed a high constitutional value on private property and market freedom. Since the New Deal had transparently repudiated *this* Founding commitment, modern courts would have to find a way of preserving those fragments of the Founding ideal that had survived the popular repudiation of the property-oriented conception of limited government. How was the Court to engage in this complex act of reinterpretation? Call this the problem of one-three synthesis, because it involves the harmonization of the first and third great turning points in our constitutional experience.

Analytically at least, this is a different problem from two-three synthesis. Once again, though, the central difficulty revolves around property ownership and free contract. As I suggested in the last chapter,[16] the courts of the middle republic were right to insist that the Civil War amendments massively reinforced these values in the new constitutional regime. Most obviously, the Emancipation Amendment worked a fundamental change in the black slave's relationship to property and contract. No longer could a person of color be treated as if he or she could be owned by others; instead, freed blacks now were guaranteed the right to acquire and transfer property on the same terms as whites. Of course, this was a very formal and abstract kind of freedom for African slaves who had been remorselessly suppressed for centuries. Moreover, the Fourteenth and Fifteenth Amendments promised Afro-Americans more than this. Nonetheless, it was hardly arbitrary for the middle republican courts to emphasize market freedoms as they set about synthesizing the constitutional meaning of the Founding and Reconstruction.

This meant that the modern Court would have its work cut out in developing a credible two-three synthesis. No longer could the Court's interpretation of the meaning of the Reconstruction amendments center on protecting each American's right to own and transfer private property. Instead, it would have to restate the meaning of Reconstruction's guarantee of "equal protection" and "due process of law" in a post–New Deal world in which the ownership and exchange of private property were less central. How was this act of interpretive synthesis to be accomplished?

This two-three question required a judicial confrontation with Republican voices that expressed different political views from those held by the Founders two generations earlier. Thus, courts engaged in two-three synthesis confronted rather different interpretive problems from those relevant to one-three synthesis. For all their analytic and substantive differences, however, modern courts have often found they cannot answer two-three questions without confronting one-three problems as well. These, in turn, often become intertwined with one-two problems raised by the continuing need to harmonize the Founding and Reconstruction. The multifaceted challenges involved in one-two-three synthesis force the modern Court beyond the simpler interpretive horizon of the middle republic.

Nonetheless, it is best to begin by confronting the synthetic problem that modern judges most closely share with their middle republican predecessors: the one-two problem involved in harmonizing the conflicting imperatives of the Founding and Reconstruction. Even this problem has been radically transformed by the New Deal. Consider, for example, the classic question of one-two synthesis raised by the relationship between the Civil War amendments and the Bill of Rights (which had applied only to the national government during the early republic). The courts of the middle republic, like those of the modern, chose the path of "selective incorporation"— imposing on the states only those aspects of the Bill of Rights they deemed fundamental. During the middle republic, the courts selected the Takings Clause of the Fifth Amendment as the central focus of its incorporationist activities.* Modern courts, however, would have to reconsider this property focus in the wake of the New Deal. They would have to emphasize new aspects of the Bill of Rights if they were to give continued meaning to the Founding in the light of the People's repudiation of laissez-faire in the 1930's. But which ones? How was the process of doctrinal reintegration to be conceived?

Of course, no single case could possibly resolve such questions once and for all. The greatest opinions could isolate only a few aspects for intensive deliberation, leaving others for other courts and other cases. Indeed, at the very beginning, the most important cases did not decide anything much at all. They gain their enduring value

---

*See Chicago, Burlington & Quincy Railway v. City of Chicago, 166 U.S. 226 (1897). The formal "incorporation" of the Takings Clause against the states occurred in the same year as the beginning of aggressive protection for "freedom of contract." See Allgeyer v. Louisiana, 165 U.S. 578 (1897). The inauguration of this more aggressive property-contract interpretation of constitutional liberty in 1897 was by no means accidental. It came immediately after the Populists tried to redefine the constitutional agenda in the election of 1896. The relationship between this failed constitutional moment and the rise of *Lochner* jurisprudence will be investigated at greater length in the forthcoming third volume, *Interpretations*.

In describing property and contract as the middle republic's central focus, I do not suggest that the Court was entirely unconcerned with other aspects of liberty that now seem more central. Compare, for example, Boyd v. United States, 116 U.S. 616 (1886), with Twining v. New Jersey, 211 U.S. 78 (1908). See also David Rabbin, "The First Amendment in Its Forgotten Years," 90 *Yale L.J.* 514 (1981).

merely by suggesting possible methods by which the new synthetic problems might be solved. Only later did the tentative suggestions of the early period motivate more self-confident acts of judicial synthesis—with particularistic solutions building upon one another over time to a more comprehensive understanding.

SAVING THE PAST: *CAROLENE PRODUCTS* AND BEYOND

Of the early efforts at redefinition, the single most significant is contained in a footnote whose provocative character has made it the most famous in Supreme Court history: footnote four of the *Carolene Products* case.[17]

Why a Footnote?

The fact that we begin with a footnote is itself important.[18] As matters stood in 1938, the Court had more pressing things to do with its text than muse on the relationship between the New Deal transformation and the fragments of the Founding and Reconstruction left scattered in its wake. One year after the "switch in time," the *Carolene* Court was still struggling to accommodate the primary thrust of the New Deal itself.

As we have seen, Roosevelt and the New Deal Congress had not chosen to codify their new constitutional principles by enacting a few formal amendments, of the sort contemplated by Article Five. Instead, the President and Congress left it to the Justices themselves to codify the New Deal revolution in a series of transformative judicial opinions, threatening to pack the Court unless it accepted this novel constitutional responsibility. When the Justices executed their famous "switch in time" in the spring of 1937, they began to execute the task Congress and the President had assigned to it. By the time the Justices rose for the summer in 1937, this new work had hardly begun.[19] Only by elaborating and reinforcing the new constitutional principles again and again in the following years could the Court reassure the still-suspicious President, Congress, and electorate that the Justices had fully accepted the constitutional legitimacy of the New Deal and had committed the judicial system to the affirmative elaboration of its higher law implications.*

Now it is precisely the New Deal Court's devotion to this codifying function that pushed *Carolene*'s suggestions about synthesis into the footnotes. The text of *Carolene* continues the prior Term's assault on the middle republic's property-oriented ideal of constitutional liberty. It denies once again that activist intervention into the economy endangers fundamental constitutional values. Henceforth, the majority announces that the Court will "presume" the "existence of facts supporting . . . regulatory legislation affecting ordinary commercial transactions." Only if the regulatory intervention lacked all "rational basis" would the Court consider its constitutional invalidation.[20]

This formulation has had a profound impact upon the law of the modern republic. *Carolene*'s "rational basis" doctrine is treated with the same kind of respect the courts accord to other formulae of fundamental importance: like the demand for "freedom of speech" we owe to the Founding or "equal protection" that we owe to Reconstruction. The fact that these latter formulae can be found, respectively, in the First and Fourteenth Amendments, while "rational basis" has its source in *Carolene,* makes no functional difference in modern legal argument.† All three formulae are taken as fixed and fundamental points in the modern legal consciousness. For this reason, *Carolene* should be numbered amongst the *transformative opinions* which the modern republic uses to memorialize the constitutional solutions of the 1930's.

---

*As I shall suggest in the next volume, this process of codification did not end until Roosevelt's third term, when a reconstituted Court *unanimously* repudiated central premises of the middle republican regime in a concluding series of transformative opinions. See, for example, United States v. Darby, 312 U.S. 100 (1941); Wickard v. Filburn, 317 U.S. 111 (1942).

†The pervasive influence of such New Deal Court formulations requires reconsideration of the commonplace claim that *stare decisis* plays an unimportant role in the law of the modern republic. Once we strip away the myth of rediscovery that presently disguises the New Deal, we shall find that *stare decisis* is particularly powerful when it comes to the landmark New Deal codifications of the activist welfare state: even conservatives who profess a dedication to the "intentions of the Framers" refuse to rethink these doctrines, despite their recognition that they do not have deep foundations in the Founding. See Robert Bork, *The Tempting of America: The Political Seduction of the Law* 216 (1990).

I will be spending lots more time on this distinctive use of judicial opinions. Right now, I am more interested in the way *Carolene*'s famous footnote moves beyond its text in the direction of intergenerational synthesis. The footnote invites lawyers to begin, once again, the process of identifying fragments of the older tradition that have endured the recent constitutional revolution. How to put these fragments into an emerging whole that does justice to the most recent transformation the Justices have witnessed?

Particularistic Synthesis

This is precisely the same question Justices asked themselves in the early days of the middle republic. But it is the answer, no less than the question, that unites the courts of the two regimes. In each case, the early Justices tried to save as much book learning as possible by characterizing the most recent transformation within the particularistic categories of lived experience. In both cases, the early Courts were reluctant to generalize the new principles validated by the People beyond the particular political context in which they were elaborated. So far as the *Slaughterhouse* case was concerned, the 1860's swept away the old law of *race relations;* on all other matters, the Court sought to reassure itself that the book learning of the older period remained (more or less) intact. So too with *Carolene.* For the New Deal Justices, it was clear that the 1930's had swept away the old law of *economic relations;* on all other matters, however, their footnote expressed a *Slaughterhouse*-like reluctance to generalize beyond the context of "ordinary commercial transactions" with which Roosevelt and the New Deal Congresses were particularly concerned. Their footnote searches for ways to express the thought that the most recent constitutional transformation had not utterly obliterated the higher law traditions handed down from the Founding and Reconstruction.

Easier said than done. Property and contract had been central to the received understanding of both Founding and Reconstruction. The new act of synthesis would require a radical reconceptualization of these earlier constitutional achievements in a way that did justice to the New Deal repudiation of laissez-faire economic relationships. From this vantage point we can begin to appreciate the remarkable capacity of the *Carolene* footnote to serve as a beacon, despite the passage of fifty years. In three short paragraphs, the footnote tentatively marked out not one, but two, paths toward intergenerational synthesis—paths that would be transformed into highways in the years ahead.

"Specific Prohibitions"

The first paragraph of the footnote suggests that there "may" (note the hesitation) be a "narrower scope" for the sweeping New Deal presumption of the constitutionality of activist intervention when:

> legislation appears on its face to be within a specific prohibition of the Constitution, such as those of the first ten amendments, which are deemed equally specific when held to be embraced within the Fourteenth.[21]

The key suggestion is that the Bill of Rights can appropriately be read as a list of "specific prohibition[s]." Once this is conceded, the courts might surgically excise the property and contract orientations of Founding and Reconstruction while preserving the other value affirmations of these earlier periods of constitutional creation.

After all, so long as one reads the Bill of Rights as if it were a list, the words "property" and "contract" don't appear very often. "Property" appears only twice[22] in the Bill of Rights, while "contract" doesn't appear at all (since the Federalists thought it so important that they did not wait until 1791 for the Bill of Rights, but protected it in the original Constitution of 1787 by forbidding the states from "impairing the obligation of contracts"[23]). Thus, if the Bill of Rights is a list of "specific prohibitions," it would appear that almost none of these prohibitions had been undermined by the New Deal's repudiation of a property-oriented understanding of constitutional liberty. To save this precious piece of the Founding, "all" that would be required was a judicial soft-pedaling of the "property" clauses as part of a general reorientation of judicial attention to the large number of other "specific" prohibitions on the list.

Even as the Court spoke, it was perfectly clear that the Bill of Rights' prohibitions against the "establishment of religion" or "un-

reasonable searches and seizures" or "cruel and unusual punish-
ments" were no more "specific" than the "property" or "contract"
clauses that the Justices were seeking to peripheralize. Moreover, the
text of the Bill of Rights itself seemed to cut off *Carolene's* approach
in the Ninth Amendment's emphatic caution that "the enumeration
in the Constitution, of certain rights, shall not be construed to deny
or disparage others retained by the People."

But all such cavils were really beside the point. In 1938, the
question for the Justices was not the "original intention" of the
Founding generation. The problem was to synthesize the Founding
into the New Deal revolution. The rhetoric of "specific prohibition[s]" seemed attractive in suggesting that modern courts might
divide the Bill of Rights into two parts: a short list of "specifics"
relating to property that had been demoted in importance by the
New Deal transformation and a much longer list of other "specific"
clauses that had survived the recent transformation relatively intact.

Given the wrenching reorientation required by the demotion of
property and contract in the constitutional scheme, the rhetoric of
"specificity" had a second great advantage. It allowed the Justices to
embark upon their task of synthesis in a suitably cautious way. Rather
than inviting broad proclamations about the enduring meaning of
the Bill of Rights in the post–New Deal world,[24] they could focus
on the meaning of one or another "specific" clause on the list:
"freedom of speech" or "unreasonable searches and seizures." Over
time, the new case law under each of these clauses would begin to
suggest larger patterns, patterns that would allow more comprehensive understandings of the relationship between Founding and New
Deal.

Substantively, this new synthesis would be very different from the
one elaborated by the middle republic. For the earlier Court, the
economic marketplace served as the paradigmatic context for the
protection of constitutional liberties. The modern Court, guided by
its "list" strategy, began emphasizing different constitutional language, changed paradigmatic contexts, to express the enduring value
of the Founding commitment to liberty in a post–New Deal world.

Three strands of synthetic activity are worth distinguishing. The
first involves criminal procedure. When considered as a list, much
of the Bill of Rights enumerates constraints on the tyrannical use of

the criminal law: restricting the authority of the government to search, seize, indict, convict, punish. Surely this concern with constitutional liberty had not been rendered irrelevant by the 1930's validation of activist government? To the contrary, wasn't it even more important now that the citizen no longer could protect his constitutional liberty through contract and property? To reduce a very complex process of case-by-case litigation to a single line: we can see the contemporary emphasis on criminal procedure as part of the process by which modern courts have filled the "constitutional vacuum" left by the collapse of property and contract.[25]

But the "list" strategy encouraged the modern Court to compensate for the New Deal devaluation of market freedom in other ways. The Bill of Rights devotes only six clauses to the First Amendment while it dedicates (roughly) fifteen clauses to criminal procedure in the Fourth, Fifth, Sixth, and Eighth Amendments. Nonetheless, by reading these majestic generalities as if they were "specific" guarantees radically dissimilar from those involving property and contract, the modern Court could once again fill the vacuum with fragments from the Founding.

Begin with the First Amendment's demand that "Congress shall make no law respecting an establishment of religion, or prohibiting the free exercise thereof . . ." Once one followed *Carolene* and pretended that Establishment and Free Exercise Clauses were chock-full of "specifics," one could lay the foundation for a powerful constitutional language preserving aspects of private liberty despite the demise of property and contract. Free exercise of religion is, of course, a different right from freedom of contract; but both doctrines insist that each American has a right to go his own way, free of state intervention, in a crucial domain of experience.[26]

Perhaps, though, it is a third set of "specifics" that has proved most important in this broad doctrinal reorientation: "Congress shall make no law . . . abridging the freedom of speech." During earlier regimes, the judicial elaboration of this clause had been notable for its scantiness.[27] This was, in part, a second-order consequence of the practical operation of other constitutional principles. So long as constitutional ideals of market freedom were ascendant, the owners of a printing press, say, could express many of their basic interests in the ascendant constitutional language of property and contract. If the producers of bread and milk had the constitutional right to sell whatever they wanted to any purchaser who found the price acceptable, did not the producers of newspapers and books have a comparable range of market freedom? The constitutional principle limiting national government also had an important constraining influence. If the limited powers of the federal government did not allow it to regulate the intrastate manufacture of iron or steel, surely it did not allow "prior restraints" on the content of local newspapers?

This meant that serious assaults on free speech by the national government were relatively rare—restricted largely, but not exclusively,[28] to pathologies during and after the Civil War and the First World War. During these extraordinary challenges, the courts did not distinguish themselves in the defense of First Amendment values. Although modern Justices endlessly recall ringing judicial pronunciamentos on behalf of free speech from early history, these famous declarations were not usually found in majority opinions.[29]

The Court's repressive precedents took on a more ominous significance with the New Deal transformation. No longer could producers of ideas demand the hefty protections accorded property owners. Given the newfound legitimacy of sweeping and ongoing efforts by the national government to manage the putatively "free market," a new rhetoric of freedom was urgently required. And it is precisely here that "specificity" could fill the vacuum. Modern courts could show respect for the New Deal and nevertheless say that the "specific" guarantee accorded by the First Amendment to speech still gave special protection to the "free market *of ideas.*"[30]

In exploring the "specifics" of free speech, however, the Court has emphasized different dimensions of constitutional freedom from the one elaborated under the clauses dealing with criminal procedure and religion. In these other areas, the Court's main concern has been to build up two new zones of private freedom in the place of the market freedoms that had been erased by the New Deal. The "free speech" cases have been preeminently engaged with the preservation of public, not private, freedom. The governmental controls most vulnerable to judicial invalidation have threatened political participation, not more privatistic forms of self-fulfillment.[31] The center of doctrinal concern has been the citizenry's right to speak its mind on matters of public concern.

The "list" strategy has, in short, provided a crucial technique by which the modern Court came to preserve two aspects of the Founding in a post–New Deal age. As an American's constitutional freedom to make private trades in the marketplace collapsed, her right to live free of arbitrary arrest and criminal prosecution, her right to define her religious and political convictions free of pervasive governmental control, has been greatly enhanced. In addition to these enhanced private freedoms, the Court has used the "specifics" of the First Amendment to emphasize the deeper importance of political self-definition in a world without the constitutional protections that private property had previously provided.

Thus far, I have focused on *Carolene*'s use of the rhetoric of specificity as it bears on a single aspect of the modern problem in synthesis: how to integrate the Founding's affirmation of constitutional liberty (Time One) with the New Deal's affirmation of activist national government (Time Three). The same rhetorical strategy played an important role in allowing the Court to rework the terms of the legal relationship between Founding (Time One) and Reconstruction (Time Two). Here, the footnote asserts that the "specific" prohibitions the Founding generation applied to the federal government are to be "deemed equally specific" if the Court holds them "to be embraced within" the very unspecific terms of the Fourteenth Amendment. In making this move, the New Deal Court was building upon an approach pioneered during the middle republic. Given the property-centered way in which the middle republican courts sought to harmonize the Founding and Reconstruction, the "specific" clause that the middle republicans thought most important was the Takings Clause of the Fifth Amendment: "nor shall private property be taken for public use, without just compensation."[32] Given the New Deal's affirmation of state intervention into the economy, different "specifics" would serve as the focus of the modern Court's ongoing effort to synthesize the Founding and Reconstruction—notably the clauses dealing with free speech, freedom of religion, and criminal procedure. By pretending that these clauses were chock-full of "specifics," the Court found it possible to redirect, but not abandon, a core insight of the middle republic. Like their predecessors, modern judges understand that the nationalism expressed by the People after the Civil War made it appropriate to look upon the Federalist Bill of Rights in a new way: henceforward the fundamental rights of Americans would be protected against state, no less than federal, infringement. Only now the Justices placed different "specifics" at the center of their synthesis of the Founding and Reconstruction than those emphasized by their property-oriented predecessors.

From Property to Democracy

In 1938, it was hardly obvious that the Court would emerge from the wreckage with any sense of its preservationist mission intact. As in the aftermath of Reconstruction's repudiation of *Dred Scott,* the Court's preeminent task was to establish there was something in the preexisting tradition worth preserving despite the last great transformation of popular sentiment. By pointing to the fact that the Bill of Rights contained a long list of "specific" liberties other than rights to private property or contract, the Court made a point that resonated broadly in American public opinion.

But *Carolene,* famously, moved beyond this initial salvage operation. This movement comes at a crucial point in the Court's evolving understanding of its problem of synthesis. To see my point, consider that the rhetoric of "specificity" could, at best, help the Court confront only two of its three fundamental problems in synthesis: in dealing with the one-three problem, the specifics of the Bill of Rights entered directly in the Court's effort to reassure itself (and the American people) that there was much more to constitutional liberty than the protection of free markets; in dealing with the one-two problem, these "specifics" entered by way of the legal fiction that the grand abstractions of Reconstruction's Fourteenth Amendment "incorporated" the "specifics" of the Founding Bill of Rights. In dealing with the third side of the synthetic triangle, however, the Bill of Rights was no use at all—for the simple reason that this third question did not involve the relationship of the Founding to some later transformative development. Instead, the two-three question invited the Court to interpret the meaning of the Reconstruction amendments (Time Two), given the New Deal's repudiation of a property-centered ideal of liberty (Time Three). If this question were to be taken seriously, the Court could not avoid a direct confrontation with the grand abstractions of the Fourteenth Amendment:

protecting all Americans against abridgment of their "privileges or immunities" as citizens of the nation, guaranteeing all persons "equal protection" and "due process of law." If these Republican ideals were something more than empty vessels incorporating selected "specifics" from the Federalists' Bill of Rights, the Court would have to propose a new way to interpret their commands—one radically different from the property-oriented theory of the middle republic. And it is precisely here that the *Carolene* footnote's concluding paragraphs made their contribution:

> It is [also] unnecessary to consider now whether legislation which restricts those political processes which can ordinarily be expected to bring about repeal of undesirable legislation, is to be subjected to more exacting judicial scrutiny under the general prohibitions of the Fourteenth Amendment than are most other types of legislation. On restrictions upon the right to vote, see [case citations omitted]; on restraints upon the dissemination of information, see [citations omitted]; on interferences with political organizations, see [citations omitted]; as to prohibition of peaceable assembly, see [citation omitted].
>
> Nor need we enquire whether similar considerations enter into the review of statutes directed at particular religious or national or racial minorities [citations omitted]: whether prejudice against discrete and insular minorities may be a special condition, which tends seriously to curtail the operation of those political processes ordinarily to be relied upon to protect minorities, and which may call for a correspondingly searching judicial inquiry [citations omitted].

As with other aspects of the opinion, the formulae introduced in these paragraphs—most notably the remarks about "discrete and insular minorities"—have been enormously influential in the development of modern law over the last half-century.[33] For introductory purposes, however, we need not consider the meaning and value of these particular doctrinal formulations.[34]

The important point goes deeper. This is the footnote's remarkable effort to reorient the meaning of the Reconstruction amendments in the post–New Deal world. Thus, the footnote does not mention the middle republican view of "equal protection"—that it guaranteed each person an equal right to own private property and to contract freely concerning its use.[35] Instead, it proposes a new area of life as the centerpiece for egalitarian concern. This is the structure of politics. While politics was always important, its significance had been enormously enhanced within the modern activist state. No longer did constitutional principles enshrining limited government and the protection of property constrain the ability of politically dominant groups to reallocate resources in their favor. Instead, politics would be the central strategic forum in the post–New Deal system. If individuals and groups were to protect and further their interests, they would have no choice but to participate actively in the ongoing political life of the state and nation. Given this fact, didn't it become crucially important to consider whether modern politics was structured in a way that was compatible with Reconstruction's egalitarian affirmations?

Not only did *Carolene* propose this political reorientation of the meaning of the Reconstruction amendments; it conceived the political process in an especially broad way. Although the footnote emphasized the importance of distributing to all citizens a fair share of crucial inputs into the political process—votes, information, and so forth—it suggested that policing the fairness of political inputs might not be enough, and that judges must scrutinize the outputs of normal politics as well. In contrast to the Justices in the middle republic, the Court in the modern era no longer feared that political power may be used to exploit the propertied classes. Instead, it redirected the Fourteenth Amendment's central concern toward the protection of "discrete and insular minorities" against majoritarian "prejudice." Once again, the Court was undertaking to preserve the egalitarian meaning of Reconstruction despite the profound transformation achieved by the New Deal: While it left the rich to take care of themselves, it suggested that the Fourteenth Amendment's concern with equality must take on a deeper meaning in the redistributional politics of the modern regulatory state.

CONCLUSION

Conclude by juxtaposing the principal rhetorical strategies deployed in the footnote—namely, the "list of specifics" strategy in the first paragraph with the "egalitarian democracy" strategy in the concluding paragraphs.[36] The contrast suggests the larger movement in interpretation I mean to chronicle. The "list of specifics" is, I think, a transparent response to the trauma induced by the shattering experience of the New Deal. Given the central place of property and contract in the Republic's first 150 years, its decisive repudiation by the People had left the courts with a host of fragments without an organizing conception of constitutional liberty. How better to preserve the higher law tradition than by detaching isolated fragments from the repudiated center and assuring oneself that many of the particular guarantees had survived the recent revolution in popular sentiment?

This particularistic form of synthesis contrasts with the interpretive suggestion in *Carolene*'s concluding paragraphs. Here the focus is on organizing constitutional ideals, not "specific" formulae. The crucial proposal is that the ideal of egalitarian democracy might in time replace the ideal of the free market as a comprehensive basis for constitutional freedom; that we might come to view much of our higher law heritage as concerned with this overarching value. As this process of doctrinal integration proceeded, it would seem less important whether one or another aspect of the ideal of egalitarian democracy first came into our constitutional law at the time of the Founding, or Reconstruction, or the New Deal (or some other moment). Instead, the crucial aim would be comprehensive synthesis: to show how the crises and transformations of the past can best be understood as a popular struggle, however imperfect and incomplete, for egalitarian democracy.

This is, transparently, a great deal for a single footnote to anticipate. To what extent have the footnote's early prophecies been realized during the life of the modern republic? To what extent should we move beyond *Carolene Products?*

I will defer a sustained answer to another volume in this series.[37] I conclude this introduction by taking up the modern problem of synthesis in a couple of concrete cases: *Brown v. Board of Education* and *Griswold v. Connecticut.*

CHAPTER SIX

The Possibility of Interpretation

GETTING DOWN TO CASES

THE LAST CHAPTER left the New Deal Court confronting the shattering consequences of the Roosevelt revolution. This one takes up the story at two later points. I first examine the single most important decision of the modern era: *Brown v. Board of Education.* I then skip from 1954 to 1965: to a time when *Brown*'s call for racial equality was finally gaining the sustained support of the President, Congress, and the American electorate. Just as the Warren Court was consolidating its egalitarian gains, it launched a new constitutional initiative, in *Griswold v. Connecticut,* that helped catalyze another political mobilization during the 1970's and 1980's. Only this time the struggle focused on the constitutional right of privacy, especially in matters dealing with sexual freedom.

Racial equality, sexual freedom: these ideals are very different in their philosophical justification and doctrinal elaboration. And yet, when we step back to questions of constitutional process, parallels emerge. In each case, the Justices destabilized traditional values with deep roots in the folkways of the country; in each case, they were accused of imposing the values of the Eastern liberal establishment without interpretive warrant in the Constitution; in each case, many of the Court's defenders implicitly conceded this charge by depicting the Justices as the nation's moral leaders; in each case, the Court's more legalistic supporters gave low grades to the opinions in *Brown* and *Griswold* and searched for better arguments that might buttress these contested decisions.

I hope to put these patterns of popular and legal reception into larger constitutional context. There will be two parts. I begin by viewing the decisions as acts of constitutional politics—in which activist Justices confronted modern America with a moral agenda that elected politicians lacked the courage to bring to the center of American political life. On this political approach, the critical question is not the interpretive validity of the decisions, but the intrinsic value of the Justices' moral vision and the political process by which the Court succeeded (or failed) to get its political pronouncements accepted. While I will ultimately reject this view, I want to do more than persuade you to do likewise. Even if you hold to the political interpretation, the general approach sketched in this part allows you to give it a new historical and theoretical discipline.

Progress will be made on this front by building upon the first two chapters—which sketched the distinctive character of dualistic democracy and the changing processes through which eighteenth-century Federalists, nineteenth-century Republicans, and twentieth-century Democrats created new higher law in the name of We the People. I shall use these historical precedents to provide a new perspective on the political interpretation: Perhaps there are striking similarities between the Warren Court's efforts to lead the American people to new constitutional values and these earlier exercises in constitutional politics by the New Deal Presidency and the Reconstruction Congress? Perhaps the similarities are sufficiently compelling to conclude that these Court-led changes in our Constitution are no less legitimate than the earlier efforts by the Reconstruction Congress and the New Deal Presidency to speak for the People?

But perhaps not. Once you compare the claims of the Warren Court to the Reconstruction Congress and the New Deal Presidency, I believe that you will be quite unsatisfied with the political interpretation of *Brown* and *Griswold*. This unease will, I hope, motivate you to consider the alternative with a new seriousness: Can/should we understand *Brown* and *Griswold* as valid—indeed profound— acts of constitutional *interpretation?*

This time I will be building on the preceding three chapters. My thesis: we can best understand both *Brown* and *Griswold* as a continuation of the project of synthetic interpretation begun in the aftermath of the Civil War in the *Slaughterhouse Cases* and redirected in New Deal opinions like *Carolene Products*. The problem lies not so much with the judges as with their commentators, who have spent more time and energy rewriting *Brown* and *Griswold* than deepening the Court's interpretive insights.

Brown and Griswold as Acts of Constitutional Politics

But first I want to explore the road not taken: Doesn't all this legalistic talk of interpretation obscure the essence of *Brown, Griswold,* and the other disputed decisions of the Warren and Burger Courts? Doesn't their real significance lie elsewhere, in the Court's courage in confronting modern Americans with a moral and political agenda that calls upon them to heed the voices of their better selves? Constitutional politics, that's what these decisions amounted to; and it is only mystifying to pretend otherwise.

For the moment, I will concede this premise and move, first, to consider how our argument illuminates a political analysis of the Court and, second, why dualist analysis cautions against too quick a disdain for the "mystifications" of legalistic interpretation. Let me begin with the obvious: I do not deny that the fundamental values of the modern republic have a foundation in successful exercises in constitutional politics. My problem is that, when measured by the great historical markers of the past, the Supreme Court's decisions in *Brown* and *Griswold* did not come at moments when a mobilized citizenry was demanding a fundamental change in our fundamental law.

Contrast the political context surrounding the Court's decision in *Brown* with the one that prevailed during the 1860's and 1930's. At these earlier moments, would-be constitutional lawmakers in the Congress or the Presidency had returned from an electoral struggle in which their conservative opponents had sought to rally the voters against their potentially dangerous reforms. Rather than heeding these cautions, the electorate had swept the innovators into office, allowing them to claim a "mandate" from the People.

Not that the constitutional system allowed either nineteenth-century Republicans or twentieth-century Democrats to gain immediate acceptance for their claim that the People had endorsed their initiatives. Their initial show of popular support only gave them the authority to place their constitutional proposals on the agenda for serious consideration. It would take years more of constitutional debate with the more conservative branches of government (led by the Johnson Presidency in the 1860's and the Old Court in the 1930's) before the constitutional reformers could earn the authority to assert that We the People had made a *considered judgment* to support their transformative initiatives.

The political scene was very different in 1953, when *Brown* was before the Court. Earl Warren was perfectly aware that President Eisenhower's recent election did not mark the rise of an aggressive new movement for constitutional reform. To the contrary: After a generation of extraordinary involvement in public life, precipitated by economic crisis and world war, the American people were returning to more normal levels of political engagement.

The parallel with developments in the middle republic is downright uncanny. After the intense mobilizations of the 1860's, the American people turned to a war hero—Ulysses S. Grant—whose political views were remarkably undefined and who refused to clarify them during the campaign of 1868, choosing to go home instead![1] Grant's lack of political vision was well known to the leaders of the Republican Party. Many would have rejected him if they believed a more ideological Republican could win. The party ran with Grant because it was unwilling to take the chance that it would lose with a more ideological candidate. By electing a war hero to the White House, at least they would not endanger the hard-won constitutional gains of the preceding period. While Grant might not lead the People onward to further constitutional reforms, his election would allow normal politics to proceed without further agonized debate over the premises of the new regime inaugurated by the three Republican amendments.

The election of Eisenhower marks a similar moment of normalization in the life of the modern regime. Moderates of both parties would seek bipartisan solutions to practical problems without challenging the premises established by the preceding generation. Like Grant, Eisenhower was a war hero whose indistinct political views allowed him to run either as a Democrat or a Republican.[2] In contrast to the 1860's, the party supporting the new regime refused to award the war hero its Presidential nomination: it chose Stevenson, who promised to continue the New Deal tradition. The opposition party proved more pragmatic. The Republicans refused to reawaken the great ideological struggles of the 1930's by nominating "Mr. Republican," Robert A. Taft, as their candidate. Instead of risking a replay of their crushing New Deal defeats, they turned to Eisenhower—a man who might not lead a frontal assault on modern activist government but would check new experiments in domestic affairs.

All this was especially clear to the new Chief Justice, Earl Warren, who gained his office by backing Eisenhower over Taft at the Republican National Convention.[3] When Warren looked beyond the White House to Congress, evidence of mobilized support for a constitutional assault on racism was also disappointingly thin. It is true, of course, that Eisenhower did not sweep into office large Republican majorities demanding an immediate return to the days of Calvin Coolidge and Herbert Hoover.[4] Regardless of their party identification, a large majority of Congressmen were not prepared to roll back the New Deal.

The consensus on Capitol Hill disintegrated, however, when the question turned to an activist assault on racism. While the Democratic Party of the North contained some strong supporters of civil rights, their efforts to lead the party had already precipitated serious Southern rebellion.[5] Given the entrenched position of Southern Democrats on crucial Congressional committees, only a mobilized mass movement might encourage progressive Democrats and Republicans to overcome massive Southern resistance to new civil rights legislation. At the time *Brown* was argued and reargued, only one thing was clear: such a mass movement did not exist. In the short run at least, a Court decision forcing the race issue into the center of American politics promised only to divide a Democratic Party that had served as the political bastion of support for the modern republic.[6] Only time would tell whether this vacuum would be filled by a new movement for racial equality; or whether a divided Democratic Party, whose vulnerability had been so recently demonstrated by Eisenhower's victory, would be displaced by very different political forces.

The most obvious threat was posed by Senator Joseph McCarthy. Whatever one may say in retrospect, the anticommunist crusade had used the early 1950's to mobilize extraordinary levels of citizen support. As we now know, this movement would fail to overcome the increasing institutional resistance in Congress and the Presidency. Senator McCarthy's efforts to mobilize further support, most notably in the Army-McCarthy Hearings of 1954, would bring about his downfall. Slowly, some of the worst McCarthyite breaches of traditional constitutional values would be repaired during the next generation.* But none of this could be clear to the Justices in 1952 and 1953 as they considered and reconsidered *Brown*.[7]

To forestall predictable misunderstanding: I do not deny the importance of the pre-*Brown* decade to the future success of the civil rights movement. Most obviously, the NAACP and its Legal Defense Fund made important organizational gains and achieved many political and legal victories.[8] On another level, both the war and the Northern migration had changed the social experience of the black community, giving it new leadership as well as new bases of political power.[9] Finally, the war against Hitler, and America's position as the leader of the "Free World," forced a rippling reappraisal of racist beliefs and practices amongst whites: How could America pretend to defend the cause of freedom abroad given its racist denials of freedom at home?[10] All this, and much more, would demand discussion if I were trying to explore the roots of the modern civil rights movement.

But this is not my aim. This book is not concerned with the generations-long process of social, political, and philosophical change that sets the stage for each of the successful constitutional movements in American history. I am focusing instead on the process through which each movement finally emerges from the background of normal politics to take the center of the constitutional stage. From this point of view, there is simply no comparison between 1954 and the times when Reconstruction Republicans and New Deal Democrats first gained the authority to place their initiatives on the constitutional agenda. While these earlier movements could point to signs that the American people were already mobilizing to consider a fundamental constitutional change, the civil rights movement in the early 1950's had not yet reached a similar stage.

This is a crucial difference for the dualist democrat—who is all

---

*Though not in ways that did much to repair the particular lives that had been shattered by the McCarthyite movement.

too aware of the ease with which elites in Washington pretend to speak for the People. As a matter of fundamental principle, the dualist insists that political elites *earn* such authority by a long effort at political mobilization. And the mere fact that Earl Warren & Co. wore black robes should make no difference—if, as the political interpretation insists, we are to consider these elderly white gentlemen as nothing other than politicians who are using the idea of "constitutional interpretation" as a mystification. Why, then, the continuing temptation to applaud *Brown* as an exercise in constitutional politics?

Because of our inveterate tendency to play constitutional history backwards. However uncertain the prospect for a breakthrough might have seemed in 1954, *Brown* did turn out to play a catalytic role. In the end, the Court was not crushed between the rocks of Southern resistance and Northern indifference. *Brown* became a symbol energizing a multiracial coalition of blacks and whites into an escalating political struggle against institutionalized racism. As the 1950's moved on, this mobilized appeal for racial justice struck deepening chords amongst broadening sectors of the citizenry— enabling the Presidency and Congress of the mid-1960's finally to transform the embattled judicial pronunciamentos of the mid–1950's into the Civil Rights Acts of 1964 and 1968 and the Voting Rights Act of 1965. As a consequence, *Brown* came to possess the kind of numinous legal authority that is, I believe, uniquely associated with legal documents that express the considered judgments of We the People.

This fascinating process of retroactive canonization deserves study in its own right; it also provides a crucial reason why today's judiciary treats *Brown* as a decisive constitutional authority possessing infinitely greater weight than it did in the 1950's when the *Brown* Court cautiously announced its intention to proceed "with all deliberate speed."[11] Nonetheless, it hardly follows that the Warren Court's *post hoc* success in gaining mobilized support should provide us with the key to *Brown* when it was handed down in 1954.

Yet it is just this assumption that lies at the core of the political interpretation. On this view, we should view *Brown* as an inspired act of political prophecy, in two senses of the word. It was prophetic in that its critique of injustice was inspired by a profound sense of moral truth; but prophetic, as well, in that the Court could somehow predict its moral critique would prove politically successful.

If this dual prophetic capacity provides the key to *Brown,* the case stands as precedent for similar exercises: Is sexual freedom morally liberating? Can Americans be taught to shed the remnants of Victorian moralism? Well, then, let the Justices begin their prophetic course of instruction. Or so one may say as the Court announced its decision in *Griswold* under political circumstances roughly similar to those surrounding *Brown* in 1954. Just as the decade before *Brown* had witnessed a broadening moral critique of racism, there was also a deepening critique of traditional sexual morality in the decades before *Griswold.* In both cases, moral questioning had moved beyond millions of disorganized conversations over the dinner table and had taken organizational form—groups like the NAACP Legal Defense Fund and Planned Parenthood had won important legal victories before the Court intervened decisively on their side. Nonetheless, as in 1954, the *Griswold* Court did not stand at the head of a transformative movement remotely comparable in breadth and depth to those led by Reconstruction Republicans and New Deal Democrats.

Granted, 1965 was a less forbidding political moment for the Warren Court than 1954. The Court decided *Griswold* in the midst of the most successful constitutional movement of our time: with Lyndon Johnson in the White House, and Martin Luther King in the streets, the American people were proceeding at long last to renew and expand its constitutional commitment to racial equality. Indeed, we may use the civil rights movement in 1965 as a contemporaneous benchmark to assess the far lower level of mobilized support that the Supreme Court might expect in response to the *Griswold* case. Lyndon Johnson had not struggled for a decade in the Senate for Planned Parenthood; nor did his landslide victory over Barry Goldwater allow him to claim a mandate from the People on such matters; nor could Planned Parenthood demonstrate the mobilized commitment of masses of American citizens in the manner of Martin Luther King.[12] As with *Brown,* the political interpretation of *Griswold* suggests that the Court was playing the prophet in the modern American Republic.

I have no doubt that this prophetic interpretation of the Supreme Court has taken deep roots within the modern legal profession. It also gains expression in some of the most important modern writers—Alexander Bickel, Robert Burt, Frank Michelman, and Michael Perry expressing these prophetic themes in important variations.[13]

Yet *Brown* and *Griswold,* understood in the prophetic mode, are tough acts for mere mortals to follow. It is hard for nine human beings confidently to locate the moral truths that authorize them to transform American society; it is even harder for Nine Old Lawyers, removed from the hustle of American life, to determine whether their initiatives will be greeted with respect or indifference or violent backlash. These concerns, of course, have not gone unnoticed in the prophetic literature. They have spawned a rich catalogue of techniques through which a prophetic Court might engage its larger publics in an ongoing dialogue which might slowly generate broad consent. Nonetheless, the greatest single contributor to this literature, Alexander Bickel, came increasingly to doubt the capacity of any court to master the necessary techniques.[14]

While I share many of Bickel's later doubts, my objection goes beyond mere matters of efficacy. The prophetic vision of the Court is flatly inconsistent with the principles of dualist democracy. Even if judges could successfully gain popular acquiescence, this kind of top-down transformation is the opposite of the bottom-up transformations prized by dualist democrats. It is not the special province of the judges to lead the People onward and upward to new and higher values. This is the task of citizens who may, after the investment of great energy, succeed (or fail) in gaining the considered assent of a majority of their fellows. What the judges are especially equipped to do is preserve the achievements of popular sovereignty during the long periods of our public existence when the citizenry is not mobilized for great constitutional achievements.

Of course, it sometimes happens that a preservationist Court may help spark a new forward-looking movement. This is my view of *Brown.* Nonetheless, on those happy occasions when a Court manages to provide constitutional symbols that new movements find inspiring, it would be a tragic irony if this success should allow lawyers to forget a crucial dualist truth: although judges are in a unique position to preserve the past constitutional achievements of the American people, many other citizens are in better positions to lead the People onward to a better constitutional future.

Before one accepts a prophetic reading of *Brown* or *Griswold,* it is only prudent to consider the interpretive alternative.

PROPHECY OR PRESERVATION?

In making this turn from constitutional politics to judicial interpretation, I take up a central theme of the last three chapters. I argued there that the present professional narrative blocks a clear appreciation of the interpretive problem that sets the modern Court apart from its predecessors. By treating the New Deal as basically uncreative, the reigning myth of rediscovery makes it impossible to formulate, let alone illuminate, the distinctive aspect of the modern Court's situation—that it must somehow make sense of a Constitution that owes its meaning to the transformative efforts of three generations: Founding, Reconstruction, and New Deal. I propose to drive this point home by suggesting that the myth of rediscovery has blocked professional recognition of the interpretive character of the opinions in *Brown* and *Griswold.*

Synthesis, Revisited

Recall the argument as it has developed so far.[15] So long as modern lawyers remain limited by the myth of rediscovery, they can recognize only two periods of regime-transforming constitutional activity: the Founding and Reconstruction. This two-solution narrative allows them to confront a single aspect of the modern problem of intergenerational synthesis—how to reconcile the nationalistic, egalitarian, and libertarian themes of the Reconstruction amendments with the more federalistic ideals expressed at the Founding?

Once we work our way free of the myth to affirm a three-solution narrative, however, we can recognize that modern synthesis is essentially a triangular affair. Given the sweeping popular affirmation of activist national government during the New Deal, it is not enough to confront the one-two problem posed by juxtaposing the Founding (Time One) with Reconstruction (Time Two). We must face up to two other issues. I called the first problem one-three synthesis: How to reconcile the Founders' affirmation of limited national government with the New Deal's legitimation of ongoing bureaucratic intervention in economic and social life? I called the second problem two-three synthesis: How does the affirmation of activist government in the twentieth century require a reinterpretation of the meaning of Republican Reconstruction?

Once we take these questions seriously, the Court's opinions in *Brown* and *Griswold* appear in a new light. In each case, the Court brings to the fore one of the dimensions we have just identified. *Brown* elaborates the problem of two-three synthesis by considering the implications of the Fourteenth Amendment for the public school—an institution that had become emblematic of the New Deal's activist use of state power for the general welfare. *Griswold* confronts the problem of one-three synthesis by reading the Bill of Rights to preserve the Founding concern with personal liberty in a way that endures in a post–New Deal world of economic and social regulation. More than most of us, the Justices have been struggling with the central issues involved in *interpreting* a Constitution that is the joint product of eighteenth-, nineteenth-, and twentieth-century exercises in popular sovereignty.

Indeed, if we read *Brown* and *Griswold* carefully, they suggest that the modern Court has been traveling an interpretive course quite similar to its precedessors. Our sketch of the middle republic emphasized the dynamic character of the Court's synthetic exercise.[16] Given the shattering consequences of Reconstruction, a majority of the Justices began their synthetic enterprise particularistically—understanding the most recent transformation as concerned only with the race problem. As lived experience of Reconstruction faded, the courts took a more comprehensive approach—trying to interpret the meaning of both Founding and Reconstruction on the same level of abstraction and to integrate the deeper meaning of each into a doctrinal whole. A similar movement is detectable in the movement from *Brown* to *Griswold:* the later opinion expresses a more comprehensive understanding of the problem of synthesis. Of course, my skill at detecting a movement from particularistic to comprehensive synthesis may be an artefact of the two cases I have selected for intensive analysis. If my interpretations are at all successful, they will encourage you to test, enrich, and modify my hypothesis by rereading other modern cases.

A Threshold Problem

Before I press onward, personal conversation suggests a preliminary objection: "If the two-solution narrative is so pervasive in professional understanding, how did it ever occur to the Justices, of all people, to see the need for three-solution synthesis?" Frankly, I haven't gotten to the bottom of this one,[17] but my answer comes in two parts. First, the Justices are, by and large, practical people who do not disdain the obvious with the nonchalance of the academic theorist or the political ideologue. And it is perfectly obvious that the wide-ranging national government established by the New Deal has had a pervasive impact upon the operative premises of American political life. Thus, the Justices shouldn't need others to point out the need to reconcile the activist principles of modern government with the constitutional inheritance of the eighteenth and nineteenth centuries.

My second answer is to refine my thesis. Although we shall see the Justices struggling with salient dimensions of the modern problem of synthesis, they have not in fact launched a full-scale assault on the two-solution narrative that lies at the core of their problem. Their insights into its inadequacy have been intermittent and framed by the particular facts of particular cases. If they are to go further, they should not be expected to travel on their own steam. Only if the rest of us take the synthetic questions raised by the Court with the seriousness they deserve, and contribute to an ongoing dialogue, can we expect the judges to confront the problem of synthetic interpretation with increasing insight over time.

BROWN AS INTERPRETIVE SYNTHESIS

Surely, if *Brown*[18] had been intended as a prophetic utterance, it was a weak rhetorical performance. Chief Justice Warren conspicuously fails to use the Declaration of Independence or other great texts to elaborate the compelling moral arguments for racial equality; still less does he provide an inspiring image of a future America freed at last from the crippling burden of race hate and subordination. *Brown* takes the form of a standard judicial opinion (stripped of some, but hardly all, of the ordinary legalism out of courtesy for its wider-than-usual readership). Its key question is the legalistic matter of *stare decisis:* to what extent is the Court bound by its 1896 decision, in *Plessy v. Ferguson,*[19] upholding "separate but equal" treatment of blacks and whites? Even this is too broad a question for the Court. Warren refuses to use *Brown* as a vehicle to denounce "separate but equal" as a general constitutional norm. He limits himself to the public schools: the question presented is not whether *Plessy* should be overruled, but whether it "should be held inapplicable to public education."[20]

The Court's answer is no less legalistic: "in the field of public education the doctrine of 'separate but equal' has no place."[21] In reaching this conclusion, Warren turns to the conventional legal sources: the intentions of the Framers of the Fourteenth Amendment, the course of the case law after *Plessy*. Perhaps the biggest surprise is the Court's use of social scientific evidence about the impact of racial segregation on black children. But this was hardly a novelty fifty years after the Court first applauded then-counsel Louis Brandeis for analogous social scientific presentations.[22] Moreover, the "scientific" evidence is used to support something the Court thinks is obvious: that segregation has a "detrimental effect upon the colored children."[23]

All in all, *Brown* stands at the opposite pole from documents we shall be rediscovering in the course of our confrontation with the Founding, Reconstruction, and the New Deal—for example, the *Federalist Papers* of the 1780's,[24] the *Congressional Globe* of the 1860's, and the *Public Addresses of President Roosevelt* in the 1930's.[25] These writings contain inspired appeals to the People for support against legalistic objections raised by leading opponents. In contrast, *Brown* is a legalistic effort to "cool" the debate, not a populist or prophetic effort to "heat" it up. It does not call upon the country to engage in a new round of constitutional politics; it tries to establish that the time had come for Americans to comply with legal principles *already affirmed* by the People in the past.

Brown's blandness has, I think, been a secret source of disappointment to the partisans of the Court's prophetic mission—who would have vastly preferred it if Earl Warren had anticipated the great "I Have a Dream" Speech made by Dr. Martin Luther King a decade later, under vastly different political circumstances. More surprisingly, it has proved unsatisfactory to the legalistically inclined. A decisive point in the opinion's reception was the Holmes Lecture given by Professor Herbert Wechsler at the Harvard Law School in 1959. One of the leading legal scholars of his time, Wechsler had devoted his life to progressive law reform. And yet he could not find a principled way to justify *Brown:* "I should like to think there is [a way], but I confess I have not yet written the opinion. To write it is for me the challenge of the school-segregation cases."[26] The expression of such anxieties by such a scholar from such a podium generated a host of responses by *Brown*'s defenders—each offering an alternative to Warren's opinion that would survive Wechsler's critique.[27]

Paradoxically, the very vigor of this response served to confirm Wechsler's low opinion of Warren's opinion. Apparently, even *Brown*'s defenders had to move far beyond Warren's feeble effort to justify the ways of the Court to thoughtful lawyers. This is not the approach I will be taking here. Far more than many of its defenders, the Court was alive to the distinctly interpretive reasons why it was legally required to repudiate "separate but equal" in public education.

The crux of the opinion involves an act of intergenerational synthesis, an explicit recognition of the need to integrate the constitutional meaning of two historical periods in reaching a valid judgment. The first period is, of course, Reconstruction: what to make of the fact that the Republicans managed, despite the fierce opposition of conservative opponents, to lead the American people to embrace the "equal protection of the laws"? Warren warns, however, that Reconstruction provides only part of the answer:

> In approaching this problem, we cannot turn the clock back to 1868 when the Amendment was adopted, or even to 1896 when *Plessy v. Ferguson* was written. We must consider public education in the light of its full development and its present place in American life throughout the Nation.[28]

This self-conscious move beyond the 1860's has often been taken as an embrace of the prophetic mission: it is here, if anywhere, that the Court declares the constitutional past too confining and imposes new values on the American people.

Yet this interpretation seems sensible only within the framework of a two-solution narrative. To see my point, reflect upon the most uncontroversial reason a Court might give for refusing to follow a prior decision like *Plessy*. This classic exception involves subsequent constitutional amendments. Consider, for example, the status of the *Dred Scott* case[29] at the time Warren wrote *Brown*. Whatever the merits of Taney's decision barring free blacks from citizenship in 1857, it was decisively discredited in 1868 when the Reconstruction Republicans enacted the Fourteenth Amendment. The question Warren's *dictum* raises is whether we can locate an analogous constitutional transformation between 1896 and 1954: Did We the People speak during the first half of the twentieth century in a way which decisively undercut *Plessy*'s interpretation of Reconstruction?

Given the reigning myth of rediscovery, the answer seems to be an easy and obvious no. After all, the formal amendments enacted during this period seem very far removed from the race question: what possible relevance does the enactment of the Income Tax Amendment (1913) or the Woman's Suffrage Amendment (1920) have on *Plessy*'s reasoning? Little wonder that the legal community has not taken Warren's *dictum* as an invitation to consider the problem of multigenerational synthesis. Once we revise our narrative to recognize the constitutionally creative aspect of the New Deal, Warren's *dictum* seems more suggestive: Is the Court struggling against the current of the official two-solution story? Has the New Deal's affirmation of activist government undercut *Plessy* just as surely as the Reconstruction's affirmation of national citizenship undercut *Dred Scott*?

When read with these questions in mind, the Court's opinion no longer seems an inept exercise in prophecy. It is a compelling exercise in two-three synthesis: explaining why *Plessy*'s interpretation of the Fourteenth Amendment is no longer consistent with foundational premises established in the aftermath of the New Deal. To explore this interpretive hypothesis, I begin by rehearsing *Plessy*'s arguments more elaborately than Chief Justice Warren does in his opinion.

Plessy's *Premises in an Activist State*

An oddity: the Court's opinion in *Plessy* was written by Justice Henry B. Brown. Stripping his opinion to its essentials, Brown gives two basic reasons for the Court's decision. The first:

> The object of the amendment was undoubtedly to enforce the absolute equality of the two races before the law, but *in the nature of things* [emphasis supplied] it could not have been intended to abolish distinctions based upon color, or to enforce social, as distinguished from political, equality, or a commingling of the two races upon terms unsatisfactory to either.[30]

There are two kinds of things to be said about this. One is that it was wrong when written. This is the line taken by Mr. Justice Harlan in his famous dissenting opinion in *Plessy*.[31] In 1954 Chief Justice Warren says something different: constitutional developments of the twentieth century have given him new reasons that Harlan lacked for rejecting *Plessy*.

Once we allow ourselves to reflect on the constitutional achievements of the 1930's, Warren's confidence seems justified. It was *precisely* the Old Court's effort to deny the New Deal authority to pursue "social, as distinguished from political, equality" that defined the great constitutional debate of the 1930's. Once the New Deal Court had authorized the state's power to guarantee a retirement pension or a minimum wage, Justice Brown's confident distinction between social and political equality was no longer tenable. Given the New Deal Court's embrace of activist government, the Warren Court could hardly respond to the petitioner's complaint by reaffirming Justice Brown's confident assertion that "the nature of things" precluded a governmental assault on social inequality.

Justice Brown's second defense of "separate but equal" survives no better:

> We consider the underlying fallacy of the plaintiff's argument to consist in the assumption that the enforced separation of the two races stamps

the colored race with a badge of inferiority. If this be so, it is not by reason of anything found in the act, but solely because the colored race choses [*sic*] to put that construction upon it.[32]

This second line brings *Plessy*'s rejection of government activism to a deeper—one might even say, metaphysical—level. Justice Brown seems to deny that law contributes to the construction of social reality. Jim Crow laws stigmatize blacks only because "the colored race chooses to put that construction" upon them. The government cannot be held responsible for these "choices." Note the extreme way in which Brown makes his point: public meaning is not produced through the interaction of government decisions and the "choices" of social groups; the stigma is "solely" a product of non-state "choices"; the state simply has nothing to do with it.

Whatever the legal plausibility of this claim in 1896, it was judicially untenable after the 1930's. The New Deal Court recognized the government as an active contributor to the process by which groups made their "choices" in American society. In the 1930's, this point had been made principally through the decisive legitimation of governmental intervention in the marketplace. No longer were workers or the elderly left to "choose" amongst the impoverished options provided by the market. This basic New Deal point, however, was also relevant to a modern assessment of Justice Brown's claim about race: Once the New Court had recognized the active role of the state in shaping "choices" in the "free market," how could the Warren Court have repeated *Plessy*'s analysis of the "underlying fallacy of the plaintiff's argument"?*

Compulsory public schooling had always challenged the rhetoric

---

*The Court's opposition to activist government is repeated in another remarkable passage: "The argument also assumes that social prejudices may be overcome by legislation, and that equal rights cannot be secured to the negro except by an enforced commingling of the races. We cannot accept this proposition. If the two races are to meet upon terms of social equality, it must be the result of natural affinities, a mutual appreciation of each other's merits and a voluntary consent of individuals." Plessy v. Ferguson, 163 U.S. 537, 551 (1896). Such passages ignored the fact that the particular statute at issue in *Plessy* did not leave segregation up to private choice but required segregation as a matter of law. Justice Brown's comment only makes clearer, however, *Plessy*'s deep intellectual indebtedness to the laissez-faire theories expressed one decade later in cases like *Lochner*.

of "choice" in two ways. First, the free public school is one long protest against the idea that the "choices" of individual parents may rightly determine whether children may be left in ignorance. Second, compulsory education supposes that children are not informed enough to "choose" whether they should go to school or seek learning elsewhere. What is a "public school" but a place where government employees "educate" children into the "truth" about social reality, whether they "choose" to be there or not?

Despite the tensions between compulsory schooling and the *Lochner* era's rhetoric of choice, the public education movement had made great strides during the early decades of the twentieth century. As Warren rightly emphasizes,[33] the public school was still in its infancy when *Plessy* was decided in 1896: many rich states did not provide a minimally adequate education; in Southern states, even the principle of universal education was incompletely recognized. While great progress occurred during the next generation,[34] public education would remain a constitutional anomaly in the law of the middle republic. So long as the middle republic remained committed to the rhetoric of free "choice" in vast domains of economic life, the courts would treat public schooling as a limited exception to more general constitutional principles developed under the Contract, Takings, and Due Process Clauses.[35]

With the New Deal, the public schools could take on a new symbolic meaning. They were no longer anomalous, but paradigmatic of the new promise of activist government.[36] They were in business precisely because black and white children were in no position to make an informed "choice" about social realities. Indeed, the very existence of public schools guaranteed that the state would be intimately involved in the way children would be *taught* the meaning of racial segregation by their teachers. Within this new activist setting, it was Justice Brown's observation that a Jim Crow law stigmatized blacks "solely because the colored race choses [*sic*] to put that construction upon it" that had become anomalous.

No court, looking at the Fourteenth Amendment after the activist affirmations of the 1930's, could repeat Justice Brown's reasons for upholding "separate but equal." As a matter of two-three synthesis, Brown's opinion had been discredited at its very foundations.

Brown on Brown

Chief Justice Warren's opinion for the Court looks a lot better than many of the scholarly "improvements" offered up over the years. The opinion turns on the crucial synthetic point: twentieth-century developments since *Plessy* have undermined the interpretive premises that informed Justice Brown's reading of "equal protection."

Warren does not make this point, however, by reflecting directly upon the meaning of the New Deal's legitimation of activist government. This effort at comprehensive synthesis would not come until later, in cases like *Griswold.* Nonetheless, the Chief Justice found a different way to express his synthetic insight. He told a story about the concrete institution in the case before him: the public school. In his opinion, the public school no longer appears as an anomalous exception to the antistatist premises of the middle republic. It serves as a compelling symbol of the modern republic's activist commitment to the general welfare:

> Today, education is perhaps the most important function of state and local governments. Compulsory school attendance laws and the great expenditures for education both demonstrate our recognition of the importance of education to our democratic society. It is required in the performance of our most basic public responsibilities, even service in the armed forces. It is the very foundation of good citizenship. Today it is a principal instrument in awakening the child to cultural values, in preparing him for later professional training, and in helping him to adjust normally to his environment. In these days, it is doubtful that any child may reasonably be expected to succeed in life if he is denied the opportunity of an education. Such an opportunity, where the state has undertaken to provide it, is a right which must be made available to all on equal terms.[37]

From constitutional anomaly to constitutional paradigm—once the public school has been symbolically transformed in this way, the Court can use it to express its intuition about synthesis:

> An additional reason for the inconclusive nature of the Amendment's history, with respect to segregated schools, is the status of public education at that time. In the South, the movement toward free common

schools, supported by general taxation, had not yet taken hold . . . .
Even in the North, the conditions of public education did not approxi-
mate those existing today . . . . [C]ompulsory school attendance was
virtually unknown. As a consequence, it is not surprising that there
should be so little in the history of the Fourteenth Amendment relating
to its intended effect on public education.[38]

Warren is trying to detach the nineteenth century's affirmation of
"equal protection" from its implicit commitments to the night-watchman state. Whatever Justice Brown in *Plessy* might have thought, it
is now absurd to dismiss the "badge of inferiority" imposed by state
officials as they shunt black children to segregated schools as if it
were "solely" the product of a "choice" by the "colored race . . . to
put [a degrading] construction upon it."

This is the point upon which *Brown* explicitly confronts Justice
Brown: The state, not the children, must bear responsibility for the
fact that school segregation "generates a feeling of inferiority as to
their status in a way unlikely ever to be undone . . . . Any language
in *Plessy v. Ferguson* contrary to this finding is rejected."[39] Given
the decisive repudiation of night-watchman ideals in the 1930's, can
there be any doubt that the Court was right in repudiating Justice
Brown's reasoning? Within the new activist order, the schoolchild's
sense of racial inferiority had become a public responsibility, not a
private choice. The Warren Court's decision to overrule *Plessy* was
not only correct as an interpretive synthesis, but obviously so.

INTERPRETING *GRISWOLD*

I choose *Griswold* as my second case study because the Court's
initiative has met a similar fate at the hands of the legal community.
As with *Brown,* the case is broadly seen as a paradigm of the modern
Court's movement beyond interpretation to prophecy—this time on
behalf of sexual freedom.[40] As with *Brown,* we reach a different view
if we take the trouble to read the opinions of the Justices. These
direct us toward interpretive synthesis. Only this time, the Court's
insights into its intergenerational problem will be clearer; its effort
at synthesis less particularistic. We shall begin to glimpse a movement

toward comprehensive synthesis, analogous to the path traveled by the courts of the middle republic.

Griswold provides an especially good test case because it seems, on the surface, so very different from *Brown*. In contrast to *Brown*'s aggressive expansion of the state's role in fighting racial inequality, *Griswold* asserts the need to contract the ambitions of activist government—by recognizing a constitutional right to privacy. If *Griswold* represents the prophetic opening of a new moral crusade, it seems odd that the Warren Court should choose 1965 to start marching off in a direction opposite from the one marked by *Brown!*

To some, the discovery of such "inconsistencies" will only confirm the inevitably political character of judicial leadership.[41] I hope to dissolve that "contradiction," however, by taking the synthetic project seriously. When treated as exercises in intergenerational synthesis, *Brown* and *Griswold* are complementary, not contradictory. Both are deep responses to the same basic problem: the transformation in constitutional values won by Americans during the New Deal. Only each case responds by exploring the New Deal's relationship to a different historical achievement of the American past. *Brown,* as we saw, is a two-three case, focusing on the nineteenth century's demand for "equal protection" in a modern world of activist state institutions. *Griswold* displays different synthetic priorities. The fact that Estelle Griswold was suing Connecticut meant that, as a formal matter, the Fourteenth Amendment was involved in the litigation. But the Court did not use the case to consider more deeply the relationship between Reconstruction and the other great turning points in the American experience. It was content to rely on other cases holding that the Fourteenth Amendment made applicable to the states the fundamental principles of the Founders' Bill of Rights, leaving other possible synthetic relationships unexplored.* By plac-

---

*Thus, the fact that Estelle Griswold was a woman did not lead the Court to consider the possible application of the equal protection doctrine. See, for example, Catharine MacKinnon, *Feminism Unmodified* 93–102 (1987). Similarly, there was no effort to reflect on the libertarian side of Reconstruction and explore the modern implications of the Republicans' concern with self-ownership expressed by the Thirteenth Amendment. See Andrew Koppelman, "Forced Labor: A Thirteenth Amendment Defense of Abortion," 84 *Nw. L. Rev.* 480 (1990).

ing Reconstruction in the background, the Court could focus on another side of the synthetic triangle: the relationship between the Founding's concern with individual freedom and the New Deal's affirmation of activist government.*

To define this one-three problem, reflect on the aspect of the Founding most obviously undermined by the New Deal.[42] This was the Federalist effort to link the constitutional commitment to individual liberty with the rhetoric of contract and private property. The Founders valued contract so highly that they protected it in the original 1787 Constitution, at a time when they believed an elaborate Bill of Rights to be unnecessary. In response to the popular demand for a further enumeration of rights, the Fifth Amendment contained an explicit guarantee against governmental takings of property without just compensation. By eighteenth-century standards, property and contract were fundamental to the constitutional language of liberty.

This left the modern Court with a formidable problem. Given New Deal activism, what remained of the Founding values of individual self-determination formerly expressed in the language of property and contract? So understood, the problem was analogous to *Brown*'s. Just as the Warren Court detached Reconstruction's affirmation of equality from the laissez-faire premises of the nineteenth century, so too it might detach the Founders' affirmation of personal liberty from the property/contract framework within which it had been imbedded before the New Deal. My thesis: *Griswold* is best understood as a critical stage in this process of *Brown*-like detachment from the abandoned premises of the middle republic.

To make this analogy persuasive, I must compensate for the fact that the Supreme Court of the middle republic did not take up the birth control question and confront it frontally, as *Plessy* did the race issue. Whatever else may be said about *Plessy*, it gave us a concrete target, identifying the antistatist premises that had been fractured by the twentieth-century triumph of activist American gov-

---

*Some cases try to make self-conscious use of all three constitutional turning points in a new doctrinal synthesis. Call these one-two-three cases. It is of the first importance to consider how the Court has confronted such issues over time, and whether its responses have made sense. Compare, for example, Gideon v. Wainwright, 372 U.S. 335 (1963), with McCleskey v. Kemp, 481 U.S. 279 (1987).

ernment. Since no similar target exists in the present case, my argument begins with a thought experiment: How would the Supreme Court of the *Lochner* era have confronted Estelle Griswold's plea for constitutional protection? Once we have constructed our hypothetical target, we can assess the extent to which Justice Douglas's opinion in *Griswold,* like Warren's in *Brown,* is responsive to the distinctive needs of interpretive synthesis in a post–New Deal world.

Griswold *and Freedom of Contract*

Suppose that Planned Parenthood had not waited until the late 1930's to begin its long series of court challenges to Connecticut's birth control statutes. Imagine that litigation had begun in 1923—when Margaret Sanger first urged repeal in the name of the Connecticut Birth Control League.[43] Were there constitutional arguments available to her at the time?

Absolutely. But they would have looked different from the ones found in Justice Douglas's opinion of 1965. In 1923, the forensic challenge was to persuade the Court to extend *Lochner*'s affirmation of freedom of contract to Planned Parenthood's effort to provide birth control services to willing recipients. After all, if the bakers in *Lochner* had a constitutionally protected liberty to contract with their employers, why shouldn't married couples be accorded the same liberty to contract with the Birth Control League? This is, at least, the question that Sanger's hypothetical lawyers would have vigorously pressed before the courts of the middle republic.

Not that they had a sure winner on their hands. Courts of the *Lochner* era hedged their libertarian principles with a number of exceptions, including one involving "protection of public morals." Given the role of sexual chastity in traditional morality, a majority might have sustained the anticontraception statutes under this "police power" exception. Nonetheless, when Planned Parenthood began its litigation campaign in 1939, its citations to *Lochner*-like cases[44] did persuade a lower Connecticut court to overturn the state ban. Even the Connecticut Supreme Court only upheld the statutes by a vote of 3 to 2 in 1940.[45]

It took a quarter of a century, however, before Planned Parenthood convinced the U.S. Supreme Court to hear its complaint. By

1965, Griswold's lawyers had reconceptualized their arguments in the wake of the popular repudiation of freedom of contract in the 1930's. Rather than relying on *Lochner,* they tried to distinguish it. Most of their brief argued that the New Deal revolution involved matters of economic regulation and did not undermine *Lochner*-like protection for "rights of a fundamental individual and personal character."[46] Talk of a constitutional right of "privacy" comes at the end of the brief, almost as an afterthought.[47] Confronted by Griswold's arguments, the Supreme Court could hardly escape an encounter with the synthetic question: How sweeping was the New Deal transformation? Should it be interpreted as obliterating the Founding affirmations of private freedom previously expressed in the terms of freedom of contract? Or could the courts preserve this Founding commitment without impugning the post–New Deal government's authority to regulate "free" markets?

Griswold's *Approach to Synthesis*

With these synthetic questions raised by the briefs, the Justices confronted them more self-consciously than they had in *Brown.* Though Warren's opinion interpreted the nineteenth century's demand for "equal protection" in the light of modern activist government, *Brown* did not pinpoint the role of the 1930's in this change of interpretive perspective. Instead, the Court discussed the rise of activist government in terms of the particular problem before it: public education. To adopt a term from literary criticism, the public school functioned in *Brown* as a metonymic placeholder: just as the history of the White House might serve as a trope expressing the rise of the Presidency, Warren used the history of public education to express the rise of the activist welfare state.

The *Griswold* Court had no use for this kind of particularistic synthesis. It began by focusing on the decisive constitutional struggle of the 1930's: "Overtones of some arguments suggest that Lochner v. New York should be our guide. But we decline that invitation as we did in West Coast Hotel Co. v. Parrish [one of the great transformative opinions of 1937]."[48] The crucial question has become the status of the myth of rediscovery itself: should the Court continue to read the entire *Lochner* period as a tragicomedy of errors dominated by capricious judges? Or was it possible to glimpse a certain kind of interpretive continuity between the courts of the middle and modern republics, despite the great break represented by the New Deal's "switch in time"?

Douglas makes a crucial turn. He views the courts of the middle republic as engaged in a valid interpretive enterprise, and one from which modern courts can continue to learn as they tried to make sense of the Founding. Instead of repudiating the entire *Lochner* era, he proposes a more discriminating view. He distinguishes between cases, like *Lochner,* that protect private ordering in economic relations and those, like *Griswold,* that protect privacy in more intimate spheres of life:

> Marriage is a coming together for better or for worse, hopefully enduring, and intimate to the degree of being sacred. It is an association that promotes a way of life, not causes; a harmony in living, not political faiths; a bilateral loyalty, not commercial or social projects. Yet it is an association for as noble a purpose as any involved in our prior decisions.[49]

A "bilateral loyalty, not [a] commercial or social project": Although the New Deal gained the support of the People to regulate these "projects" for the general welfare, Douglas refuses to read the New Deal precedents so broadly as to include "bilateral loyalties" within the sphere of governmental management. He can, therefore, still mark out marriage as an appropriate context for re-presenting the continuing constitutional value of liberty inherited from the Founding.

To buttress his case, he proposes a more discriminating view of the middle republic. He "reaffirm[s]" two *Lochner*-ian decisions of the 1920's, describing one as protecting the family's "right to educate a child in a school of the parents' choice—whether public or private or parochial . . . ," another as according "the same dignity . . . [to] the right to study the German language in a private school."[50] Similarly, the Court makes much of an 1886 opinion in *Boyd v. United States,*[51] describing the Fourth and Fifth Amendments as protecting "against all governmental invasions 'of a man's home and the privacies of life.'"[52]

Building on this rediscovered continuity with the Justices of the middle republic, Douglas explores how the constitutional value of privacy has served as a leitmotiv in the modern effort to make sense of the Bill of Rights. Looking at the First Amendment and at the Bill's multiple commands regulating the criminal process, Douglas finds that the idea of privacy has given these specific provisions "life and substance."[53] This recurring concern with privacy provides, in turn, the basis for a comprehensive reading of the Founding text itself:

> Various guarantees create zones of privacy. The right of association contained in the penumbra of the First Amendment is one, as we have seen. The Third Amendment in its prohibition against the quartering of soldiers "in any house" in time of peace without the consent of the owner is another facet of that privacy. The Fourth Amendment explicitly affirms the "right of the people to be secure in their persons, houses, papers, and effects, against unreasonable searches and seizures." The Fifth Amendment in its Self-Incrimination Clause enables the citizen to create a zone of privacy which government may not force him to surrender to his detriment. The Ninth Amendment provides: "The enumeration in the Constitution, of certain rights, shall not be construed to deny or disparage others retained by the people."[54]

At the heart of *Griswold* is the act of synthetic interpretation—an effort to integrate Founding text with New Deal transformation to make sense of both parts of our evolving heritage. Douglas rejects particularistic efforts to look upon the Bill of Rights as a series of disjointed rules.[55] He views the rules as expressive of more abstract Founding values—values that retain their constitutional meaning despite the transformations and contingencies of two centuries. Making this effort at comprehensive synthesis, he finds that "[t]he present case, then, concerns a relationship lying within the zone of privacy created by several fundamental constitutional guarantees. And it concerns a law which, in forbidding the *use* of contraceptives rather than regulating their manufacture or sale, seeks to achieve its goals by means having a maximum destructive impact upon [the marital] relationship. Such a law cannot stand . . . ."[56]

The Chorus: Concurrences and Dissents

The distinctive character of the Court's opinion is displayed by contrasting it with others entered in the case. There were three concurrences[57] and two dissents, and I cannot do them justice here. As for the concurrences, it is enough to say that none focused on the problem of synthesis with the same intensity as did the Court. None begins with *Lochner* and asks whether, despite its repudiation, the Justices may yet find a way to re-present the Founding commitment to personal freedom using concepts and contexts distinguishable from those repudiated in the 1930's. Instead of emphasizing the centrality of one-three synthesis, the concurrences sketch more open-ended kinds of inquiry in which the Court roams broadly to elaborate the substance of constitutional value.

In contrast, the two dissenters—Justices Black and Stewart—take on the synthetic challenge raised by Douglas. Like the Court, they recognize that they must define the meaning of the constitutional transformation of the 1930's in order to decide Griswold's case. Only they offer up a much broader interpretation of the New Deal than does the majority. For them, the 1930's did not merely repudiate the constitutional value of private ordering in "commercial or social projects." It amounted to a rejection of the very idea that some spheres of life should be insulated from pervasive management by the activist state. On this statist interpretation the People not only decisively authorized their government to regulate sweatshops in the 1930's. They also authorized state management of free choice in any and all areas of life. Any judicial effort to construe the New Deal more narrowly is tainted by "the same natural law . . . philosophy found in *Lochner v. New York* [and] other discredited decisions."[58]

Taken to its extreme, this statist interpretation implies the end of all constitutional limitations on normal government. But the dissenters did not go to this extreme. No less than the majority, they see the need to synthesize the New Deal into a broader narrative embracing the Founding and Reconstruction. Only they propose to read these earlier constitutional solutions in a very different spirit. Justice Douglas read the Founders' Bill of Rights as part of a comprehensive synthesis—providing constitutional principles which might be harmonized with the concerns of the modern activist state. In contrast, the statist dissenters read the Bill of Rights as Raoul Berger reads the Fourteenth Amendment—as a superstatute containing "specific prohibitions"[59] with fixed and relatively straightforward meanings.[60] So long as the newly empowered activist state does not violate any of these "specifics," the dissenters would sustain the challenged statute.

On this approach to one-three synthesis, the meaning of Time One has been reduced to a series of very concrete superstatutes, whereas the New Deal victory at Time Three has been inflated into the grant of an almost plenary power to the activist state. Indeed, the dissenters understand the New Deal victory in metaphysical terms. They do not think the 1930s involved something as humdrum as the grant by the People of new governmental powers over economic and social life. For them, it amounted to nothing less than the repudiation of something called "natural law philosophy."

These differences between the majority and the dissenters are of great importance—both practical and theoretical. But there is something more important than deciding who is right. It is recognizing that both sides are talking about the same problem: one-three synthesis.

FROM *BROWN* TO *GRISWOLD* TO . . .

In re-presenting the exchange in *Griswold,* I have had two aims. The first is to deny that the case is yet another venture in judicial prophecy. At the very least, this is not what the Court, nor the dissenters, think it is about. Instead, they are arguing about very fundamental *interpretive* questions that all of us should face in making sense of a Constitution that has been transformed, and transformed again, through two centuries of constitutional politics.

The second is to suggest that, as in *Brown,* the *Griswold* Court had a firmer grip on its interpretive problem than most commentators have had. A decade onward, the Court has become yet more self-conscious. While *Brown* was emphatic about harmonizing modern activist government with the nineteenth-century ideal of "equal protection of the laws," its approach remained particularistic. It focused narrowly on the facts of its problem—black schools—and did not try for a premature statement of comprehensive principles that might integrate Reconstruction with the New Deal.

The *Griswold* Court gets closer to the core of the problem. It squarely confronts the popular repudiation of free market constitutionalism in the 1930's and asks how to make sense of the Founding texts in a constitutional regime no longer committed to the strong protection of property and free contract. From this point of view, *Griswold*'s reinterpretation of the Founding texts in terms of a right to privacy, rather than a right to property and contract, is nothing less than a brilliant *interpretive* proposal. Granted, when the Founders thought about personal freedom they used the language of property and contract; given the New Deal repudiation of this language, doesn't the language of privacy provide *us* with the most meaningful way of preserving these Founding affirmations of liberty in an activist welfare state?[61]

A satisfactory answer must, of course, confront the challenges raised by the very different approach to one-three synthesis advocated by Black and Stewart—one reinvigorated recently by the appointment of a surprisingly large number of statists to the courts by a Reagan Administration that, on the surface, championed individualistic rhetoric.* As with *Brown,* however, my aim here has been to begin a story, not to end it.

Synthesis and Interpretation

I hope I have said enough to suggest my larger ambition—to define a model of interpretation which can do justice to the complexity of American judicial practice. When viewed in its largest terms, this practice bears some striking resemblances to other great interpretive enterprises—most notably those that derive from the major religious traditions.

The most obvious analogy is with Christianity: as with interpreters of the American Constitution, Christians do not suppose that their tradition is the product of the religious experience of a single historical era. In one way or another, they must synthesize the meaning of the Old Testament of the Jews and the New Testament of the Christians into a single whole if they are to hear the voice of God. From a formal point of view, we should also be looking to Islam for insights. Our modern problem of constitutional interpretation is one

---

*Evidenced by the majority opinion in Bowers v. Hardwick, 478 U.S. 186 (1986), refusing to generalize the principle of privacy to include homosexual, as well as heterosexual, intimacies.

involving the synthesis of *three* different generational experiences and hence has the same structure as the Islamic narrative, in which Mohammed is viewed as continuing, but transforming, the inspired teachings of Christ and Moses.

And yet, there are hazards involved in too quick a leap over the hermeneutic wall separating interpreters of We the People from interpreters of the will of God. Most obviously, the American tradition is born in the spirit of the Enlightenment. American lawyers are forbidden, by command of the First Amendment, to suppose that the Constitution is but a continuation of the divine project described in one or another sacred text.

Equally important, Americans do not look upon the movements led by James Madison, Abraham Lincoln, Franklin Roosevelt, or Martin Luther King in the same way that believing Christians look upon the relationship between Christ and Moses or that Moslems view the relationship between Mohammed and his predecessors. For these believers, the last movement served to close the canon and reveal, once and for all, the last word of God (before the end of time). For citizens of a secular Republic, the past expressions of We the People have a different status. None of them provide the last word that makes further human revision unthinkable. Our latter-day amendments represented profound, but partial, transformations of the vision first elaborated by our Enlightenment Founders. So long as the Republic lives, there will remain the possibility of further critique and popular reconstruction.

In the meantime, we are left to piece together the different contributions of different generations—none of them complete, all of them important. While Reconstruction Republicans and New Deal Democrats shattered the Founding vision, no generation has mobilized its political energies to reconcile these disparate achievements into a comprehensive whole, in the manner of the Philadelphia Convention. Perhaps some future generation will make this effort at a second Constitutional Convention. Only one thing is clear: The Supreme Court cannot simply shut up shop until this happens. The flow of concrete cases forces the Justices to confront and reconcile, without divine inspiration, the disparate historical achievements of the American people.

The more we take the Justices' struggle seriously, the more we see a persistent pattern to their synthetic activities. At the beginning of both the middle and modern republics, the Justices responded to the recent transformation by trying to preserve those fragments of the older tradition in which they were trained. Thus, the majority in *Slaughterhouse* could not bring itself to rethink the basic principles of federalism that were at the foundation of the early republican order; the majority in *Carolene Products* sought to convince itself that the popular validation of activist national government "only" implied the repudiation of the Court's interpretation of a few clauses of the Constitution dealing with contract, property, and the regulation of interstate commerce, but had not discredited the Court's efforts to preserve other aspects of the Bill of Rights and the Reconstruction amendments from the ebb and flow of normal politics.

Over time, a different approach to synthesis comes to the fore. As the last transformation recedes in collective experience, as a new generation of lawyers and citizens arises, as the first generation of case law accumulates, a new and more comprehensive perspective on multigenerational synthesis becomes more available. Here the Justices no longer content themselves with salvaging fragments of the old regime; they try to integrate the new principles added by the last transformation into the older tradition in a comprehensive way. I have tried to show how this process was at work in *Brown* and *Griswold,* just as it was in the middle republic. And it is just this process I mean to assist by this book.

If I am successful, perhaps the next generation of citizens, lawyers, judges might, over time, gain a more sympathetic understanding, and genuine assistance, from those of us who are lucky enough to earn our keep as academic commentators. As we reflect together on the complexities of one-two, two-three, one-three, one-two-three synthesis, we will not miraculously converge on a single neat doctrinal answer. Even the most deliberate answers reached by the greatest courts in our history have not served as the last word in the past, nor will they in the future.

My reading of American history suggests a more dialectical relationship between the People and the Court. By offering up the deepest synthesis of the past constitutional achievements of which they are capable, the Justices provide today's Americans with a dialectical mirror, as it were, in which to look at themselves. Does the re-presentation of the People by the Court reveal a picture of our constitutional identity that we are prepared to live with? Or has it come time again to mobilize our political energies to transform our fundamental principles? If the time for serious constitutional politics is now, which aspects of our higher law need critique and transformation? Which aspects need further development?

The better the legal community does its job of interpretive synthesis, the more useful we will be to our fellow citizens in the present and future—as they carry on the project of constitutional lawmaking which will end only with the death of the Republic.

CODA

Discover the Constitution: as a distinctive idea, as a political regime, as a rule of law. I have been trying to introduce the multiple, and interacting, aspects of the American people's historical exercise in dualistic democracy.

But I have only scratched the surface. No single work—no single mind—can do justice to the spirit of the Constitution. The best I can do is encourage you to move to the next round in the cycle of reflection. I will be going more slowly now, taking up some of the leading ideas we have inherited from the past, assessing how well they have survived the journey to the present.

I shall begin, unsurprisingly, with the Founding. We shall be mining Federalist thought in search of a deeper understanding of dualist democracy—both as the basic ideas emerged from the experience of the Revolutionary generation and as they continue to structure, with many transformations, modern political life. A second volume, *Transformations,* will take up the contributions of Reconstruction and the New Deal in a similar spirit. Only after deepening our understanding of dualist ideas, in their evolving political context, will the third volume, *Interpretations,* return the Supreme Court to center stage: How well has the Court discharged its preservationist functions over the last two centuries? By what techniques did Marshall seek to preserve 1787 from Jefferson's "Revolution of 1800"? How did the Taney Court respond to the problem posed by Jackson's engagement in constitutional politics? And on and on . . . to the struggle by the Reagan Republicans to transform the shape of constitutional law.

PART TWO

Neo-Federalism

CHAPTER SEVEN

Publius

OVERVIEW

THIS PART TRACES the historical taproots of American dualism to the Founding. To follow dualism to its source, we must learn to see the Founders as they saw themselves: as successful revolutionaries who had managed, time and time again, to lead their fellow citizens in public-spirited collective action, even at great personal cost. So far as the Founders were concerned, these revolutionary acts of mobilized citizenship gave their public life a special quality—far removed from the pushings-and-shovings of normal life.

In charting their constitutional future, the Founders did not turn their back on their revolutionary past. They recognized that much of American politics would lack the quality of mobilized public deliberation they associated with the spirit of the Revolution. Much of their Constitution was elaborated with the pathologies of normal politics in mind. But not all of it. The Founders recognized that their new constitutional machine could not operate indefinitely without further exercises in mobilized deliberation by the people at large. Thus, their constitutional text inaugurates the American experiment in dualism by defining a higher lawmaking process through which future generations might concentrate their political energies to make fundamental law in the name of We the People of the United States.

My first aim is to place these Founding dualisms in historical context—exploring the remarkable way our eighteenth-century predecessors grappled with the problem of constitutionalizing their experience of the American Revolution. My second aim is different, though not (I hope) inconsistent. I propose to use the Founding as the beginning of a dialogue between past and present which will serve as our central technique for constitutional discovery. I mean to ask whether the Founding still remains a meaningful act for us today.

The very question conjures up the enormous chasm that separates us from the spokesmen for a million or so white male planters and merchants, farmers and mechanics, who spoke in the name of the People of 1787. What can hundreds of millions of men and women living in a postindustrial and polyglot America learn about governing a world power from these imperfectly liberated Englishmen of long ago?

The problem transcends the obvious social, economic, and political gap separating an agrarian republic on the European fringe from a continental powerhouse at the center of the world political economy—though these differences make meaningful communication hard enough. The deepest difficulty, as always, involves values. The Founders compromised with slavery and religious intolerance; many were positively enthusiastic about sexism and economic inequality. It is easy to use these, and many other, moral disagreements as excuses for refusing to engage them in serious dialogue, to treat these gentlemen in funny clothes as if they had no more intimate connection to our political identity than Martians. What can we possibly learn from such arrogantly self-satisfied Anglo-chauvinist folk?

This moralizing dismissal of dialectical engagement is curiously abetted by a different kind of estrangement. This has its source in the small, but devoted, band of professional historians who give their lives to the study of the American past. These academicians are so intent on elaborating the vast gulf separating 1787 from 1987 that they verge on condemning as unhistorical any suggestion that modern Americans may have something to learn about themselves by establishing a meaningful relationship to the Founding. From this professionalistic point of view, the effort to learn from the Founding is just a fancy kind of shadowboxing—the world of 1787 is so distant from our own that the "Founders" we discover are entirely our own creation. There is just nothing that Americans living two centuries apart have in common, except a few scraps of paper whose meaning has been divorced from their originating contexts. If this be so, the very exercise in dialectical engagement can seem historically flawed no less than morally suspect.

And yet, the fact is that today's constitutional language and practice can be traced back to the Founding. Americans will lose a vital resource for political self-understanding if we estrange ourselves from these origins. The challenge is clear enough: can we recognize the historical and moral ways in which *we* are different from *them* and nonetheless work out points of dialectical contact that genuinely illuminate our continuing connection to our origins?

This chapter invites you to reread the *Federalist Papers* with this question in mind. I have focused on these essays by Hamilton, Madison, and Jay—writing under the evocative pseudonym Publius—because they represent the Founders' most reflective effort to convince their fellow Americans that the Constitution is worthy of "reflection and choice."[1] From the very beginning, the *Federalist* has served as a dialectical mirror through which Americans have glimpsed their constitutional identities. For now I won't describe the path of interpretation over the centuries, or locate the Papers in the larger field of late-eighteenth-century thought—deferring these questions to the next chapter. I propose to plunge into the Papers at once, searching for commonalities that may remain after we have bracketed the more obvious moral differences that separate us. In confronting *Federalist* No. 10, I shall not be focusing on Publius's impassioned diatribe against the "rage for paper money, for an abolition of debts, for an equal division of property, or for any other improper or wicked project."[2] Whatever Publius may have thought, we know that the constitutionalization of paper money was one of the achievements of Republican Reconstruction;[3] the legitimation of the welfare state, the triumph of New Deal Democracy. Similarly, the *Federalist*'s embarrassed apology for the Constitution's compromise with slavery[4] can only serve to remind us how much more struggle remains before blacks, women, and other subordinated groups can become full citizens of the country they inhabit. The question is not whether the Founding Federalists are to be put on a pedestal, but whether we can still learn something from them that might illuminate our search for constitutional self-definition.

CONSTITUTION AND REVOLUTION

"We the People of the United States . . ." Begin with the remarkable act involved in writing these opening words. Only six years before, all thirteen states had unanimously agreed on the Articles of Confederation, which they solemnly proclaimed the basis of "perpetual Union." Now, after a short summer of secret meetings, thirty-nine "patriots"* at the Convention were not only proposing to destroy this initial hard-won effort. They were also claiming authority, in the name of the People, to ignore the rules that the Articles themselves laid out to govern their own revision. The Articles explicitly required the agreement of all thirteen states before any constitutional change was enacted;[5] yet the Founders declared that their new Constitution spoke for "We the People" if only nine states give their assent. This revolutionary redefinition of the rules of the game extended further—to the manner in which the nine states were to signify their approval. As the Convention looked ahead to the struggle over ratification, it refused to permit existing state governments to veto its authority to speak for the People. Only special "constitutional conventions" would be allowed to determine the fate of the new Constitution.[6] What justified the Federalists in asserting that this end run around legal forms gave them a *better* claim to represent the People than the standing governments of the day?

I begin with Publius's answer to this question—not only because the struggle to establish one's own authority is always revealing; not only because this same answer has reverberated throughout our constitutional history; but also because it provides a distinctive perspective on a central puzzle of modern politics: the nature of revolution. Despite the hopes and fears the word conjures up, revolution has become one of the great banalities of late-twentieth-century life. We have seen the surging masses, the assertive slogans, the charismatic leaders, so many times before—if only on our television tubes. Indeed, modern revolutionaries often seem content to play out minor variations on scripts first written in Paris or Saint Petersburg or Peking. For all its proud talk of new beginnings, is there anything more familiar than revolution?

And yet, there was a time when all this was not so cut-and-dried.

---

*There were fifty-five delegates dispatched to the Convention, but only thirty-nine stayed to sign the final proposal. Two of the three New Yorkers abandoned the Convention in response to its Federalist drift, leaving Hamilton alone to sign on behalf of the state. This was better than Rhode Island, which boycotted the Convention from the very beginning. See Max Farrand, *The Framing of the Constitution of the United States* 11–12 (1913).

By some uncanny accident, Washington, Madison, and the other American revolutionaries convening in Philadelphia chose the last possible moment at which their deliberations would be unaffected by the events that shook Paris, and the world, in 1789. Unlike their modern counterparts, they were incapable of viewing themselves as second-rate imitations of Robespierre or Napoleon, Lenin or Mao. They were obliged to think for themselves about the possibilities for political order opened up by the American Revolution. The result was the construction of a dualistic conception of government very different from the visions explored by later revolutionaries in Paris, Moscow, and Peking. We will not understand this achievement by reading history backwards: looking upon the Founding Federalists as if they were acting out one or another scene from the French or Russian revolutions.

Speaking broadly, this has been the fate of the Founding during the twentieth century. Many of our most brilliant historians have allowed images of later revolutions to shape their approach to the Federalists—sometimes blatantly, sometimes subtly.[7] This academic failure mirrors a general malaise. The French, Russian, and Chinese revolutions have had a profound impact on the popular, no less than the academic, mind. Because these revolutions failed to generate a vision of constitutional order that resembled the American type, their high visibility allowed modern Americans to lose sight of the revolutionary roots of their own Constitution.

To regain perspective, I will begin with a statement of the constitutional predicament encountered by all successful revolutionaries—a statement sufficiently general to cover the case of Peking no less than Philadelphia. Only in this way can we grasp the distinctiveness and creativity of the Federalist response.

The Problem of Revolutionary Legitimacy

Turn your mind's eye to revolutionary scenes that have become, through endless repetition, a part of common consciousness. Do not begin at the climactic moment at which you and your fellow revolutionaries triumphantly explore the wreckage of the old regime. Start at a point when final victory seems more doubtful.

Time One. You are surrounded by an ongoing regime—people occupying government offices, declaring themselves rightful rulers of the territory; others plotting and scheming to replace the present incumbents; the masses looking on with resigned indifference: politics as usual.

All this, so far as you are concerned, stinks. Though the government says it represents the people, you think the opposite. Despite its undisputed mastery of established legal forms, you and your comrades—not the government—are the true representatives of the People. Now such a claim requires courage, no less spiritual than physical. After all, who do you think you are? The New Messiah?

Religious zealots might stop the conversation at this point. But for secular folk, things are more complicated. Predictably, political revolutionaries will respond to the question of their own legitimacy in three different ways. First, they will say that the established government is *subverting the public good.* This requires an ideology that specifies the public good that is being subverted. Second, they will portray themselves as possessing *special virtues* qualifying them as the People's true representatives over other applicants for the position. Third, the leadership's claims to legitimacy must be validated by the *concrete assent* of fellow citizens, who recognize them as the true representatives of the People despite their illegality. Without such validating conventions, you cannot be a revolutionary leader— only a leader in search of a revolution.

Time Two. The old regime has collapsed; established legalities have disintegrated. You and your comrades have seized the commanding heights and proceed with the business of government. Quite remarkably, you are now in control of the forms of legal authority. While this, in a way, was what the struggle was all about, victory brings its own embarrassments.

Revolution is a game any number can play. Just as you challenged established authority, so can the next fellow. He too can proclaim his superior virtue and your subversion of the public good before irregular conventions speaking in the People's name. Vigilance, and the effective use of force, is part of the successful revolutionary's answer to such rivals. But there is another part too—an explanation why it is wrong for others to usurp the usurper's crown.

Two Simple Solutions

There are two obvious answers. The first is "permanent revolution." Here, the revolutionary elite denies that anything really important has happened with its accession to legal authority. After all, the elite did not require legal forms earlier to declare themselves the People's true representatives. It was enough to present themselves to irregular assemblies as people of special virtue in pursuit of the public good. And the "revolutionary legality" that was good enough for those great times of glorious victory is certainly good enough today. So hip-hip-hooray: onward in the People's service. Anybody who stands in the way is a counterrevolutionary, who must be consigned to the past or reeducated for life in a brave new world.

The other obvious answer is "revolutionary amnesia." Now that we have seized power, let us forget how we got here. The law is the law. If you do not like the law, try to change it through the (newly) established forms. Anybody who ignores the forms and violates the law is a criminal. Criminals belong in jail.

Reading the *Federalist*

Now the first reason the *Federalist* is worth reading—not merely by Americans but by all thinking people—is that it proposes a third way to solve the problem of revolutionary legitimacy. While rejecting the desirability of permanent revolution, it places a high value on public-regarding political activity involving citizen sacrifice of private interests to pursue the common good in transient and informal political assemblies. While rejecting revolutionary amnesia, it insists that mobilizational forms of mass engagement should dominate the constitutional stage only under certain well-defined historical situations. When these conditions do not apply, governmental officials should not be allowed to pretend that they speak with the full authority of the People. During periods of normal politics, they must be constrained by the constitutional forms imposed during rare periods of constitutional creativity, when the People mobilize and speak with a very different voice.

But if the People do not speak all the time, how to recognize the rare moments when Americans have hammered out a considered political judgment? The *Federalist* draws its line with the aid of a dualistic theory of political life. Only one side of the dualism is familiar from everybody's class in high school civics. In *Federalist* No. 10, Publius presents a profound analysis of the politics of faction: "By a faction I understand a number of citizens, whether amounting to a majority or minority of the whole, who are united and actuated by some common impulse of passion, or interest, adverse to the rights of other citizens, or to the permanent and aggregate interests of the community."[8] Though factional politics is naturally distasteful to a successful revolutionary, Publius thinks the cure will be worse than the disease. The only sure way to suppress faction is to force everybody to think alike. Such a destruction of liberty is inconsistent with everything for which the American Revolution stands. The best we can hope for is an amelioration of the evil consequences of faction. Here is where constitutional law comes in: By a clever manipulation of legal forms, we may play different factions off against one another so that they do relatively little damage to the rights of citizens and the permanent interests of the community.

For the moment, we need not analyze the substance of Federalist constitutional science. The important points go deeper. According to Publius, constitutional wisdom begins by recognizing that the future of American politics will not be one long glorious reenactment of the American Revolution. The *Federalist* constructs the foundations for a different kind of politics—where passion and interest will drive Americans apart rather than emphasize the permanent interests and fundamental rights they have in common. So far as this politics is concerned, the new constitutional forms should trump ordinary political outcomes.

Yet we cannot allow Publius's brilliant sketch of faction in No. 10 to blind us to the larger vision of political life displayed in the *Federalist* as a whole. This will deprive us of Publius's insights into the politics with which he is best acquainted: his own. Does he suppose the Constitutional Convention to be a factional assembly of the kind he condemns in No. 10? If so, why does he expect its constitutional proposals to gain the consent of his fellow Americans? If not, why not?

Constitutional Politics

A key paper is No. 40, where Publius confronts the Convention's decision to rip up the Articles of Confederation and change the rules for constitutional ratification the Articles had established six short years previously—in ways that greatly enhanced the Federalists' prospects for success.

Publius launches a two-part defense. So far as the decision to new-model the constitutional order, he meets his critics head on. Taking up the relevant legal documents, he tries to persuade them that the Convention had the legal authority to propose sweeping changes in the preexisting system. These arguments have their share of problems, but it isn't necessary to examine them. It is more important to contrast this legalistic exercise with Publius's treatment of the Convention's end run around the rule requiring unanimous state consent for constitutional amendments. Here we have a flat confession: "In [this] one particular it is admitted that the Convention have departed from the tenor of their commission."[9]

This explicit confession of illegality motivates the Paper's remarkable reflections defining "how far considerations of duty . . . could have supplied any defect of regular authority."[10] The answer is worth pondering:

> Let us view the ground on which the convention stood. . . . They must have reflected that in all great changes of established governments, forms ought to give way to substance; that a rigid adherence [to forms] would render . . . nugatory the transcendent and precious right of the people to "abolish or alter their governments . . .," since it is impossible for the people spontaneously and universally to move in concert . . .; it is therefore essential that such changes be instituted by some *informal and unauthorized propositions,* made by some patriotic and respectable . . . citizens. . . . [The Convention] must have recollected that it was by this irregular and assumed privilege of proposing to the people . . . that the States were first united against the danger with which they were threatened by their ancient government; . . . nor could it have been forgotten that no little ill-timed scruples, no zeal for adhering to ordinary forms, were anywhere seen, except in those who wished to indulge, under these masks, their secret enmity to the substance contended for. They must have borne in mind that as the plan to be framed and proposed was to

be submitted to *the people themselves,* the disapprobation of this supreme authority would destroy it forever; its approbation blot out antecedent errors and irregularities.[11]

Hear the voice of the successful revolutionary: the highest form of political expression is not found in formal assemblies arising under preexisting law, but through an "irregular and assumed privilege" of proposing "informal and unauthorized propositions." If such proposals were accepted by irregular, but popularly elected, conventions, we are to understand that *the people themselves*—the words are italicized in the original[12]— had spoken; and if the People approved the revolutionary elite's considered proposals, this could "blot out . . . errors and irregularities."

Strong stuff. At present, I am less interested in evaluating Federalist theory than in recovering it from the dustbin of history. From this perspective, it is important to recognize that Publius is saying nothing here that his audience would have considered idiosyncratic. To the contrary, *the very meaning of "convention" was tied up with illegality in the eighteenth century.*[13] The Americans had appropriated the word from English constitutional practice—where "convention" was used to designate a legally defective parliament, most notably the convention that presided over the Glorious Revolution of 1688. This convention consisted of Lords and Commons, meeting without the King; and through it, on the Americans' whiggish understanding, the people of England preserved their freedom by ousting a tyrannical king and imposing a Bill of Right on his successors. So far as the Americans were concerned, *this* legally imperfect convention represented a high point of English history. And it was only natural for them to use this word to denote their own revolutionary assemblies meeting in defiance of the King's officials: just as the English people represented themselves in convention during the Glorious Revolution, so too would the Americans during their even more glorious revolution.

In borrowing the word "convention," the Americans changed English practice in one crucial respect. Even though it might oust a tyrant-king and impose conditions on his successors, the 1688 convention's legal defects haunted the participants.[14] As soon as William and Mary were seated in their proper place, the convention-turned-parliament reaffirmed the convention's work in the form of a "proper" statute.[15] For the seventeenth-century English, the legally defective status of the convention meant that its products were *legally inferior* to those of a proper parliament.[16]

The Americans transvalued this relationship. To them, the legally anomalous character of the "convention" was not a sign of defective legal status but of revolutionary possibility—that a group of patriots might speak for the People with *greater* political legitimacy than any assembly whose authority arose only from its legal form. Within their revolutionary setting, it made sense to deny that "mere" legislatures could legitimately revise constitutional law. As the revolutionary years moved on, Americans insisted that the People could deliberate on constitutional matters only in special bodies whose very name— "convention"—denied that legal forms could ultimately substitute for the engaged participation of citizens.[17]

It is precisely this revolutionary usage that Publius is self-consciously invoking to justify the Convention's decision to take the law into its own hands. By conceding illegality, *Federalist* No. 40 was not undermining the Convention's authority but, if anything, enhancing it—linking it to the institutional form that Publius's contemporaries associated most intimately with We the People.*

The Conditions for Constitutional Creativity

For all this, Publius does not succumb to the self-intoxications of "permanent revolution." He is clear that the Convention's effort to

---

*A bit more of No. 40, for those so inclined: "Had the Convention . . . taken the cold and sullen resolution of . . . sacrificing substance to forms, of committing the dearest interests of their country to the uncertainties of delay, and the hazard of events; let me ask the man, who can raise his mind to one elevated conception, who can awaken in his bosom one patriotic emotion, what judgment ought to have been pronounced by the impartial world, by the friends of mankind, by every virtuous citizen, on the conduct and character of this assembly? Or if there be a man whose propensity to condemn is susceptible of no control, let me then ask what sentence he has in reserve for the twelve States who *usurped the power* of sending deputies to the convention, a body utterly unknown to their constitutions; for Congress, who recommended the appointment of this body, equally unknown to the Confederation; and for the State of New York, in particular, which first urged and then complied with this unauthorized interposition?" *Federalist* No. 40, at 253–54 (J. Madison) (C. Rossiter ed. 1961). We shall find remarkably similar expressions at later constitutional turning points, most notably during Reconstruction and the New Deal. See volume 2, *Transformations*.

speak for the People can be credible only under very special conditions. The core of his analysis appears in an important paper explaining why all constitutional disputes shouldn't be submitted to the general public for resolution:

> Notwithstanding the success which has attended the revisions of our established forms of government and which does so much honor to the virtue and intelligence of the people of America, it must be confessed that the experiments are of too ticklish a nature to be unnecessarily multiplied. We are to recollect that all the existing constitutions were formed in the midst of a danger which repressed the passions most unfriendly to order and concord; of an enthusiastic confidence of the people in their patriotic leaders, which stifled the ordinary diversity of opinions on great national questions; of a universal ardor for new and opposite forms produced by a universal resentment and indignation against the ancient government; and whilst no spirit of party connected with the changes to be made, or the abuses to be reformed, could mingle its leaven in the operation. The future situations in which we must expect to be usually placed do not present any equivalent security against the danger which is apprehended.[18]

A grim theory: Americans can be expected to transcend factional politics only "in the midst of a danger which represse[s] the passions." It is the old saw about the power of the hangman's rope to concentrate the mind, raised to the level of collective political consciousness.

In case the point was missed, Publius devotes the following Paper to important variations. Since a constant appeal to the People only permits the destruction of constitutional forms by selfish and passionate pressure groups, why not a regularized legal procedure under which the general public may undertake the task of constitutional review? Every seven years or so, a group of censors might be assembled to discover and sanction all violations of the Constitution that have occurred since the People last assembled.[19]

Publius's response is predictable but revealing in its comments upon the limitations of legal form. He derides the idea that a mobilized politics of citizenship will flourish on legal command. To the contrary: the spirit of self-interest will degrade the constitutional forms of censorship—with the most powerful factions manipulating their amplified power to speak in the name of the People. Instead of using law to suggest that the People might regularly stand in judgment on their representatives, a collective effort to transcend faction should "be neither presumed nor desired; because an extinction of parties necessarily implies either a universal alarm for the public safety, or an absolute extinction of liberty."[20] The first possibility explains the success of the revolutionary generation; the second can be avoided only if Publius persuades his fellow citizens to use Federalist constitutional science to prevent some future faction from suppressing freedom.

For all this grim emphasis on the role of "universal alarm" in jolting Americans into civic activity,* Publius refuses to learn the same lesson which Burke was to draw from the crowds of the French Revolution. Publius is aware that mass anxieties "for the public safety"[21] may precipitate paroxysms of extreme irrationality and brute oppression that make the pathologies of normal politics seem tame by comparison. Nonetheless, in a crucial move, he focuses on a more constructive possibility—the revolutionary experience of his generation has shown that public danger can "repress the passions most unfriendly to order and concord," not inflame them. Though it is a "ticklish" business, the American people have channeled mass energy into a deliberative politics that is *more* rational and public-spirited than the norm. For Publius, then, the image of a constitutional convention joins together four features in an altogether remarkable way: formal illegality, mass energy, public-spiritedness, *and* extraordinary rationality are fused in a combination fateful for the dualist enterprise.

Given its remarkable attributes, it is not surprising that the *Federalist* treats constitutional conventions as if they were perfect sub-

---

*No. 46 is also important on this point. It describes the way the American people would respond if critics proved correct and the new national government became an engine for a centralizing tyranny at the expense of the states. Such "encroachments . . . would not excite the opposition of a single State, or of a few States only. They would be signals of general alarm." *Federalist* No. 46, at 298 (J. Madison) (C. Rossiter ed. 1961)—from which, as in No. 49, Publius expects salutary consequences. The passage continues: "Every Government would espouse the common cause. A correspondence would be opened. Plans of resistance would be concerted. One spirit would animate and conduct the whole. The same combination, in short, would result from an apprehension of the federal, as was produced by the dread of a foreign, yoke. . . ." Id. The entire scenario that follows is well worth reading.

stitutes for *the people themselves*. Consider Publius's description of the Convention's end run around the Articles' demand that all amendments gain unanimous state consent:

> In one particular it is admitted that the convention have departed from the tenor of their commission. Instead of reporting a plan requiring the confirmation *of the Legislatures of all the States,* they have reported a plan which is to be confirmed by the *people,* and may be carried into effect by *nine States only.*[22]

But this is not what the constitutional text actually says. Article Seven stipulates that "The Ratification of the Conventions of nine States shall be sufficient . . ." Publius, who generally quotes accurately, sees no gap between the text's mention of "convention" and his own description of ratification by the "*people.*" Given his revolutionary background, how could the People be represented better than through an illegal, public-spirited, deliberative body that successfully calls upon the engaged citzenship of those beyond the convention chamber?

Not that Publius is confident that his fellow Americans will respond in the good old revolutionary way to the call of the Convention from Philadelphia. The Papers are full of indications that the revolutionary impulse is on the wane—the English have gone and, with them, the anxiety for the public safety that fueled the rare mixture of mass energy and collective deliberation that could support a healthy constitutional politics. If this Convention fails, the Union will be torn apart by self-serving politicians and interest groups who will use the language of state sovereignty to advance their factional projects:

> Was then the American Revolution effected, was the American confederacy formed, was the precious blood of thousands spilt, and the hardearned substance of millions lavished, not that the people of America should enjoy peace, liberty and safety, but that the governments of the individual States . . . might enjoy a certain extent of power, and be arrayed with certain dignities and attributes of sovereignty? We have heard of the impious doctrine in the old world, that the people were made for kings, not kings for the people. Is the same doctrine to be revived in the new, in another shape—that the solid happiness of the people is to be sacrificed to the views of political institutions of a different

form? It is too early for politicians to presume on our forgetting that the public good, the real welfare of the great body of the people, is the supreme object to be pursued; and that no form of government whatever has any other value than as it may be fitted for the attainment of this object.[23]

"It is too early for politicians . . .": this is no rhetorical flourish. As No. 10 reminds, the normal situation is one in which factions *will* thrive. And a faction is defined precisely by its members choosing to "forget," as it were, that "the public good, the real welfare of the great body of the people, is the supreme object to be pursued."

Publius is engaged in a grim race against time. In the afterglow of the most successful revolution in world history, have the American people stored up a reserve of public-spirited rationality sufficient to support a culminating act of constitutional creation offered to them by their revolutionary leaders?

Even if the answer is yes, Publius does not suppose that his generation has spoken the last word in the name of the People. At the same time he emphasizes the naivete implicit in constant or formalized efforts to place constitutional issues at the tender mercies of factionalized politics, he recognizes "that a constitutional road to the decision of the people ought to be marked out and kept open, for certain great and extraordinary occasions."[24] There will be future crises, new calls by future statesmen to put aside the pettiness of factional politics. It is to be hoped that the People will, in their irregular way, prove equal to the challenge.

But this, understandably, was not Publius's first concern. His more immediate preoccupation was the politics of faction—which, precisely because of the Revolution's success in expelling the British, seemed inevitably on the rise.

Representing the People

Of course, it was always possible for Washington, Madison, and the rest to do nothing after the British left the scene. The successful revolutionaries might remain passive as they were engulfed by the tide of faction. But Publius is no fatalist. He is a legal activist—through the reflective use of constitutional law, the Revolutionary generation may channel the flow of normal politics in ways consistent with revolutionary principle.[25]

Yet Publius is no Pangloss. Almost everything he knows suggests that he will fail. America is a country of imperial dimension. Already there are millions of inhabitants; especially if the new Constitution is "successful," the nation's population will, in half a century, rival the largest countries of the Old World. This prospect does not bode well: the kingdoms of Europe are hothouses of despotism.[26] The *Federalist,* moreover, is refreshingly free of any claim that Americans will be exempt from the moral diseases afflicting the rest of mankind.[27]

When Publius turns from the monarchical present to the classical past, the lesson is different, but no less disconcerting. Republican government is a creation of the Greek polis, a micro-state so small that citizens could meet together and discuss their political future in face-to-face assemblies. These city-states were transparently unequal to the military and economic challenges of aggressive empires.[28] Their efforts at confederacy were pathetic failures; heroic victories at Thermopylae, precisely because they were miraculous, could not compensate for this failure in political organization.[29] Worse yet, when Publius inspects the democratic politics of the polis, he can reach only more despairing conclusions. These micro-polities were notoriously unstable—constantly degenerating into turmoil and despotism as each group tried to seize exclusive power to oppress the others. And even when the democratic forms were maintained, the outcomes were offensive to the principles of the American Revolution. The democratic polis was hardly a steady friend of individual freedom: Athens killed Socrates, after all.[30]

In trying to channel the flow of normal politics, Publius does not suppose he can adapt a blueprint that has succeeded elsewhere. There is no effort to recapture a golden age; no notion that somebody else has built a better mousetrap. The closest model is England and we all know how corrupt it has become.[31] Upon considering the materials at hand, the soberest political scientist of the age, Montesquieu, concluded that republican government could not survive without constant calls upon its citizenry's public virtue.[32] Yet the *Federalist* is very clear that this appeal to public virtue could not, and should not, serve as the exclusive resource in constructing a tolerable normal politics.

The Problematics of Representation

Against all these reasons for despair, the *Federalist* can place only one weighty factor in the balance: the peculiarly modern institution of political representation. It was this invention, not any increase in the quantity of human virtue, which permitted the rational hope that Americans might succeed where the ancients failed.[33] Representative institutions will permit us to establish a regime encompassing millions of people, with different religious and economic interests. Though each interest would gladly use political power to subordinate the others, their multiplicity permits the constitutional architect a new kind of political freedom. Rather than suppress faction at the cost of individual liberty, one may hope to neutralize the worst consequences of faction by playing each interest group off against the others. Hence, the supreme importance of constitutional law. By manipulating the forms of constitutional representation, Publius hopes to drive normal politics into directions that do not endanger the principles of the American Revolution—principles elucidated by the irregular methods of constitutional politics.[34]

How to preserve the principles of the Revolution? This is the master question of constitutional design. Only one thing is clear—disappointment awaits all who fail to understand the distinctive character of representative institutions and strive to create a national government that resembles, as much as possible, the face-to-face democracies of the ancient past.[35] The temptation is strong to simulate the ancient polis by calling together a few hundred people to "re-present" the whole and reenact the ancient ritual of direct democracy. They, not us, will gather together in one place, discuss the pros and cons, count heads, and declare the majority to be winner in our name. The rhetoricians have a name for this solution to the problem of representation: synecdoche. In this figure of speech, the part (Congress) replaces the whole (the People of the United States): "The representatives of the people, in a popular assembly, seem to fancy that they are the people themselves and betray strong symptoms of impatience and disgust at the least sign of opposition from any quarter. . . ."[36]

All is lost if we are captured by this naive synecdoche. If we mistake Congress for the People Assembled, and give it supreme power, it will act in a way that belies its populist rhetoric:

The concentrating of [all power] in the same hands is precisely the definition of despotic government. It will be no alleviation that these powers will be exercised by a plurality of hands, and not by a single one. One hundred and seventy-three despots would surely be as oppressive as one . . . As little will it avail us that they are chosen by ourselves. An *elective despotism* was not the government we fought for . . .[37]

Representation not only promises a solution to the ancient problem of democracy but provides the source of an entirely new problem—misplaced concreteness or reification. No institution of normal politics can be allowed to transubstantiate itself into the People of the United States.

Publius is most explicit about this in *Federalist* No. 63. He rejects the popular belief that the ancient world was ignorant of the institution of representative government; in doing so, he clarifies the distinctive conception of representation upon which the *Federalist* pins its hopes:

In the most pure democracies of Greece, many of the executive functions were performed, not by the people themselves, but by officers elected by the people, and *representing* the people in their *executive* capacity. . . . From these facts, to which many others might be added, it is clear that the principle of representation was neither unknown to the ancients nor wholly overlooked in their political constitutions. The true distinction between these and the American governments lies *in the total exclusion of the people in their collective capacity,* from any share in the *latter,* and not in the *total exclusion of the representatives of the people* from the administration of the *former.* The distinction, however, thus qualified, must be admitted to leave a most advantageous superiority in favor of the United States. But to insure to this advantage its full effect, we must be careful not to separate it from the other advantage, of an extensive territory. For it cannot be believed that any form of representative government could have succeeded within the narrow limits occupied by the democracies of Greece.[38]

This text contrasts with Publius's earlier emphasis. Before, we heard him explain how the "irregular and assumed" procedures of constitutional conventions provided access *"to the people themselves."*[39] Now he proudly declares that *"the total exclusion of the people in their collective capacity"* is the hallmark of the American Constitution—which, together with the country's large size, will permit the success of representative democracy during periods of normal politics. We must systematically reject the idea that Congress (or the President or the Court) speaks with the *genuine* voice of the American people. During periods of normal politics, the political will of the American people cannot be "represented" by such naive synecdoches.

Yet, at the same time, Publius insists that his constitutional creations—Congress, President, Court—*do* "represent" the People in some other, nonsynecdochical, way. If we are to understand the Federalists' hopes for American government, we must be clear about the sense of "representation" Publius has in mind.

Beyond Mimesis

Reflect more generally upon the idea of representation—the process by which one thing is made to "stand for" another. A thought experiment: Imagine you were planning a long and hazardous journey and wanted to commission a painting which would "represent" you to your loved ones in your absence. Two options are open. On the one hand, you may find somebody with photographic aspirations. Her effort at mimetic representation will have familiar advantages and disadvantages. Precisely because it tries to present a realistic copy of your appearance, it is easy for others to read at a glance. For the very same reason, the snapshot will be unsatisfactory. Perhaps an artist who self-consciously appreciates that he *cannot* reduce your living reality to a piece of paper, that he is *only* making a representation, will provide a portrait which, though less realistic, will convey a deeper meaning to its viewers. Call this semiotic representation, because it communicates by self-consciously exploiting its audience's recognition that the picture is only a symbol and not the thing the symbol symbolizes.*

---

*This paragraph has been written in a way that gives maximal credibility to the mimetic aspiration. By defining semiosis as requiring self-conscious exploitation of the "audience's recognition that the picture is only a symbol and not the thing which the symbol symbolizes," I have left open the possibility that mimetic representation does not involve a similar form of symbolic self-consciousness. Like many others, I do not believe that this naive mimetic claim can withstand scrutiny. See, for example, Arthur

Publius adopts the semiotic understanding in his effort to "represent" the people of the United States by means of a written text—the Constitution. There can be no hope of capturing the living reality of popular sovereignty during normal politics. The text does not aim for phony realism by allowing you to suppose that Congress *is* the People. It provides a picture of government which vigorously asserts that Congress is merely a "representation" of the People, not the real thing itself.

And what better way to do this than by proliferating the number and kind of "representative" institutions within the constitutional ensemble? Thus, the House "represents" the People in one way, by direct election of all citizens; the Senate "represents" the People in another, by giving the power of selection to state legislatures; the Presidency "represents" the People in yet another, by means of the Electoral College. By manipulating the term of office and constitutional function of each "representative," the system endows each with virtues the others lack. Thus, the House will have an incentive to reflect every perturbation of popular opinion; the Senate will have a capacity for knowledgeable judgment; the President, energy and decisiveness. When these "representatives" disagree, each will predictably invoke its special virtues to support its claim to be acting for the public good.[40]

If, however, Publius is successful, the other "representatives" will not respond by ceding power to the assertive branch, but will resist and say that *they* speak for the People, and so forth. The result will be the opposite of each protagonist's hopes. The exchange of claim and counterclaim between House, Senate, and President will only emphasize the problematic character of each branch's effort to represent the People in some simplistic, synecdochical way. *No small group can ever be transubstantiated into the People by virtue of legal form. The constitutional forms are only a device to ameliorate the unavoidable evils of normal politics.* If normal political actors can

---

Danto, *The Transformation of the Commonplace* 1–32, 54–89 (1981). I think that mimesis is best defined as the effort to *suppress* the interpreter's self-conscious recognition that the symbol is not really the thing symbolized, while semiosis conveys meaning by *provoking* the interpreter's recognition of the symbol's symbolic character. But it is not necessary to go this far to support the claims made in the text.

somehow be induced to undermine each other's pretensions to speak in the commanding voice of the People, this would be the best way of representing the true state of affairs: *"the total exclusion of the people in their collective capacity"* during periods of normal politics.

But the rhetorical pattern of affirmation and negation exchanged in Washington, D.C., is only a part of a larger whole that includes the individual states. Federalism is another powerful technique for problematicizing representation. Consider Publius's response to his opponents' charge that he is not a "Federalist"[41] but a nationalist who aims for nothing less than the *"consolidation* of the States" into a single center.[42]

Publius does not respond by confessing his nationalism, nor by establishing that he is a federalist in the classic sense used by his opponents.[43] Instead, he urges us to look at his Constitution from multiple perspectives—beginning with the way it will be ratified; then observing how the House, Senate, and President will be selected; then considering how the center's powers will be defined and administered; then glancing at the manner of constitutional amendment. This tour will show that it is impossible to say whether the whole is "really" national or federal. The matter depends entirely on one's angle of vision. His triumphant conclusion:

> The proposed Constitution . . . is in strictness neither a national nor a federal Constitution; but a composition of both. In its foundation it is federal, not national; in the sources from which the ordinary powers of the government are drawn, it is partly federal, and partly national; in the operation of these powers, it is national, not federal; in the extent of them, again, it is federal, not national; and finally in the authoritative mode of introducing amendments, it is neither wholly federal, nor wholly national.[44]

By multiplying perspectives, Publius deflates the claims of normal officials sitting either in Washington *or* in the states to speak for the People. Each official effort is just one of a number of competing representations. The People, in contrast, reveal themselves only through an amendment process that can best be categorized negatively—"neither wholly federal, nor wholly national." Then, but only then, can we begin to hear the irregular, but public-spirited and rational, voice of the citizenry, deliberating and deciding on fundamental principle as they did during the conventions of the Revolutionary era.

Yet, while Publius begins his sketch by emphasizing that government is normally only a representation of the People, he does not end there. After all, there are many ways of representing something—whether that something be an absent lover or an absent People. And Publius is determined to design a system that, given the available human materials, will do as good a job as possible in re-presenting the kind of public-spirited deliberation that the People themselves can attain only during rare constitutional crises that "repress the passions." How, then, to proceed with this ambitious project in constitutional design?

Constitutional Science

Not by traveling down the path smoothed by so many other revolutionaries. All too often, the revolutionary vanguard has responded to the threat of faction by monopolizing power on a permanent basis. So far as they are concerned, *they* were the heroes who had risked their lives for the People when it really counted. If, then, one wishes to re-present these great moments of communal effort, why not authorize these heroes to rule forever on the basis of their past revolutionary virtue?

No, says Publius in No. 10, with an analysis that has won a permanent place in the annals of human freedom. Such authoritarian cures are "worse than the disease," destroying the personal liberty that is one of the greatest achievements of the American Revolution. Rather than succumbing to the delusions of revolutionary elitism, the *Federalist* insists that all principal officials trace their authority, directly or indirectly, to a regular system of popular elections.[45] The crucial question is how to organize the electoral system so that, despite the realities of faction, winners may be encouraged to govern in the deliberative, public-spirited way exemplified by the People meeting in constitutional convention during their finest revolutionary hour.

The Anatomy of Faction

To make progress here, we must examine Publius's theory of faction more closely. Thus far, I have been content to describe Publius's concern in general terms: during normal times, groups will form on the basis of passion or interest to use state power at the expense of the rights of other citizens and the permanent interests of the community. It is time to make some necessary distinctions.[46] In Publius's description, factions acting out of "passion" look different from those acting out of "interest."

As No. 10 explains, "passionate" factions come in two basic varieties:

> A zeal for different opinions concerning religion, concerning government, and many other points, as well of speculation as of practice; an attachment to different leaders ambitiously contending for pre-eminence and power; or to persons of other descriptions whose fortunes have been interesting to the human passions, have, in turn, divided mankind into parties, inflamed them with mutual animosity, and rendered them much more disposed to vex and oppress each other than to co-operate for their common good.[47]

Adapting today's usage, I will call the factions described in the first clause *ideological* and the ones described subsequently *charismatic.**

Though these two may look very different from one another, they have one important similarity: "passionate" factions won't have much staying power. Publius's point is not that passions are intermittently

---

*Of course, nothing prevents a faction from being ideological and charismatic at the same time, since the first term describes a group's program and the second, its leaders. Indeed, such an ideological/charismatic combine begins to look similar to the one Publius represents: are not the Federalists themselves a group who are proposing, with Washington at their head, a "different opinion concerning Government"?

See how tightly Publius's famous arguments in No. 10 interlock with the themes we have explored previously. Since the Federalists have a novel political program and many attractive leaders, Publius's argument requires him to explain why they are not merely trying to "inflame" their fellow citizens "with mutual animosity." Though Publius doesn't try to do this within the short space of No. 10, the other Papers we have explored demonstrate that he is very much aware of the need to do so; and that his effort yields a dualistic theory of political life.

expressed in politics. Indeed, when "no substantial occasion presents itself, the most frivolous and fanciful distinctions have been sufficient to kindle their [the citizenry's] unfriendly passions and exercise their most violent conflicts."[48] His point is that particular passionate factions will have a short half-life—popular leaders will die, ideological zeal will ebb as well as flow. This will prove important later on[49]— it helps explain the importance Publius gives to the separation of powers. Checking and balancing will take time, bursting many factional bubbles in the process.

In contrast, factions grounded in "interest" will be more durable: these are based on the "various and unequal distributions of property."[50] Once again, Publius divides this category into two: those emphasizing the "variety" of economic interests and those emphasizing economic "inequality." The first look like the interest groups of modern pluralism: landowners, manufacturers, merchants, bankers, and the rest compete with one another to use government power for their narrow advantage. The second sort of faction looks like our modern egalitarians—championing the interests of the poor against the propertied. Publius thinks both are bad—he is neither a proto-pluralist nor a proto-redistributionist. He is a successful revolutionary with an eighteenth-century, not a twentieth-century, agenda. Whatever modern Americans may think, *he* speaks for a People of white male merchants and planters, farmers and mechanics who fought a Revolution for life, liberty, and property—but not for the end of slavery or the triumph of the welfare state.

At a later point, these differences in constitutional values will be crucial.[51] For now, I want to bracket them in search of remaining commonalities: though many of Publius's constitutional values are different from ours, we can still learn from his anxiety at the prospect that factions will endanger the principles that prior generations had put into higher law after so much public-spirited effort. How, then, to use the Constitution to prevent faction from subverting the will of the People?

Transcending Faction

Here is where No. 10's famous challenge to Montesquieu enters. The great political scientist thought republics should be small.

Publius thinks they should be big—because deliberative and public-spirited representative government is more likely in the large republic.

For two reasons. The first is that revolutionary heroes, and men like them, will be more likely to win popular elections in big republics.[52] Since deliberative assemblies can't get too large, a big republic implies big election districts. This puts people like Publius at a relative advantage. In small districts, factional types will find it easier to mix bribery, friendship, and narrow appeals to local prejudice and interest to gain victory. With big districts, voters will be obliged to look beyond their immediate neighborhood; their gaze will be "more likely to center on men who possess the most attractive merit, and the most diffusive and established characters."[53] If things work as Publius hopes, the large-district system will operate "to refine and enlarge the public views by passing them through the medium of a chosen body of citizens, whose wisdom may best discern the true interest of their country and whose patriotism and love of justice will be least likely to sacrifice it to temporary or partial considerations."[54]

Publius doesn't let his hopes get in the way of his head. He is perfectly aware that bigness is only one of a host of factors that will affect the quality of representatives—hence the probabilistic way in which he makes his point: the voters are "more likely to center" on the best and the brightest patriots in bigger districts. Prospects look a bit brighter when one recalls that "[i]f a faction consists of less than a majority, relief is supplied by the republican principle, which enables the majority to defeat its sinister views by regular vote."[55]

Nonetheless, Publius places more weight on a second argument in praise of bigness:

> Extend the sphere, and you take in a greater variety of parties and interests; you make it less probable that a majority of the whole will have a common motive to invade the rights of other citizens; or if such a common motive exists, it will be more difficult for all who feel it to discover their own strength, and to act in unison. Besides other impediments, it may be remarked that, where there is a consciousness of unjust or dishonorable purposes, communication is always checked by distrust in proportion to the number whose concurrence is necessary.[56]

Passion against interest, interest against interest, passion against . . .
—in numberless combination. Notice that Publius does *not* favor
big government because he wants it to express the shifting balance
of passion and interest in the polity. To the contrary: the proliferation
of factions will allow the constitutional architect to make creative
use of the old tactic of divide and conquer. While each faction will
wish to oppress citizens outside its particular orbit of concern, different factions will be pushing the government in competing, and
mutually inconsistent, directions. This may give elected representatives maneuvering room to transcend faction, rather than mimic it—
that is, if Publius's first argument is working, and bigness is operating
to get enough public-spirited candidates into power. In later Papers,
Publius also tries to show how the different institutional perspectives
supplied by House, Senate, President, and Court enable the deliberative whole to be more reflective and public-spirited than any one
of its parts.[57]

When things are going well, then, Americans will not see their
representatives mimicking the shifting balance of power amongst the
competing factions. Instead of mimesis, there will be semiosis. Despite the factions swirling around the periphery, the center of the
stage will present a picture of We the People in action: a group of
public-spirited representatives engaging in the kind of deliberation
that the people themselves can achieve only in rare circumstances
which "suppress the passions."

Fail-safe Mechanisms

But, as Publius is well aware, things will not always go well. Even
at his most triumphant, he cannot suppose that the separation of
powers will inexorably achieve its intended aim:

> In the extended republic of the United States, and among the great
> variety of interests, parties and sects which it embraces, a coalition of
> the majority of the whole society could *seldom* take place on any other
> principles than those of justice and the general good . . . [Emphasis
> supplied][58]

Seldom is not never. The artful distribution of lawmaking powers
between House and Senate, Congress and the President is no guarantee of public-spirited deliberation. Surely, then, it is best to design

some back-up mechanisms into the system? Even when factional strife is on the rise, the separation of powers may provide a more modest, but crucial function. At least each branch may check the factional aims of the others:

> [T]he great security against a gradual concentration of the several powers in the same department consists in giving to those who administer each department the necessary constitutional means and personal motives to resist encroachments of the others. The provision for defence must in this, as in all other cases, be made commensurate to the danger of attack. Ambition must be made to counteract ambition. The interest of the man must be connected with the constitutional rights of the place. It may be a reflection on human nature that such devices should be necessary to control the abuses of government. But what is government itself but the greatest of all reflections on human nature? If men were angels, no government would be necessary. If angels were to govern men, neither external nor internal controls on government would be necessary. In framing a government which is to be administered by men over men, the great difficulty lies in this: you must first enable the government to control the governed; and in the next place, oblige it to control itself. A dependence on the people is no doubt the primary control on the government; but experience has taught mankind the necessity of auxiliary precautions.[59]

Do not overread this great dark passage. Publius is serious in describing the checking role of the separation of powers as "auxiliary." Indeed, this famous passage comes at the end of the very argument in which Publius earlier recognized that "a constitutional road to the people, ought to be marked out, and kept open, for certain great and extraordinary occasions."[60] It is only after emphasizing, for reasons we have canvased,[61] why "the people" cannot plausibly be expected to transcend faction under *normal* conditions that Publius brings in the separation of powers as an "auxiliary precaution." However important checks and balances may be, the system ultimately relies on the People's capacity to organize themselves in times of crisis for mobilized deliberation and decision.

Judicial Review

But is there a final "precaution" that might strengthen the constitutional forms at moments of factional vulnerability? Can't we design an institution that gives incentives to its incumbents to intervene on the side of the Revolutionary generation when factional leaders assault the People's earlier constitutional achievements?

Here is where the judges enter. When Publius takes up the Supreme Court late in the series of Papers, he treats it for what it is—just another institutional implication of the general theory of dualistic politics that has been developed throughout. When factional politicians break through constitutional constraints, the judges should invalidate their proposed statutes and expose them for what they are: mere stand-ins for *"the people themselves."* Only the People can change the Constitution, and the judges must prevent Congress from making basic changes unilaterally:

> Nor does this conclusion by any means suppose a superiority of the judicial to the legislative power. It only supposes that the power of the people is superior to both, and that where the will of the legislature, declared in its statutes, stands in opposition to that of the people declared in the Constitution, the judges ought to be governed by the latter rather than the former.[62]

The problem with this argument is obvious enough. What is to prevent the Court from abusing its power to interpret the Constitution? Rather than seeking to preserve the achievements of the Revolutionary generation, why won't the Justices use their power to further one or another factional interest?

Publius's optimism is based on a realistic assessment of the Court's position: "beyond comparison the weakest of the three departments of power."[63] Without control over "the sword or the purse," it must "depend upon the aid of the executive arm even for the efficacy of its judgments."[64] Given these facts, he thinks it silly to suppose that the Justices could successfully endanger "the general liberty of the people." The danger is just the reverse: despite their life tenure, they will be unduly timid when a master politician somehow induces our so-called representatives to betray the People's constitutional commands. In elaborating this danger, Publius invites us to reflect again on the dualistic foundations of his entire enterprise. Despite the fame of Publius's treatment of judicial review, this passage is rarely treated with the attention it deserves:

This independence of the judges is equally requisite to guard the Constitution and the rights of individuals from the effects of those ill humours which the arts of designing men, or the influence of particular conjunctures, sometimes disseminate among the people themselves, and which, though they speedily give place to better information, and more deliberate reflection, have a tendency, in the meantime, to occasion dangerous innovations in the government, and serious oppressions of the minor party in the community. Though I trust the friends of the proposed constitution will never concur with its enemies in questioning that fundamental principle of republican government which admits the right of the people to alter or abolish the established Constitution whenever they find it inconsistent with their happiness; yet it is not to be inferred from this principle that the representatives of the people, whenever a momentary inclination happens to lay hold of a majority of their constituents incompatible with the provisions in the existing constitution, would, on that account, be justifiable in a violation of those provisions; or that the courts would be under a greater obligation to connive at infractions in this shape than when they had proceeded wholly from the cabals of the representative body. Until the people by some solemn and authoritative act, annulled or changed the established form, it is binding upon themselves collectively, as well as individually; and no presumption, or even knowledge of their sentiments, can warrant their representatives in a departure from it prior to such an act. But it is easy to see that it would require an uncommon portion of fortitude in the judges to do their duty as faithful guardians of the Constitution, where legislative invasions of it had been instigated by the major voice of the community.[65]

This passage provides a wonderful summary of all the themes we have rehearsed: Publius's dualistic understanding of the People, his semiotic concept of representation, and his complex analysis of faction interact to yield a distinctive view of the Court's responsibilities. Thus, such texts will seem utterly antidemocratic to those who fail to recognize that, for Publius, the People convene only under rare circumstances that "repress the passions."[66] Since these monistic democrats[67] fail to make qualitative judgments about popular will formation, they will read Publius's concession that "the legislative invasions . . . had been instigated by the major voice of the community" as fatal to the democratic exercise of judicial review.

In contrast, we have seen that Publius emphasizes that the Constitution is trying to re-present a People which normally does not exist—a People both mobilized and capable of sober deliberation. Given this semiotic understanding, it is not undemocratic to recognize that officials *fail* to represent the People when they yield to those "ill humors" which, "though they speedily give place to better information and more deliberate reflection, have a tendency in the meantime, to occasion dangerous innovations in the government, and serious oppressions of the minor party in the community."

Further, Publius's analysis of faction in No. 10 provides the political science needed to motivate the belief that some "ill humors" will indeed be temporary. Recall that, in addition to the "durable" factions based on economic interest, No. 10 suggests that factions based on "passion"—those I called charismatic or ideological—will often have little staying power. Hence Publius's call to the Court to resist "the arts of designing men, or the influence of particular conjunctures" is hardly a piece of *ad hoc*-ery. He has already provided reason to believe that, if the public is given adequate opportunity for reflection, some factional coalitions will fail to sustain popular support.

Yet, for all this, Publius has no inclination whatever to deny that there will be times when the People can and should get into the act. To the contrary: the very point of his Papers is to establish that one such time is NOW. Thus, the same text that emphasizes the need for sober second thought also twits his Anti-Federalist opponents for "questioning the fundamental principle . . . which admits the right of the people to alter or abolish the established constitution whenever they find it inconsistent with their happiness." In making this remark, Publius is building on more elaborate foundations developed earlier. Recall his explicit vindication of the Convention's authority to violate "the established constitution" by taking an end run around the existing legislatures and proposing ratification by nine of thirteen state conventions. Rather than denying the possibility of popular sovereignty, he is proudly insisting that the Federalists have *earned* the authority to call the People to act decisively in convention to safeguard their great revolutionary achievements before they are eroded by the passions and interests of normal politics.

Even if Publius turns out to be successful, the passage once again emphasizes that the Federalists have not spoken the final word on behalf of the People. In speculating about the future of constitutional politics, Publius's advice to the judges is cautious: be skeptical when "representatives" claim to know that the People support their projects in constitutional transformation; continue to resist "[u]ntil the people have by some solemn and authoritative act annulled or changed the established form."

"Solemn and authoritative." Note the absence of a very important word: legal. Publius does not say that the judges should resist until the transformative movement satisfies all the *legal rules* for constitutional amendment that are contained in his new Constitution. He leaves open the relationship between these new rules and the kinds of "solemn and authoritative" action that should convince the judges. This failure to insist on strict legality makes sense, of course, given Publius's own frank confessions that the Philadelphia Convention's own actions are illegal.[68]

We will have abundant reason to recall Publius's silence on this score as we investigate the great constitutional achievements of later generations of Americans. During both Reconstruction and the New Deal, the Court recognized that the People had spoken even though their political leaders refused to follow the technical legalities regulating constitutional amendment.[69] Legalities aside, Publius expresses a deeper concern. He is doubtful that the judges will prove steadfast enough to oppose factional leaders who demand constitutional change in the absence of deep and considered support among the People. Instead of awaiting "solemn and authoritative" actions that evidence considered popular support, the judges may cave in too quickly: "it is easy to see that it would require an uncommon portion of fortitude . . ." Only time would tell whether Publius's anxieties were justified.

Some Concluding Questions

We have come full circle: from Publius's description of the special character of his generation's exercise in constitutional politics, to his effort to shape the future of normal politics through constitutional science, to his advice to the Court as he contemplates future efforts to mobilize the People for authoritative acts of constitutional creation. Now that we have glimpsed the course of a Publian life cycle, a few questions may help prepare the way for further exploration.

The Causal Question

Begin with Publius as prophet. Though the *Federalist* is littered with predictions that have been falsified by history, Publius's grim theory of constitutional transformations isn't one of them. The two most sweeping in our history have indeed occurred "in the midst of danger" that raised the "general alarm." The Reconstruction Republicans won the constitutional authority to break with the Federalist past only after a war of unprecedented sacrifice; the New Deal Democrats gained a comparable authority only after an economic disaster of unprecedented intensity and duration. At least at the level of regime change, there is something to Publius's point: wrenching social crisis has been instrumental in leading masses of Americans to support efforts to move beyond normal politics and articulate new principles of constitutional identity.

If we turn to constitutional movements that have had an important, but somewhat less sweeping, impact on constitutional values and structures, the causal story is richer. The civil rights movement of the modern republic, the women's suffrage movement of the middle republic, the Jeffersonian and Jacksonian "revolutions" of the early republic all serve as important examples of successful constitutional politics. None was precipitated by crises on the scale of the Civil War or Great Depression. We must surely move beyond Publius's "crisis" theory to gain an adequate understanding of the causes of American constitutional politics.

The Translation Question

Lots of people since Publius have noticed that modern political life is characterized by bursts of popular involvement. Publius is distinctive, however, in the way his response eludes familiar dichotomies. On the one hand, he is no hard-line conservative. He denies that these intermittent infusions of mass energy need fuel a nightmare politics in which demagogic elites cynically compete to channel mass irrationality to achieve evil and selfish ends. He sees these episodes of revolutionary engagement as the moments of great constitutional achievement—our higher law.

On the other hand, Publius is no knee-jerk partisan of the mob. His theory of faction emphasizes the possibility of mass irrationality—where people get carried away by charisma or ideology, or both, to do serious damage to the community as a whole or to minority rights. Rather than glorifying the fluidity and excitement of the revolutionary moment as an end in itself, he is a rationalist: "it is the reason, alone, of the public, that ought to control and regulate the government. The passions ought to be controlled and regulated by the government."[70]

This joint commitment to reason *and* popular mobilization[71] leads Publius to emphasize the role of institutions in separating the demagogue from the statesman, the mob from the People. We saw him urging the Supreme Court to resist initial assaults on received constitutional principles so as to give the People time to collect their thoughts and energies for the "solemn and authoritative" act appropriate for a considered change in constitutional fundamentals. More generally, he insists that "a constitutional road to the people, ought to be marked out, and kept open, for certain great and extraordinary occasions."[72] It is this road, and what has and may become of it, which will be an abiding concern here: How to organize a process of public reasoning between the mass of Americans and their political representatives so as to identify those occasions when a movement has *earned* the authority to speak in the higher lawmaking voice of We the People?

Call this the *translation question*—since it inquires into the appropriate conditions under which American institutions have translated, and should translate, the excited rhetoric of constitutional politics into the considered judgments of constitutional law. What kind of institutional tests should Americans impose on a political movement before it is conceded higher lawmaking authority? Why should the achievements of constitutional politics have a special place in our political arrangements?

I will take up each of these questions in turn in later chapters.[73]

Deliberation and Preservation

But it is important to remember that there is another side to the neo-Federalist story: normal politics. In his approach to this subject, Publius is an unashamed partisan of public-spirited deliberation. Just as he hopes to marry mass energy with reasoned deliberation in constitutional politics, so too he aims to encourage a deliberative spirit in the more factional environment of normal politics. To borrow Cass Sunstein's happy formula,[74] the maximal goal here should be *deliberative democracy:* try to design a system that both encourages the election of "enlightened statesmen" and gives them incentives to govern according to their conscientious definition of the public interest.

Publius is, however, appropriately cautious in his expectations. He has a minimal goal that falls far short of his maximum. Here the aim is *preservationist.* "[E]nlightened statesmen will not always be at the helm":[75] let's make it tough for factionalists to undermine the constitutional solutions already reached in the name of the People. How successfully has the Constitution discharged these goals—both maximal and minimal—over two centuries of transformation?

This too is a question that deserves a chapter of its own.[76]

The Economy of Virtue

Consider, finally, the single theme that unites the diverse aspects of the Publian enterprise, as we have come to understand it. In response to the perception that public-regarding deliberation is in short supply, the *Federalist* proposes a democratic constitution *that tries to economize on virtue.*

The first great economy is, of course, purchased by the distinction between constitutional and normal politics. The second is gained by a scheme of representation that gives each popularly elected official incentives to engage in public-spirited deliberation despite the proliferation of faction. The third seeks to provide fail-safe mechanisms by encouraging each representative to undercut the claim of the others to speak for the People during normal politics. The fourth economy establishes judicial review to uphold the integrity of earlier constitutional judgments against the centrifugal forces of faction.

In proposing a constitutional economy of virtue, Publius does not take a simple Hobbesian view of the human condition. His entire enterprise supposes a dualistic psychology:

> The supposition of universal venality in human nature is little less an error in political reasoning than the supposition of universal rectitude. The institution of delegated power implies that there is a portion of

virtue and honor among mankind, which may be a reasonable foundation of confidence.[77]

The task is to economize on virtue, not do without it altogether; to create a constitutional structure that will permit Americans, in both normal and extraordinary times, to make the most of the public spirit we have. Our success in continuing the conversation begun by Publius is ultimately to be measured by our success in pursuing this objective under very different historical circumstances. But not so different that the entire enterprise has lost its meaning?

CHAPTER EIGHT

The Lost
Revolution

TWENTIETH-CENTURY SKEPTICISM

THE FOUNDING was accompanied by an immense national dialogue—in pamphlets and newspapers, letters and diaries, Americans struggled to express their hopes and fears about self-government. Two centuries later, only the *Federalist* remains in general circulation. If I have been at all successful, perhaps you will pick up a paperback copy when you are next in a bookstore? Isn't it about time for you to encounter the Founding at first hand? Of course, the *Federalist* is only one of many such collections—albeit the most comprehensive and profound. Given the rich store of historical materials, a lifetime of intensive reading and reflection beckons.[1]

This will cause a problem for many Americans. While they may want to think through their relationship to the constitutional past, present, and future, they have lots of other projects—practical as well as intellectual. They simply don't have the time, energy, or interest to become professional historians of the eighteenth century. They want to be knowledgeable citizens, not professors. It is not too much to ask such people to spend a few evenings with the *Federalist,* seeing whether it does serve as a profound introduction to dualistic democracy. But it is too much to ask them to dedicate their lives to intensive readings of many other worthwhile Founding texts.

I suggest a different course—one that invites you to deepen your understanding of the eighteenth century by taking a detour through the twentieth. Modern historians have made immense contributions to our understanding of the Founding—generating insights that might evade the most heroic autodidact. I propose, then, to deepen our initial encounter with Federalist thought by turning to images of the Founding contributed by modern scholarship. To what extent do they support the dualist interpretation? To what extent do they challenge it?

The answer requires us to reflect on one of the slipperiest words in the modern political vocabulary: revolution. I have been presenting Publius as a successful revolutionary, giving a distinctively dualistic answer to a crucial question: How to reconstruct political order after destroying the ancien régime? In contrast, a great deal of modern scholarship proceeds from a different premise. It treats Publius as an enemy of the American Revolution, not its friend. As a result, I expect some scholars to greet my dualist interpretation with skepticism: Isn't it naive to take Publius at his word when he so loudly protests his revolutionary ardor? Doesn't Publius come to bury the American Revolution, not to praise it?

This predictable response, I suggest, has less to do with "the facts" than one might suppose. The scholars who call Publius counterrevolutionary do so mostly because they have a different concept of revolution, not because they have a different idea of "the facts." To make my case, I distinguish two concepts of revolution which frame competing images of the Founding. Having clarified the conceptual confusion, we shall see that much modern scholarship supports the dualist interpretation.

Before we proceed with the conceptual argument, a bit of historical background into its origins may be illuminating. After all, during the nineteenth century, Americans had no trouble recognizing Publius as a successful revolutionary. Indeed, they endlessly contrasted their own successful Revolution with the sad failures of the Europeans to make a decisive break with entrenched despotisms.[2] While this orgy of self-congratulation was laced with distasteful Schadenfreude, it kept the revolutionary character of the American Founding at the forefront of the public mind. Only in the twentieth century did the image of the counterrevolutionary Publius come to the fore.

The second decade of the century marked a crucial turning point. This is the decade of Charles Beard's *Economic Interpretation of the Constitution.*[3] On his view, the Framers' secret meetings and illegal procedures were but the outward sign of a harsh truth: our Constitution was a counterrevolutionary document, deviously imposed upon the revolutionary masses by a propertied elite. His work tried to strip away the Founders' rhetoric to reveal the conflicting class interests that lay beneath. Beard's initial explorations inspired an entire generation of Progressive historians, who sought to establish that the Framers' masquerade in the name of the "People" was nothing but a bad joke. For them, the really interesting question was why the Federalists were so much more successful as counterrevolutionaries than were their hapless counterparts in Paris and Moscow.

But Beard's book was hardly the only event that spurred reappraisal during the second decade of the century. The First World War and the Russian Revolution set new terms for national self-understanding. The shattering success of the Communists reinforced the agonizing reappraisal already going on in intellectual circles: If the Bolsheviks were entitled to call themselves "real" revolutionaries, perhaps the Founders *were* the counterrevolutionaries the Progressive historians said they were?

This question resonated more deeply with the passing decades. After the Second World War catapulted America to the center of the world stage, the triumph of the Chinese Communists emphasized how far the forces of revolution had strayed from the early days of the American Republic. The public symbolism of the time cast America as the leading counterrevolutionary power, engaged in an epic struggle with a worldwide Marxist insurgency threatening to destroy the liberal West.

For all this, a more positive image of revolutionary achievement runs deep in our tradition. Although I am bad at crystal ball gazing, the time seems ripe for its reassertion, beginning with the Founding. Certainly, the intellectual scene has changed a lot since Progressive historians confidently expected hardheaded analysis of the economic data to reveal that the struggle over the Constitution had systematically set the masses against the classes. By the 1950's, most historians became convinced that a state-by-state canvas of the data did not support this simple-minded story.[4] By the 1960's, the main line of historical research began to take the ideas and debates of the Founding period with a most un-Beardian seriousness.[5]

As American historians were reappraising Beardian methods and metaphors, there was a much broader change in the direction of political thought throughout the West. The specter of Worldwide

Marxist Revolution has simply disintegrated. By the 1990's, it is hard to find intellectuals who seriously believe that Communist revolution is, or ought to be, the wave of the future—even in places, like Latin America, where Marxism has long provided the intellectual classes with their principal tools of analysis. For the first time since 1848, it is the liberal West that waits with great expectation for the revolutionary news from Warsaw and Prague. Will Moscow or Peking be next? South Africa or Cuba? The specter of revolution is, once again, haunting Europe and the world—but it seems closer to the liberal spirit of Philadelphia than Americans had expected during the Cold War.

It is too soon to say what will come of all this. At the very least, it should lead to a thoroughgoing critique of Beard's image of Publius as a counterrevolutionary.

TWO CONCEPTS OF REVOLUTION

Try to separate two different ideas of revolution jumbled together in modern usage. The first looks upon revolution as a social phenomenon. In the familiar Marxist interpretation, the crucial question is what happens to the class structure: only if a new class gains control over the means of production has a "real" revolution occurred; otherwise, there was much ado about nothing. This Marxist view has been enormously influential; Beardianism itself can be seen as a quasi-indigenous variation. Nonetheless, Marxism does not have a monopoly over the social interpretation. One may reject an emphasis on the means of production and yet insist that the revolutionary character of a transformation be measured by other social indicators: power within the family, between the races, and so forth. When the Founding is viewed from such perspectives, skeptical doubts about its revolutionary character abound. In many ways, the Founding Federalists were fighting a rearguard battle against social forces that would dominate nineteenth-century life.[6]

Things look different if the key to revolution is the political consciousness of the engaged participants. On this political interpretation, the crucial question is the extent to which a revolution inspires large numbers of people to invest their energies and identities in the collective process of political redefinition. So long as people treat revolutionary politics as a sideline, incidental to the main business of life, no "real" revolution is going on. If large numbers come to take revolutionary politics with deep seriousness, this transformation in political consciousness marks out a distinctive revolutionary reality, regardless of the polity's success in transforming one or another social relationship.

If Marx provides the archetype for the social interpretation, Hannah Arendt is the preeminent modern spokesman for the political view. She does not value revolution for its social consequences, but for its transformative impact upon the modern political consciousness. As we shall see, it will be perilous to treat Arendt, any more than Marx, as the last word on these matters. Nonetheless, her book *On Revolution*[7] is a genuinely profound work, which locates the American Founding within a political, rather than a social, interpretation of revolution. Since there is a need to redress the balance between the two interpretations, Arendt's work provides the obvious starting point.

ARENDT, AND BEYOND

The modern West, Arendt suggests, has been quite unoriginal in its basic political vocabulary: much of our talk about democracy, representative government, and individual freedom goes back thousands of years. But not when we talk revolution. The claim that an entire People might plausibly break with its past, and construct a new political identity for itself, is something genuinely new—though, of course, it could not have been built without preexisting cultural materials. Most proximately, the Christian West already believed itself capable of making a fundamental break with its past through a belief in Christ. The coming of the Savior marked a revolutionary event, breaking time in two—allowing Christians to believe that their self-understanding was, in principle, superior to the greatest of the heathens and Jews who lived before the great divide. There is an obvious difference, however, in the mechanism through which the American and French revolutionaries broke with their past. No longer would the divine hand mark out the terms of the new beginning. Ordinary human beings now claimed the authority to define, debate, and transform their received political tradition.

This revolutionary claim permitted a new sense of the special dignity of political life. Revolutionary politics presented itself as a special domain of meaningful action, whose significance could not be grasped in non-political terms—whether these be religious, economic, or psychological. Like any other ideal, this revolutionary promise of a "new beginning" could be distorted or degraded in numberless ways. The crucial point, for Arendt at least, was the way it provided modern Westerners with a new language of committed citizenship. After a millennium during which the meaning of political life was subordinated to Christian faith, the modern revolutionary might once again affirm a Greek-like sense of the independent value of politics—the intrinsic dignity and joy of engaging one's fellow citizens in an effort to define and achieve the political good.

Greek-like, but not Greek. While the classics were full of praise for citizenship, there was little suggestion that moments of political transformation brought out the best in the political animal. Even less classical is the modern revolutionary's belief that a nation might create something valuable by attempting a radical break with its past. For the Greek philosophers, the best polities owed their beginnings to mythic founders endowed with semi-divine insight and self-control; if your polity was lucky enough to have been graced with a Lycurgus or Solon, it would be foolhardy for you to join a bunch of latter-day citizens in an effort to transform your inheritance. The Greeks were, of course, familiar with drastic regime change. But they associated such breaks with political decline, not renewal and creation.

It is here where the first modern revolutions in America and France mark new ground. The special dignity of political life, the special promise of citizenship, resided in a revolutionary act of collective redefinition: the construction of a novo ordo seclorum. This fateful understanding is evident from the very first paragraph of the *Federalist Papers:*

It seems to have been reserved to the people of this country, by their conduct and example, to decide the important question whether societies of men are really capable or not of establishing good government from reflection and choice, or whether they are forever destined to depend for their political constitutions on accident and force. . . . [T]he crisis at which we are arrived may with propriety be regarded as the era in which that decision is to be made; and a wrong election of the part we shall act may, in this view, deserve to be considered as the general misfortune of mankind.[8]

This reassertion of the dignity of political action marked the American Founding, in Arendt's eyes, as the most successful revolutionary act of the modern era. After a generation of agitation against the pretensions of the Crown, Americans had done more than win the first guerrilla war of modern history. They had, time and again, entered the public forum to debate the nature of their "new beginning," and they had discovered that they actually loved this ongoing entry into public life, this great agon of collective self-definition that was revolutionary politics. With the Constitution, they proposed to give self-conscious structure to the great public stage they had built for themselves. Having learned to speak in the name of We the People, the Founding generation would provide their successors with a series of public spaces within which they too could learn to love the ongoing struggle for the common good.

Now Arendt finds lots to criticize in the details of the Founders' constitutional design. More important for us is her basic disagreement with Beard. Beardians are skeptical of the Founding because they embrace the social interpretation of revolution, and suspect the Federalists' class origins and aims. For Arendt, the true spirit of revolution has nothing to do with social outcomes, but with the rediscovery of the value of citizenship. Within this political interpretation, a group's claim to speak for "the People" cannot be impugned by a consideration of their social origins or program. The crucial question is whether the Founders successfully mobilized the inhabitants of the Eastern seaboard to break with their colonial past and win a new understanding of themselves as *American citizens,* proud of their revolutionary new beginning and determined to enable their posterity to enjoy this newfound sense of political meaning. On this interpretation, the revolutionary impulse is not conceived as antagonistic to the construction of constitutional order: *a Constitution is a natural culmination of a successful revolution.*

To put the point conceptually, Arendt challenges the way Beardians define their key political terms, and hence the way they relate them to one another. The "People," for Arendt, is not a name for the three-million-odd featherless bipeds who inhabited the Atlantic coast in 1787. Instead, the People consisted of those former colonists who had mobilized themselves politically to establish a new world of political meaning for themselves. Those who failed to join in this revolutionary work of communal self-definition were at best inhabitants of the United States, not real citizens.

The Beardian understands "the People" in a very different way—as represented by the Paris mob demanding bread, not the constitutional assembly deliberating on the public good. Once this paradigm shift is allowed, it becomes easy to impugn a constitution as counterrevolutionary even if it is deeply rooted in processes by which citizens came to understand themselves as citizens. So long as a constitution does not fulfill the social interests of the "People"—now meaning the mass of the population—it stands condemned as counterrevolutionary.

Of course, in order to make use of this social criterion, the Beardian critic must define the "true interests" of the masses. At its core, however, Arendt's protest does not involve the variety of tricky problems implicated by this effort to define "true interests." It is the very shift from a political to a social interpretation of revolution that serves as the crux of her critique.

This protest, in turn, motivates her effort to loosen the grip that the French Revolution has exercised upon the modern political imagination: "The sad truth of the matter is that the French Revolution, which ended in disaster, has made world history, while the American revolution, so triumphantly successful, has remained an event of little more than local importance."[9] If "real" revolutions are modeled on the French, they cannot end—for the most obvious historical reasons—with the triumphant construction of a political order by the revolutionary generation. Instead, the "real" revolutionary script runs along very different lines: tragedy, not triumph, as brave talk of a "new beginning" dissolves in the blood of the revolutionaries themselves. As the general citizenry sicken of the bloodbath, years of political struggle succeed in giving birth to modern bureaucratic dictatorship—in which a strongman, at the head of a bloodless bureaucracy, parodies the revolutionary ideals that inspired the original effort to break with the past.

If the French, and not the American, Revolution provides the model of a "real" revolution, only two attitudes remain plausible. One is self-consciously counterrevolutionary. After all, it's hard to keep up one's revolutionary ardor as one sees Napoleon and then Louis XVIII serve as the residuary legatees of the Declaration of the Rights of Man; and surely, a glimpse at political life under Lenin-Stalin-Brezhnev or Mao-Deng-? only reinforces this anxiety. The second approach sustains a positive attitude toward (French-style) revolutions, but at the cost of downplaying the political conception in favor of the social interpretation: Granted, the Revolution did not inaugurate a new world of political meaningfulness, but did it not transform social relations in progressive ways?

Once again, Marxism has served as the most influential apologetic. It famously views the French Revolution as the historical moment at which the bourgeoisie consolidated itself as the new hegemonic class. The bloodbaths and political disillusionments can then be seen as the "historically necessary" price of a great change in social relationships—a transformation which Marxists consider "progressive" in liberating the forces of nineteenth-century industrialization. This sets the stage for dismal Marxist apologies for Stalin, Mao, and countless two-bit totalitarians of the twentieth century. Politics may be reduced to a desert of dead slogans, bloodless bureaucracy, and mass murder—but consider, comrade, the "progressive" social consequences!

Writing in the early 1960's, Arendt takes this Marxist apologetic very seriously—undoubtedly because Marxism (in a proliferating variety of watered-down forms prophetic of decline?) remained a powerful, often an overwhelming, presence in many intellectual circles. And yet, did she, like so many others,[10] allow Marxism to distort her own affirmative vision?

I cannot resist this suspicion as I puzzle at Arendt's eager willingness to push her argument to absurd—or so it seems to me—extremes.[11] She is not content to reassert the political promise of revolution, nor to distinguish it from the social interpretation. She insists that the very effort by revolutionaries to place "the social question" on the political agenda inevitably destroys the sense of meaningful public participation created by the effort to construct a "new beginning." According to her, citizenship can thrive only if citizens do not try to use politics as a means for achieving economic and social ends.

This is the lesson she draws from the French Revolution. She holds that the Revolution destroyed itself by pandering to the needs of the Paris masses. Its focus on the "social question" debased it into a mere instrument for the satisfaction of the mob's desires for bread. Such needs are insatiable. Once the revolutionaries tried to satisfy them, they opened themselves up to a deadly bidding war between competing demagogues promising the masses bread, more bread. The revolutionary impulse exhausted itself as the Parisian mob learned to distrust the capacity of demagogues to deliver on their promises. Disappointed by the politics of welfare, diverted from the politics of citizenship, the masses turned away from the public space—leaving it to generals and bureaucrats who do not need the arts of citizenship to impose their will on an exhausted population.

A grim picture—and surely Arendt is right to insist that this modern nightmare can spring into life with awful consequences. My problem is with Arendt's necessitarianism—her claim that, once the "social question" is placed on the political agenda, revolutionary politics inevitably degenerates into demagogy and dictatorship. Obviously, such a strong conclusion cannot be established by pointing to the success of a Napoleon or a Stalin in catapulting himself to power by military-bureaucratic means after revolutionary agitation. The question is whether such a downward spiral is inevitable.

Consider America as a leading counterexample. From the "Revolution of 1800" led by Thomas Jefferson to the civil rights movement led by Martin Luther King, a concern for the "social question" has served as the principal engine for engaged public participation by the American people. Both in their successes and in their failures, all these social movements called out to their fellow Americans to transcend factional interest and respond to the call of the public good; in all of them, success was measured by the extent to which Americans entered into the public space to support the social vision offered up by committed activists; it is through these movements that Americans have tasted the special joys of citizenship that Arendt so eloquently evoked in her own work.

How sad, then, that Arendt's deep hostility to the "social question" blinded her to the civic significance of these movements in American history.* On her reading, the Founders led the last successful revo-

---

*Perhaps I am too hard on Arendt here? There are moments in her work when she

lutionary movement in the history of the Republic. Worse yet, her portrayal of the Founders is oddly truncated. She ignores the fact that the Federalists, no less than their successors, were intent on committing the American people to a social vision: their ideal of a large commercial republic has remained vital, but controversial, to the present day. She applauds the Federalists for refusing to use the Constitution to solve social problems—ignoring the way the Contract Clause, the Commerce Clause, and many other aspects of the Federalist Constitution codified the Founding affirmation of a market-oriented society. In her hands, the Federalists take on the frozen character of bad neo-classical statues. Bloodlessly staring out at us, they created a constitutional structure for a remarkably sterile politics—devoid of the social and economic concerns that have in fact inspired Americans to put aside their narrow self-interest and mobilize themselves for great political achievements.[12]

Something has gone wrong. And yet we should not allow Arendt's extreme views on the social question to blind us to two other aspects of *On Revolution*. The first is the recovery of the political meaning of revolution: the way in which men and women may reinvigorate their identity as citizens by calling upon one another to mark a "new beginning" in their political life together. Arendt's second point is a warning: do not succumb to the anachronistic temptation of using the French revolutionary experience of 1789–1815 as a model against which to measure the American experience of 1776–1789. Once we begin treating the French scenario as if it defined the inevitable course of "real" revolutions, then the Beardian move is all but inevitable. We will lose sight of the way in which the American Constitution was seen by its participants as culminating, rather than negating, their political experience as revolutionaries.

Indeed, so long as we do not go to Arendtian extremes, perhaps we can reformulate her cautionary point about social revolutions. While Arendt is wrong in suggesting that American revolutionaries—of the eighteenth, nineteenth, or twentieth centuries—have lacked a social and economic program, there is a distinctive character to the initiatives that have proved most successful. None of them envisioned

---

glimpses another view; see, e.g., Hannah Arendt, "Civil Disobedience," in Arendt, *Crises of the Republic* (1972). Nonetheless, she fails to integrate these passing insights into her general interpretation of American history.

a total revolution in social and economic relationships. Each has followed the Federalist example of revolutionary reform—proposing to use state power in limited, but strategic, ways to achieve fundamental, but partial, social and economic objectives.

As we shall see, even these exercises in revolutionary social reform placed immense strains on preexisting constitutional traditions. Especially during Reconstruction and the New Deal, the strains became so great that preexisting strands of the constitutional tradition visibly begin to unravel. At these moments of constitutional crisis, the ground rules themselves become the self-conscious object of revolutionary reform. The contestants glimpse the precipice: Had the nation emerged from Civil War only to fight again about the terms of Reconstruction? Would the country respond to the Great Depression by following Germany down the road to dictatorship? Rather than plunging down the path of total revolution, the response both times was revolutionary reform. Like the Federalists themselves, latter-day revolutionaries neither played by the old rules nor ripped up the entire institutional system in a show of disdain. They combined old ideas and institutions in new ways—ways that finally allowed them to gain wide acceptance of their claim that *the People themselves* have endorsed their transformative social initiatives.

Centuries of struggle over revolutionary reform—both social and political—have generated a distinctive legacy that must be preserved against two kinds of critique. On the one hand, it is easy for totalizing revolutionaries to condescend to the American experience. Even the achievements of the most successful generations seem so remarkably incomplete. Today's Americans continue to struggle with the structural inadequacies we have inherited from the Founding, the failed promises of racial equality we have inherited from Reconstruction, the inadequate protections against social injustice we have inherited from the New Deal. In the eyes of the totalizing revolutionary, these failures establish the inadequacy of partial reform. Let us move on and try to transform the entire system in a single blow!

On the other hand, it is too easy for traumatized exiles like Arendt to wring their hands at the very prospect of social reform, lest the revolutionary demand for utopia disintegrate into barbarism. Surely it is better to empty politics of all serious social content, lest we let the genie out of the bottle?

But American experience teaches a different lesson. Time and again, the great reform movements of our past have displayed the precious political capacity to shape partial, but deep-cutting, constitutional solutions in ways that finally win broad consent. However inadequate these triumphs may seem from the vantage of utopia, surely they will repay study as we struggle to make our own constitutional contribution?

WOOD, AND BEYOND

Arendt has, I think, won recognition as one of the most important thinkers of her generation. *On Revolution* is still on the shelves of "better bookstores everywhere" a quarter-century after its publication. Yet the book has had remarkably little impact on its most obvious audience: American historians and political scientists who make the Founding a principal academic concern. This is not because the field has been especially sleepy. To the contrary: Adair, Appleby, Bailyn, Banning, Dahl, Diamond, Diggins, McDonald, Morgan, Pocock, Robbins, Wiebe, Wills, White, Wood[13] are among the important scholars who have made genuine contributions over the last few decades. It is impossible to pick up a new book on the Founding without seeing the mark of these people on the final product. But it is easy to read book after book that gives no sign whatever of serious encounter with Arendt. Why?

Because American historians are still not prepared to confront her basic complaint about their work: "[i]t is odd indeed that twentieth-century American even more than European learned opinion is often inclined to interpret the American Revolution in the light of the French Revolution, or to criticize it because it so obviously did not conform to lessons learned from the latter."[14] In writing these lines, Arendt was challenging the Beardian predispositions of the American academy. When she published *On Revolution* in 1963, she had every reason to believe that her call for revision would gain a positive response. The 1950's had not been kind to Progressive preconceptions. Important work by Robert Brown and Forrest McDonald had convinced professional historians that the economic data simply did not support the simplistic "classes against the masses" view of the ratification struggle.[15] As the academy cast about for a new perspective, some leading scholars challenged the Beardian view of the

Founders as brilliant counterrevolutionaries. Were not the likes of Madison and Hamilton better conceived as "young men of the Revolution" who had reached an age where they could continue the revolutionary project of political construction begun by the older generation of Washingtons and Adamses?[16] Wasn't the Philadelphia Convention best seen as the greatest "reform caucus" in American history?[17] These suggestive essays were not written in the grand philosophico-historical style natural to a German refugee like Arendt, but they bespoke, in plain American prose, a similar appreciation of the Founders as political revolutionaries, and proud of it.

And yet, surprisingly little came of these exploratory reappraisals.[18] With the publication of Gordon Wood's great book of 1969, *The Creation of the American Republic,* the main line of historical research moved in a related, but different, direction.[19] Before identifying these differences, I want to emphasize how Wood's work supports my effort to view the Federalists as political revolutionaries struggling with the consequences of their success. First, and most important, his book takes political culture seriously. His six-hundred-page study does not contain a single statistical tabulation of the economistic kind. Instead, Wood undertakes a painstaking progress through the countless pamphlets, debates, and political artefacts left by Americans between 1776 and 1787. We are invited to locate ourselves in the distinctive symbolic universe of late-eighteenth-century America; to grasp the changing way in which Americans understood the nature of politics as they moved from the Declaration of Independence to the Founding. This interpretive method would make no sense if Wood looked upon political culture as a mere reflex of underlying economic and social "realities."

So much for the common methods that link Wood's work to my own. Turning to substance, I cannot do justice to Wood's sustained encounter with the rich legacy of popular debate left by the American revolutionaries—let alone the interpretive work that his example has inspired over the last generation. To suggest this scholarship's potential contribution to the neo-Federalist project,[20] I shall confront it with the framework the last chapter used to recover the dualistic aspirations of Federalist constitutional thought. Recall, then, the two-period schema that exposed the legitimation problem raised by all successful revolutions. Time One: a group of outsiders challenge the legal authority of the ins, proclaiming their superior dedication to the public good before irregular assemblies claiming to speak in the name of the People. Time Two: outsiders become insiders, and struggle with their revolutionary past as they seek to legitimate their present authority. How does Wood's book allow us to embed this schema, and the Federalists' response to it, into a rich account of the political languages and practices current in late-eighteenth-century America?

Time One, Contextualized

Wood's study does not begin with 1787, but 1776—which can serve as a rough-and-ready equivalent for Time One in my model. His initial aim is to recover the symbolic world which made revolution seem a sensible response to many Americans. This universe of meaning largely derived from the revolutionary struggles of Radical Whigs and Commonwealthmen of seventeenth-century England.

I shall strip Wood's rich account of this revolutionary legacy down to a very few elements.[21] The first is the basic Whig contrast between a corrupt, self-aggrandizing Court and a virtuous, yeoman Country. This contrast provided Americans with a diagnostic framework defining both the English threat and the revolutionary cure. Assertions of power by the metropole would not be judged on their particular merits and demerits. Whig ideology invited the colonists to view them as symptoms of corrupt central power which, if left unchecked, would culminate in the pathologies of despotism. Rather than passively await this fate, the Country should organize itself before it was too late. There was virtue in the yeomanry—so long as the self-aggrandizing center was not allowed to poison the well of civic goodness.

This Whig world view provided a remarkably straightforward answer to a crucial question defined by our simple two-period model: what gives would-be revolutionaries the authority to challenge the legally constituted powers that be? Because *they* are corrupt and *we* are virtuous—where "virtue" does not refer to some privatistic code but to the yeoman's capacity to put the public good over his own. The Radical Whig legacy also provided a rich storehouse of ideas through which revolutionary Americans could elaborate the substance of the public good that the corrupt center was threatening. For the present, I am not interested in describing these Lockean and Harringtonian ideas, or tracing the fascinating way this seventeenth century inheritance mixed with more modern notions coming from the Scottish Enlightenment into a complex and evolving whole.

It is more important to see how these revolutionary definitions of the public good, together with Whig ideas of the virtuous Country, interacted with a third feature: the American experience in self-government, then already 150 years old. This experience played a crucial role in providing the revolutionaries with the materials they needed to confront a final aspect of their problem: How to organize bodies that could *credibly* claim to represent the Country against the corrupt center despite the fact that these popular assemblies could not, in the nature of the case, drape themselves with the legal symbols that normally stabilize claims to political authority?

Most obviously, colonial self-government provided Americans with preexisting institutions—the colonial assemblies—that might serve as the springboard for a gradual break with the old legality: first the colonial assembly might engage in an escalating set of challenges to the Crown, then the *same assembly* might sometimes join the People by meeting in a tavern to issue "resolves," "recommendations," and the like, that gained public recognition as having something like the force of law.[22] More fundamentally, the tradition provided each of the colonies with a host of informal organizations, leaderships, political practices, that could serve as building blocks for the construction of new authorities that might *credibly* claim to speak for the Country against the tyrant. People already knew how to run elections; they already knew a lot about the self-proclaimed patriots competing for popular approval—these same men had been seen and heard for years (if not contending for such dominant positions) under the old regime. The disintegration of the old legality did not reveal a political vacuum—atomized egos struggling to impose themselves on one another without restraint or mutual recognition. It revealed *a People* capable of organizing their own political affairs—arguing, reacting, deciding—even as these citizens of America struggled for their political existence against the most formidable empire of the Old World.

This context allows us to locate a final Whig contribution to the emerging American political vocabulary: the idea that an illegal convention of virtuous citizens might speak in the People's name with an authority that had fundamental constitutional significance. The last chapter, already building on Wood's work,[23] emphasized how the Federalists moved beyond Whig precedents in promoting the supreme authority of the Convention. While eighteenth-century Whigs gloried in the achievements of the Convention of 1688, they did not claim that this convention's work had the force of law— insisting, instead, that the terms of the new constitutional settlement be reenacted by a perfectly legal Parliament.[24] In contrast, the Federalists asserted that an illegal convention could be a source not only of law, but of higher law.

This was by no means a Federalist innovation. Wood perceptively explores the complex ways this new understanding of popular conventions developed on the state level in the years immediately after the Declaration of Independence. As Americans deliberated over new constitutions in the states, the authority of revolutionary legislatures over the content of higher law became an increasingly contested matter. Building on their Whig inheritance, the dominant opinion in most places came to insist that the legislatures, as organs of normal government, had no business defining their own powers, that only a special convention of the People could lay down higher law.[25]

Time Two, Contextualized

The virtuous Country, defending the public good against the corruptions of power, by means of an illegal convention. Wood's account allows us to see the Federalists as they saw themselves: as successful revolutionaries, adapting ideas and institutions that had already become a part of their generation's experience, imagery, self-understanding. It also permits us to grasp the framework which enabled the Founders to provide dualistic solutions to some basic problems in constitutional government.

The first involved sovereignty. It was an elementary principle of eighteenth-century political science that every nation had to have one—and only one—sovereign. Who was ours? A flat-footed answer would endanger the entire enterprise. On the one hand, to proclaim

the national government as *the* sovereign would alienate large portions of the public committed to their state's political identity and
fearful of the prospect of centralizing tyranny. On the other hand,
to identify the state governments as unequivocal "sovereigns" undermined the point of the Federalist initiative—which was to construct a new central government that could wield limited, but substantial, power. The Federalists brilliantly saw that Radical Whig
ideology permitted a third answer: deny that any government should
be viewed as "sovereign"; insist that, in America, the only legitimate
sovereign was *the People,* who could delegate different powers to
different governments in any way that would serve the common
good.[26]

The fact that the Federalists shifted the locus of "sovereignty"
from government to the People is widely appreciated. Too often,
however, it is viewed as part of a legalistic shell game which allowed
the Founders to dispense with the notion of sovereignty entirely.[27]
Wood provides historical resources for a different understanding.
Rather than some lawyer's trick, the shift of sovereignty to the People
expressed a fundamental aspect of the Americans' revolutionary
experience: that it *was* possible for informal groups of Americans to
mobilize themselves for political action and redefine the aims and
nature of ordinary government.

This revolutionary redefinition of sovereignty allowed a second
conceptual innovation, involving the separation of powers. The idea
is a very ancient one. On the traditional understanding, however,
each of the separate powers represents a different constituent element in society. Thus, the House of Lords did not owe its place in
the English constitution to some functional analysis concerning its
likely contribution to the quality of decisionmaking; instead, it represented the lords as a distinct social estate, entitled to insist that its
corporate interests be protected as a constituent element of the
kingdom; and the same was true of the Crown. While it would have
been tough to create an American nobility in 1787,* it was a good

---

*Not that it was unthinkable. It was widely feared that the Society of the Cincinnati,
composed of officers of the Revolutionary army, harbored just such pretensions. In one
of his finest moments, George Washington opposed such a program, signaling his
republican commitments by chairing the Philadelphia Convention rather than presiding

deal easier to reconceive this traditional idea of the mixed constitution in terms of economic classes: insisting that any legislative proposal gain the assent of an upper house selected by citizens who satisfied a property requirement, as well as a lower house representing all citizens.[28]

But this is precisely the move the Federalists refused to make. They conceived the relationship between the branches and the People in a radically different way. Each branch of government was just that: a part of the government, not an organic expression of the People. Since the People expressed itself through revolutionary mobilization, it was impossible to predict the precise institutional route the next movement would take in exercising popular sovereignty.[29] No longer did the separation of powers provide an organic representation of the different classes of the People. Instead, it was now a device for problematicizing representation: Since *all* governmental power was potentially corrupting to the governors, the aim of constitutional design was to check and balance, to economize on the scarce supply of virtue likely to be available. The old idea of mixed government by the estates of the realm had been displaced by the revolutionary idea that governors should check and balance each other, at all times aware that the People might intervene decisively if the corruptions of power led them to betray the basic principles of the Revolution.

Now the last chapter encouraged you to explore these dualist themes by picking up the *Federalist Papers* at your local bookstore and giving them a close (re-)reading. While it may be harder to get your hands on Wood's magisterial work, try to do so: his comprehensive canvas of the enormous outpouring of pamphlets, debates, and correspondence of the era will allow you to put the Papers in context. Publius's dualistic preoccupations—rule by the People, control of the governors—are by no means idiosyncratic. He is instead speaking directly to the concerns of his fellow revolutionaries and explaining, in a common language, why the Convention's effort to speak for the People was worthy of "reflection and choice."

---

over the national meeting of the Cincinnati called for Philadelphia at the same time. See Garry Wills, *Cincinnatus: George Washington and the Enlightenment* 92–148 (1984).

Beard's Ghost

And yet, for all of Wood's great merits, there is one respect[30] in which his book's publication set back historical understanding. This has to do with Beard's picture of the Founders as the most successful Thermidorians of all time. While the early 1960's had seen the beginnings of a deep-cutting critique, Wood's book does not take it seriously. Somehow or other, Arendt's *On Revolution* eluded his otherwise remarkably comprehensive grasp of primary and secondary sources. The reason for this failure lies, I suspect, in *The Creation*'s origin as a doctoral dissertation. Wood's hero was not Hannah Arendt but Bernard Bailyn, his dissertation supervisor; his central text was not *On Revolution,* but Bailyn's *Ideological Origins of the American Revolution.*[31] This path-breaking study brought to life the Radical Whig world inhabited by the early revolutionaries; Wood's thesis took the story from 1776 through 1787, exploring how the Federalists reworked the earlier world view as they sought to legitimate new forms of constitutional authority. In taking this job on, Wood wrote a model dissertation. He is not to be faulted for missing the challenge raised by a German exile speaking in an historico-philosophical idiom alien to the no-nonsense, original-source style of the American academy. Nobody's perfect.

Not that Wood's work remains faithful to the old picture of the Founders in all its Beardian details. Given his heroic excavation of the Federalists' revolutionary world, he no longer supposes that the Founders thought of themselves as enemies of the People, cynically using the symbols of popular government to secure their class interest. He recognizes that Washington, Madison, and the rest believed that they were continuing, rather than aborting, the revolution for which so many had fought and died.

Just as he approaches an Arendtian appreciation of the revolutionary roots of the Founding, however, he swerves into Beardian orbit. After devoting almost six hundred pages exploring the marvelously creative way the Federalists adapted the language and practices of the Revolution to confront the legitimation crisis engendered by its success, Wood becomes anxious. Detaching himself from his historical context, he warns his modern readers against getting the wrong idea: we, the sophisticated folk of the twentieth century, should realize that, in claiming to speak for the People, the Founders "appropriated and exploited the language that *more rightfully belonged* to their opponents."[32] Whatever else may be said about these concluding remarks, they do allow Wood to make his peace with Progressive historiography. In the end, *The Creation* invites us to view the Founders as afflicted with a massive case of false consciousness. They remain the counterrevolutionaries Beard said they were, *even though they thought of themselves as revolutionary spokesmen for the People, and got most of the politically active citizenry to agree with them.* But, in making this turn, has Wood bought intellectual peace at too high a price?

His appeal to false consciousness implicitly accepts the social interpretation of revolution in its most question-begging form. Before we can even begin to assess Wood's claim, we must suppose, first, that history is best understood as a process in which one social class gains hegemony over another in a fixed sequence and, second, that revolutions gain their meaning only insofar as they either advance or retard this sequence. Only within this framework does it even make sense to consider, third, whether Wood is correct in believing that the Anti-Federalists, more than the Federalists, "rightfully" expressed the interests of the historically "progressive" social groups that would rise to ascendancy during the nineteenth century.[33]

I reject the framework which makes Wood's inquiry sensible. I deny that revolutions are principally to be assessed by their success in advancing or retarding a predetermined "march of progress." Whatever my differences with Arendt, she is right on the most important point: the true significance of the language of revolution is its invitation to modern men and women to take citizenship seriously, to consider whether the public realm is in such perilous condition as to require a dedicated common effort of renewal and redefinition: a "new beginning." From this political point of view, there can be no gainsaying the Founders' success in gaining broad credibility for their claim to speak for the People on matters of fundamental national identity. The Philadelphia Convention did not appropriate and exploit "the language that more rightfully belonged to their opponents." It creatively elaborated a revolutionary language and practice in ways that allowed future Americans to take to the higher lawmaking track to challenge many of the verities held by the Founders themselves—while at the same time authorizing government to undertake the normal tasks of daily life. Not bad for a single generation. Can we say as much for ourselves?

As always, Wood *is* onto something in questioning the Founders' capacity to anticipate the future course of American history. The Federalists' confidence in their ability to speak for the People had a lot to do, no doubt, with the hubristic belief of the white, propertied, male, Protestant gentry of the South and New England that they could count on the deference of the lesser orders of mankind.[34] Much of the constitutional politics of the future—from Thomas Jefferson through Martin Luther King—would involve campaigns against many of the patterns of deference that the Founders took for granted.[35] Though we have begun with 1787, we shall have to move far beyond it if we hope to understand how Americans built a modern dualist democracy.

For now, though, it is enough to stand on the broad shoulders of Arendt and Wood to glimpse a view of the Federalist achievement that neither author quite manages to attain. Arendt's fear of the "social question" blinded her to its role in shaping subsequent generations of constitutional politics in America. Wood's Beardian suspicion of the Federalists' substantive agenda blinded him to their success in providing Americans with models of political behavior and constitutional concepts through which future generations could test, and sometimes gain credibility for, their own projects in revolutionary reform.[36] The challenge is to affirm what both Arendt and Wood, for very different reasons, deny: that the spirit of 1787 is not dead, that neo-Federalism is very much a live option for our own time.

FROM FEDERALISTS TO *FEDERALIST PAPERS*

As with the study of the Founding period generally, the modern interpretation of the *Federalist Papers* begins with Charles Beard. During the late nineteenth century, the Papers had suffered an eclipse. Disenchanted with constitutional politics by the failure of Reconstruction, many American intellectuals found it hard to share Publius's revolutionary faith in the powers of human reason to shape normal politics through constitutional law. Rather than returning to Enlightenment models of rationality, they were far more impressed with the new evolutionary science of Darwin and sought to use it as a guide to constitutional reflection.[37]

Woodrow Wilson is exemplary:[38] his life and work is one long effort to deal with the fact that American government after the Civil War had moved beyond the Founding pattern.[39] Only he expressed this insight in the Darwinian language of his time: evolution, not revolution; organism, not mechanism. Turning away from the revolutionary Founding, Wilson found the slow evolution of parliamentary democracy in England the key to the future success of the American Empire.[40] Within the increasingly Anglophile world inhabited by leading constitutionalists, the *Federalist Papers* were not so much forgotten as drained of their deeper meanings. Bits and pieces of the text might be cited in discussing one or another practical problem; what was missing was an appreciation of the revolutionary spirit informing Publius's dualistic enterprise as a whole.

Against this background, Beard's reassertion of the *Federalist* was very much a mixed blessing. His emphasis on the Papers did give them renewed centrality in the ongoing debate about the meaning of the American Constitution. Unsurprisingly, however, Beard revived the Papers because he found in them evidence for his more general view of the Founding as counterrevolutionary. Thus, we have Beard to thank for the extraordinary prominence of *Federalist* No. 10 in twentieth-century thought—to the point where it is probably the only essay in American political theory that is actually read and discussed in most high school civics classes. As Douglass Adair has brilliantly shown, No. 10 never preoccupied commentators during the checkered 125-year history of *Federalist* interpretation preceding Beard.[41]

For Beard, however, No. 10 served as the "smoking gun" clinching his case. It not only marked the spot where Madison, as Founder in Chief, elaborated the economic foundations of modern politics in a way that, according to Beard, made him a brilliant anticipator of Marx.[42] It also indicated unequivocally—at least for those who cared to read the original sources rather than the hagiographies—on which side of the barricades Madison stood. There it is, in black and white: his express fear of the "rage for paper money, for an abolition of debts, for an equal division of property, or for any other improper or wicked project. . . ."[43] Isn't this the kind of evidence professional historians dream about, but almost never find? What more can one really expect?

Even within his own terms, there was one thing Beard never could explain: Why were the Founders so up-front about their counter-revolutionary intentions? It was one thing to share conspiratorial confidences with one another at secret meetings in Philadelphia; quite another for Publius to proclaim his antipopular convictions in election propaganda like the *Federalist*. Whatever else Madison was doing in writing No. 10, he certainly wasn't founding Madison Avenue!

But there is now no reason to take Beard on his own terms. The past half-century of *Federalist* interpretation has discredited—as well as anything can—Beard's particular readings. And yet Beard's ghost continues to haunt. Here, as elsewhere, his image of the counter-revolutionary Founding casts its spell. Even critics who have done the most to liberate us from particular mistakes remain entranced by Beard's basic picture. The consequences become clearest as the major contributors move from critique to their own constructive interpretation of the Papers. Here disagreements abound, as each writer appropriates the Papers for his or her own programmatic purposes; despite the cacophony of voices, all fail to hear the voice of the revolutionary Publius calling upon his fellow citizens to join in a constitutional politics that might enable them to transcend faction and speak in the name of the People.

Adair

We owe to Douglass Adair the first sustained attempt to rid the Papers of their Beardian gloss. In the style of intellectual historians, Adair set out to show that it was Hume, not Marx, who provided the master key to *Federalist* No. 10. Beard's claim that its talk of faction amounted to a theory of "economic determinism"[44] carried more than a hint of that most dreaded of historical sins: anachronism. Whatever else may be said about Hume, at least it was possible for Madison to read him!

Adair suggests that Hume's "Idea of a Perfect Commonwealth," first published in 1752, provided Madison with much of the material he uses in No. 10.[45] Indeed, Madison might have lifted Beard's pride and joy—No. 10's theory of faction—straight from Hume's *Idea.* Adair establishes, moreover, that neither Hume nor Madison understood "faction" in proto-Marxist fashion. While both Hume and Madison think economic self-interest is important, they both stress the role that factions based on competing ideologies, sentiments, or personalities can play. The last chapter built on this insight in elaborating Publius's theory of normal politics.[46]

I follow Adair on another crucial point: Madison does not believe that there is anything inevitable about government's reflecting the will of the dominant economic faction. To the contrary: the aim of constitutional science is to check and balance competing factions to allow the People's representatives leeway to deliberate and pursue the public good. Once again, Adair makes these points by charting Hume's influence. It is Hume's *Idea,* not Madison's No. 10, that first proclaims big republics as the hope of the future. It is Hume's *Idea,* not Madison's, to use the processes of representative government as a filtering device to select the best and the brightest for service in the nation's republican elite.

For all this, and much more, I am greatly in Adair's debt. There is, however, one great danger in approaching the Papers through Hume. I can think of no great philosopher[47] who has less sympathy for the revolutionary enterprise—who denies the power of large ideas to move human beings in any way whatever, let alone to inspire constructive revolutionary reform. The aim of Humean philosophy is to transcend such naive enthusiasms—not embrace them. Thus, Adair's emphasis on Hume blocked his recovery of the Founders' higher lawmaking voice. Rather than successful revolutionaries, the Federalists appear as Humean skeptics, exceedingly proud of their success in placing the Republic in the hands of the best and the brightest gentlemen-skeptics to be found this side of the Atlantic. As with Wood, an inspired effort to break free of the conventional wisdom ends by describing another Beardian epicycle.[48]

Diamond

I find the same imbalance in Martin Diamond's important contributions. Although an early essay pointedly questions the "predominant" view that had made the Federalists into "quasi- or even anti-democrats,"[49] Diamond never does justice to the revolutionary reasons that the Founders supposed they could speak for the People.[50] This failure is especially curious because Diamond, like Hannah Arendt, emphasizes the role of classical Greek ideals in interpreting the *Federalist*. He differs dramatically, however, in the lessons he learns from the Greek experience. For Arendt, the Founders' engagement in successful revolution allowed them to come close to recapturing a Greek-like dignity for politics. For Diamond, the contrast with the classics only reveals how far Enlightenment America had fallen from the Greek original. While the ancients aimed for virtue, Diamond's *Federalist* is distinctive precisely in its appreciation of the unvarnished vulgarity of American politics.

He makes his case by building on Adair's reading of No. 10.[51] Adair emphasized that Madison's text treats economic self-interest as only one of four principal causes of faction. Other Madisonian factions form around attractive personalities, or sentiments, or ideologies. Diamond explores this fourfold typology further and finds a disturbing bias in No. 10's treatment. Though Madison condemns all types of faction, his tone shifts with his subject. He vigorously opposes all ideological factions that inflame the citizenry with a "zeal for different opinions concerning religion" or other matters that the ancients would have considered fundamental. By the time he gets to economics, however, Madison is more cagey. Since property serves as "the most common and durable source of faction," Diamond's Madison urges a more discriminating approach: though all factions are bad, some are worse than others. The ones that are really threatening arise from the "unequal distribution of property." Factions that organize the poor against the rich, debtors against creditors, seem as perilous to Publius as those that set Protestants against Catholics.

Compared to class war, a second prospect seems almost benign. If the citizenry is not diverted by appeals to religious salvation or economic equality, Madison expects them to form special interest groups to gain favors for their own particular economic activity: cotton growers, shippers, manufacturers, each trying to increase their share of the pie at others' expense. Diamond points out that Madison does not oppose this kind of faction with the same fervor as others. Instead, Madison wants to use them as part of his constitutional design. Publius hopes that proliferating special interest groups will push and pull in different directions, canceling each other out. This will increase the capacity of elected representatives to transcend the competing factional viewpoints and take the rights of citizens and the permanent interests of the community as paramount. Of course, this divide-and-conquer strategy will work only if the constitutional scheme is subtly structured to encourage the selection of "enlightened statesmen" and to reward them to take the public good seriously in their deliberations.[52] The proliferation of special interest groups is hardly the whole story—nor does Diamond suppose otherwise. He simply wants to isolate an important aspect of Madison's genius: he had discovered "a novel way of channeling the stream of politics"[53]—one that promised the modern commercial republic a stability that had tragically eluded the classical polis.

And yet, Diamond cannot help but be impressed by the vulgarity of it all. No. 10's "deliberate tilt" against "the grand, dramatic, character-ennobling but society-wrecking opinions about justice and virtue";[54] its eager embrace of the "modern world, the substratum of which consists of these narrow, fragmented interests."[55] Stability yes, but at such a price? Despite his admiration for the grandeur that was Greece, Diamond does not suppose there is any going back. He consoles himself by reflecting that things could be worse. At least the Madisonian polity allows some private space for the philosophical few to devote themselves to ideas; at least the commercial republic encourages its citizens to cultivate a modest set of virtues if they hope to succeed in the marketplace. It's not classical Greece, but it isn't Stalinist Russia either.

There is a depth in Diamond's resignation—one that sets his essays apart from the mass of *Federalist* scholarship. There is also important insight—into the distinctive way the American system gains stability by enticing myriads of special interests to play the game of normal politics. But there is great blindness as well. Diamond is so taken by the figure of the huckster that he does not seem to notice the likes of Abraham Lincoln or Martin Luther King.

Or Publius himself. Diamond simply ignores those portions of the *Federalist Papers* that would allow him to hear the voice of the revolutionary Publius—the voice calling upon Americans to mobilize themselves for an arduous struggle to reconstruct the foundations of their constitutional identity. In this crucial respect, Diamond remains in the thrall of Beard's image of the Founding.*

From Progressivism to Neo-Federalism

The time has come to put Beard in his place. He and his fellow Progressives spoke some important truths and won some important victories. But we cannot allow his truths, now rendered into platitudes, to block our own search for self-understanding.

The Progressives cannot be understood apart from their target: the unregulated capitalism of the early twentieth century. Given their struggle for reform, the Progressives viewed the Founding with deep suspicion. Their opponents, after all, were making the Constitution's commitment to property and contract into potent weapons in the defense of the status quo. It was only natural to react by demystifying the Founding—by stripping the Federalists' pretensions to civic virtue.

But it is time to recognize that the Progressive battle against unregulated capitalism has been won. Fifty years after the New Deal, even conservative Americans have learned to live in an activist welfare state. Doubtless, the modern mix of regulated markets and social welfare will be reshaped through generations of political debate, mobilization, decision. The America of 2090 will be as different from today as from the America of 1890.

Nonetheless, this *is* 1990, and the world has changed in the century

---

*There is a paradox here. Diamond is not generally cast in Beard's shadow. He is seen as a distinguished follower of a very different éminence grise of postwar America: Leo Strauss. Indeed, the power of Diamond's reading of No. 10 is itself a tribute to Strauss—for the themes Diamond found are the very same leitmotivs that Strauss himself elaborated in his encounter with many other great texts of the Western political tradition.

It is equally true, however, that Diamond inherited Strauss's failings: in this case, his master's deep hostility to the revolutionary spirit of modern times. Here is where the path marked out by Strauss paradoxically converges on the path marked out by Beard. Both deny, if for very different reasons, the importance of the revolutionary aspect of Federalist thought. They disagree merely on whether Publius is a brilliant anticipator of Marx or a no less brilliant mourner of lost classical virtue.

For other essays in the Straussian mode, see David Epstein, *The Political Theory of The Federalist* (1984), and Thomas Pangle, *The Spirit of Modern Republicanism: The Moral Vision of the American Founders and the Philosophy of John Locke* (1988).

since Beard formed his critique. Thanks in part to Beard and his fellow Progessives, most Americans no longer find it so threatening to recognize the obvious: the Founders held notions of property rights different from those that prevail in America today. They would have been profoundly disturbed by our modern "rage for paper money, for an abolition of debts, for an equal division of property," and other "improper or wicked" projects.[56] Rather than flogging this dead fact, the question is whether we can move beyond it and still learn something from the Founders that remains vital?

My positive answer distinguishes two aspects of the Founding's achievement that the Progressives jumbled together—the *revolutionary process* through which the Federalists mobilized popular support for their constitutional reforms, and the *property-oriented substance* of their particular social vision. Since the New Deal, modern Americans have profoundly revised the property-oriented substance of the Federalist vision; but have they rejected the Federalist process?

I do not think so. We still have a good deal to learn about dualist democracy from the *Federalist*. If we are to take these teachings seriously, however, we must let another one of Beard's sacred cows out to pasture. This is the reductionist tendency to trivialize the entire domain of politics by looking upon it as a reflex of more fundamental things going on elsewhere in the society. This reductionist tendency is by no means limited to Marxists or old-fashioned Progressives; nowadays it is at least as common on the right as it is on the left.*

Right, left, or center, it is to be resisted on behalf of a better view. Politics is a relatively autonomous domain of life, with its own symbolic meanings, practices, and dynamics. This does not mean that we should embrace Arendt's absurdly idealistic view that political discourse is or ought to be entirely autonomous from social and economic interest. It is enough to be resolutely non-reductionist:

---

*The kind of crude reductionism formerly practiced by "vulgar Marxists" is now to be found, in properly mathematicized form, in the work of leading members of the Chicago School of Economics. See Gary Becker, "A Theory of Competition Among Pressure Groups for Political Influence," 98 *Q. J. Econ.* 371 (1983); Sam Peltzman, "Toward a More General Theory of Regulation," 19 *J. Law & Econ.* 211 (1976). For a less mathematical form of reductionism, see John Diggins, *The Lost Soul of American Politics: Virtue, Self-Interest, and the Foundations of Liberalism* (1984).

just as economic interest doesn't predetermine politics, so too political meanings don't predetermine economic interests. There is, quite simply, no single aspect of life that serves as the "engine of history"—not even in the "final analysis." We must take the complex interaction between social, economic, psychological, and political domains seriously and allow no single domain to monopolize our effort at causal explanation or philosophical self-understanding.

Given the roles both constitutional politics and constitutional law have played in America's struggle for power, for self-understanding, don't we owe it to ourselves to take this domain seriously? Not because it contains the last word on what it means to be an American—no single domain is rich enough for that. But surely an important piece of the puzzle would be missing without Publius, and what has become of his revolutionary spirit?

CHAPTER NINE

Normal Politics

From Successful Revolutionary
to Private Citizen

WE HAVE BEEN LOOKING upon the Constitution as the work of successful revolutionaries. For such people, the good life *is* the political life; the paradigm of virtue is somebody, like George Washington, who gains his greatest fulfillment in sacrificing private interest for public good.[1] Despite this gratifying starting point, Publius transcends his historical situation to glimpse another possibility: a world of private men and women who gain their deepest satisfactions in a life far removed from the public forum.

Unsurprisingly, he views this world with anxiety. These private people spell public trouble—factional indifference to the public good. Publius's greatness is revealed in his response. He does not try to suppress these distasteful forms of life. He uses constitutional law to reach an accommodation with privatism in the name of civic freedom. He proposes dualistic democracy in an act of self-transcendence—reaching out to people living in vastly different historical circumstances.

Notably ourselves. Putting aside all the obvious social and economic differences, we do not live in the triumphant afterglow of successful revolution. When we say virtue, we do not think of George Washington or his living equivalent (and who might that be?). We have had our share of political successes—and failures. But, for contemporary Americans, the political life is only one of many in which virtue can be found. A person who manages to preserve her integrity and make her mark in politics is, doubtless, somebody who merits great praise—but any more so than somebody who contributes to art, or science, or industry, or the less exalted business of decency, love, and thoughtfulness? If somebody concluded that the life of politics is not for him, we would not think of condemning him, straight out, as a moral failure. Perhaps he is right to think he has better things to do than emulate Publius. The political domain simply does not dominate our moral consciousness as it did for the Revolutionary generation.

In a sense, this only makes the Federalist economy of virtue more relevant to our political situation. If politics is not the preeminent path to virtue, it is even more important for the Constitution to make the most of what little we can expect. Yet, on a superficial level, the dominating importance Publius assigns to the political life may be an interpretive stumbling block for moderns whose moral consciousness gives it a less central place. Dualist democracy will be more convincing if we can see how it makes sense within our own, more pluralistic, conception of the good life.

This chapter makes the effort at modernistic adaptation by reversing perspective. Despite our distance from Publius, perhaps we can find common ground in an awkward desire to achieve credibility in two very different worlds of meaning. Of course, the world most modern Americans find secure is precisely the place which Publius views with anxiety. It is a place where we devote ourselves to a host of things that often crowd out politics—sport or science or religion, friends and family and the business of life. And yet, despite our manifest concern with our personal destinies, we continue to assert our capacity to speak about "the rights of citizens and the permanent interests of the community."

To mark this political capacity, we call ourselves *private citizens,* effortlessly eliding the two words into a single phrase. While such self-identification may seem part of second nature, there is something puzzling about private citizenship. By puzzling over it we can come to a renewed appreciation of the dualistic system of democracy we have inherited from the Founders.

I shall introduce the puzzles by contrasting the private citizen with two other political types: the *public citizen* and the *perfect privatist.* Both characters do indeed play recognizable roles in the political world we inhabit. Only they bulk larger in book learning than they do in life, and cannot be allowed to obscure the distinctive kind of political animal Americans call the private citizen. By reflecting upon the distinctive tensions experienced by this American political type, we shall find ourselves traveling down a more modern path toward the dualist Constitution.

A THIRD TYPE

I shall introduce the private citizen by considering the bad things that two competing political types will predictably say about him.

The Critique of the Public Citizen

The first critique comes from high-spirited sorts who rebel at the countless compromises the *private* citizen makes in his ongoing commitment to the enterprise of self-government. They look with disdain as Joe American constantly glances at his watch, anxiously measuring the minutes of his political engagement lest they crowd out his pressing private commitments. This ever-present need to economize on one's investment in the enterprise of government is a basic feature of private citizenship, as it is commonly understood.

For purists, however, this omnipresent trimming on time and energy makes private citizenship too shabby and compromised an affair to be really valuable. They call upon us to look upon citizenship as a higher calling, the source of the deepest values to which men and women can ordinarily aspire. Rather than trimming the demands of citizenship to fit our more humdrum needs for personal satisfaction, we must learn to put the private sphere in its place. Compared with public citizenship, private life represents an inferior plane of existence.

The last chapter introduced this view in its encounter with Hannah Arendt.[2] For present purposes, a glance at political practice, not theory, may help. A good recent example: Ralph Nader, who combines an emphatic asceticism in personal life with a more-than-full-time commitment to the public good as he understands it. Note, moreover, that Nader deliberately refuses to earn his keep by running for public office. He prefers to rely on the voluntary contributions of those who support his effort to serve, in his words, as a Public Citizen.[3] This Naderite self-description contrasts perfectly with the *private* citizenship of most Americans—so long as we emphasize that

Naderism is hardly the only -ism that inspires high levels of public commitment from high-minded men and women who disdain high salaries to work eighty-hour weeks in crummy offices in Washington and many other places across the nation. Left, right, and center, there are more public citizens at work today than at any time in our history. I have no doubt that such people will play crucial roles in the constitutional politics of our future, just as they have in our past.

For the present, I am more interested in pointing out the contrast between these public citizens and the millions of Americans who watch television, read the papers, talk politics with their families, friends, and fellow workers in a bewildering variety of unions, churches, voluntary organizations. If anything allows us to say that America remains a democratic republic, rather than some new-fangled mix of aristocracy and oligarchy, it is the ongoing involvement of these millions in the life of the nation. However much (or little) one may admire the handful of public citizens in our midst, only a sympathetic understanding of private citizenship will provide a framework for the assessment of the democratic state of the Republic—and bring us to a neo-Federalist appreciation of dualist constitutionalism.

The Critique of the Perfect Privatist

Now let's demarcate our subject by approaching it from a second, and opposite, direction. From this extreme, the problem with the private citizen is that she is *too* serious about the collective effort to define "the rights of individuals and the permanent interests of the community." For the perfect privatist, as I shall define her, the right way to respond to the question

(1) What is good for the country?

is by treating it as a fancy way of asking

(2) What is good for me?

While the Greeks called such people *idiots,* we need not adopt such an uncomprehending view. Rather than doing business with a selfish amoralist, we may be dealing with a deeply religious person who utterly refuses to allow conversations about the earthly common-wealth to divert him from the things that really matter; or somebody who believes in personal morality but is skeptical about the place of morality in politics; or . . .

My aim here is not to "refute" such skeptical doubts. It is to contrast them with the more affirmative commitments of the private citizen. Though this character type does not follow the public citizen in considering politics to be her highest calling, she isn't identifying herself with the skeptical doubts of the perfect privatist either. She is saying something different. She is giving value to citizenship with-out conceding that it should *always* trump the values of her private life.

The Dilemmas of Private Citizenship

While most Americans answer to the name of private citizen, they have learned not to take their protestations of civic virtue *too* seri-ously. Even gaining a rudimentary empirical understanding of a national problem often requires a lot of work. Although we may occasionally make this effort, an ongoing commitment to informed citizenship may unduly deflect our energies from the struggles of everyday life.

Beyond the problem of information towers the moral dilemmas of American citizenship. A sober consideration of the national interest may indicate that personal and local interests must be sacrificed to the general good. Yet this message will be met with bewilderment, or worse, by friends and neighbors who fail to look beyond their parochial interests. It is little wonder, then, that most people rarely shoulder the full burden of Publius.

However understandable his limited engagement in public life, the thoughtful private citizen must recognize that it generates three interrelated problems for a democratic polity. The first is apathy. The existence of many *private* citizens may demoralize those who might otherwise invest greater energy into private *citizenship:* If so many others give only a passing concern to national politics, isn't it silly of me to maintain the struggle? The second problem is igno-rance. Given their limited engagement, most Americans will not be in a position to make a considered judgment on most—sometimes all—of the issues that preoccupy politicians in Washington, D.C. And finally there is the problem of selfishness. Without undertaking a serious examination of "the rights of citizens and the permanent interests of the community,"[4] isn't it all too likely that the private citizen's first political impressions will give too much weight to narrowly selfish interests?

COERCIVE DEMOCRACY

Apathy, ignorance, selfishness—without belittling these misfortunes, consider the disaster that would follow upon a thoroughgoing effort at their eradication. Call the cure coercive democracy. If most people don't take national politics seriously, simply force them to pay attention. Every day each private citizen should be compelled to spend an hour or two discussing current events. Over time, this will encourage all of them to form considered political judgments. And if the discussions reveal the masses to be caught up in the protection of petty local interests, perhaps we might rely on specially trained public citizens to lead their fellows onwards and upwards to a genuinely national and public-regarding view of the country's problems?

It is easy to find this chilling vision of coercive democracy entirely unacceptable. Today's private citizen joins Publius in condemning coercive democracy as "a remedy . . . worse than the disease."[5] Doubtless there are times when a liberal democracy may rightly call upon its private citizens to die in the defense of their country.* The demands imposed in times of crisis are not to be confused, however, with the normal place that citizenship occupies in the ordinary American's self-understanding. Generally speaking, it is up to each American to decide how much time and energy he will devote to private *citizenship,* how much to *private* citizenship. If this means that national politics will often suffer from apathy, ignorance, and selfishness, we will all have to learn to grin and bear it.

---

*Though there are occasions when people should conscientiously reject this demand in the name of some ideal that is higher than democratic citizenship. My own views may be found in Bruce Ackerman, *Social Justice in the Liberal State* §62, at 293–301 (1980).

Normal Voting

Which is not to say that even the most *private* citizen should be confused with the perfect privatist. Even during normal politics, the dualist Constitution cannot dispense with public virtue entirely. Following Publius, we must aim for a realistic sense of the limited supply of citizenship that is available in normal politics. We must then make a determined effort to structure our lawmaking institutions in ways that make the best use of the existing supply.

The following sketch seeks to redeem some basic Federalist insights into the political economy of virtue. On the one hand, I shall present a picture of American government that insists, against some fashionable economistic views,[6] on the absolute necessity of a certain kind of virtue in the normal operation of the democratic system. On the other hand, I shall try to recapture a Publian perspective on the problematic character of democratic representation during normal politics. My aim will be to describe, as unmystically as possible, the sense in which our normally elected representatives are only "stand-ins" for the People and should not be generally allowed to suppose that they speak for *the People themselves,* to indulge in some Publian italics. This, in turn, will set the stage for the next chapter's discussion of constitutional politics—which seeks to define the conditions under which this higher lawmaking claim is appropriate.

Voting as an Act of Private Citizenship

Begin with the baseline: how much and what kind of public-regarding virtue is required before normal American government can go on?

Start from the bottom up with a thought experiment:

> *The Last Election.* Suppose the polls opened some future Tuesday in November and only a few hundred thousand voters showed up to cast their ballots for President; the other hundred-million-plus went about their normal business and ignored the event.

Conclusion: Democracy has died in America, not with a bang but a whimper—just as surely as if the Marines had seized the Capitol.

Indeed, the demonstration of such apathy and unconcern would probably provoke a coup—but an Election Day that revealed so little public involvement would already have made a mockery of the winners' claims to democratic legitimacy. If our aim, then, is to plumb the depths of public-regarding virtue necessary for normal government, we can begin here: How much of this scarce commodity must the general citizenry possess if it is to avoid the Last Election?

The answer: more than one might naively suppose. The villain is the free-ride problem, whose analysis has been taken to new depths by the last generation of political economists.[7] For present purposes, the point is simple enough.[8] Even if a few hundred thousand people are voting, the chance of my vote deciding the winner is vanishingly small—let's call it epsilon, ϵ. This simple fact generates the free-ride problem.

To see how, consider the matter as it appears from the perspective of the perfect privatist. Since, by definition, he is only looking out for Number One, he will go to the polls only if the personal benefits to him outweigh the costs. And while the costs of voting might seem small—the loss of half an hour traveling to the voting place, standing on line, pulling levers—the benefits seem even smaller. Our privatist may, of course, gain many personal benefits if candidate A wins over candidate B—gains that (for purposes of illustration) he may value at 10,000 dollars. But this large number does not measure the benefit he stands to gain by voting, since A's electoral fate will not normally be decided by a single vote. And in all other cases, the privatist either will or will not get his 10,000 dollars regardless of whether he actually goes to the polls. Thus, the clear-thinking privatist will factor in epsilon—the chance of his vote making the difference—into his personal cost-benefit equation before heading to the polls. And since epsilon is vanishingly small, numbers bigger than 10,000 will be cut down to such a small size that even the waste of half an hour will seem a huge expenditure. After all, there are lots more pleasant and/or profitable ways of killing time than standing on line and flicking a few switches. Why not go to church or mow the lawn or search for a good stock market tip? Won't these investments be more rewarding than $(10,000)(\epsilon)$ = almost zero?

And don't say: But if everybody thought that way, the American people *would* confront the last Election Day. The perfect privatist will refuse to be moved. Even if he did make the personal effort to go to the polls, this would only increase the turnout from 600,000 to 600,001. His personal decision would not be enough to avoid the Last Election; normal democracy will survive only if tens of millions of people take the trouble to cast their ballots. And nothing he personally can do will make this happen. Even if the privatist values highly the personal benefits of continued democracy, the discounted value of *his* voting will remain near zero.

It follows that a sizable election turnout would not exist in a world of perfect privatists. Normal elections require tens of millions of Americans to move beyond privatism and declare themselves as private citizens.[9] They must be prepared, some of the time at least, to sacrifice for the public good. Granted, the half-hour or so spent flipping levers at the polls isn't much of a sacrifice. The public citizen wouldn't think twice before making it. But before the private citizen recognizes an obligation, he will require additional argument.

It is easy to see why. In contrast to the public citizen, our private citizen denies that he is under an obligation to maximize the production of any and all public goods—since accepting such an onerous obligation would make it impossible for him to pursue the private goods he also values highly. Before convincing him that he has an obligation to go to the polls, we must explain what is so special about voting—something that sets it apart from the countless other public goods whose pursuit is praiseworthy, but not obligatory. What could that something be?

Three things, taken together, make voting special. The first is humdrum, but important. This involves the temporally limited character of voting. Most other demands of good citizenship are more open-ended. Consider the public interest in citizens' acquiring adequate information about the issues currently on the agenda in Washington, D.C. This task can easily devour enormous quantities of time and energy. In contrast, the simple act of voting requires you to go to the polls two or three times a year; indeed, many private citizens recognize an obligation to vote only at the most important elections.

Second, voting is obviously strategic to the operation of the system as a whole. While normal constitutional government can and does endure despite widespread citizen ignorance, apathy, and selfishness, the Last Election scenario would signal its destruction. Moreover, voting takes on a different, but equally strategic, role during periods of constitutional politics, where it provides a crucial mechanism for testing the claim of one or another movement to speak in the name of *the People themselves*.[10] Thus, in spending half an hour from time to time, the private citizen is getting good value for a very limited expenditure. While the vulgarity of this kind of cost-benefit talk deeply offends the public citizen, for whom the political life is the good life, it cannot but influence the *private* citizen, who must forever be economizing on his public virtue to find room for other valuable aspects of life.

Third, voting is something that all citizens do together. Many other civic activities are discharged either individually or in smallish groups. Either you do or you don't read a daily newspaper or a news magazine to keep up on current affairs; whatever you do, you don't do it in public, for all the world to see. Even if you attend a "crucial" meeting of the zoning board or join a march on Washington, you don't expect to find every private citizen with you. In contrast, voting is the paradigmatic form of *universal* citizenship participation. If you don't even take the trouble to vote, are you any kind of citizen at all?

This is no rhetorical question. The perfect privatist will predictably answer it in the negative. But that is, in a sense, just my point: while a modern democracy must learn to economize on public-regarding virtue, there can be no hope of doing without it entirely—even in normal politics, where the mass of the citizenry are not gripped by the compelling character of the issues at the center of the agenda. If large numbers of Americans do not answer to the limited, strategic, but universal obligation that voting imposes on private citizens, there can be no hope of sustaining the American constitutional tradition of republican government.

By this marker, the modern republic isn't in very good shape. The logic of perfect privatism hasn't escaped half the voting population— who are "too busy" with their private lives to spare half an hour even for Presidential elections. While these numbers aren't quite as bad as they look,[11] they are plenty bad enough. Nonetheless, we are still pretty far away from the Last Election. The Presidential contest between Bush and Dukakis—which surely raised as few gripping issues as any election within living memory—still drew tens of millions of voters to the polls.

In saying this, I'm not saying much. In particular, I'm not saying that the paltry amount of self-sacrifice required to avoid the Last Election is *sufficient* to sustain the life of the American Republic— only that it is necessary. If we hope to move from necessary to sufficient conditions, and glimpse all the occasions upon which the Constitution requires the exercise of private citizenship during both normal and abnormal times, we have our work cut out for us. Nonetheless, this first exercise in a neo-Federalist economy of virtue has taken us down a distinctive path. It has already allowed us to refute the remarkably common view that our Constitution is best conceived as a "machine that would go of itself"[12] without constant, if limited, infusions of public virtue. It will, moreover, permit us to take a second step and regain a renewed appreciation of a fundamental Federalist insight—into the problematic way in which the winners of normal electoral competitions represent the People.

The Soft Vote

The root of the difficulty is this: while our private citizen may have enough virtue to get her to the polls, she doesn't necessarily have enough virtue to cast a ballot that represents her *considered judgment* on the central issues raised by the candidates in the election.[13]

The villain, once again, is the free-ride problem. But this time the costs of transcending it are far more substantial than the half-hour needed merely to go to the polls. Not only does it take time and energy to get a rough-and-ready sense of the facts and value alternatives raised by a political campaign. No less crucial is the moral questioning involved in defining the appropriate stance: it is not enough for a private citizen to ask herself which candidate better fulfills her personal interests; the question is which will, all things considered, further the "rights of citizens and the permanent interests of the community." Approaching such a question requires lots of talk with people you know and trust—over the dinner table and on the job, at your church or union hall, at the P.T.A. or the local bar.

Yet the fact is that, for most people most of the time, normal political talk is pretty perfunctory. The upcoming election is treated as a distant event that will not profoundly change the shape of one's world—with anything like the shattering impact of a divorce, or a big promotion, or a personal disgrace before one's friends. The normal American's self-identification as a private citizen is not enough, by itself, to generate the kind of probing conversation that would be appropriate, say, in deciding whether one should change jobs or living quarters—let alone spouses or religions. Such active engagement in private *citizenship* does not seem demanded simply because you will soon be casting a ballot for President with tens of millions of fellow citizens. It would be a very different matter, of course, if your vote decided the outcome. But it won't. So isn't it O.K. to economize on virtue?

This logic leads millions of *private* citizens to go to the polls and cast a "soft" vote for their candidates. In calling their votes "soft," I do not mean that they are based on nothing at all. Indeed, modern political science has usefully explored the complex ways in which traditional party and ethnic identities, retrospective judgments on the incumbents, a general sense of the country's prosperity, impressions of the particular candidates and issues interweave in the process of forming the American voter's judgment.[14] My crucial claim is this: as she goes to the polls, *the normal private citizen is under no illusions about the quality of reflection that lies behind her ballot.* She normally does not view her ballot as the expression of a considered judgment about one or another fundamental choice confronting the nation. Instead, she thinks of it as a much softer statement:

> As a *private* citizen, I've had a lot of other things to worry about lately— my job, my husband, where my kid is hanging out after school. Despite all these private concerns, I'm not copping out. Here I am, going into the voting booth, trying to figure out what's best for the country—on the basis of my inherited political beliefs, my glimpses into the present state of the Union, and my impressions of the character of the candidates and issues. Sorry, but that's the best I can do right now. Surely it's better than nothing? Surely we have enough perfect privatists without my joining them?

In putting these words into my *private* citizen's mouth, I am not trying to judge her on some Platonic standard of high seriousness which few, if any, mortals ever satisfy. I am making a more mundane claim: most private citizens have no trouble recognizing that most of their voting decisions do not measure up *to their own standards* *of deliberateness;** and that, if they took the trouble to think about the issues more carefully, their judgments might well be different from the relatively superficial views they now hold.

This softness of the normal vote enters into the neo-Federalist argument in two different ways. First, it helps explain why the modern dualist joins Publius in insisting on the problematic way statutes enacted by the electoral victors represent the considered judgments of We the People of the United States. The problem does not arise because these statutes may run counter to the considered judgments of most citizens (though this may, of course, happen as well). The problem is that the mass of the *private* citizenry may not have judgments that they themselves take to be considered. What they have are opinions that they recognize might not stand up very well to the kind of scrutiny they reserve for their considered judgments. In this very common situation, we must begin our study of normal government with a Publian sense that We the People are absent from the scene, and that there can be no hope of capturing, in some simple snapshot, what the citizenry really think about an issue. Nobody can plausibly predict what the People would say if they devoted a lot of time and energy to scrutinizing their received opinions in the process of hammering out a new collective judgment about the "rights of citizens and the permanent interests of the community." Normally, the People just aren't spending the time and energy; and we had better design our normal lawmaking system with this in mind.[15]

This leads to my second point about softness: it is not inevitable.

---

*Think, for example, of a time you made an important decision in private life: which career should I pursue? where should I live? whom should I marry? How did you go about making up your mind? Should you have looked more carefully before you leaped? If so, what should you have been looking for?

As you ask these questions, it should be easy to avoid an obvious mistake—call it perfectionism. There can be such a thing as undue deliberation, worrying a decision to death without coming to closure. Nonetheless, without falling victim to perfectionism, all of us are perfectly aware of the distinction between considered and unconsidered judgments. Some of the time we look back to an important turning point and say, "Even if things turned out badly, at least I knew what I was getting into . . ." Sometimes all we can say is, "What a fool I was!" It is this rough-and-ready distinction, familiar enough in private life, that I mean to invoke here. For further discussion, see Chapter 10, pp. 272–274.

Over time, millions of private citizens may be provoked by their fellow Americans to scrutinize some of their received political opinions with care. Not, mind you, that they become public citizens, whose commitments may lead them to become full-time activists. Nonetheless, during periods of successful constitutional politics, there is an important difference in their political conversations, actions, attitudes. Their questions become more urgent, their conversations more energetic; their actions move beyond the ballot box to include money contributions, petitions, marches—all to express the fact that they now have a *considered* judgment that they want their would-be governors to recognize. If italics will do the trick, *private* citizens become private *citizens*. If jargon is any better, distinguishing between passive and active citizens will serve, so long as it is firmly recalled that even the passive citizen is not a perfect privatist, nor is the active one a public citizen—we are distinguishing between shades of gray.

This leads us to the problem of higher lawmaking that we will take up in the next chapter: how to design a credible higher lawmaking system to test and finally to express those constitutional principles that represent the considered judgments of a majority of active citizens? But first let's focus on the problem of institutional design under more normal conditions.

Normal Political Resources: An Inventory

Can we define, in the manner of the *Federalist Papers,* how constitutional structure may ameliorate the worst pathologies of normal politics, if not effect a miracle cure? To give these neo-Federalist reflections some structure, allow me three sets of simplifying assumptions. The first has to do with the citizenry; the second, electoral processes; the third, the character of representatives. The first set should be straightforward enough. I shall assume a population composed principally (but not exclusively) of *private* citizens—Americans who recognize the meaningfulness of the Publian enterprise but content themselves with conduct they themselves recognize as insufficiently informed, public-regarding, and politically active to fulfill their own aspirations as private *citizens.*

The second set assumes that we have already taken steps to assure a free and fair electoral process of the American type—where two major parties struggle for victory in winner-take-all electoral districts, with only the indistinct threat of a serious third-party challenger on the horizon.

The third set involves the likely behavior of would-be representatives. These politician/statesmen, as I shall call them, display a dualistic character of a kind that should be becoming familiar. On the one hand, our politician/statesmen are not perfect privatists willing to sell their legislative influence to the highest bidder (after taking due account of the risk of criminal prosecution). On the other hand, they are unwilling to devote themselves single-mindedly to the public good, as they might define it if they were public citizens who were not interested in winning and holding electoral office. Instead, as a *politician*/statesman, each representative is interested in getting reelected. Subject to this constraint, they will try to use their influence on behalf of the "public good," as they conscientiously define it. But they will be reluctant to play the role of politician/*statesman* when it seriously endangers their reelection chances. Perhaps some politician/statesmen will rise to the occasion on occasion. But "[e]nlightened statesmen will not always be at the helm."[16]

The challenge, then, is this: How to design a system that will make the most of the political virtue that exists in a world dominated principally by private citizens and politician/statesmen?

Begin by considering how politician/statesmen will go about seeking electoral victory in the world we have described. There is one technique our would-be representative cannot use. By definition of normal politics, she cannot rely exclusively upon a successful *constitutional movement*. Such a movement draws upon the energies of large numbers of private *citizens* in its ongoing activities of political discussion, recruitment, organization, and mobilization. Widespread activity of this kind is excluded by our model of normal politics— in which *private* citizens are the preponderant political type.

Yet, it would be a mistake to banish all thought of constitutional politics from the model. Even in normal times, both Democratic and Republican parties still bear marks of the fact that they have served the cause of such movements at one or another time in their checkered histories. The historical residues left behind by these earlier popular movements may well provide an era of normal politics with much of its party infrastructure and symbolism. While these will help get out the vote on Election Day, they will not provide our would-be representative with all the resources she will require to assure her electoral victory. She will also want to call upon electoral resources generated by a diverse set of organizations which manage to prosper despite the mass ignorance, selfishness, and apathy characteristic of normal politics. The challenge is both to see why these organizational types can achieve effectiveness under normal conditions and to understand how their existence constrains the representative process.

Private Interest Groups

The first way to transcend the general ignorance, apathy, and selfishness is through a *private interest* group. Here a political organization piggybacks upon enterprises that had initially been formed to satisfy perfectly private desires. Assume, for example, that when you next enter the market for a car, you make your decision as a perfectly private person—trying to maximize your own good without thinking of yourself as casting a vote for the car whose production best serves the national interest. Acting in this perfectly private way, suppose you and millions of others buy Chryslers; and thanks to these decisions, Chrysler becomes a large and complex organization which can, if it so chooses, divert some of its energy from car manufacturing to political influence. Surely you have not authorized Chrysler to act on your behalf as a private citizen by buying one of its cars: and yet Chrysler may well take advantage of the organizational vacuum created by citizen passivity to gain bailouts, protective tariffs, or an imperialist foreign policy that its consumers would never approve if they were acting as private *citizens*. The only trouble is that you aren't investing heavily in active citizenship right now; nor are tens of millions of your fellow Americans. As a consequence, our *politician*/statesmen have a powerful incentive to pander to private interests in order to get the resources they will require for normal political victories.[17]

It should not be imagined that this problem can be solved by some simple "campaign reform"—limiting campaign contributions, licensing lobbyists, or the like. While these may be desirable,[18] they will not get to the core of the problem. Even if Chrysler or the United Auto Workers can't give big bucks to politicians directly, they will find it relatively easy to divert some of their organizational resources to the task of shepherding an ignorant, selfish, and passive bunch of Chryslerians through the polls on Election Day. This grass-roots organizational muscle cannot help but be important to the normal politician/statesman—for whom a vote is a vote is a vote. If he can induce Chryslerians to flick the lever in his direction by pandering to the company or the union by declaring, against his Publian judgment, that Chrysler's salvation is in the national interest, he will be tempted to do so—provided, of course, that he will not suffer an offsetting loss of support from some other organized group.[19]

As we have seen,[20] Publius was well aware of this pathology, and did not seek its total eradication. His hope was to ameliorate the oppressive character of these rip-offs by proliferating the number and variety of privatistic interests. By bumping against one another in their rush to the public trough, perhaps they will check and balance each other, making it easier for a majority of Congressmen to liberate themselves from undue subservience to any single pressure? At the very least, the proliferation of privatistic factions will make it harder to organize a solid coalition of "ins" who will use their majority power to rip off the same bunch of "outs"? If the citizens of Detroit may succeed in getting a federal bailout for Chrysler, perhaps they will find themselves paying a good portion of the disaster relief bill suffered by Floridians after the next hurricane?

Not that I have a grudge against the good citizens of Detroit or Miami. Perhaps a bunch of private *citizens* might conclude, after devoting time and energy to the matter, that either or both subsidies are in the national interest. My point is simply that private interest groups have organizational resources that will generate pressure in this direction independently of the judgment of private *citizens,* or even *private* citizens. This is pathological.[21]

Bureaucratic Interests

So too is a second kind of organizational pressure. This one does not come from the private sector, but the public. Once created, bureaucracies will develop an interest in self-preservation that will endure independently of the public need for their continued existence. Acting on this interest, they will try to use the resources at their disposal to create powerful constituencies on their behalf— groups that will fight to maintain the private benefits they receive from the programs regardless of the broader public interest.[22]

This kind of bureaucratic logrolling is especially serious in the modern republic, where activist government intervenes on a broad front in the name of the public interest. Thus, the Defense Department designs its weapons programs so that lots of Congressional districts will gain lucrative private contracts, as does the Agriculture Department, as does the . . .

Once again, my point is not that a majority of private citizens do not support a steady stream of defense contracts to the Boeing Corporation. It is that the representatives from Boeing's hometown, Seattle, will push for more contracts independently of their Publian judgment about the "permanent interests of the community"—because the people in Seattle, especially during normal politics, won't be making much of an effort to scrutinize these benefits from a national point of view. Instead of taking on the burden of statesmanship, they will be tempted to club together with the relevant bureaucrats to bring home the bacon.

As in the first case, much of modern political science has detailed the varieties of such pathological behavior.[23] Again, the neo-Federalist does not hope for its eradication. Nonetheless, its control should be a very high priority for constitutional design.

Public Interest Groups

A third political organization enters the normal political scene from a different direction. In picturing the world of normal politics, I did not ask you to imagine a place entirely populated by *private* citizens; merely one dominated by them. This leaves the model open for smallish groups of private *citizens* who are, indeed, actively concerned about one or another aspect of the public interest, and who have successfully transcended the free-ride problem to make themselves an organizational presence on the lawmaking scene. So far as they are concerned, the times imperatively demand a general mobilization of private *citizens* on behalf of the cause that has impelled them into political activity.

Despite their failure to pierce the veil of ignorance, selfishness, and passivity that surrounds their fellow citizens, these "single-issue" groups may be a significant force in normal politics. Given the size of the American population, a group drawing on the allegiance of a few hundred thousand private *citizens* can be considered "smallish." Depending upon their geographical location, one or another group of activists may be in a position to cast a swing vote in close elections. They can also contribute a disproportionate amount of the available energy that can be brought to bear on Election Day to induce the passive *private* citizenry to go to the polls and vote.[24] All things considered, politician/statesmen will not antagonize such groups unnecessarily; indeed, it may prove prudent to endorse a position one recognizes is opposed to the "permanent interests of the community and the rights of citizens."

Prudence may seem too weak to describe such adaptive behavior—isn't it the job of a statesman to make the best of unattractive political realities? After all, if a smallish group of moralizers succeed in replacing a representative with somebody who uncritically espouses their wrongheaded view, who will be the better for it? Isn't it the better part of statesmanship to mouth some faction's moralisms for a time if this is what it takes to keep in office?

Hard questions. Of course, the neo-Federalist hope is that because of the number of factions espousing different moralisms, most normal politicians will avoid becoming hostage to any particular one—especially at the same time. But, once again, perfection is not to be expected.

Mass Media

The emphatic moralisms of public interest groups often contrast sharply with the transparent selfishness of private and bureaucratic interests. Nonetheless, all these different organizational types have one thing in common. They can monitor would-be representatives quite closely and provide their memberships with detailed assessments of their future promise and past performance. Not so the fourth type of organization: the mass media. Newspapers and television have little incentive to monitor politician/statesmen on an ongoing, issue-by-issue, basis. Such reports will overwhelm the information-processing capacities of the *private* citizenry that constitutes the mass audience. What this public wants is "news": bits and pieces of current events that require little in the way of unfamiliar background.

And yet, given the prevailing passivity of the *private* citizenry, the mass media provide an essential mechanism by which would-be representatives can reach out, however superficially, to the bulk of their constituents. If "news" is what they want, "news" is what politician/statesmen will give them.

This leads to a number of familiar distortions. First is the cultivation of a "media personality"—a politician must cultivate the talents necessary to convey a favorable impression on a fifteen-second T.V. spot. Conversely, a cinematic gaffe—a moment of tearful frustration or a failure to use the right makeup to suppress a "sinister" five o'clock shadow—can damage a good name built up through years of public-spirited service.

Second, moving from style to substance, the mass media reward the most superficial kind of sloganeering—for it is only such stuff that will be assimilable within the audience's exceedingly modest attention span. The slogans, in turn, will be of two kinds. Most obviously, the private citizenry will receive a steady diet of political banalities inherited from the past—for these slogans are sufficiently familiar so as not to require elaborate explanation. The unremitting banality will be punctuated, in turn, by evocative simplicities so outrageous that they will arrest attention. The hardest thing, however, will be to engage the media in a long and serious process of public education on an issue of genuine social significance. In normal times at least, the mass public simply finds such things too tedious to hear; investigative reporters will be better advised to spend their time on topics that are more readily accessible: like personal scandal. So long as the normal politician keeps his nose clean, and takes his acting lessons seriously, he has little incentive to use the media to talk to his constituents, in a serious way, about the nature of the fundamental problems that press upon them as private *citizens* of the United States. He may serve himself best by beaming benign banalities through the mass media while sending very different signals to the public and private interest groups he seeks to mobilize on his behalf.[25]

Political Parties

A final way of mobilizing electoral support is through the political party—which, in normal times,[26] is largely a service organization helping local constituents with their personal dealings with the government. Here is where political patronage comes in. By increasing the number of full-time operatives in his employ, each representative can increase the effectiveness with which he can discharge this service function. The larger his "home office," the more grateful constituents there will be to remember the representative on Election Day when, as *private* citizens, they go to the polls to make their distracted decisions. Indeed, effective constituency service might, in theory at least, make an incumbent's stand on all national issues entirely irrelevant to his future electoral success. He might simply gain reelection by saying: Vote for me, and I'll make sure that your Social Security check gets delivered on time.[27]

The Brighter Side of Normal Politics

But surely, I hope I hear you say, there is more to normal politics than this! Despite the aggressiveness of private and bureaucratic interests, the self-righteousness of public interest groups, the banality and image-mongering of the media, the crude efforts by political hacks—indeed all and sundry—to secure a place at the public trough, surely there is something more that is going on—the representation of We the People of the United States in the good old democratic American way?

I do not deny this for a moment. Even during the normalest moments, people at all levels of the political system are assuring themselves—and others—that they are more than the single dimensional parodies they sometimes allow themselves to seem.[28] And it is crucial to catch the half-hidden tokens of a more complex understanding of private citizenship—without them, the Republic could not survive. Thus, however intently private and bureaucratic interests work to deliver the goods for their constituents, they betray signs of Publian self-restraint. For one thing, most do not stoop to outright corruption. Indeed, most lobbyists would be loathe to admit that they are engaged in *purely* factional activity. Though they may rue-fully recognize that they lavish a rather large share of their energies upon the pursuit of a rather narrow aspect of the public good, only the most cynical lobbyists confess that there is absolutely nothing to their case from a Publian point of view; lobbyists aside, certainly most Chryslerians back home *do* honestly believe that the interests of Chrysler and America coincide—though they certainly don't ad-dress the question with an open mind.

An equal and opposite form of dualistic consciousness can be found amongst public interest groups. However strident their de-nunciation of existing abuses, they refuse to break with the normal political system by engaging in illegal revolutionary activity. Many partisans are uncomfortably aware that their stentorian tone is attrib-utable, at least in part, to their fear that they might go unheard by a passive citizenry if they spoke more reasonably; and that, until they actually do succeed in mobilizing a widespread movement behind their cause, they will have to settle for much less than half a loaf. In short, our organized private *citizens,* no less than our organized *private* citizens, go about their activity with a more complex self-understanding, and greater self-restraint, than an initial impression suggests.

And the same is true as we go down the list of normal political actors. However cynical media specialists have become about the gap between appearance and reality, they spend more time and energy on the Publian side of politics than a hard dollar-and-cents accounting would justify. Even the most hardened party hack is aware that there *is* another side to his business; indeed, American history is full of examples of seeming hacks rising to the Publian occasion against all expectations (though there are lots of cautionary tales as well). Most of all: however grateful Americans may be for their Social Security checks, many remain conscious of themselves, if ever so privately, as citizens, and may unpredictably repudiate politicians who pander too obviously to their private interests.

THE PARLIAMENTARIAN'S CRITIQUE

All this is very crude—but there is a real danger in greater detail. Constitutional assessment cannot depend on particularities that will change in a couple of years or even a decade or two. The basic question is this: Two centuries ago, Publius claimed that his new constitutional order could control the operation of faction in normal government. Does this claim still make sense today?

Ever since Woodrow Wilson's time, mainstream political science has tended toward skepticism. Rather than admiring the Federalist legacy, Wilsonians have looked across the Atlantic and found the British parliamentary model superior. Since this Anglophile critique has been important in diverting American constitutional thought from its Federalist roots,[29] we must confront it here. I shall summarize the critics' bill of particulars under three interrelated heads—responsibility, transparency, decisiveness—before considering what, if anything, a neo-Federalist response might look like.[30]

Responsibility

The modern British constitution concentrates authority in the Cabinet in general, the Prime Minister in particular. During normal times, the House of Commons is not an independent power center, but a sounding board—through which the leading parties seek to organize public opinion for support in the next general election.[31] This means that the Prime Minister, and her party, cannot escape responsibility for their conduct in office. If there is a fiasco, it is their fiasco; their successes are their successes. They have the power and everybody knows it.

Publius's testimony notwithstanding, this focused sense of responsibility is superior in controlling faction. Most importantly, it breeds mature deliberation by seasoned politician/statesmen who know they cannot evade the judgment of their peers, their fellow citizens, and history. In contrast, the American system invites buck-passing: President blames Congress, House blames Senate, the Court condemns them all, only to be excoriated in turn. Since nobody is in charge, everybody claims credit for successes and blames everybody else for failures. Sometimes it seems that nobody is even trying to make a considered judgment about the merits of a programmatic initiative—so long as somebody else can be stuck with the blame for the costs, why should I care?

Transparency

The flip side of irresponsibility is a lack of transparency. With everybody in Washington blaming everybody else, it's awfully hard for the normal citizen to figure out who is really at the bottom of a particular affair. While this is an especial problem during periods in which different political parties dominate different branches, the separation of powers increases opacity of government even when the same "party" dominates everywhere. So long as Senators and Congressmen win their elections independently of the President, they will have powerful incentives to differentiate their appeals from those coming out of the White House. After all, a Representative wants to convince the voters to reelect her even when they don't much like the President. Under normal conditions, this will mean that the "Congressional party" will be saying very different things from the "Presidential party."[32]

In contrast, the centralized structure of British government breeds transparency. Since there is no separation of powers between the Executive and the Legislative, the only way a voter can express a preference for Prime Minister is by voting for the M.P. who is running in her name in the district. Thus, individual M.P.s can only hope to win by focusing on the programs and personalities presented by the potential Prime Ministers. While the American party normally goes to the electorate with a cacophony of voices, each candidate running for parliament seeks to defend the top of the ticket.

Decisiveness

Little wonder, then, that the English can get things done. Once the Prime Minister gets an electoral mandate, she can expect the House to support her statutory initiatives without endless pressure for exceptions and special treatment. Rather than dealing with hyper-aggressive back-benchers seeking to prove to the folks back home that "they can do more for Manchester," the P.M. can rely more on experts in the bureaucracy that will be charged with the implementation of her program. Unsurprisingly, this means that statutes are not only more coherent ideologically, but also designed for effective administration.

Contrast this with the familiar deadlock of American politics: the President, claiming a mandate, proposes a statutory initiative only to see it sink in Congress without a trace. Even if a Presidential initiative emerges from the Congresssional committees, it has lost its programmatic edge—battered about by powerful Congressmen who demand *ad hoc* concessions to their local interests and ideological idiosyncrasies. By the time both Houses have done their "deliberating," the President may find his call for a "comprehensive initiative" transformed into a chaotic assemblage of interstitial compromises.

To make matters worse, the statute will be unresponsive to the needs of effective administration. The Congressmen who draft the statutes will be hostile to clear lines of authority in the executive branch. They will want to assure their continued influence by encouraging bureaucrats to look to Congress, rather than the President, as their boss. They will succeed just enough to undercut executive efforts at coordination, without substituting penetrating oversight of their own.

Incoherent legislation implemented incoherently. If this is what Publius's economy of virtue has come to mean in the modern world, isn't it time for agonizing reappraisal?[33]

A NEO-FEDERALIST RESPONSE?

There can be no hope of magically dissolving these doubts. They point to real pathologies. While there may well be neo-Federalist cures for some of the worst symptoms, the basic diseases—irresponsibility, opacity, indecisiveness—are endemic to a system of checks and balances.[34] Rather than wishing them away, a neo-Federalist response must begin by redefining the question: Sure, there are serious problems with the Publian system. But that's true of any system. The real issue is whether the vices of the Publian system are more or less vicious than those generated by the British[35] system of concentrated authority?

Begin by reflecting on the misleading way the parliamentarian sets the political stage. On a good day in the House of Commons, an observer will find hundreds of mobilized back-benchers loudly giving the Prime Minister their enthusiastic support. Yet, by definition of normal politics, nothing like this is going on in the country. Most people are giving the the parliamentary debates only passing attention; at best, the Prime Minister's policies may enjoy the soft support of a majority of the *private* citizenry. This is not to say that Her Majesty's Loyal Opposition is doing any better. Indeed, the very idea that public opinion is neatly divided between a single majority view and a unified minority view is often an utter fabrication.

In short, the parliamentary system tries to ignore the dualist's crucial point about normal politics: *the People themselves* have retired from public life. Rather than emphasize the problematic way in which politician/statesmen normally represent a predominantly *private* citizenry, the parliamentary system allows the governing party to project an image of mobilized national commitment that doesn't really exist. Every day, the Party Whip herds the majority of M.P.s into the winning lobby to show their support for the Prime Minister for the umpteenth time. This emphatic and repeated show in Parliament contrasts oddly with the mass apathy and fractional conviction swirling about the country. Despite their best efforts, the P.M. and her friends in Parliament are only *stand-ins* for the People; they do not *stand for* the People themselves.[36]

Whatever its deficiencies, at least the Publian system forces the problematics of representation onto the surface of normal political life. Every politician/statesman loves to claim that the People themselves have given him, and him alone, a mandate for every jot and tittle of his program. But only the American Constitution takes the decisive step that can effectively undercut this cheap talk. It refuses to grant *any* single governor an effective monopoly over lawmaking in the manner of a victorious Prime Minister. Within the dualistic system, no statute can hope to succeed if it remains the product of a single mind—even if it is the mind of the President (supported by his brains trust). Every initiative must appeal to the interests and ideologies of a host of independent politician/statesmen, who themselves have gained the soft support of popular majorities. Doubtless, the outcome of this process may lack the clean hard lines that can come out of the parliamentary system.* But why *should* the Prime

---

*No necessity of this: there have been as many Harold Wilsons as Margaret Thatchers living at 10 Downing Street.

Minister have the power to take decisive action on the basis of soft popular support? Isn't it *more democratic* to require her to convince independent politician/statesmen that, despite the softness of support amongst the *private* citizenry, her proposal serves the permanent interests of the community?

Granted, the separation of powers may make it harder for a far-seeing Prime Minister to take decisive steps to solve a problem before it reaches crisis proportions. Even here, however, there is something to be said on the other side. Instead of depending so heavily on the Prime Minister, the separation of powers allows a host of politician/statesmen to play the role of policy initiator. Perhaps there is more fresh thinking on more problems under the American system? It may even be a mistake to exaggerate the ideological incoherence that comes out of a genuinely collaborative process in statute writing. There are many problems that profit from a healthy eclecticism; perhaps, over time, the American system encourages lawmakers to move beyond the narrow limits of "clear" ideologies?[37]

We have thus far been allowing our parliamentarian to suppose that "enlightened statesmen will always be at the helm" of her concentrated system. In the worst case, the British system will exhibit vicious pathologies of its own. Parliamentary oppression may take two forms. First there is the garden-variety rip-off: taxes may be designed so that the social groups supporting the Opposition are forced to pay the bulk of the revenue; benefits may be distributed so that Government supporters appropriate the lion's share. By constantly funneling wealth from Opposition to Government, the Prime Minister may try to build her electoral support on the most tangible of foundations. Her appeal: If the Government's supporters desert her at the ballot box, they will be killing the goose that lays the golden egg.[38]

Then there are the more intangible rip-offs. Perhaps the Prime Minister can cement her coalition by pandering to some "single-issue" groups that have gained some active support amongst the general citizenry. This may be an especially attractive strategy if the moralisms espoused by the activists oppress groups who support the Opposition party in any event. In such a case, the P.M. may have little to lose, and much to gain, by catering to an ideological fraction's intense convictions—despite the fact that these would be repudiated by a majority of private *citizens* if they were ever induced to take the issue seriously.[39]

Publius had a name for these parliamentary diseases: tyranny by factional majority. In recalling this concept for modern use, I propose to reserve it for a special sort of tyranny. I am not describing the nightmare case in which a political movement successfully mobilizes the mass of private *citizens* behind a program of overwhelming evil— the extermination or enslavement of blacks or Jews or aliens. Tyranny by *factions* focuses on a more humdrum kind of viciousness—where the mass of private citizens, distracted by their private concerns, allow *politician*/statesmen to build a winning parliamentary coalition by oppressing minority out-groups.

Though the oppressions here will not generally reach Nazi-like monstrosity, this does not mean we shouldn't worry about them. Indeed, it seems plausible to suppose that constitutional structures might control political viciousness born of citizen apathy, ignorance, and selfishness better than they can control viciousness which has the mobilized support of a malevolent majority. The cleverest constitutional designs will be swept away by a people that has lost all sense of decency.

THE ECONOMY OF VIRTUE

Which is better: a far-seeing Prime Minister taking decisive steps to resolve a problem before it reaches crisis proportions or a bunch of eclectic Congressional types slowly coming to grips with a problem that might have eluded a more centralized political apparatus? Which is worse: irresponsibility, opacity, and indecisiveness or factional tyranny by the parliamentary majority?

Surely, the right answer is that there is no right answer for all times and places. This may seem bland, but it is pretty controversial. The Wilsonian tradition treats the Publian system as so deeply defective as to make the case for British-style centralization seem obvious. Once we move beyond the "obvious," there is obviously lots to be said on both sides. I can only point to a couple of factors that keep me in the neo-Federalist camp.

First, the British system looks better in a place where almost all Prime Ministers are trained at Oxbridge and then subjected to a

long probationary period of scrutiny by a stable political elite. Whatever the vices of this class system, it makes it less likely that a Prime
Minister will be selected who will use her parliamentary majority in
the ruthless way I have described. The reigning class ethos may also
increase the chances of up-side performance—where the Oxbridge
P.M. takes the tough decisions that her Oxbridge peers recognize
are required for the long-term good of the country.

In contrast, the system would operate very differently in America.
My point updates the old Publian emphasis on the vast size of our
Republic. The country is *so* large and heterogeneous that it outstrips
the governing pretensions of the American leadership class generated
by Oxbridge universities. Many modern Presidents depend heavily
on regional, not national, elites. President Carter's victory promoted
Georgians to the White House; President Reagan's, Californians. In
contrast to Britain, there is a lower chance that the chief executive
here will be an experienced national statesman who will seize the
opportunity to make hard short-term decisions that will greatly re-
dound to the nation's long-term advantage; instead, we will often
find regional politicians using their power on the basis of very soft
national mandates. Generally speaking, it seems wiser to force the
President to try to use the great resources at his disposal to convince
politician/statesmen from other regions of the country of the wisdom
of his proposals.

Especially, and this is my second point, when we take the weaknesses of the Washington bureaucracy into account. Once again, it
seems a fair guess that a smaller percentage of the best and brightest
are to be found there than in Whitehall. There is no reason to think
that superior bureaucratic leadership will stabilize the erratic mechanisms of Presidential selection.

There is a circularity here. Probably, Americans would have developed stronger traditions of elite leadership—both for politicians
and bureaucrats—if we had had a British system over the last two
centuries. But we didn't; we have relied, more than the British have,
on a mobilized citizenry to correct the mistakes of circulating regional
elites. At the very least, the Wilsonian reformer should confront this
central difficulty—and explain how his centralized system of parliamentary power fits into a society without a hegemonic national elite
of the British type. Certainly Wilson himself never gave a satisfactory

answer to this question; until somebody does, I remain a neo-Federalist.

Beyond Publius:
The Modern Separation of Powers

Thus far, we have been exploring the question of first principle: Does the separation of powers continue to make sense as a governing idea? Even if your answer is yes, it doesn't follow that the *Federalist Papers* can serve as the last word on the subject. As the first part of this essay explained, many of the Founders' more concrete expectations about the House, Senate, President, and Court have been transformed, and transformed again, over the course of two centuries. While the modern separation of powers continues to problematicize representation as Publius hoped, it does not do so in the precise ways he anticipated.

Begin with the House of Representatives. The Federalists expected it to be the place where popular movements that aimed to speak for the American people would first make their tumultuous presence known. At that time, the House was the only part of the national government directly elected by the voters. Given this fact, it seemed sensible to expect the Senate and the President to serve as ballast. They should not be too easily overwhelmed by a few House demagogues who claimed to speak for *the People themselves.* Senate and President should serve as bulwarks of deliberation, demanding that the hotheads submit their proposals to cool analysis from competing perspectives.

Two centuries onward, a lot has changed. Nowadays, the principal populist impulse comes from the Presidency, not the House. In turn, the House has become a bulwark for skeptical doubts about the latest Presidential pronunciamento: It's all very well and good for the President to say that we must wage war against inflation/drugs/ you name it; but do the folks back home in the Nth District agree? How important are these national issues anyway, compared to local and regional concerns beneath Presidential attention?

The Senate has also undergone a profound, if subtler, transformation. Surely Senators continue to serve as the distinctive voice of the states that elect them. But they have also become a principal home for would-be Presidents fashioning their own appeals to the People. As a consequence, the Senate is often the focus of a critique of the Presidential program from a relatively national perspective—though, of course, Presidential aspirants in the Senate will characteristically be skeptical of White House proposals.

As I suggested in Part One, these changes in the normal orientation of our modern institutions have deep roots in the nation's history.[40] The crucial point is to see how, for all these changes, the basic Founding idea endures. A glance at the constitutional stage in Washington continues to emphasize the problematic character of the effort to speak for We the People during normal politics. Behold: the President calling on Congress to embrace his brave new vision of American government—in the name of the People. Behold: the Senate subjecting the Presidential initiative to scrutiny, and proposing counterinitiatives—in the name of the People. Behold: the House doubting whether these large initiatives really serve the interests of the folks back home, and pushing lots of localist agendas—in the name of the People. Who, then, *really does* speak for the People?

None of them. They are just stand-ins, that's all. The mass of *private* citizens are too busy right now to engage in the kind of sustained and mobilized debate and decision that would justify any of their stand-ins declaring that they have a decisive mandate for fundamental change. President, Senate, House are merely stand-ins for the absent People; none of them should be allowed to pretend they stand for *the People themselves*.

This does not imply that normal political functions are unimportant. Mobilized or not, America's private citizenry confront serious problems at home and abroad. Their representatives have been constitutionally empowered to deliberate together and figure out statutory solutions to emerging problems. Indeed, given the seriousness of normal lawmaking, there is a very real question whether the Founding allocation of powers amongst the different branches continues to make sense. Given the profound changes in the policy-making perspectives of House, Senate, and Presidency, it would be very surprising if the Founders had given each of the branches just the lawmaking powers that promoted the goal of public-spirited deliberation under modern conditions. To take but one example, the President's aggressive use of his veto power in the modern republic is radically different from its use in the early republic.[41] Such shifts in the balance of lawmaking power and institutional perspective open up a rich agenda for a neo-Federalist critique of existing arrangements: Which changes in the lawmaking balance make sense, given the changing ways in which House, Senate, and President represent "the People" in normal politics? Which changes in the balance endanger deeper dualist commitments—most notably, that *no* branch of normal government can be allowed to become so powerful that it can force all the others to recognize it as the *unproblematic* spokesman for the People?

These are, transparently, tough questions, requiring a mix of philosophical and practical judgments worthy of Publius himself. My only point is that the Wilsonian tradition prevents modern political science from making its necessary contribution. So long as many political scientists believe that the very effort to depart from the British-style concentration of power is conceptually confused and deeply antidemocratic, we cannot ask, let alone answer, the right questions involved in restriking the balance of powers in the modern republic.

THE SUPREME COURT

The same is true in reaching a balanced assessment of the modern Supreme Court. The Wilsonian's anxieties about the separation of powers reach a maximum when he confronts this most peculiar of American institutions: what gives Nine Old Lawyers the democratic authority to veto the statutory conclusions of Our Elected Representatives? It is bad enough for lawmaking responsibility to be diffused amongst our representatives in a way that generates buck-passing, confusion, and indecisiveness. But it is even worse when the Supreme Court then invalidates the result. Although the House, Senate, President may not be as democratic as the House of Commons, at least the leading actors are elected. That's more than one can say of the Supreme Court. Little wonder there is no judicial review in England, where they know what a proper democracy looks like!

Such Wilsonianisms have shaped the dominant school of modern constitutional theory. These monistic democrats, as I called them,[42] begin by placing each and every exercise of judicial review under the cloud of the "countermajoritarian difficulty." In Alexander Bickel's classic statement, judicial invalidation of a Congressional statute puts the Justices on a collision course with "the actual people of the here and now."[43] Given this breach, the task for constitutional theory is inevitably apologetic: Is there any way to rehabilitate the Court's legitimacy, given its frontal assault on the very foundations of America's democratic identity?

This is far too melodramatic a question for the neo-Federalist. In rejecting a normal statute, the Court is aiming at a smaller target than Democracy Itself. It is questioning the popular mandate of the five-hundred-odd politician/statesmen in Washington, D.C. While these folks have all won election, they have normally done so on the basis of soft ballots by a majority of *private* citizens who themselves recognize that they have not given the key issues the kind of sober consideration they deserve. President and Congress normally do not have the *considered* support of the American people in assaulting the principles established by past successes in constitutional politics. If the Court is right in finding that these politician/statesmen have moved beyond their mandate, it is furthering Democracy, not frustrating it, in revealing our representatives as mere "stand-ins" for the People, whose word is not to be confused with the collective judgment of *the People themselves.*

In rejecting the countermajoritarian difficulty, I hardly wish to give the modern Supreme Court a blank check. I do not deny that it is undemocratic for Nine Old Lawyers to force the country to embrace the moral ideals that win their approval by a vote of 5 to 4. I mean, instead, to suggest a third possibility: that the modern Court has been doing a credible (not perfect) job interpreting the constitutional principles hammered out by We the People at the Founding, Reconstruction, and the New Deal (as well as at lesser constitutional moments). Of course, I do not expect my introductory treatment of this theme in Part One to resolve all your doubts. My aim has been to suggest how much we may learn from the past once we reorient constitutional theory away from the "countermajoritarian" difficulty toward the possibility of interpretation. The challenge is to deepen our insight into the Court's interpretive practice—from *Marbury* through *Brown, Lochner* through *Griswold*—so as to help the courts make the most of our constitutional legacy in the future.

Even if, in the end, you are convinced to take the possibility of judicial interpretation seriously, it is important not to exaggerate the dualist claim about judicial review. I do not suggest that even a Court that discharged its interpretive responsibilities with great insight can pretend to represent the People *better* than the President or the Congress. My point is quite different: During normal politics, *nobody* represents the People in an unproblematic way—not the Court nor the President nor the Congress nor the Gallup polls. Given the "softness" of normal public opinion, it is simply impossible to say how the people of today would decide an issue if they mobilized their political energies and successfully hammered out a new constitutional solution. In the very process of mobilized debate and decision, many minds would change, many new directions would be explored before a new constitutional solution was reached. Only a fool would predict the outcome of this hypothetical higher lawmaking process on the basis of the "soft" opinions expressed during a period of normal political life. We must instead face up to the Publian truth: during normal politics, the People simply do not exist; they can only be represented by "stand-ins."

Let me make this crucial point about representation in terms of the endless jokes we tell each other about good news and bad news. The good news about the President and Congress is that they represent the democratically expressed will of the present generation; the bad news is that today's citizenry is distracted from public life and unwilling to give the fundamental issues the kind of considered judgment they deserve. The good news about the Court is that it is interpreting the constitutional principles affirmed by the American people at times when their political attention and energy was most focused on such matters; the bad news is that the Americans who made these considered constitutional judgments are dead.

It would be nice, I suppose, to live in a world in which all the news was good. There will be times in the future, as in the past, when one or another group of private *citizens* will begin to strike a responsive chord amongst a larger group of fellow Americans; the weak, fragmentary, disconnected political talk around dinner table and workplace will begin to focus on a particular movement's constitutional agenda, and will give shape to the debate in more public forums; increasingly, the transformative initiative will dominate the country's political life; elections will be fought on the movement's agenda, in the process transforming the public's understanding of the nature of the issues, as well as the character of possible solutions; then, after long struggles in many different public places, a movement may at last gain the constitutional authority to speak, once again, for We the People. At such moments, the Supreme Court should bend to this new expression of constitutional will—seeking to integrate the new constitutional solution into the older structures which the People have left intact. But, during more normal times, isn't it better for the Court to represent the *absent* People by forcing our elected politician/statesmen to measure their statutory conclusions against the principles reached by those who have most successfully represented the People in the past?

Within this neo-Federalist framework, judicial review can commend itself without requiring its partisans to engage in spurious talk about the Justices communing with a "contemporary community consensus." If such phrases are meant to suggest the existence of a set of principles of public morality that have been self-consciously affirmed by the mass of today's Americans in a considered manner, they beg the question. Rather than supposing that such a consensus usually exists, the question is how it can be formed and how best to govern democratically during those periods when people are focused on other things.

From this angle, the Supreme Court's backward-looking exercise in interpretation will begin to seem a fundamental aspect of a larger future-oriented enterprise of popular sovereignty. By trying to represent the concrete implications of past principles affirmed in the name of the People, the Court invites the reigning group of politician/statesmen, and the public more generally, into a critical dialogue about the future: if there is something seriously wrong with the higher law legacy inherited from the past, what precisely is it? Can We the People of today articulate our proposed re-visions in a language which will stir the mass of passive citizens into mobilized political activity?

When faced with the Court's challenge, our elected representatives may, of course, find themselves unable or unwilling to overcome the Supreme Court's defense of the past judgments of the People by successfully taking to the higher lawmaking track—and leading the People to hammer out a new constitutional solution. Yet such failures should not in themselves delegitimate judicial review. They simply express the hard Publian truth about the difficulty of mobilizing a majority of private *citizens* in a liberal democracy.

Nor will it do to respond by denouncing an interpretivist Court as unduly conservative, if not downright undemocratic. This easy condemnation ignores the extraordinary consequences that follow when, after years of long and hard struggle, a political movement does gain the constitutional authority to speak for the People. Once this happens, the popular movement will no longer be obliged to call so extravagantly upon the political energies of the American people. Its constitutional achievement will remain intact even when most private citizens lapse into relative passivity. Despite the inexorable return of normal politics, the movement's legal achievements will remain at the center of the consciousness of America's constitutional lawyers, who will recognize a high responsibility to scrutinize normal politics in terms of the movement's constitutional principles. From this point of view, the Supreme Court is hardly a conservative friend of the status quo, but an ongoing representative of a mobilized People during the lengthy periods of apathy, ignorance, and selfishness that mark the collective life of the private citizenry of a liberal republic.

CHAPTER TEN

Higher Lawmaking

FROM NORMAL POLITICS TO
HIGHER LAWMAKING

T HE LAST CHAPTER approached the Founding dualisms from a direction Publius would have found uncongenial. He spoke of constitutional politics in the confident voice of the successful revolutionary, and looked upon the prospect of normal politics with anxiety. My exercise in neo-Federalism began by reversing interpretive field: perhaps modern Americans will find their dualist heritage more approachable if they begin with the more mundane realities of normal politics?

So long as higher lawmaking remains mysterious, however, we remain far away from our goal. This chapter returns to the problem, placing it against the preceding sketch of normal politics. I shall be following the life cycle of a successful movement in constitutional politics, beginning at the point when it has gained sufficiently deep and broad support amongst the private citizenry to warrant admission to the higher lawmaking process. During this signaling phase, the movement earns the constitutional authority to claim that, in contrast to the countless ideological fractions competing in normal politics, its reform agenda should be placed at the center of sustained public scrutiny.

This leads to the second phase of the process: proposal. Here the higher lawmaking system encourages the movement to focus its rhetoric into a series of more or less operational proposals for constitutional reform.

As this process matures, the stage is set for the third phase: mobilized popular deliberation. Here the movement's transformative proposals are tested time and again within the higher lawmaking system. The result may be very disappointing to movement activists:

the movement's success at the signaling phase may only catalyze a powerful backlash—in which a previously "silent majority" organizes in energetic defense of traditional constitutional prerogatives. The outcome, in this case, will be a failed constitutional moment—in which the higher lawmaking system rejects the movement's pretensions and returns its partisans to the humbler triumphs and defeats of normal politics.

If, however, the movement emerges from its period of institutional trial with an even deeper and broader base of support, the higher lawmaking system shifts into its final phase: legal codification. Here the Supreme Court begins the task of translating constitutional politics into constitutional law, supplying the cogent doctrinal principles that will guide normal politics for many years to come.

My aim will be to define, at each phase of this process, the basic functions that should be discharged by higher lawmaking institutions in a credible dualist democracy. This functional assessment will provide a critical perspective on America's existing higher lawmaking machinery. After two centuries, how do our institutions presently discharge the crucial signaling, proposing, deliberating, and codifying functions?

I think we are in pretty bad shape at present, and that the reform of our higher lawmaking institutions should be high on the neo-Federalist agenda. Although I have floated a concrete proposal in Part One,[1] this chapter is not concerned with its defense. It is more important to provide a framework for further analysis. The entire question has drawn so little attention recently. A much fuller debate is required before the stakes involved in particular reform measures are fully understood.

My framework builds upon the sketch of constitutional history presented in Part One. I suggested that Americans have built up two distinct higher lawmaking systems over the last two centuries. The *classical* system operates along the lines sketched by the Founding Federalists in Article Five of the original Constitution. Here the decisive constitutional signal is issued by a deliberative assembly meeting on the national level; the ratification process is conducted by popularly elected assemblies on the state level; and the process of judicial codification is guided by a formal constitutional amendment.

The *modern* system has historical roots stretching back to Thomas Jefferson's "Revolution of 1800," but it came into its own in the modern regime inaugurated by the Democratic Party of Franklin Delano Roosevelt. Here the decisive constitutional signal is issued by a President claiming a mandate from the People. If Congress supports this claim by enacting transformative statutes that challenge the fundamentals of the preexisting regime, these statutes are treated as the functional equivalent of a proposal for constitutional amendment.

The stage is then set for the third phase: mobilized deliberation. Here the Supreme Court invalidates the initial wave of transformative statutes and challenges the ascendant movement to refine its vision and go to the People for another show of deep and broad popular support. If the President and Congress rise to this challenge by passing a new wave of statutes and demonstrate broad and deep electoral support at the next general election, the matter returns to the Court for reappraisal: Should it invalidate the second wave of transformative statutes and escalate the constitutional struggle yet further? Or should it recognize that the People have spoken in a deliberate and sustained way, and that further resistance would be counterproductive?

If it reaches this second conclusion, the Court executes a "switch in time" without awaiting a formal constitutional amendment. Following New Deal precedents, the Justices proceed to the codification stage by issuing a set of transformative opinions validating the second wave of statutes despite their inconsistency with bedrock legal principles that were foundational during the previous regime.

While this modern system is poorly understood by lawyers, it is now at the very center of the constitutional consciousness of the American People. Thus, when the Reagan Republicans sought to repeal the principles of activist national government first constitutionalized by the New Deal Democrats, they did not use the classical system. In an ironic recognition of the New Dealers, they sought to use the Rooseveltian system of Presidential leadership to repeal the substance of the New Deal. Once again, we saw a President claiming a mandate from the People to enact transformative statutes, in this case ones that challenged the fiscal foundations of the welfare state and the basic principle of progressive taxation. Once again, we saw a President calling upon the Supreme Court to make a switch in time that would reverse fundamental doctrines of the existing constitutional regime—supporting this effort by nominating Justices who, like the New Dealers Frankfurter, Douglas, and Jackson, were able and willing to revolutionize constitutional law in a series of transformative opinions. Unlike Roosevelt, Reagan failed to gain authority for his transformative judicial appointments. But this does not make his effort any less instructive. Apparently the New Deal system is so entrenched in the public mind that even those who would reverse other aspects of the Democratic achievement are willing to make use of it.

How then does the modern system of Presidential leadership compare with the classical one in discharging the basic functions of signaling, proposing, deliberating, and codifying that are crucial in an ongoing dualistic democracy?

THE STARK VIEW, AND BEYOND

But we are getting ahead of ourselves. Before distinguishing classical from modern systems, we must first examine some broader conceptual issues. Most notably—what is it, precisely, that distinguishes the rare success in higher lawmaking from the exercises in normal lawmaking which go on every day in the country's life?

Begin by avoiding a tempting oversimplification. It becomes too easy to define the distinctive character of higher lawmaking if we take an overly grim view of normal government. This dark picture treats normal politics as if it yielded statutes that were nothing more than deals by selfish interest groups, each looking out for itself without a thought for the general welfare; it paints legislators as if they were nothing more than brokers gratifying the selfish interests currently dominant in their districts. Against this grim background, higher lawmaking seems very high indeed: it is the only kind of lawmaking in which anybody is taking the public interest at all seriously.

I reject this stark view. As the last chapter suggested,[2] it cannot explain some basic aspects of normal politics, such as why tens of millions of Americans take the trouble to go to the polls on Election Day. This regular, if formalized, participation is inexplicable if we really did live in a world of perfect privatists, each looking out for Number One. It is in the name of realism, not idealism, that my model of normal politics marked the existence of millions of *private* citizens as central to the operation of American democracy. Though they would admit that they haven't given national politics the sustained deliberation it deserves, they do recognize that there is more to public life than the pursuit of private interest (otherwise they wouldn't have gone to the polls in the first place).

My model's economy of virtue did not end with the massive presence of a passive citizenry on Election Day. Even during normal politics, it envisioned more active types organizing and agitating for large projects of political renewal and redefinition. Some of these organizing efforts may well gain the support of thousands and thousands of private *citizens,* willing to sacrifice money and time to establish one or another "public interest" group as a significant presence in the process of normal legislation. If we added all these groups together, there would be hundreds and hundreds of thousands—probably millions—of citizens seriously concerned with one or another project for national redefinition.

The presence of both active and passive citizens in the normal political process suffices to undercut the stark view. The line between normal and higher lawmaking must be drawn in a subtler way. How to proceed?

The beginnings of my answer: During normal politics, no "public interest" grouping is powerful enough to force its agenda to the center of political concern, to make normal politician/statesmen treat *its* questions as *the* critical questions they *must* answer if they hope to continue to represent the People.

This lack of political salience can be measured along two different if related axes. The first compares the "public interest" agendas proffered by competing groupings. In a free society, different fractions will identify different issues as the focus of their mobilizational concerns—from the right to bear arms to nuclear disarmament, from the right to abortion to the preservation of endangered species, from the rights of minorities to the sanctity of property. During normal politics, the partisans of these, and many other, issues will be jostling against one another in calling attention to their competing agendas. Their efforts to push the legislative process in so many different directions only emphasizes the lack of a broad and deep consensus on the direction of future change.

At the same time they compete with one another for ideological primacy, all citizen groups must struggle against a very powerful undertow that deemphasizes the entire domain of policy and principle. During normal politics, most politician/statesmen have learned the dangers of strong ideological commitment. Taking sides can earn the undying enmity of mobilized opponents. Even activist "friends" can cause long-term trouble—as they may make increasingly extreme demands as a condition for sustaining their support. Politicians will often find it more prudent to give a bit to both sides, to cover their ultimate position in a fog of ambiguity. After all, most of the voters aren't nearly as engaged in the Cause as the overheated rhetoric of activists suggests. Rather than invest heavily in ideological politics, isn't it wiser to appeal to the bread-and-butter interests of constituents: Vote for me, I can do more for Massachusetts! This emphasis on constituency service is especially attractive for incumbents so long as seniority counts in the House and Senate. If the folks back home send somebody new to Capitol Hill, they will have to wait a long time before she can do as much for them as the old-time incumbent. So long as the incumbent keeps on bringing home the bacon, isn't it silly to unseat him because of one or another policy dispute?

Of course, these narrow appeals to constituency advantage may come to mean less to voters during times of political mobilization. Suddenly, incumbents may learn that years of yeoman's service to their Congressional district matters a lot less than whether they are standing up for the Right Things on Capitol Hill. At such moments, the reigning politician/statesmen may be found falling all over themselves to make strong statements on behalf of causes with which they formerly had the most nodding acquaintance.

But this in no way defeats the main point: normally the mass of the *private* citizenry will not be focusing on any single cause with anything like this degree of political seriousness; and it will only be prudent for most politician/statesmen to deemphasize controversial principles for fear of picking the wrong ideological horse to ride during long periods of more passive mass engagement.

SIGNALING

"We are not mere politicians. We come in the name of the People to demand a fundamental revision of our higher law." Of course, spokesmen for every interest group would love to be given the constitutional authority to make this claim. But a dualist constitution seeks to ensure that such pretensions will be taken seriously *only* when our representatives in Washington have extraordinary support for their initiative in the country at large. Extraordinary in three senses: depth, breadth, and decisiveness.

Depth

Depth points to the quality of public involvement, and is best explored by returning to two central dilemmas of private citizenship.[3] First, citizens normally haven't gathered enough information for an informed opinion. Second, they haven't conscientiously probed their initial reactions: Do these give too much weight to their selfish interests? Have they *seriously* considered the "rights of citizens and the permanent interests of the community"?

The depth of a movement's popular support is measured by the extent to which its adherents have made special efforts along these lines. Assessing such matters does not, of course, allow for sharp yes/no answers: There is no magic moment at which a private citizen shouts *Eureka!* and announces that he has come to a *considered judgment* on a problem that has been bothering him, no single instant at which a passive *private* citizen transforms himself into an active private *citizen*.

Nonetheless, the notion of reaching a "considered judgment" is neither arbitrary nor unfamiliar. All grown-ups constantly use the notion in everyday life. Consider, for example, how you might go about hunting for a new home or apartment: Would you take the first one that came along? For some, the answer is yes. But even they would recognize that they are not acting in a considered manner.

The thoughtful person tries to find out about his alternatives. No less important than raw data is some self-scrutiny. The search for an apartment rarely proceeds without requiring the house-hunter to reconsider what he is *really* about: Do I need this extra room at the cost of doing without something else? How important is the fact that this apartment is located in a school district that is awful/great/only so-so? Whatever your answers, you must confront questions like these before you have made a *considered* choice about your future home.

And the same is true when you act as a private *citizen*. Before voicing a judgment about the "rights of citizens and the permanent interests of the community," you must scrutinize your inclinations with the kind of intensity you might give to a house-hunting decision. Of course, the kind of questions are different. Rather than defining what's "really" important to you and your loved ones, you must now deliberate about the best interests of the United States. My point goes to the degree of scrutiny you have invested in the process: Have I struggled with myself on the issue of national self-definition as much as I would in deciding about the house I will be making a home for the next few years?

Perhaps this way of putting the question stacks the deck a bit against private *citizenship*. Deliberation in house-hunting requires a relatively intensive, but short-term, engagement with the facts of the real estate market. Learning about a political issue is typically a more cumulative affair—conversations around the dinner table and on the job, reactions to T.V. specials and newspaper articles may add up, over time, to a rough-and-ready understanding of the basic options confronting the American people, a considered judgment about the national interest.

Not that the private *citizen* imagines that he is searching for some ideal deliberative perspective. To the contrary, the quest for perfection can become disabling: it is always possible to obtain more relevant information, always possible to scrutinize one's citizenship commitments more closely. A time will come when you must quit deliberating and start deciding: This house or that one? This ideal for the nation or that one?

I shall say that a private *citizen*'s support is "deep" when she has deliberated as much about her commitment to a national ideal as she thinks appropriate in making a considered judgment on an important decision in her private life.

Breadth

But it is not enough for a movement to have depth; it must be broad as well. Numbers count. Before a group can be allowed to place its initiative on the higher lawmaking agenda, there must be lots and lots of private citizens who think that the reform should be taken seriously. How many?

In principle, this question cannot be answered by a single number. We must disaggregate the movement's adherents into at least four types. First, there are a relatively few public citizens devoted full-time to the cause. Next, there are the private *citizens* whose character we have just been describing. Then, there are *private* citizens who support the cause on the basis of judgments that do not satisfy their own standards of deliberative seriousness. Finally, there are perfect privatists who support the movement because they find it in their self-interest to do so.

Every political movement attracts all four types, in different mixtures to be sure. In claiming to speak for the People, a movement asserts that it has more than the usual percentage of private *citizens* among its number—as well as gaining the softer support of a large number of *private* citizens. How large must these numbers be before a movement should be allowed to signal its ascent to the higher lawmaking stage?

In setting your numbers, keep in mind that we are addressing only the first stage of a lengthy process. Even after a movement places its initiative on the agenda, it will have to win many victories before its proposal will become a part of our higher law. As a consequence, it would be wrong to set the threshold too high at this stage. There is lots of room for good-faith disagreement on the right numbers, but let me fix a few for purposes of exposition. Let's say that a dualist Constitution should demand that a movement have the deep support of 20 percent of the citizenry, and the additional support of 31 percent of *private* citizens,[4] before it may place its initiative on the higher lawmaking agenda.

Decisiveness

Depth, breadth: is it reasonable to demand more? I think so. The problem lies in a famous paradox of voting first elaborated by Condorcet two centuries ago. Even if a movement has gained 20 + 31 percent in support, Condorcet established that there may still be a serious problem with its democratic claim to legitimacy.

To grasp the foundational character of Condorcet's point, stipulate that the higher lawmaking system is otherwise operating freely and fairly—for the conceptual problem can arise even then. In the same spirit, stipulate that elected representatives are accurately reflecting the division of opinion amongst the citizenry. Having simplified away so many practical problems, we can now confront the conceptual issue that forces the dualist democrat beyond breadth and depth—to something I will call decisiveness.

To illustrate the paradox,[5] suppose that Americans found themselves divided into three groups when confronting a problem on the public agenda. Say, one-third of the population thinks the best response to the race problem in this country is Meritocracy—judging each person on the merits, in a color-blind fashion; one-third believe in Affirmative Action, giving traditionally oppressed groups a compensatory opportunity in hiring and promotion; and one-third believe in Separate Development—in which resources are given to minority leaders to build up their own communities, while leaving the institutions in the dominant community relatively untouched. Suppose moreover—and this is critical—that these three groups not only disagree about the best strategy, but also disagree about the second-best strategy. Though Meritocrats object to Affirmative Action, they find it less evil than Separate Development—since Separatism, in their view, will ultimately increase rather than diminish Americans' estrangement from one another. Separatists, in contrast, find Affirmative Action the worst of the three alternatives—since it will drain the minority community of its most vital members. Finally, Affirmativists think that Separatism is morally superior to Meritocracy—which they consider a sham form of Tokenism. To put these rank orderings in a picture:

Meritocrats (less than 50%)	Affirmativists (less than 50%)	Separatists (less than 50%)
M	A	S
A	S	M
S	M	A

This breakdown is, of course, only hypothetical. I do not claim it describes past, present, or future realities. So long as it can occur, however, we must consider its implications for higher lawmaking design. Imagine that one of the three groupings—say, the Affirmativists—mobilizes the deep support of 20 percent of the citizenry and demands that the Constitution allow it to place A on the higher lawmaking agenda. Will they win?

It all depends on their cleverness in manipulating the legislative agenda. Consider: Meritocrats and Affirmativists can get together to vote A into law over S; Separatists and Meritocrats, however, can collaborate to defeat A and make M the majority winner; while Affirmativists and Separatists can join to defeat M, and replace it with S. So long as the assembly keeps on voting on the alternatives in a pairwise fashion, the cycle will proceed endlessly. More realistically, voting will not be permitted to cycle endlessly. Instead, the legislative leadership will fix the pairwise order of voting. In this case, victory will be determined by the way the agenda is manipulated: if the last vote pairs A against S, then Affirmativists will win; if A against M, the Meritocrats; if M against S, then the Separatists.

Seeing this, the Affirmativists place themselves in the crucial agenda-controlling positions. They successfully manipulate the order of voting to gain the "soft" support of the Meritocrats in the final vote against the Separatists. This triumph, I suppose, would allow the Affirmativists to claim that they have successfully satisfied the depth and breadth conditions: after all, they have managed to gain the deep support of 20 percent, and the shallower support of 31 percent, of their fellow Americans to their higher law initiative!

But this should not be enough: for the Affirmativists do not owe their victory to the fact that a majority of the American people think their proposal is better than the rival ones. They owe it merely to their leadership's superior success in manipulating the legislative agenda. Such successes in legislative leadership may suffice to win normal political victories. But they should not be sufficient for higher lawmaking, whose very point is to identify principles that represent something more than the opinions that happen to be dominant in the halls of power in Washington. If, then, a proposal deserves a place on the higher lawmaking agenda, its support in the country should not only be deep and broad. It should be in a position to decisively defeat *all* the plausible* alternatives in a series of pairwise comparisons—in the terms of the trade, it should be a Condorcet-winner.[6]

The Inadequacy of Voting as a Signaling Mechanism

We can now approach our first problem in higher lawmaking design: how to create an institutional mechanism that will allow lawmakers to make proposals on the higher lawmaking track *only* if these proposals have the requisite depth, breadth, and decisiveness?

One thing is clear. A British-style parliamentary design is entirely unequal to the task. The dualist cannot allow the Prime Minister to ram constitutional amendments through the House whenever she

---

*I add the notion of "plausible" alternatives to address (inadequately) the challenges to democratic theory introduced by the "chaos theorems" propounded by Richard McKelvey, "Intransitivities in Multidimensional Voting Models and Some Implications for Agenda Control," 12 *J. Econ. Theory* 472 (1976), and Norman Schofield, "Instability of Simple Dynamic Games," 45 *R. Econ. Stud.* 575 (1978). These writers have established that the existence of Condorcet-style cycles in one area of policy space may be used strategically to create voting cycles in other policy areas that would otherwise have been governed by unambiguously decisive majority-winners. Thus, a Condorcet-style cycle existing on the question of the design of traffic lights might conceivably disturb an otherwise decisive judgment on race relations!

To respond to this conceptual possibility, the text suggests that a constitutional movement need only beat alternatives that, given the public discussion, seem to be "plausible" competitors; and that opponents should not be allowed to defeat the movement by creating complex "tie-ins" between policy spaces that seem unrelated to one another in public debate, merely for the purpose of exploiting strategic possibilities opened up by Condorcet-manipulation. (Note to aficionados of modern public choice: this problem deserves far more work than a footnote will allow.)

thinks she can whip the majority party into support for her initiative. There is simply no reason to presume the existence of deep and decisive support amongst the People for each and every one of the Prime Minister's initiatives.

Instead, the dualist Constitution employs a strategy of institutional resistance. It makes higher lawmaking much harder than normal lawmaking. Consider, for example, the obstacles that the original Constitution placed in front of a higher lawmaking movement. Spokesmen for the People must gain the support of either two-thirds of state legislatures to call a second Constitutional Convention or two-thirds of both houses of Congress to propose an amendment. Both of these institutional paths to signaling authority are steeper than the ones that lead to normal lawmaking legitimacy. It takes two-thirds of Congress to pass an ordinary statute over the President's veto, but two-thirds can only *signal* the rise of a movement for constitutional change.

As I have suggested,[7] these Federalist mechanisms have been supplemented by an alternative signaling system revolving around the Presidency. From Jefferson to Reagan, movements for constitutional revision have used Presidential elections to mobilize citizen support for their campaigns to redefine and renew American political identity. Under this more modern system, if a President can convince Congress to support the enactment of transformative statutes that challenge the constitutional premises of the preexisting regime, the American public treats his success as a higher lawmaking signal similar to the proposal of a formal constitutional amendment under the classical system. This signaling system has very different risks and rewards from the classical one. Right now, though, I am more interested in exploring a feature that all signaling mechanisms— whether they be keyed to the Presidency or Congress or Conventions—have in common.

False Positives and False Negatives

And that is their tendency to make mistakes. Of two kinds. Following the statisticians, one kind is the *false positive*. Here a movement successfully gains control over the signaling mechanism despite the fact that it has failed to gain the decisive kind of 20 + 31 support I have envisioned. The other kind is the *false negative*. Here a movement has won a decisive majority but fails to gain access to a higher lawmaking signal. Given the impossibility of a perfect signaling device, the dualist faces a basic trade-off. The harder it is to signal, the lower the probability of a false positive; but the higher the probability of a false negative. And vice versa.

Neither type of error can be completely eliminated at an acceptable cost. The only way to eliminate all false positives is to make the Constitution completely unamendable. But this would require dualists to reject the very idea of democracy and base the Constitution on sheer ancestor worship. The Founders were clever fellows, but they made serious mistakes, moral no less than instrumental. And so will every generation. In a democracy, the People of today must have the chance to change their minds about the fundamental choices made by preceding generations. The object of higher lawmaking design is not to frustrate this process, but structure it—so that it occurs when a mobilized citizenry wants it to occur, so that it will proceed in a deliberate and focused fashion, so that changes in constitutional identity will occur, when they occur, in a deliberate and weighty fashion that will gain respect as a *considered* judgment of We the People.

At the same time, if the Constitution tries to eliminate all risk of false negatives, it will make signaling too easy. While movements that satisfy the 20 + 31 test will almost surely gain institutional access to the signal, so will many other normal political interests. The proliferation of so many false negatives will discredit the entire signaling system. The general public will no longer believe that a group that gains access to a higher lawmaking signal is any different from the countless ideological fractions that participate in the pushing-and-shoving of normal politics. The point of the signaling system—which is to give higher lawmaking legitimacy to citizen movements that have managed to penetrate the barriers of ignorance, apathy, and selfishness in an extraordinary way—will be undermined by the proliferation of fraudulent signals.

So: signaling can't be made too hard or too easy. And even then there will be mistakes. Conventions or Congresses or Presidents may signal the need to consider sweeping constitutional changes when there isn't anything like 20 + 31 support for their agenda in the country at large; or there may be such a movement abroad in the land but the existing set of institutional signals have eluded its grasp. Which kind of mistake is worse? False positives or false negatives?

The answer seems pretty easy, once you recall that we are only considering the initial phase of a multi-stage problem in constitutional design. Within this framework, an occasional false negative seems far worse than frequent false positives. Consider the consequences: Even if a movement manages to gain access to a signal too easily—say, its support is only 15 + 36 rather than 20 + 31—it isn't the end of the world. If the movement crosses the initial threshold in a relatively weak condition, it is unlikely that its initiative will survive the obstacle course that awaits on the higher lawmaking track (though, of course, nothing is certain in politics).

The consequences of a false negative are much worse. The heart of dualism is the belief that a mobilized citizenry may, on appropriate occasions, take the law into its own hands and give governors new marching orders. If established institutions successfully block the movement at the threshold, they betray the Constitution's foundational commitment to popular sovereignty. Worse yet, they will alienate the movement's many partisans from the ongoing process of government. These people will not passively accept the fact that the door to higher lawmaking has been slammed in their face. If existing institutions refuse to hear the voice of the People, they will be tempted to take more radical steps to gain the center of the political stage—abandoning entirely the higher lawmaking structures intended to organize the debate and seeking more violent and elitist forms of fundamental change.[8]

THE PROPOSAL FUNCTION

When should a movement be afforded access to a higher lawmaking signal—how deep and broad should, in principle, its popular support be? *Which* institutions have won signaling authority in American lawmaking practice—Conventions, Congresses, Presidents—and under what conditions can each of these generate credible signals? Should the present signaling system be reformed?

However perplexing these questions, they are only the first to greet us. Even if a movement appropriately gains access to a credible signal, it must still define *what* it wants to propose in the name of the American people. How should the system structure this process?

Consider the problem in all its intractability. Political movements gaining signaling authority will have a complex and tension-filled intellectual history stretching back decades, generations, sometimes centuries. Some leaders will be activists who have given their lifetimes to the Cause, others will be Johnny-come-latelies who have risen to prominence as the Cause began to strike a responsive note amongst the more general public. These competing elites will appeal to an equally variegated mass of supporters—some loyalists have stuck with the Cause through thick and thin, many more are just beginning to define their positions on the issues. Getting these diverse types behind a common proposal is no easy matter. To make the task harder, it is not enough for the movement's proposal to gain the wholehearted support of its present adherents. It must be framed in a way that will prove acceptable to the millions of Americans who have yet to take the matter seriously, but whose support will be decisive at later stages in the higher lawmaking process.

Given the difficulty of the task, much will depend upon the insight and the spirit the would-be constitutional reformers bring to their task: Will they allow petty personalities and ideological niceties to split them into factional chaos? Or can they work together to develop an incisive set of principles that the larger body of Americans will find meaningful? There can be no substitute for leadership if the movement's initiative isn't to disintegrate into ideological chaos at the very moment it comes to the forefront. But statesmanship can be helped or hurt by the extent to which constitutional structure rewards leaders who wish to present a cogent proposal for collective deliberation.

This is especially true in the American setting, which has traditionally lacked some of the nongovernmental structures that European movements use to render their transformative impulses coherent. The most important difference involves the role of the political party in channeling reform movements. Modern European movements for fundamental reform have tended to affirm the need for hierarchy in ways that mock their populist rhetoric. The "democratic centralism" practiced by Leninist parties represents an extreme example of a general European tendency toward hierarchy—on the right no less than the left. Whatever the disadvantages of this "strong-party" approach to fundamental change, it tends to minimize the incoherence problem. Thatcherites no less than Leninists take de-bates on the party platform seriously—since, given the parties' hier-archic structure, both expect them to guide transformative activity on the Great Day the party gains governmental authority.

Things are different in America, though we must not exaggerate. Since the Founding, parties have played a strategic role in almost all important exercises in constitutional politics. Federalists, Jefferson-ians, Jacksonians, Republicans, New Dealers—all used the party as a principal tool in their exercises in political mobilization. Many failed constitutional movements have done so as well.*

The American difference lies more in its nonhierarchical under-standing of political parties. Even when a party gains signaling au-thority, its internal organization will seem chaotic by European stan-dards. Washington or Lincoln or Roosevelt may have had high moral standing amongst their countrymen at the time they chaired the Constitutional Convention of 1787 or issued the Emancipation Proc-lamation of 1863 or proposed the National Industrial Recovery Act of 1933. They were also tied to political groupings that called them-selves Federalists or Republicans or Democrats. Nonetheless, they possessed nothing like the disciplinary techniques that European party leaders use to keep their followers in line. They confronted other movement leaders who possessed their own independent bases of support, and who felt free to elaborate their own opinions about the movement's program. Rather than presenting a disciplined lead-ership cadre marching under the banner of the Party Platform, the Federalists, Republicans, and Democrats were groupings of more or less like-minded people who shared common political experiences in the past and broadly similar perspectives on the future.

But broad similarity is notoriously consistent with concrete and bitter differences. Since the typical American movement-cum-party does not resolve these differences before taking office, the structure

---

*From this vantage point, the women's movement of the middle republic and the civil rights movement of the modern republic seem rather exceptional—while these movements certainly had complex relationships to the party systems prevailing in their eras, they seem a good deal more autonomous in their organizational self-understandings.

of the higher lawmaking system importantly influences the nature of the movement's proposals. On the one hand, it selects the officials who will be the prime movers in the operation. The classical system designates Congress or a Constitutional Convention as the prime mover; the more modern one gives the Presidency a larger role. On the other hand, the structure of the system affects the form of the proposal—in two different ways.

First, the classical proposal mechanism culminates in a decisive moment of truth. Either the Convention or Congress votes to propose a constitutional amendment; or they don't. In contrast, the modern mechanism is more gradual. The process begins when the President, claiming a mandate from the People, convinces Congress to enact transformative statutes which give legal substance to the new movement's program for fundamental change. Precisely because of their revolutionary character, many of these statutes will be invalidated by the Supreme Court. This will return the burden of initiative back to the political branches: Does the constitutional movement have sufficient strength in the country to challenge the Court with a second round of statutes that refine and deepen the legal meanings adumbrated the first time around?

Second, the classical system invites reformers to speak in a laconic voice that invokes highly abstract legalisms: "[N]or shall any State deprive any person of life, liberty, or property, without due process of law . . ." The modern system invites a more concrete process of articulation. The legal meaning of the new constitutional solution is first elaborated in several waves of transformative statutes, which are typically more detailed than the classic constitutional amendment. Later on, the Supreme Court takes on more of the burden of abstracting the core constitutional doctrines from the mass of statutory material that has gained popular support. These *transformative opinions* come to express much of the movement's higher law contribution. Thus, rather than forcing the movement to speak abstractly at a relatively early stage in the process, the modern system allows reformers to begin relatively concretely and slowly to move to more abstract principles as the constitutional debate proceeds.

While this modern approach has some significant strengths, I believe it has even more serious weaknesses. First for its strengths: It allows the movement more time to deliberate upon the legal formulae through which it will codify the constitutional meaning of its transformation. Indeed, when we turn to inspect this process during the New Deal period, the advantages of this kind of evolution will seem substantial. If, for example, Roosevelt had proposed formal constitutional amendments in 1933, the text might well have been far cruder than the constitutional solutions that eventually emerged from the great struggle between the New Deal and the Old Court during his first term.[9]

Nonetheless, this evolutionary approach contains great dangers. Since the movement isn't forced to pin its transformative message down in a formal amendment, the modern system relies very heavily on the good judgment of courts. After making their "switch in time," they must reflect upon the deeper meanings of transformative statutes and seek to codify them in transformative opinions that will guide constitutional development in the regime ahead. If the courts fail to discharge this function sensitively, the system will suffer greatly. Is it wise to rely so heavily on judges in this way?

It is true, of course, that even the classical system relies heavily on the courts. While the Republican Congress did lay down some formulae in its Fourteenth Amendment—"privileges or immunities of citizens of the United States," "equal protection"—it fell to judges to give doctrinal meaning to these broad commitments. The fact that the Congress provided them with a few formulae did not make this task an easy matter. Indeed, if we take a practical view, I do not think the courts have done a better job interpreting Reconstruction principles than they have in making doctrinal sense of the New Deal. The presence or absence of a few textual formulae hasn't made much of a difference in giving doctrinal expression to these two great popular transformations.[10]

Nonetheless, there is danger involved in the informality of the process by which the New Deal translated constitutional politics into constitutional law. Given the precedent of 1937, some future Court may decide to embark on a "switch in time" without the kind of broad and deep groundswell that accompanied it in the 1930's; without the aid of formal amendments, it might grotesquely distort the meaning of some future transformation. Is there anything practical we can do to control such dangers?

This has been a central concern in my own proposals for reform.[11]

Right now, though, my concern is with the unreformed system as it is—warts and all. We must understand it much better than we do if we hope to change it for the better.

MOBILIZED DELIBERATION

Suppose that American institutions have responded to the initiative of a mobilized movement in either the classical or the modern way— Congress or a Convention has proposed a constitutional amendment; or the President has convinced Congress to enact transformative statutes despite the clear and present danger of judicial invalidation.

In both cases, full-time politicians and the mass of the private citizenry will interpret the institutional triumph in a distinctive way. On the one hand, Congressional endorsement of the transformative amendments or statutes will place the movement's initiative at the very center of the political debate. People in and out of Washington will recognize that our so-called representatives are up to something special, something that is best approached with high seriousness: a self-conscious challenge to our fundamental law. On the other hand, this political success in Washington by no means concludes the struggle over re-vision. It only inaugurates a new stage of public mobilization and deliberation.

This insistence on a further period of mobilized deliberation is one of the most distinctive features of American higher lawmaking. Many other nations have adopted dualistic mechanisms for consulting the People on special occasions of high importance—typically using plebiscites for this purpose.[12] These practices differ from the American, however, in supposing that the People can make up its mind in a rather short interval: in other countries, the space between proposal and final referendum is often a couple of months. In contrast, the period between proposal and ratification in the American system is usually measured in terms of years. Does this make sense?

The need for such a lengthy interval is certain to meet with great resistance—not to say incredulity—from the most committed partisans of constitutional reform. So far as these activists are concerned, constitutional conservatives have already had plenty of time to convince the People to support the status quo. While the reformers were spending decades, generations, trying to mobilize a deep and broad movement during normal politics, the conservatives held the high ground of Constitutional Orthodoxy. Most obviously, they had the Supreme Court on their side, time and again giving aid and comfort to the partisans of the existing Constitution both in word and deed. No less importantly, the spirit of Tradition dominated most other institutions most of the time. Despite these great symbolic and practical advantages, the conservatives have finally proved incapable of sustaining the logjam. The reformers have at long last gained access to the higher lawmaking path. The People's elected spokesmen have solemnly indicated the need for reform. And now that the reformers' exhausting errand into the wilderness of normal politics seems to be coming to an end, how do the conservatives respond? By demanding more time! When will this effort to stifle the living voice of the People end?!

And yet we should resist this impatient demand for immediate vindication—for two reasons. The first returns us to the problem of decisiveness. A movement's victory at the signaling stage need not imply that a mobilized majority actually supports its constitutional proposal against all plausible competitors. Instead, the initiative might have succeeded largely by its leadership's strategic manipulation of Condorcet-style paradoxes. By forcing the movement to undergo a second round of institutional testing, the dualist Constitution seeks to reduce this risk to acceptable proportions. Throughout the period of mobilized deliberation, the movement will have to gain support for its initiative time and again in lawmaking assemblies. Such repeated successes will be unlikely if a majority of citizens does not support it decisively against all the plausible alternatives.[13]

The second reason returns us to the depth of popular support that should be required. To fix ideas, I suggested earlier that 20 percent of the voting population should provide deep support at the signaling stage—though I have no great stake in this particular number. As we turn from signaling to final ratification, it seems reasonable to insist that a larger fraction of the American people give the proposal deep support. By insisting on a second round of deliberation, the Constitution has hit upon an excellent device for implementing this demand. The key, paradoxically, is the likely behavior of constitutional conservatives. Now that the reformers have gotten together to propose a serious transformative initiative, these conservatives have new incentives to pour lots of energy into a mobilized defense of the status quo. As they appeal to the People to rally to the conservative Constitution, two things may happen. Perhaps the "silent majority" responds by springing into political life—giving new popular vitality to constitutional principles that the Court and other traditionalistic elites had defended in more normal times. Perhaps the conservatives find, to their horror, that popular faith has eroded over the decades or centuries since the days when Madison or Lincoln or Roosevelt first proclaimed them in the name of the People. Rather than rising to the defense of the traditional Constitution, the private citizenry respond with doubt and uncertainty. Maybe the reformers are right; maybe the substance of our higher law has outlived its time and needs self-conscious reconstruction for a new age?

In either event, conservative countermobilization will vastly broaden and deepen the political engagement of the People on the fundamental issues at stake. A year or two or three after the first higher lawmaking signal, much of the softness of normal public opinion will dissolve. The apathy, ignorance, selfishness that occlude the judgments of tens of millions of Americans will have been dissipated by hundreds of millions of arguments, counterarguments, insults, imprecations. Apathy will give way to concern, ignorance to information, selfishness to serious reflection on the country's future—at least this is how many a private *citizen* will see it.

Not that this period of mobilized deliberation is anything like a philosophy seminar. It is much more democratic; much more energetic; much more multivocal. There will be a great deal of passion and personality, action as well as argument, drama as well as debate—the stakes are much too high to imagine otherwise. This is the point at which the higher lawmaking system confronts its greatest challenge: Can it channel the contending parties into an energetic exchange of public views, inviting them to address each other's critiques as they seek to mobilize deeper and broader support from the general citizenry? Or will it allow partisans to dissipate political energy in an almost random series of public scenes—in which first one, then another, group of activists give voice to their grievance, interspersed by shows of outrage by conservatives? In a single line: will the system encourage the protagonists to talk *to* one another or *past* one another?

Obviously, there will be a lot of both going on—there can be no stopping extremists on all sides who can only preach hate and violence. All things considered, however, I think it is downright remarkable how well Americans have managed this challenge in the past. Under the classical system, the ratification struggles before state legislatures have been powerful tools for focusing debate. Under the modern system, the Supreme Court's invalidation of the first wave of transformative statutes forces the debate to a new level of seriousness: Now that the Court has flagged the fundamental principles at stake, how should reformers respond? Should they accept the Court's judgments and reluctantly concede that the People will not support a mobilized effort to repudiate the traditional principles? Or should they challenge the reigning doctrine head-on, in a second Hundred Days of transformative legislative activity, and return to the People for support in the next election?

Of course, under the modern system, this second round of constitutional politics is conducted on the national, not the state, level. No less than the classical system, however, it envisions a temporally extended, and institutionally complex, debate—first amongst the President and Congress as they devise suitable responses to the first round of judicial invalidation, and then as they go to the People at the next elections to gain support for their second round of transformative statutory activity.

CODIFICATION

If the higher lawmaking system is working right, by this point something special is going on. Representatives and citizenry are speaking a *common* language redefining and renewing the foundations of American government. This language has been tested time and time again in deliberative assembly and popular election. Its partisans have emerged victorious despite strong opposition.

Not that anybody supposes that this moment can last forever. Nothing lasts forever, least of all a mobilized majority of private *citizens*. Soon enough, the popular mind will turn to other things.

The time has come for sober legal codification of the new constitutional solution. We must act before it is too late; before the moment passes, the leading officials of government must solemnly commit themselves to the new constitutional commitments. They must pledge to remain faithful to the new constitutional solutions even when the People turn their minds to other public and private pursuits. No matter how powerful officials may be, they are not to allow the pressures of normal politics to erode the meaning of these constitutional solutions. And it is the special obligation of lawyers and judges to remind the powers that be that they are only the People's servants, not spokesmen for the People themselves—unless, of course, the political leadership wishes once again to take to the higher lawmaking path to win the mobilized citizenry's consent to another exercise in fundamental re-vision.

It is at this point that the courts become central in both the classical and modern systems. In the classical system, they confront a laconic text of high abstraction inscribed in a formal constitutional amendment. Over time, litigants seek to use the new abstractions to their advantage in the press of litigation. If these abstractions are not to become dead letter, the courts must give them concrete meaning: Which traditional doctrines must now be cast onto the junk heap of history? Which must be radically rethought before they can be safely used in the new order? Which endure relatively un-scathed? It is only as the new abstractions are worked up into "middle-level" doctrines defining operational principles and rules that they can serve as reliable constraints upon normal politics. If the process of legal translation is proceeding apace, the courts will be issuing a series of landmark opinions that seek to elaborate the middle-level principles and rules needed to provide practical guid-ance for the resolution of the countless disputes generated by the fundamental transformation of the constitutional landscape.

Codification proceeds in a different way—but to a similar end—in the modern system. The crucial moment begins as the courts confront concrete statutes they would have invalidated under the traditional principles of the preceding regime. But now, by hypoth-esis, the Justices have embarked on a "switch in time" comparable to 1937. In the light of the sustained popular support for President and Congress, a majority of the Justices have concluded that it would be counterproductive to continue the constitutional crisis until the new movement ratifies formal constitutional amendments. Instead, they uphold the last wave of transformative statutes in a series of landmark opinions, which inaugurate the radical revision of pre-existing doctrine.

In contrast to the classical system, these opinions do not begin with spare abstractions like "equal protection" or "due process"—since, by hypothesis, the Justices have made their switch without insisting on a formal Article Five amendment. Instead, the revisionary effort begins concretely: the judges confront particular transformative statutes and explain how preexisting doctrine must be revolutionized to accommodate the new innovations that have won the support of the People. For all the differences between these classical and modern processes, earlier chapters pointed to deeper similarities in the dynamic of judicial synthesis as it emerges over time.[14] Regardless of the abstract or concrete nature of the starting point, the Justices must ask and answer the same basic questions if they hope to integrate new and old into a compelling set of doctrinal directions for the resolution of the mass of cases: What does the heady new constitutional rhetoric mean in the practical resolution of day-to-day disputes that come forward for judicial decision? Which older doctrines must be rejected? Which must be radically reconceptualized? Which survive the new redefinition of the nature of American government?

Tough questions. My point is simply that they must be taken seriously by the courts of a well-ordered dualist democracy. Otherwise, the effort to control normal governors by the constitutional achievements of the American people will disintegrate with the return of normal politics.

THREE SKEPTICISMS

This chapter has isolated four critical functions that must be discharged by a credible higher lawmaking system. First, it must reliably signal the rise of movements whose transformative agendas promise to gain the deep, broad, and decisive support of the American people. Second, it must encourage the movement's political leadership to elaborate its basic proposals in language that the majority of the population can support. Third, it must provide a substantial period for mobilized deliberation during which popular support for these initiatives is tested time and again. Fourth, the courts must translate the rare successes of constitutional politics into cogent doctrinal principles capable of controlling normal politics into the indefinite future—until such time as the People themselves mobilize once again to redefine the organizing purposes of American government.

Corresponding to each of these functions is the possibility of malfunction. Congress or a Convention might propose a formal constitutional amendment, or the President might convince Congress to enact transformative statutes, without anything resembling the deep, broad, and decisive support appropriate for a constitutional signal. Or the leadership may fail to devise a proposal that incisively conveys the nature of its initiatives to the broader public. Later on, a constitutional amendment may be approved by three-quarters of the state assemblies, or the Supreme Court may constitutionalize a second round of transformative statutes, without the transformative initiative gaining the requisite kind of support of the mobilized People. And even later, the Supreme Court might betray the organizing principles affirmed by the People by failing to develop appropriate doctrinal formulations at the codification stage.

These ever-present possibilities can only provoke deep anxiety for all concerned with the fate of the dualist project begun in Philadelphia—anxieties which, I think, are quite healthy if they are kept within reasonable bounds. They serve to impress upon all Americans—and especially those who find themselves at key points in the higher lawmaking process—with the high seriousness of the decisions they are called upon to make. There is simply no escaping the fact that the fate of the Constitution is in our hands—as voters, representatives, justices. If we allow ourselves to abuse the tradition of higher lawmaking, the very idea that the Constitution can be viewed as the culminating expression of a mobilized citizenry will disintegrate. After all, the American Republic is no more eternal than the Roman—and it will come to an end when American citizens betray their Constitution's fundamental ideals and aspirations so thoroughly that existing institutions merely parody the public meanings they formerly conveyed.

And yet, as with most anxieties, this one can get out of hand. When we reflect upon Washington presiding over the Convention, or the Reconstruction Congress demanding ratification of the Fourteenth Amendment, or President Roosevelt demanding support for his proposal to pack the Supreme Court in 1937, can we say for sure that these representatives *really* spoke for a mobilized citizenry that deserves the respect owing to We the People?

It all depends on what we mean by "really." I am not suggesting that a glimpse inside the innermost psychic recesses of Americans supporting the new constitutional solution would reveal hearts entirely purged of self-interest and minds fully focused upon the "rights of citizens and the permanent interests of the community." To the contrary, an accurate portrait of a triumphant constitutional movement requires a much richer palette—to capture both the vain ambition of the leadership in Washington and the continued distraction of followers who remain enmeshed in the daily tasks of changing diapers and bringing home the bacon. Indeed, if it were possible for any of us to experience—and reveal to others—a pristine purity of motive, we could dispense with the complex legal rituals of higher lawmaking. We might simply display the purity of our motives and get on with the public business at hand. Precisely because we are psychologically complex creatures, such "sincere" protestations of simon-purity seem naive ways of establishing our claims to private *citizenship.* Since talk is so cheap, and human nature so complex, political leaders can never hope for constitutional credibility merely by *saying* that they represent one of those rare movements through which citizens have hammered out a specially considered judgment on America's future. Instead, if they want to make this claim, they must *earn* it—by subjecting themselves to a specially rigorous set of public tests as their higher lawmaking pretensions are signaled, deliberated upon, and codified.

If, however, a movement does survive these demanding tests, its claims should not be denied merely because some skeptic points out impurities of motive, residuals of ignorance and apathy. It is because real-world citizens are always impure that they need public procedures for separating out shades of gray—indicating when, for all the world's distractions, they mean to invest the political side of their personalities with special significance. In responding to skeptical doubts, the dualist does not deny that, even during America's moments of greatest higher lawmaking triumph, there will be evidence of ignorance, apathy, selfishness swirling about the center of the political stage. Rather than undermining the point of higher lawmaking, it is precisely the continued existence of human ambiguity and complexity that makes higher lawmaking processes such a precious resource.

A domestic analogy will help make the point. Imagine that we lived in a place where the legal institution of marriage was unknown. In such a world, couples would still agonize over their decisions to live together, and devise countless subtle mechanisms to signal the special meanings they attach to their relationship. Yet this ongoing effort at communication would be immeasurably enhanced by the legal form of marriage—through which parties self-consciously expose themselves to heavy costs if they later act inconsistently with their protestations of love and affection. The point of such a costly ceremony is not primarily to serve as a snapshot of the love and hate that attract and repel the parties to the ongoing relationship; it is to provide a symbolic system through which psychologically complex people can give a special meaning to a form of interaction and thereby *constitute* it as a special kind of community, distinct from the ordinary relations of everyday personal life.

Constitutional dualism provides a similar symbolic system in the public realm. By providing a higher lawmaking system, the American Constitution succeeds in constituting something more than a government in Washington, D.C. It constitutes a system of political meanings that enables all Americans to indicate the rare occasions when they mean to present themselves to one another as private *citizens,* and mark them off from the countless ordinary occasions when they are content to understand themselves as *private* citizens— for whom political life is but one of many diversions in their ongoing pursuit of happiness.

Not that every effort at establishing our claim to private *citizenship* is fated to meet with Publian success. We must expect that most of our fellow citizens will look upon most political efforts at national renewal with the apathy, ignorance, and selfishness characteristic of normal life in a liberal democracy. And yet, from time to time, some would-be Publians begin to strike a resonant chord. The rising movement is taken seriously by more and more Americans—even when they find its message deeply repugnant. The movement's success in penetrating political consciousness provokes a general effort to assess its ultimate significance: Is it a passing fad or something of lasting significance? Slowly the half-remembered rituals of higher lawmaking begin to take on a deeper meaning, for it is through these rituals that Americans test the seriousness of their fellows' efforts at

national renewal and redefinition. When put to the test, most movements will fail to generate the deep and decisive support required
before they can constitutionally speak in the special accents of We
the People of the United States.

But that, in a sense, is just the point. If it were cheap and easy
for higher lawmaking to succeed, we would be debasing the remarkable collective achievement involved when millions of Americans do
manage, despite the countless diversions of liberal democratic society, to engage in an act of self-government with a seriousness that
compares to the most outstanding constitutional achievements of the
past.

CHAPTER ELEVEN

Why Dualism?

DEMOCRACY:
DEATH AND TRANSFIGURATION

DEMOCRACY. For the eighteenth century, the word called up images of the Greek city-state. Democracy was possible within a face-to-face community in which all citizens might directly participate in public affairs. Only then could the People rule (*demos-kratos*) in any meaningful sense. Imperial scale implied imperial government—with monarchs, bureaucrats, and nobility arranged in endless permutations. Though these governments were not democratic, they were powerful. Their larger resources and more centralized power structures typically permitted them to dominate the pathetic confederacies that city-states might organize in self-defense. Except for an odd Swiss mountain canton, democracy was obsolete in the modern world.

In the last two centuries history has rescued the term, only to transform it into banality. Nowadays, only the most backward empires do without the protective coloration of Democracy; some insist on the emphatically redundant People's Democracy. This transformation occurred after a radical reconceptualization: the image of the Athenian polis has been displaced from the center of democratic thought and practice.

The American Constitution played a role in this transformation. Publius rejected the Greek polis as a model for popular government in the modern age, and offered dualism as an alternative. Over time, Americans have used their Federalist inheritance to redefine themselves as a people along increasing democratic lines, including an ever more diverse group of men and women within the scope of citizenship. This ongoing effort in self-government has helped convince the world that democracy is no utopian fantasy, that there *is* a meaningful sense in which a few politicians in the nation's capital can speak for a vast people, one-quarter of a billion strong.

I have no desire to whitewash the dark side of this achievement: the Constitution's celebration of political freedom has been mocked ceaselessly by its coexistence with human slavery and domination. Nonetheless, there is something special about the American experience in modern democracy, something that we should not give up. My aim has been to recover that something—by distinguishing dualistic democracy from its theoretical alternatives, by tracing its development through three constitutional regimes, by reflecting upon its source in the revolutionary tradition, and by exploring the way it continues to control normal and constitutional politics in America. Perhaps we have now seen enough of dualist democracy, from enough different angles, to confront the ultimate question: Is the dualist tradition worthy of America's continued support?

My answer is: yes and no. Yes, the dualist tradition is sufficiently sound that Americans should accept it as imposing a legitimate set of constraints on our political practice. No, it is not good enough to allow us to rest comfortably on its achievements. If we do not ourselves renew the foundations of the American Republic, the constitutional narrative I have told will lose credibility for the next generation—who will, for good reason, be increasingly impressed with the dark side of the dualist "achievement." Indeed, I shall conclude by asking whether there is something lacking in the basic idea of dualistic democracy that should give Americans pause. All things considered, perhaps we should view the first two centuries of dualistic practice as the prologue of our ongoing effort to build a sounder constitutional democracy—one which moves beyond the outermost limits of the dualistic ideal?

The utopian character of this final question should not blind you to the anti-utopian spirit of this essay. We have been searching for the spirit of *this* Constitution, not some better one. The ultimate question is not whether this Constitution meets the standards of our highest moral ideals—no constitution in world history has ever come close—but whether it is good enough to warrant respectful and conscientious support. "Good enough," in terms of the moral quality of its past achievements; "good enough," in providing reasonably fair methods for resolving existing disputes; "good enough," in opening up the future to popular movements that promise further political growth. If the existing tradition is good enough along these lines, we will make more progress by building upon it rather than destroying it. And that seems to me to provide a good enough reason to accept its claim to legitimacy.

This is an open-ended and contestable argument, one that depends on a host of factors, and I won't pretend otherwise. Nonetheless, I shall limit myself to a single theme that focuses upon the distinctive political character who has been lurking these pages: the private citizen. I will be exploring the way in which the dualist tradition gives life and substance to the American practice of private citizenship. This link, to my mind, will provide you with the single best reason for giving your conscientious support to the American Constitution.

My argument will be in three parts. The first presents a spare conceptual account of the link between private citizenship and dualistic democracy. The second presents the case for preserving the dualistic traditions we have inherited from the past. The third considers the claims of private citizenship itself: Why is it important to sustain and renew this aspect of American identity?

After making the affirmative case for conscientious support, I turn to the darker side of dualism, the side that challenges us to make further progress, lest our children find the entire enterprise unworthy.

TRACKING PRIVATE CITIZENSHIP

What is good for me? What is good for the country? The private citizen takes both these questions seriously. She does not assert, in the manner of the public citizen, that only the second question is "really" important. She does not suppose, in the manner of the perfect privatist, that the public good does not exist apart from the pursuit of private interest.[1]

What is more, she recognizes that her two master questions may yield conflicting answers: What is good for me may not be good for the country, and vice versa. Of course, such conflicts do not always arise. Pursuit of my self-interest may be in the public interest. But the private citizen does not suppose this true by definition. This is why Charles Wilson earned a special place in history by famously insisting that "What's good for General Motors is good for the country"—as if it were unimaginable that these two goods might ever diverge. For the private citizen, such a breach is, alas, always conceivable.

The Labor of Citizenship

Which leads to the next basic question: How does one identify the occasions upon which public and private goods diverge from one another? By a special kind of work, the work of private citizenship.

To define its character, I shall contrast it with the way a perfect privatist[2] might go about responding to an issue on the public agenda. The privatist need not decide "What's good for me?" by consulting his material interests. His understanding of the good may be far richer than this, extending to the pursuit of spiritual and associational ideals. So long as these are distinct from the good of the United States, there is always the possibility of conflict. I may be a devout Catholic, deeply concerned with the welfare of my fellow workers and my family. It is these things, not lining my own pockets, that are really important. And yet, as a private citizen, I must recognize that these great goods may be in conflict with the national interest: perhaps it is in the public interest for my fellow workers to run the risk of unemployment, or my Church to be denied tax revenues, or my income taxes to provide social security even for those Americans who look upon the pope as an anti-Christ.

How, then, does the private citizen try to move beyond perfect privatism? First and foremost, she recognizes that other Americans have very different understandings of their own self-interest—and yet remain perfectly decent citizens. This may make the divergence between private and public good agonizing. One might, for example, find the establishment of one's religion deeply gratifying—and yet conclude that it does not respect the "rights of citizens and the permanent interests of the community." Apart from the special need for tolerance, the citizenship perspective will often require you to reflect on the vast size of your country, the need to give interests of Americans on the other side of the continent equal weight to your neighbors'. As citizens, all of us are equals; no region, race, or sect can be ruthlessly sacrificed to the rest. And then there is the question of national security, the harsh fact that other nations find the American dream a threat to their fundamental interests. Other perspectives—moral, religious, personal—place national security in the background. But the private citizen must take it seriously—otherwise who will?

Doubtless, there are other aspects of the citizenship perspective that set it apart. But I have said enough to suggest the crucial point: It requires work to be a private citizen, work of a spiritual kind. You're not a private citizen if you never find the time and energy to deliberate about the public good—either by yourself or, more commonly, with other would-be citizens. Even after you've put in some time and effort, you should not expect to reach effortless agreement with your fellow Americans. The citizenship perspective is wide enough for large and passionate conflicts. And it will require even more work to hammer out common solutions to the big problems we face together. For present purposes, however, the need for all of us *to work* at private citizenship suffices to push the argument to the next stage.

The Expressive Needs of a Private Citizenry

Quite simply, American citizens don't work equally hard all the time. This point lies at the foundation of the two-track lawmaking system. The higher lawmaking track is designed to structure deliberation when we are working especially hard and productively as citizens; the normal lawmaking track, when we are not. If, as I am now assuming, these institutional systems are in good working order, they respond to a fundamental fact about modern political existence: mass involvement in political life is a variable, not a constant.

Indeed, two-track systems are best viewed as examples of a much wider class of *n*-track systems. Once a community of private citizens confronted their problem in public deliberation, they might design three or more tracks, each track calibrated to a different level of citizenship engagement: the lowest for the issues that must be resolved without very much deliberative activity by the larger citizenry; the next track for somewhat more; and so on up to the highest track—in which the general citizenry has invested a very great deal of time and energy in deliberative activity.

Of course, increasing the number of tracks increases the level of institutional complexity. A two-track system "merely" requires pre-servationist institutions like the Supreme Court to eliminate lower-track laws that are inconsistent with higher-track principles. An n-track system demands lots more layers of review. Preservationist institutions check laws passed on the lowest track for their compatibility with those on middle tracks, which in turn must be checked for compatibility with the highest track. The whole thing can begin to resemble a Rube Goldberg machine pretty quickly. Nonetheless, I believe that the modern American Constitution is best understood as containing three basic tracks rather than two—below the level of normal Congressional statutes lies a third track containing the thousands of rules issued by modern bureaucracy. Much of modern administrative law struggles with ways in which the principles of law announced on the two higher tracks can be deployed to constrain bureaucratic rule-making.[3]

This is not the place to extend my two-track analysis to the three-track realities of modern administrative government. I introduce the problem here because it usefully illustrates the relative importance of two basic ideas that have kept reappearing in this essay: private citizenship and two-track lawmaking. It is the former, not the latter, that is foundational. From the vantage point of a community of private citizens, there is nothing special about two tracks. Two may be better than one, but it may not provide a private citizenry with all the expressive resources they need to mark the different democratic values they place on different sorts of legislation. Although the costs of complexity are substantial, it may well be worth discriminating among several grades of breadth and depth of citizen engagement, not just two.

THE CLAIMS OF TRADITION

We have been looking upon the basic idea of two-track lawmaking from the vantage point of the private citizen: Given her shifting involvement in the enterprise of government, doesn't it make sense to support a multitrack effort to separate those occasions upon which she has hammered out a *considered* judgment with a decisive *majority* of her fellows from the many other occasions upon which she hasn't worked as hard, or as productively, on the definition of the public good?

Our next step brings this question down to earth. The ultimate issue is not whether Americans should conscientiously support the abstract idea of dualist democracy; it is whether they should support the particular version that has come down to us after two centuries of historical practice. The abstract idea might be worthwhile; but its historical execution might be awful. Why should Americans think their particular dualist Constitution is good enough to warrant conscientious support?

A considered answer requires the larger exploration suggested by this multivolume project: How well has the dualist system functioned over time? What are its internal resources for reform? For the moment, I shall assume that this survey leads you to conclude that the future is not hopeless; and that, with some effort, we might use these traditional materials to build a decent dualist democracy. (The second half of this chapter returns to this question in a more skeptical spirit.) Within this framework of cautious optimism, I continue to explore the link between private citizenship and two-track democracy—but this time in a way that points to the particular dualistic practices that Americans have constructed for themselves.

I will be presenting two arguments. They call upon different aspects of the private citizen's complex character. The first asks her to view the tradition as a crucial resource for her active engagements in private *citizenship*. The second urges her to remark upon the way it helps protect the values expressed by her more passive moments of *private* citizenship. In each case, I will be trying to convince my hypothetical interlocutor that her deepest interests are best served by accepting the baseline provided by the historical tradition, rather than rejecting it as unworthy of a thoughtful American's commitment.

The Dialectical Argument

I draw my first argument, perhaps paradoxically, from our revolutionary tradition. The American variant of this tradition, as we saw,[4] does not glorify violent social transformation for its own sake—though there has been more violence and transformation than is generally recognized. It focuses upon the idea of political renewal, the possibility that American citizens can mark a new beginning by mobilizing themselves for sustained political deliberation about their future as a nation.

Surely this is a great thing for men and women to attempt? Greater still, when they succeed—not perfectly, of course, but in a manner that allows the contending sides to confront one another, rather than blindly flail about; to struggle for the support of a mobilized majority in ways that even losers will recognize, however grudgingly, authorize the winners to speak in the name of the People.

Such successes don't happen very often. There are just too many ways for constitutional politics to misfire. But it is right to honor its paradigmatic achievements. By testing normal statutes against inherited constitutional principles, our institutions are constantly putting normal politics in perspective, allowing us to see it for what it is—one of the prices we must pay for life in a free society, a price well worth paying, but *not* the best Americans can do when they work most productively at their common project of citizenship. By calling normal politics by its proper name, we do honor to our revolutionary tradition of popular sovereignty by refusing to confuse it with normal democratic life.

This is not only a question of respect for the past. In holding up the paradigms of successful constitutional politics, we emphasize a present and future possibility: no less than our predecessors, we too may find it within ourselves to speak with the voice of We the People—so long as we keep the language alive. If, however, we allow ourselves to forget the very distinction between constitutional and normal politics, by obliterating the institutional practices organized around that distinction, will we still possess the language and practice needed to speak in the name of the People when we want to?

It is naive to respond that Americans can just make up a new language of popular sovereignty when the spirit moves us. This is not how things happen in history, even revolutionary history. However creative the Philadelphia Convention may have been, it did not construct its dualistic language and practice out of sheer imagination or speculative insight. It spoke for the People by adapting ideas and

practices current at the time, many inherited from the English revolutionaries of the preceding century.[5] The Founders' genius resided mostly in the brilliant way they combined these ideas and
practices into new constitutional patterns that promised to renew,
while redefining, the meaning of popular sovereignty to their fellow
Americans. By speaking a language that resonated in existing vocab-
ularies and practices, the Federalists managed to avoid the tragedy
of so many "successful" revolutionaries, whose language loses all
touch with indigenous traditions of government and so alienates the
People for whom they try to speak.

This capacity to deepen and revitalize democratic meanings
through the artful recombination of received ideas and practices is
very precious, and is by no means a monopoly of the Founding
generation. Nineteenth-century Republicans reworked eighteenth-
century patterns in renewing their commitment to the Union; so did
twentieth-century Democrats in asserting the meaningfulness of the
democratic welfare state against Nazi and Communist alternatives.
Will this remarkable exercise in democratic renewal through creative
recombination of traditional ideas continue in the next century? Only
one thing is clear: it won't if, during more normal times, Americans
obliterate the dualistic materials available for further reconstruction
in the name of the People. If we allow our higher lawmaking tradition
to sink to the depths of the collective unconscious, the notion of
popular sovereignty will become trivial or scary or both. Trivial, if
our institutions come to accept the President's claim that he has
received a "mandate" from the People on every detail of his program.[6] Scary, if they allow demagogues to exploit momentary outbursts of popular passion without exposing their constitutional initiatives to a sustained period of institutional deliberation and
electoral testing before they are admitted to the canon of higher law.

These twin dangers have informed my treatment of the Supreme
Court, as the leading (but not the only) preservationist institution of
the dualist Constitution. By striking down recent statutes which seem
inconsistent with the constitutional solutions of the deep past, the
Court begins but does not end the popular debate. It warns the mass
of private citizens that something special is happening in the halls
of power; that their would-be representatives are attempting to legislate in ways that few political movements in American history have

done with credibility; and that the moment has come, once more, to determine whether their generation will respond by making the political effort required to redefine, as private *citizens,* their collective identity. By re-presenting the conclusions reached by the People in the past, the Court calls upon the citizenry of the present to reflect upon the image of the People's past decisions revealed in its mirror. If we do not like what we see, it remains within our power to do something about it—by mobilizing our energies as private *citizens* to amend the Constitution. In making this effort to redefine ourselves, it is always possible to smash the mirror, in the hope that the America of the future will look nothing like the America of the past. But surely this notion of total revolution is a fatal delusion? Far better to use the mirror to help figure out what is worth saving, what is in need of revolutionary reform?

This is, at any rate, the key to my first argument in defense of accepting the historical Constitution as the starting point for our own generation's efforts at democratic self-definition. To retrieve a much-abused idea, the Court's use of the deep past is best understood dialectically. Its interpretive thesis[7] about the historical meaning of the Constitution forces political movements of the present to move beyond the fluff of normal political rhetoric to explain more incisively what they find wanting in the Court's thesis—and state their counter-theses in constitutional language which has some realistic promise, if accepted, of effecting their transformative ideals over the long haul. As the Court's statement of its historical thesis generates political efforts to state counter-theses, the heightened dialogue enables the American people to consider its future with greater self-consciousness about its alternatives than it might otherwise possess: If we are to break with the past, how big a break? What kind?

By dramatizing the character of the historical thesis and proposed antitheses, the institutionalized dialogue between the Court and the political branches allows for a more deliberate and popular choice defining the broad synthesis of past and present principles that should guide the Republic in the next phase of its development. Thesis, antithesis, synthesis—each generation's dialogic activity providing in turn the new historical thesis for the next generation's ongoing confrontation with the constitutional future of America.*

---

*Thesis, antithesis, synthesis: perhaps I'm making a mistake invoking these dialectical

Granted, the Supreme Court is hardly the only institutional mechanism for organizing this conversation between the present and the past about the future. In Europe, for example, the effort at historically rooted redefinition is driven by ideological debate within tightly organized political parties and the more subtle dialectical challenges of elite bureaucracies. But are Americans really prepared to say that these alternatives are better? Others? Surely it would be premature to destroy the resources for collective reflection that we possess, in the hope that better ones will spring up in the political wilderness?

The Bargain between Personal Freedom and Constitutional History

My first argument has taken the point of view of the private *citizen*. Perhaps this perspective may not be at the forefront of your consciousness right now, but you should not take your present passivity as a fixed part of the human condition. There may come a time when you hope for a more active engagement in public life—and you are well advised, in the interim, to support the preservation of dualistic languages and practices that will make the deliberate exercise of active citizenship a meaningful possibility.

My second argument, in contrast, is more appreciative of the *private* citizen as she is, not as she might become. Surely we cannot take her measure simply by noting her distracted glances toward the national political stage. While her passivity as a citizen doesn't invite admiration in itself, her life may have many other valuable aspects. It is these other values and interests, she explains, that *appropriately* distract her from a single-minded concern with the public good of the nation as a whole—her work, her family, her friends, her religion,

---

terms, however lightly. Perhaps they are too encrusted in famous Teutonic efforts to chart the course of History from Berlin or the British Museum. Lest there be any mistake, I reject the whole idea that society is moving down some predetermined historical track whose shape can be known if only we were clever and learned enough in dialectical science. I use these unhappy Germanisms only to provoke reflection upon the constitutional consequences of rejecting the nineteenth century's pursuit of a science of historical necessity. Once we realize that we are not playthings of some larger destiny, it becomes more, not less, important for American citizens to figure out where we should be going—for if we don't deliberate together, History isn't going to reveal its meaning on its own. Our choice, instead, is the one Publius described between "establishing good government from reflection and choice, or . . . depend[ing] . . . on accident and force." *Federalist* No. 1, at 33 (A. Hamilton) (C. Rossiter ed. 1961).

her culture, all weaving together to form the remarkable patchwork of American community life.

This incredible diversity of lived experience is itself one of the great glories of America; and it could not be achieved if everybody placed national citizenship first all of the time. Rather than looking upon the shifting involvements of private citizenship as a concession to human frailty, we should see it for what it is: as part of the price we pay for freedom—freedom to explore the depth and breadth of the human spirit; freedom to live within one of the countless frameworks of meaning opened up by the modern world, without excessive interference from Washington, D.C.

From this point of view, the greatest moments of constitutional creativity in American history can never be viewed as unmixed blessings. Even the successes take all of us away from too much that is too close to home. Little wonder that so many (but not all)* of our great constitutional turning points have been associated with terrible wars or economic disasters. Surely it is a great and good thing for us to work productively as citizens, when the times or our consciences require it. But it is no less important to explore very different worlds of meaning—with only a few intimates, or a thousand fellow workers; worlds that invite us to move beyond geographic boundaries to seek religious or cultural association with different and distant people. These disparate values are placed in jeopardy by too great a fixation on constitutional politics, private *citizenship*.

Normal politics is, in short, not only a predictable part of the cycle of American history; we should not want to break free of the cycle even if we could. We would lose much too much of value if we were constantly debating the future of America with one another. While the political future of the country is placed in jeopardy by too much passivity, more activity isn't always better.

This path of reflection opens the entryway to my second argument. Given all the other claims on his time and energy, isn't it reasonable for each private citizen to ask his fellows for a certain degree of restraint in calling upon him to invest heavily in public deliberation? Only if a *substantial* number of citizens believe that

---

*For example, the civil rights movement—surely the most notable recent success in constitutional politics—took place during a period of extraordinary American prosperity.

there is something *really wrong* with the higher law tradition is it appropriate for them to force the rest of us to engage actively in the arduous enterprise of collective renewal and redefinition.

But this is, of course, precisely the effect of the dualist's backward-looking Constitution. So long as it is working well, our *private* citizen can gain the reasonable assurance that he seeks. He will not be jolted into extraordinary activity merely because elected politicians find it expedient to exploit the apathy, ignorance, and selfishness of normal politics in ways that endanger fundamental traditions. Since the Supreme Court (and other preservationist institutions) will resist such cheap and easy efforts to revolutionize higher law, elected politicians will normally pursue their electoral advantage without engaging in such fundamental challenges. Only when a substantial movement for revolutionary reform arises in the country will elected politicians begin to signal the advent of a constitutional moment by openly challenging traditional principles.[8]

At this point our *private* citizen will be faced with a hard choice. He is now on notice: if he passively remains on the sidelines, fundamental aspects of his social situation may be revolutionized without his serious participation. The receipt of this signal will not, of course, magically dissolve the dilemma experienced by private citizens who will lose a great deal of value if they begin to invest heavily in political participation. The dualist, however, does not hope to "solve" this dilemma. He simply provides constitutional resources that allow all of us to live with it as sensitively as we can. At least the two-track Constitution tries to assure our *private* citizen that he is not being called to active engagement for some normal reason of electoral advantage, but because lots of other private *citizens* think that the time is ripe for serious collective labor. Can you really ask for more than this?

If you like,[9] you can put your answer in the language of consent: By voting for normal politicians, *private* citizens do not understand their ballots to signify their consent to a change in fundamental principles; if such a change is sought, the general citizenry must be put on notice and given a fair chance to deliberate upon the transformative proposal in a sustained way; otherwise, elected politicians cannot presume that they have earned the People's consent to their cheap talk of a brave new world.

THE ULTIMATE QUESTION

Can we now move on to the third stage of the argument? Stage one was abstract: it explained why two-track democracy fulfilled the expressive needs of private citizens as they shifted their political engagements over time. Stage two was more concrete: it explored the ways in which the particular American tradition of dualistic democracy provided resources for the practice of private citizenship in both its active and passive phases. Stage three confronts the ultimate question: Does private citizenship make sense as a lifetime project? What's so good about it?

The Deflections of Democratic Theory

It is a shame that so much modern democratic theory has deflected our attention away from this question. The sources of distraction are many and various. On one side, private citizenship is under constant threat from the excessively high-minded, who shake their head in disdain at the general level of apathy and ignorance, selfishness and narrowness of vision prevailing amongst the private citizenry. From their lofty pinnacle, the remorseless economy of civic virtue makes the American engagement in self-government seem a shabby and pathetic affair. Better far to keep this involvement on the level of pure symbol, and consolidate the authority of an educated elite who know enough to take the business of government seriously.[10] Or perhaps the right answer for the elite is to wash its hands of democratic politics and retreat into the university to contemplate its own wisdom.[11]

Aristocratic disdain can dissolve, by degrees, into outright fear. Mass mobilization hasn't had a happy history in the twentieth century. Think of the Bolsheviks, the Nazis, the Maoists. With these examples in mind, the last thing you want to encourage is private citizenship—popular engagement will only degenerate into perverse combinations of hysteria and bureaucratic tyranny. Perhaps the deepest spokesman for this view is Joseph Schumpeter. Reeling from his confrontation with Nazism and Bolshevism, his *Capitalism, Socialism, and Democracy*[12] remains committed to the importance of free and fair elections. But Schumpeter understands their function in a way that detaches the case for democracy from the promise of private citizenship. For him, it is enough that a democratic electorate is a notoriously fickle beast. While "ins" may beat "outs" in one or two or three elections, their efforts to monopolize power will eventually be disrupted—if only because the opposing candidates have managed to convince the voters of the superior brilliance of their smiles or the profundity of their advertising copy. Even if elites are destabilized by almost-random electoral shocks, this may be enough to disrupt the tyrannical ambitions of permanently entrenched political cliques.[13] And with this, for understandable reasons, Schumpeterians remain content.

As in Europe, fear of the masses is detectable in much American political science. Nonetheless, the main line has seemed downright optimistic, if only by comparison. Modern scholars have continued to emphasize the capacity of Americans to act collectively in a constructive way. Only they have not given pride of place to the masses' problematic engagement with private citizenship. Instead, academic attention took a pluralist turn, focusing on the extent to which Americans understood themselves as members of a host of interest groups—defined principally along economic, ethnic, and religious lines. On this pluralist view, democratic politics is principally a process by which interest groups bargain with one another. Each issue on the public agenda engages the interests of different groups, with different intensities. Politicians serve as brokers, devising outcomes that express the shifting balance of interest group pressure. At least in places like America, the right answer to the question *Who Governs?*[14] is that nobody does all the time. Since different groups invest their scarce political resources in different issues, no single group always calls the shots.

While pluralist analysis sometimes degenerated into sheer apologia, it positively invited one powerful form of critique: the search for suppressed interests. This involved the identification of groups which, for one structural reason or another,[15] experienced profound difficulties in finding a place at the pluralist bazaar. Blacks and other impoverished groups headed the list—which over time has expanded to include more diffuse interests like environmentalism and consumerism. As the number and variety of these weak groups became apparent, American pluralism began to seem less benign.

No less important, this critical diagnosis suggested its own cure. Should we not take steps to modify the political structures to allow all groups to compete with one another on roughly equal terms? This ideal—I shall call it perfected pluralism—has proved attractive to a host of different audiences, ranging from grass-roots organizers to the Supreme Court of the United States.[16]

My own response is mixed. Interest groups do, of course, have an important place in normal politics; given this fact, I agree that the gross imbalance of organizational resources available to different groups is a matter of concern; and that we should take creative institutional steps to correct the grossest imbalances. But there are dangers here. Steps to correct organizational imbalances can erode more fundamental dualist commitments. Most important, such reforms too easily allow us to forget that we are not merely members of a race, religion, class, region, industry. We are also citizens of the United States—concerned with the rights of all Americans and the permanent interests of the entire community. *This* is the voice that the constitutional structure aims to encourage Americans to develop. We should not content ourselves with perfected pluralism. Like Madison, our constitutional game is divide and conquer: Let thousands of interest groups proliferate so that their narrow objectives will cancel one another out and allow some breathing room for the effort by politician/statesmen and private citizens to focus, however distractedly, upon the public good. Too much effort to correct the imbalance between interest groups encourages the impression that what is "really" important is the narrow pursuit of partial interests rather than the good of the whole.

It also threatens the future development of constitutional politics. Aiming for "fairness" amongst existing interests can entrench the existing system of normal politics in ways that will make it too resistant* to subsequent popular movements for political redefinition. The pluralist—perfected or otherwise—is blind to the significance of these movements, once again because she is blind to the

---

*Note that I say "too resistant." A transformative movement should not expect its claims to speak for the People to be accepted too easily. See Chapter 10, pp. 285–288. Like many questions of constitutional design, this is one of maintaining proper balance— a balance that is lost by an undue fixation on interest group imbalance.

fundamental importance of private citizenship as distinct from narrower group associations.

If anything, the dualist critique of pluralism applies more forcefully to the even narrower focus adopted by a recent tendency in political science: the so-called public choice school.[17] This economistic tendency begins with the individual, not the group, and seeks to describe a politics that would emerge if all participants were exclusively concerned with the pursuit of self-interest. Once again, I hardly want to deny the importance of this focus. Doing so would ignore the existence of the millions of perfect privatists in American life who think it a waste of time to make any effort to focus on the public good. The problem comes when the "public choice" perspective mistakes this part of politics for the whole. Perfect privatism is a crucial part of the problem of American politics, not the keystone of its constitutional solution.

Private Citizenship?

So long, that is, as it still makes sense for Americans to answer the call of private citizenship. But does it? Why not reject the project entirely?

An affirmative answer requires defense on two fronts. On the one hand, we must explain why we should not join the privatists who scoff at those benighted folk who continue to ask themselves, however distractedly, what *is* good for the country? On the other hand, we must counter the public-spirited sorts who condemn private citizenship as intolerably shabby: its distracted glances, its shallow commitments, its episodic engagements.

Begin with the second hand. Three big points should make us think twice before joining in a revival of an ideal of citizenship that would rival the classical Greek in its intensity. The first has to do with work. The Greeks didn't like it much: work was for slaves, women, foreigners—anybody except citizens, who would be happy to talk, fight, exercise, but work as little as possible. Now Americans don't especially like to work either; but we see in it a fundamental source of value. Labor has a dignity. And this alone changes our attitude toward citizenship, in two different ways. First, all people who work—in the factory or the farm, at the office or at home—

deserve to be citizens; second, the normal duties of citizenship had better not be so onerous as to make it impossible for Americans to put in a full day's work.

This single point goes very far toward justifying the most distinctive characteristic of private citizenship: the fact that it is a loose-fitting garment that Americans can wear as we act out a variety of other roles in social life. A second difference with the Greeks drives the same point deeper. This is the legacy of Christianity, which emphasizes the supreme value of spiritual exercises far removed from the public forum. This inward turn has been redefined, but not abandoned, by people like myself who do not look to traditional religions for inspiration.[18] For both modernists and the religious, it would seem intolerably shallow to place *too* high a value on something so public as citizenship. Yet this, paradoxically, suggests that a relatively undemanding conception of citizenship best fulfills our highest aspirations for ourselves. Only by designing private citizenship along dualist lines can we preserve spiritual space for matters of ultimate concern that transcend the secular state.

And finally, there is the modern idea of freedom. Each of us is entitled to decide how to live without Big Brother forcing our hand or looking over our shoulder. Tolerance is too weak a word to describe this ideal. The diversity of life choices is a positive good, symbolizing the inexhaustible fecundity of human freedom, the impossibility of any single person, or any concrete community, to master the totality of value. But this, once again, leads to a cautious view of the responsibilities of citizenship. Civic obligations must be designed to allow very different sorts of people—radically different sorts—to take it up. Loading responsibilities upon private citizens without compelling reason shows disrespect for freedom.

The dignity of labor; the inwardness of value; the value of freedom: these are no trivial things, and they all lead me down the dualist's path toward private citizenship, rather than up some steeper slope toward Greekish virtue. Some of us, of course, will choose a more full-time commitment to the public service; but the bedrock of private citizenship must be placed at a different level.

As we have seen, even this level will seem too lofty for perfect privatists. What are we to say to them?

Three things. The first speaks in the language of long-term self-interest. Politics may seem an annoying sideline right now; but consider, my privatist, how it may loom up and grab you quite suddenly. Are you quite sure that it is in your self-interest to scoff at the very idea of citizenship, when you may later want to protect your own hide by appealing to others to take a broad view of the public good?

A second argument moralizes this appeal to brute self-interest through the metaphor of social contract. Following the pioneering work of John Rawls,[19] think of the problem from the vantage of an original position in which your social vision is not distorted by knowledge of your concrete advantages. Once you have placed yourself behind a veil of ignorance, would you sign a social contract which imposed the duties of private citizenship? There are at least two reasons for thinking that the answer is yes. The first looks upon the universal practice of private citizenship instrumentally: You would accept these obligations because you think that they will, in general, serve to protect you against the imposition of severe disadvantage. Consider the alternatives: are you willing to trust a more elitist regime behind the veil of ignorance, now that you don't have any reason to think you will be a member of the elite? Are you willing to trust to a politics of pure self-interest, once you don't know how often your own ox will be gored? The second approach is more foundational: Use the veil of ignorance as a conceptual device for clarifying your fundamental self-interests, once narrow questions of strategic advantage have been obscured from view.[20] Now that you have done this, isn't it clear that you have a fundamental interest in participating with your fellow citizens in the ongoing project of self-government—at least when these obligations have been constrained by a due appreciation of the competing claims of work, inner spirituality, and freedom?

The final approach takes up this question without inviting you to abstract yourself from the particularity of the human predicament in the way Rawls recommends. There is no need for a veil for you to figure out that you're stuck with a problem that won't go away.

It is simply this: You are not alone on Earth; you share your time and space with others, lots of others, who differ with you about lots of things. How to come to terms with this basic fact? You may simply seek to oppress others through force and fraud. Or you may try to come to terms with them about the best way to associate together. Isn't there a certain dignity in the second course? Isn't there something noble in calling upon yourself, by calling upon others, to put some intelligible form upon your social life together? If we are not to live as mere brutes, grunting past one another in the night, surely we owe at least this much to each other?

After all, the construction of a public order does not seem utterly impossible. People like us, inhabiting this brave new world of North America, have been struggling for political meaning for quite some time. They have been diverted from this struggle, to be sure, by countless distractions, and their greatest achievements have been scarred by injustice.

And yet we may take heart in the thought that the American Republic has not come to an end. At least, not yet. Surely it is better to struggle for a new beginning than turn away to the private celebration of the death of citizenship?

A New Beginning

But it is not enough make a personal commitment to private citizenship. The American experiment in self-government cannot endure unless tens of millions of your fellow citizens do the same.

This simple thought is enough to prompt anxious reappraisal. It is all very well for a Yale law professor to see the bright side of the American constitutional achievement and to call his fellow Americans to live out its dream of private citizenship. The question is whether this traditional ideal can commend itself to lots of Americans who don't spend their time teaching constitutional law at Yale in exchange for a big salary.

Especially people whose first reaction to the Founding is naturally one of suspicion: blacks, who cannot forget that these Enlightenment gentlemen established the most powerful slave-ocracy of the nineteenth century; Indians and Hispanics, who cannot forget the slaughter of their ancestors in the name of "manifest destiny"; working people, who wonder how aristocrats like Madison could be of any possible use to them; women—the Founding Fathers indeed!

I am asking a great deal when I ask these people to join me in telling a story of American constitutional achievement that begins with the Founding Fathers. If this is the common history which we share as private citizens, aren't we better off without it? Isn't it time to face up to the hard truth that Beard and later Progressives established: that the "great moments" of American constitutional history were so compromised by deceit and evil that they are part of the problem, not the solution. There is nothing exceptional about American constitutional history, other than the pretentious lies we tell about it. Americans—and especially progressive Americans—should continue the debunking operation the Progressives so nobly began. Only by tearing down the constitutional past can we confront the oppressions of American history—and find the courage to build a better future.

Isn't neo-Federalism a big mistake? Doesn't it blind us to two transparent failings of our past—its oligarchic politics, its toleration of social injustice? Let us consider these evils in turn.

Beyond the Founding

The Founders established an oligarchy. While they spoke for the People, they only tried to win the mobilized consent of white men.

This is, of course, true; and it is one of the principal reasons why I have been urging a thorough reworking of the professional narrative which guides modern judges in interpreting the Constitution. By ignoring or trivializing the higher lawmaking achievements of the twentieth century, the received narrative gives too oligarchic an aspect to our constitutional history. This oligarchic slant is extended further by treating the nineteenth-century Republicans as if they were content to make three formal amendments to the Federalist scheme, rather than reconstructing the Union in the name of a redefined People. The net result is to heighten the impression that the Founding oligarchs are ruling us from the grave with relatively little assistance from folks who are not only closer to us in time but closer to us in democratic spirit.

Of course, if our Constitution had not been fundamentally changed since its Founding by white male oligarchs, we would simply have to confront the dark implications of this fact. The facts, however, are quite otherwise. Without the constitutional politics of Reconstruction Republicans and New Deal Democrats, our modern

Constitution would not exist. These nineteenth- and twentieth-century spokesmen for the People refused to follow the rules for constitutional amendment specified by the omniscient, if oligarchic, Founders. Modern lawyers embrace a legal fiction when they pretend otherwise. The legal culture's addiction to such fictions is nothing new. Nonetheless, it is odd to find lawyers spinning fictions that make their entire project of constitutional law *more* illegitimate than it would seem if they tried to tell the truth.

Not that the truth will make for an easy argument. But at least it will permit a reasoned response to today's black or female American who wants to know why she should give any respect at all to old-time politicians who thought they could speak for "the People" without even making an effort to consult people like her. After all, at least she can vote for the normal politicians of today. Don't they speak for her better than oligarchs who didn't even try?

My answer: these old-timers provided a constitutional language and institutions through which later generations of women and blacks have won fuller citizenship. In gaining their victories during the twentieth century, neither the women's movement nor the civil rights movement has sought to repudiate the country's higher lawmaking heritage. Instead, they used the inclusionary potential of this tradition to advantage—finally allowing Americans, after two long centuries, to struggle their way to a regime in which every adult citizen is granted at least a formal political equality.

Not that We the People have reached some democratic height merely because we don't bar blacks or women from the polls any longer. The question, alas, is not whether we live in Utopia. It is whether we can deepen our commitments to government by the People by building up, or tearing down, the dualist conception of democracy laboriously constructed over the past two centuries.

It seems odd to give up on the higher lawmaking tradition just at the moment that it has provided us with the means to affirm the common citizenship of all Americans. Given the resources for self-criticism available in our constitutional tradition, are those most estranged from ancient history by reason of race or sex or class best served by repudiating the Founding and Reconstruction? Does it not make more sense to use this language to call Americans to make a new beginning by reforming the foundations of their common life together?

The Legacy of Injustice

Whatever your answer, do not mistake it for a response to a second distinct, if related, question. This one does not focus on political process, but on social outcomes. Its complaint is not that blacks and women and many others have been excluded from past exercises in constitutional politics; it is that they are *still suffering* from their centuries of powerlessness in everyday life right now. From this point of view, the dualist's insistence on the priority of the past can seem a vicious apologia for the toleration of social injustice.

Consider: even if oppressed social groups could gain a normal political victory at the polls, the dualist still insists that they have much more political work to do before they can inscribe their vision of social justice into our higher law. Rather than proceeding immediately to social reform, as in the parliamentary system, the ascendant coalition would have to confront the resistance of the courts, and other preservationist institutions, if their program strikes at the heart of traditional constitutional values. Isn't building a more just society hard enough without the cumbersome complexities of higher law-making?

The power of this critique will depend a lot on your own vision of social justice. Some people will deny the premise—that America remains deeply scarred by racism, sexism, poverty. More people will deny that this legacy of injustice can be effectively remedied through more and better government intervention into social life. On their view, activist government does more harm than good—destroying precious individual freedoms without achieving much in the way of real social justice. For those impressed with these ripostes, there isn't much that needs to be said before rejecting this critique as misconceived.

For me, though, this critique comes closest to the mark. Ten years ago, my book *Social Justice in the Liberal State*[21] explained the sources of my opposition to the gross maldistribution of wealth that prevails in today's America. Over the last decade, I haven't been persuaded

to change my mind by fashionable neo-conservatisms that cast activist government as the most potent source of injustice in contemporary
social life. There is no Invisible Hand out there leading America
upwards and onwards. If Americans want to build a more just life
for themselves, there is no substitute for engaged national politics
and activist government.

My problem with this second critique has less to do with its
premises than with its institutional conclusions. It strikes me as facile
to suppose that social justice will come to America in a single burst
of lawmaking that follows a single electoral victory in the style of
British parliamentary democracy. I believe that dualism is far sounder
in its instincts. *Lasting* progress will require an extended period of
citizen mobilization through which reformers confront the doubts
of their fellow Americans and win the consent of many, if not all,
to the need for fundamental change in the name of justice.

I do not understate the magnitude of the task. At no time since
the 1920's has the movement for social justice in America been as
fractionated as today. Rather than bonding with one another, the
labor movement and the peace movement, blacks and ethnics, fem-
inists and environmentalists look upon each other with anxiety and
suspicion. The very thought they might find common ground—much
less common ground with more mainstream Americans—seems to
many a vain illusion. But is it an illusion that we can afford to live
without?

There can be no knock-down answer to this question. I have been
trying to reassert the revolutionary promise of the constitutional
tradition, not guarantee its performance—which will depend on lots
of things beyond our power to predict or control.

But it will also depend on us. We may reach out to one another—
across the lines of class and caste and race—and work together to
build a more just foundation for our life together; or we may not.
Our generation may be numbered amongst those that found meaning
in the work of private citizenship; or we may hand down to our
children a history in which the constitutional achievements of the
past become ever more distant, the distractions of normal politics
ever more present, the call for a new exercise in common citizenship
ever more hollow.

All I know is this: Americans have in the past answered this call, and have successfully worked together to build a community more inclusionary and more just than the one they entered. There is no reason to say that this history has come to an end.

BEYOND DUALISM?

I write at a time of normal politics: a time best used for reflection on the needs of the future, as well as the promise of the past.

I say we need a new Bill of Rights, one that moves far beyond the first ten amendments ratified in the aftermath of the Founding, one that builds on the achievements of Reconstruction, the New Deal, and the civil rights movement to give new substance to each American's right to pursue life, liberty, and the pursuit of happiness.

It would be a Bill that recognizes the inclusionary thrust of American history by giving each American an effective guarantee of equal opportunity—in schools, on the job, in public places and public life. It would be a Bill that commits the American people to secure each citizen against the vagaries of unemployment, disability, sickness, and old age.

It would be a Bill that strengthened the Founding concerns with individual freedom in a bureaucratic society very different from the eighteenth century's. We must confront the fact that the overwhelming majority of Americans go to jail today on a "plea bargain" that allows prosecutors to short-circuit the jury trials that the Founders thought central to the Bill of Rights. We must protect traditional rights of free expression in a world of concentrated mass media and pervasive state regulation. We must carve out new spheres of privacy and autonomy to protect individuals from technocratic oversight and control.

This is not the place to go into details. The crucial point is to urge the variety of progressive movements and causes that today swirl about in normal politics to seek a common platform: a modern Bill of Rights that might unite *all* Americans in a renewed sense of national commitment to individual freedom. If we should succeed in this, I am sure that the particular substantive provisions of the Bill that would emerge from a generation's debate and decision would be very different from any blueprint that you or I might formulate before the event.[22]

For present purposes, then, I shall take up a single question that speaks to process, not substance—for the purpose of testing your commitment to the very idea of dualist democracy. The question—admittedly visionary at the time of this writing—can be posed by a contrast with the present constitutional situation. While the Federalist First Congress went along with the popular demand for a Bill of Rights, it did not seek to entrench its Bill against subsequent modification through constitutional politics. To this day, it remains possible to amend the First Amendment—as the recent flap over President Bush's proposal of a flag-burning amendment illustrates. Suppose, then, that a movement did arise in support of a Bill of Rights for the twenty-first century. In seeking to move beyond our eighteenth-century Bill, should We the People seriously reconsider the Founders' failure to entrench fundamental rights against constitutional revision?

More modern constitutions have taken this step. In the aftermath of Hitler's defeat, the German people made it unconstitutional for subsequent majorities to weaken their founding commitment to a host of fundamental freedoms. The text's guarantees of basic human dignity were proclaimed unamendable.[23] Since we are (by hypothesis) moving beyond the Framers in other respects, why not in this one? Why not make our new Bill of Rights unamendable? Couldn't a Hitler arise in America, no less than in Germany?

Not that a decision to entrench a modern Bill of Rights by the year 2000 would be enough to guarantee the enjoyment of these freedoms by Americans in the year 2050. Constitutional history is full of eloquent warnings against putting too much faith in legal rules limiting the power of future Americans to redefine the popular will. Nonetheless, entrenching the Bill might make the triumph of a Nazi-like movement more difficult. It would serve as a reminder to all future generations of a time when Americans solemnly recommitted the nation to the *unconditional* protection of fundamental rights. Perhaps this solemn act of rededication might reverberate in the collective memory for many generations to come? And if, despite this memorial, a Nazi-like movement should arise, the unconditional character of the modern Bill would encourage courts—and the rest of us?—to make a last stand against a Hitlerian movement with greater determination, giving more time for the People to reconsider their support of such an awful tyranny.

Of course, a decision to support German-style entrenchment should depend on many things—most importantly on the substance of the new Bill of Rights that gained deep and decisive popular support. For all we know, a mass movement for a new Bill might converge on constitutional solutions that are worse, not better, than those found in the traditional Bill of Rights. Even if today's Americans might find it in themselves to make moral progress—brave words—the new constitutional solutions might not seem sufficiently incisive to warrant unconditional entrenchment. Nonetheless, the German example does suggest that entrenchment might be used for valuable purposes: Must Americans be forced to endure a Holocaust before they follow the Germans in solemnly recognizing that there are some individual rights that a majority of the citizenry, however mobilized and deliberate, can never legitimately suppress?

I myself would be proud to be a member of the generation that took this burden upon itself—finally redeeming the promise of the Declaration of Independence by entrenching *inalienable* rights into our Constitution. At the same time, this thought experiment emphasizes how far away we are from such a moment. Civil libertarians today are not building bridges to other movements with self-confidence. If anything, they are struggling to preserve what Americans have won in the past, not redefine and deepen the national commitment to inalienable rights. It will take a generation of work before we can hope for a new constitutional solution along the lines I have imagined—and even then, who knows how the American people might decide?

In any event, crystal-ball gazing isn't my specialty. Nor have I been trying to glimpse the shape of Utopia. My aim has been to capture the spirit of the existing historical enterprise—to persuade you that this spirit is better captured by the dualist emphasis on rule by the People than any competing theory of American government.

Whatever the ultimate limitations of this enterprise, it has one great strength. It offers Americans a distinctive solution to an ongoing problem of self-definition posed by the struggle between two great Western traditions for hegemony over the modern spirit. The first tradition, recalling the grandeur of the Greek polis, insists that the life of political involvement serves as the noblest ideal for humankind. The second, recalling a Christian suspicion of claims of secular community, insists that the salvation of souls is a private affair, and that the secular state's coercive authority represents the supreme threat to the highest human values. When faced with this ongoing struggle for ascendancy in Western thought and practice, the American Constitution does not seek an easy victory of one part of ourselves at the cost of the other. It proposes to use the conflict to provide the energy for a creative synthesis.

As Americans, we are neither perfectly public citizens nor perfectly private persons. The Constitution of the United States constitutes us as private citizens equipped with a language and process that may, if thoughtfully used, allow for democratic self-government of a remarkably self-conscious kind. Like all languages, this one may be used to accomplish great evils as well as great goods.

The choice, my friends, is yours.

NOTES

INDEX

Notes

1. Dualist Democracy

1. Woodrow Wilson, *Congressional Government* (1885); Woodrow Wilson, *Constitutional Government in the United States* (1907).
2. James Thayer, "The Origin and Scope of the American Doctrine of Constitutional Law," 7 *Harv. L. Rev.* 129 (1893).
3. Charles Beard, *An Economic Interpretation of the Constitution of the United States* (1913).
4. Lochner v. New York, 198 U.S. 45, 74 (1905) (Holmes, J., dissenting).
5. Robert Jackson, *The Struggle for Judicial Supremacy* (1941); Railway Express Co. v. New York, 336 U.S. 106, 111 (Jackson, J., concurring).
6. Alexander Bickel, *The Least Dangerous Branch* (1962).
7. John Ely, *Democracy and Distrust: A Theory of Judicial Review* (1980).
8. For a balanced statement see Jesse Choper, *Judicial Review and the National Political Process,* ch. 1 (1980).
9. For the classic statement, see Alexander Bickel, supra n. 6, at 16–23.
10. See Alexander Bickel, supra n. 6; Alexander Bickel, *The Supreme Court and the Idea of Progress* (1970).
11. John Ely, supra n. 7.
12. Richard Parker, "The Past of Constitutional Theory—And Its Future," 42 *Ohio St. L.J.* 223 (1981).
13. Richard Epstein, *Takings: Private Property and the Power of Eminent Domain* (1985).
14. Ronald Dworkin, *Taking Rights Seriously,* ch. 5 (1978); Ronald Dworkin, *Law's Empire,* chs. 10–11 (1986).
15. Owen Fiss, "Groups and the Equal Protection Clause," 5 *J. Phil. & Pub. Aff.* 107 (1976).
16. John Rawls, "Kantian Constructivism in Moral Theory," 77 *J. Phil.* 515 (1980).
17. Robert Nozick, *Anarchy, State, and Utopia* (1974).
18. Not that monists necessarily oppose all exercises of judicial review. As I have suggested, the school has been quite ingenious in justifying the judicial protection of one or another right as instrumental for the ongoing democratic functioning of the regime. See authors cited at nn. 6, 7, 12, supra.
19. I will focus here only on the objections of the strong foundationalist, deferring a more elaborate defense of the democratic character of dualism to Chapter 11.

20. Technically, this might be done within the framework of the present Basic Law (Grundgesetz), which allows for its replacement by a completely new Constitution (Verfassung) in art. 146. Since the drafters of the Basic Law took this step to emphasize the provisional character of West Germany, and not the provisional character of fundamental rights, it would be a great abuse of art. 146 to use the occasion of a new Verfassung to modify the entrenched provisions on human rights. Nonetheless, this technical possibility does provide an escape hatch through which German dualists might conceivably modify their Basic Law's foundationalist commitments.

21. The second entrenching provision stipulates that no State shall be deprived of equal representation in the Senate without its express consent. U.S. Const. art. V. This effort to entrench federalism caused all sorts of trouble in the aftermath of the Civil War. See the second volume in this series (forthcoming).

22. I will return to this question in Chapter 11.

23. Although Alexander Bickel became an eloquent spokesman, he died before he had a fair chance to develop his evolving views. But see, Alexander Bickel, *The Morality of Consent* 1–30 (1975).

24. See, for example, Anthony Kronman, "Alexander Bickel's Philosophy of Prudence," 94 *Yale L.J.* 1567 (1985); Charles Fried, "The Artificial Reason of the Law or: What Lawyers Know," 60 *Tex. L. Rev.* 31 (1981).

25. See Alexander Bickel, supra n. 23. For eloquent spokesmen in allied disciplines, see, Friedrich Hayek, *Law, Legislation and Liberty* (1978); Samuel Huntington, *American Politics: The Promise of Disharmony* (1981); Michael Oakeshott, *On Human Conduct* (1975).

26. As my discussion of judicial interpretation in Chapters 4–6 will suggest.

27. See Paul Kahn, "Reason and Will in the Origins of American Constitutionalism," 98 *Yale L.J.* 449, 453–73 (1989).

28. Edmund Burke, "Speech on Moving His Resolutions for Conciliation with the Colonies," in *Edmund Burke: Selected Writings and Speeches* 147 (P. Stanlis ed. 1968) (enumerating the distinctive aspects of the American people).

29. The historical Burke is a far more complex figure than the conservative incrementalist of modern fiction. See Robert Kelley, *The Transatlantic Persuasion: The Liberal Democratic Mind in the Age of Gladstone*, ch. 3 (1969).

30. See, for example, Richard Hofstadter, *The Paranoid Style in American Politics* (1965); Richard Hofstadter, *The Progressive Historians* (1969).

31. Robert Dahl, *A Preface to Democratic Theory* (1956); Robert Dahl, *Who Governs?* (1961).

32. Daniel Bell, *The End of Ideology* (rev. ed. 1962).

33. Bernard Bailyn, *Ideological Origins of the American Revolution* (1967).

34. Gordon Wood, *The Creation of the American Republic* (1969).

35. Frank Michelman, "Law's Republic," 97 *Yale L.J.* 1493 (1988); Frank Michelman, "The Supreme Court, 1985 Term—Foreword: Traces of Self-Government," 100 *Harv. L. Rev.* 4 (1986).

36. Suzanna Sherry, "Civic Virtue and the Feminine Voice in Constitutional Adjudication," 72 *U. Va. L. Rev.* 543 (1986).

37. Cass Sunstein, "Beyond the Republican Revival," 97 *Yale L.J.* 1539 (1988); Cass Sunstein, "Interest Groups in American Public Law," 38 *Stan. L. Rev.* 29 (1986).

38. Mark Tushnet, *Red, White, and Blue: A Critical Analysis of Constitutional Law* (1988).

39. Curiously, republicanism has not been mined by constitutional conservatives— despite their putative concern with the "intention of the Framers." Doubtless, this deficiency will be remedied in time.

40. Louis Hartz, *The Liberal Tradition in America: An Interpretation of American Political Thought since the Revolution* (1955).

41. J. G. A. Pocock, *The Machiavellian Moment: Florentine Political Thought and the Atlantic Republican Tradition* (1975).

42. For a good contemporary critique of the familiar Marxist account of the French Revolution, see J. F. Bosher, *The French Revolution* (1988).

43. Louis Hartz, supra n. 40, at 5, 66.

44. J. G. A. Pocock, supra n. 41, at ch. 15.

45. Suzanna Sherry has a wonderful footnote that accurately summarizes the present historical perplexity surrounding the date when republicanism died in America:
    See, for example, G. Wood, [*The Creation of the American Republic*] at 606 (1787 and the adoption of the Constitution signaled "the end of classical politics"); L. Banning, *The Jeffersonian Persuasion: Evolution of a Party Ideology* (1978) (liberalism triumphed no earlier than the end of the War of 1812); R. Ketcham, *Presidents Above Party: The First American Presidency, 1789–1829* (1984) (classical politics ended with rise of Jacksonian democracy); D. Howe, *The Political Culture of the American Whigs* 301–05 (1979) (republican or Whig values lasted until after Civil War); Ross, "The Liberal Tradition Revisited and the Republican Tradition Addressed," in *New Directions in American Intellectual History* 116, 122–29 (J. Higham & P. Conkin eds. 1979) (republicanism lingered through 1880's); J. Pocock, [*The Machiavellian Moment*], at 526–45 (classical influence and awareness of the "Machiavellian moment" continues to present day); cf. M. Horwitz, *The Transformation of American Law, 1780–1860,* at 253 (1977) ("Law, once conceived of as . . . a paramount expression of the moral sense of the community, had come [by 1850] to be thought of as facilitative of individual desires . . .").
    Sherry, supra n. 36, at 551, n. 23.

46. See, for example, Sherry, supra n. 36.

47. Liberalism and republicanism are treated as dichotomies by Sherry, supra n. 36, at 544–47; Tushnet, supra n. 38; and Horwitz, "Republicanism and Liberalism in American Constitutional Thought," 29 *Wm. & Mary L. Rev.* 57, 66–67 (1987). Critiques of this dichotomous treatment may be found in Richard Fallon, "What Is Republicanism, and Is It Worth Reviving," 102 *Harv. L. Rev.* 1695, at 1704–13 (1989), and Larry Simon, "The New Republicanism: Generosity of Spirit in Search of Something to Say," 29 *Wm. & Mary L. Rev.* 83, 86–90 (1987).

48. David Gauthier, *Morality by Agreement* (1986); Robert Nozick, supra n. 17.

49. See, for example, John Stuart Mill, *Considerations on Representative Govern-*

ment, ch. 3 (1861); John Dewey, *Liberalism and Social Action* (1935); John Rawls, "Justice as Fairness: Political Not Metaphysical," 14 *J. Phil. & Pub. Aff.* 223 (1985). My own work builds on this tradition, see *Social Justice in the Liberal State* (1980), and "Why Dialogue?," 86 *J. Phil.* 5 (1989).

50. This theme is explicit in Sunstein's recent "Beyond the Republican Revival," supra n. 37, at 1566–71, and implicit in Michelman's recent explorations, see supra at n. 35.

51. See Part Two.

2. The Bicentennial Myth

1. The distinction between ceremonial and effective constitutions comes from Walter Bagehot, *The English Constitution* 1–2 (2d ed. 1872), who passes it to Woodrow Wilson, *Congressional Government* 7 (1885), who passes it to countless moderns.

2. I borrow this term from Robert Cover, "The Supreme Court 1982 Term— Foreword: Nomos and Narrative," 97 *Harv. L. Rev.* 4, 11 (1983).

3. See Chapter 5, pp. 119–129.

4. See, for example, Sanford Levinson, *Constitutional Faith* 130–31 (1988); David Kay, "The Illegality of the Constitution," 4 *Const. Commentary* 57 (1987); David Kay, "The Creation of Constitutions in Canada and the United States," 7 *Canada–United States L.J.* 111, 124–36 (1984). But see Akhil Amar, "Philadelphia Revisited: Amending the Constitution Outside Article V," 55 *U. Chi. L. Rev* 1043, 1047–54 (1988). Professor Amar concedes that ratification of the Constitution "obviously violates Article XIII of the pre-existing Articles of Confederation," but suggests that the Articles should be viewed as a treaty whose obligations had lapsed as a result of state violations. Given this asserted lapse, Amar does not believe that the Convention was acting illegally in calling upon nine or more states to secede from the Confederation.

While some Federalists undoubtedly held Amar's view in private, even they were reluctant to rely on it in public. Compare *Federalist* No. 40, at 252, 254 (J. Madison) (C. Rossiter ed. 1961) (illegality explicitly conceded), with No. 43, at 279–80 (noting that "[p]erhaps, also" [emphasis in original] justification for ratification procedure "may be found" in breach-of-treaty theory). And, as Amar recognizes, many Anti-Federalists denied that the Articles' pledge of "perpetual" Union could be evaded so easily after so short a trial. See Herbert Storing, *What the Anti-Federalists Were For,* Ch. 2 (1981).

Overall, I find Profesor Kay's arguments establishing the illegality of the Constitution more persuasive than Professor Amar's. At the very least, Amar's confidence in the legality of the Convention's end run around the state legislatures was not shared by the Federalists themselves—who recognized that their "legal" argument for secession would not get them very far in popular debate, and that they would have to invoke other, more fundamental, principles of popular sovereignty to defend their act of constitutional creation.

Indeed, the rest of Amar's article usefully emphasizes how important the principles of popular sovereignty were to the Revolutionary generation—though, once again, I think he goes overboard in suggesting that the Convention's call for ratification by state conventions, rather than state legislatures, was *legal* under the laws of all thirteen states. While some states, like Massachusetts, had given great authority to constitutional conventions in their domestic law—see Amar, supra, at 1049–51—others, like Rhode Island, were much more backward in conceding that constitutional conventions, meeting in the name of the People, might legally modify preexisting state charters. See Luther v. Borden, 48 U.S. (7 How.) 1 (1849).

5. Since this chapter's sketch will be fully documented in the next volume, I have refrained from extensive footnoting here. For those who would like to review some of the supporting sources before the next volume is published, they are presented in my "Constitutional Politics/Constitutional Law," 99 *Yale L.J.* 453, 486–515 (1989).

6. See Chapter 5, pp. 113–119. I will be treating this theme at greater length in subsequent volumes.

7. See Robert Dahl, "Myth of the Presidential Mandate," 105 *Pol. Sci. Q.* 355 (1990).

8. Surely the decisive majorities commanded by the New Deal Democrats in all sections of the country would have been the envy of the Reconstruction Republicans and the Founding Federalists.

9. I address the questions raised by my proposal at somewhat greater length in "Transformative Appointments", 101 *Harv. L. Rev.* 1164, 1182–84 (1988).

10. I take up the question of basic criteria in Chapter 10. I attempt a more elaborate appraisal of my particular proposal for constitutional referenda in the next volume.

3. One Constitution, Three Regimes

1. In characterizing American history as a series of distinctive regimes, I share a common enterprise with other recent writers. See, for example, Theodore Lowi, *The Personal President: Power Invested, Promise Unfulfilled* xi, chs. 2–5 (1985); Stephen Skowronek, *Building a New American State* 19–46, 285–92 (1982). In making this effort, I have sought to integrate important insights of students of "critical elections" in American history. See Walter Burnham, *Critical Elections and the Mainsprings of American Politics* (1970); James Sundquist, *Dynamics of the Party System: Alignment and Realignment of Political Parties in the United States* (rev. ed. 1983).

2. See Chapter 1, pp. 7–24.

3. See, for example, Philip Bobbitt, *Constitutional Interpretation* (1991); Robert Bork, *The Tempting of America: The Political Seduction of the Law* (1990); Ronald Dworkin, *Law's Empire* (1986); Stanley Fish, *Doing What Comes Naturally: Change, Rhetoric, and the Practice of Theory in Literary and Legal Studies* (1989); Owen Fiss, "Objectivity and Interpretation," 34 *Stan. L. Rev.* 739 (1982), and the critique of his arguments in Fish, "Fish v. Fiss," 36 *Stan. L.*

Rev. 1325 (1984). An interesting set of essays is collected in "Interpretation Symposium," 58 *S. Cal. L. Rev.* (1985). For a skeptical perspective, see Mark Tushnet, *Red, White, and Blue: A Critical Analysis of Constitutional Law* (1988).

4. See, for example, Gerald Gunther, *Constitutional Law* 1–104 (11th ed. 1985) (introducing the constitution through a series of Marshall Court opinions). The structure of the reigning professional narrative is perhaps most visible in books, like Gunther's, which are used in first-year law school courses introducing students to "the professional" approach to constitutional law. Since Gunther's book has dominated the market for a generation, it is an especially valuable document for purposes of illustration.

5. For fine sketches of the early regime at different stages of its development, see James Young, *The Washington Community, 1800–1828* (1966); Richard McCormick, *The Second American Party System* (1966); William Freehling, *The Road to Disunion: Secessionists at Bay* (1990).

6. Even reactionaries who long for the "good old days" of *Lochner* recognize, however reluctantly, that they are gone forever. See Richard Epstein, "The Proper Scope of the Commerce Power," 73 *Va. L. Rev.* 1358, 1454–55 (1987).

7. Dred Scott v. Sandford, 60 U.S. (19 How.) 393 (1857).

8. Lochner v. New York, 198 U.S. 45 (1905).

9. Robert Cover, *Justice Accused: Antislavery and the Judicial Process* (1975).

10. For different aspects of this transformation, see James Ceasar, *Presidential Selection: Theory and Development* 170–353 (1979); Samuel Kernell, *Going Public: New Strategies of Presidential Leadership* (1986); Theodore Lowi, supra n. 1; Benjamin Page, *Choices and Echoes in Presidential Elections: Rational Man and Electoral Democracy* (1978). The very notion that the President should begin each legislative session by advancing a comprehensive program is an innovation of the modern republic. See Richard Neustadt, "Presidency and Legislation: Planning the President's Program," 49 *Am. Pol. Sci. Rev.* 980 (1955).

11. See James Ceasar, supra n. 10, at 41–83 (1979); *Federalist* No. 68 at 414 (A. Hamilton) (C. Rossiter ed. 1961): "It will not be too strong to say that there will be a constant probability of seeing the station filled by characters preeminent for ability and virtue." Richard McCormick, *The Presidential Game* 7, 16–27 (1982), stresses the Founders' desire to insure executive independence against popular influence.

12. See James Ceasar, supra n. 10, ch. 1. For an insightful study of the early nonpartisan ideal of the Presidency, modeled on Bolingbroke's patriot-king, see Ralph Ketcham, *Presidents above Party: The First American Presidency, 1789–1829*, 89–140 (1989). The ideal's remarkable survival, with some notable exceptions, throughout the nineteenth century is suggested in Jeffrey Tulis, *The Rhetorical Presidency* 25–93 (1987).

13. See Charles Black, "Some Thoughts on the Veto," 40 *Law & Contemp. Probs.* 87, 89–91 (1976). There are two arguable exceptions. One, a pocket veto by Madison of an immigration bill, was based on an objection of expediency, not policy. Madison thought it would allow too much fraud, and signed an amended

bill the next session. The other involved Madison's veto of a bill providing for a Second Bank of the United States. The President's veto message does not, however, claim a broad prerogative to reject legislation on policy grounds. The veto is based on Madison's fear that the proposed bank would not provide sufficient financial support for a war. Given the context of Madison's war with England, Professor Black is right to suggest that, "without stretching too much, such a veto may [be viewed as] . . . connected with protection of the Presidency's role as Commander-in-Chief, and with the effective execution of that power." Id. at 90–91.

14. The executive veto is discussed only once in the Federalist Papers. In *Federalist* No. 73, supra n. 11, Hamilton offers two rationales: principally, to protect the office from legislative encroachment; secondarily, to provide a check against improper laws passed as the result of "passion" or faction in the legislature. Though Hamilton's definition of "improper laws" is vague, it did not envision the veto as a tool to promote programs arising from Presidential "mandates." To the contrary, the veto is presented as a device to allow an independent, disinterested executive to inhibit the passage of poorly considered legislation by partisans of popular movements in the Congress. Hamilton also suggests that Presidents would utilize the veto rarely, a belief subsequently confirmed by the actions of the first holders of the office. See n. 13, supra, and *Federalist* No. 73, supra n. 11, at 442–47 (A. Hamilton).

15. David Mayhew, *Congress: The Electoral Connection* (1974), provides the best analysis of the localist impulses that find maximal expression in the House.

16. In contrast to the "national" House, "[t]he Senate will derive its power from the states as political and coequal societies, and these will be represented on the principle of equality . . . ." *Federalist* No. 39, supra n. 11, at 244 (J. Madison). *Federalist* No. 62 suggests that the Senate would act as repository for state interests against the more nationalistic House: "[It] may be remarked that the equal vote allowed to each state is at once a constitutional recognition of the portion of sovereignty remaining in the individual states and an instrument for preserving that residuary sovereignty. . . . No law or resolution can now be passed without the concurrence, first, of a majority of the people, and then of a majority of the states." *Federalist* No. 62, supra n. 11, at 378 (J. Madison). Similarly, Publius argues that the House, not the Senate, should select the President when the Electoral College reaches impasse, on the ground that the House is the "most popular" branch of the government. *Federalist* No. 66, supra n. 11, at 403–404 (A. Hamilton). See also William Riker, "The Senate and American Federalism," 49 *Am. Pol. Sci. Rev.* 452 (1955).

17. See chap. 2, pp. 44–47.

18. For thoughtful accounts, see Lance Banning, *The Jeffersonian Persuasion* 94–302 (1978); Richard Hofstadter, *The Idea of a Party System,* ch. 3 (1969).

19. The best single discussion of these matters is by James Ceasar, *Presidential Selection,* supra n. 10, ch. 2.

20. Marbury v. Madison, 5 U.S. (1 Cranch) 137 (1803).

21. Compare, for example, Julius Goebel's legalistic search in his *History of the*

Supreme Court of the United States: Antecedents and Beginnings 50–142, 778–84 (1971), with Alexander Bickel's political treatment in *The Least Dangerous Branch: The Supreme Court at the Bar of Politics* 1–14 (1962).

22. See George Haskins & Herbert Johnson, *History of the Supreme Court of the United States: Foundations of Power, John Marshall 1801–15,* chs. 5, 7 (1981)

23. See, for example, Ralph Ketcham supra n. 12, at 108–13, who persuasively argues that despite his role as party leader, Jefferson retained, both in his official capacity and in his personal conception, most of the significant features of the Founders' ideal of nonpartisanship.

24. McCulloch v. Maryland, 17 U.S. (4 Wheat.) 316 (1819).

25. Dartmouth College v. Woodward, 17 U.S. (4 Wheat.) 518 (1819).

26. For the early history of party nominating conventions, culminating in Jackson's Democratic nomination in 1831, see James Chase, *Emergence of the Presidential Nominating Convention, 1789–1832* (1973).

27. See James Ceasar, supra n. 10, ch. 3.

28. "It was no accident that the first president to break decisively from the Inaugural Day custom of attributing his election to some modestly, abstractly stated call of Providence and his fellow citizens and declare that he had been swept into office by 'the will of the American people' was Andrew Jackson, back from the bruising partisan battle over his bank policies in 1832." Daniel Rogers, *Contested Truths* 89 (1987).

29. Though, of course, not as far as Southern extremists desired.

30. The veto message cites *McCulloch v. Maryland* and never directly challenges Marshall's broad construction of the "necessary and proper" clause. The President argues that Marshall's opinion left the question of whether the bank was "necessary and proper" to the President and Congress. His determination that the bank was not necessary authorized him to veto the bank bill as unconstitutional. See 3 *Messages and Papers of the President* 1139 (J. Richardson ed. 1897).

31. See Worcester v. Georgia, 31 U.S. (6 Pet.) 515 (1832), whose relationship to the Jackson Presidency is thoughtfully discussed by G. Edward White, *History of the Supreme Court of the United States: The Marshall Court and Cultural Change* 715–39 (1988).

32. I am omitting another important part of the story—in which the Presidency and the State of South Carolina were leading actors in a struggle defining the limits of decentralization.

33. The events summarized in this paragraph are developed by Carl Swisher, *History of the Supreme Court of the United States: The Taney Period* 15–127 (1974).

34. New York v. Miln, 36 U.S. (11 Pet.) 102 (1837).

35. Charles River Bridge v. Warren Bridge, 36 U.S. (11 Pet.) 420 (1837).

36. For the shock of an engaged participant, see R. Kent Newmeyr, *Supreme Court Justice Joseph Story,* 196–235 (1985).

37. Swift v. Tyson, 41 U.S. (16 Pet.) 1 (1842).

38. See, e.g., Michael Rogin's remarkable account in *Fathers and Children: Andrew Jackson and the Subjugation of the American Indian* (1975).

39. Though I disagree with some of its interpretive premises, the best book on the subject is by Don Fehrenbacher, *The Dred Scott Case: Its Significance in American Law and Politics* (1978).

40. The best book on this debate is by Harry Jaffa, *Crisis of the House Divided* (1959).

4. The Middle Republic

1. See Chapter 2, pp. 44–47.

2. See Chapter 3, pp. 76–77.

3. A full generation before *Lochner,* federal courts were intervening to control the process by which states financed railroad development. See, for example, Gelpke v. Dubuque, 68 U.S. (1 Wall.) 175 (1864); C. Fairman, *History of the United States Supreme Court: Reconstruction and Reunion, 1864–88,* 918–1116 (1971).

4. See Chapter 2, pp. 46–47. The analysis of this constitutional struggle will serve as a centerpiece of the next volume.

5. A first turning point in the emancipation of the executive from Congressional control was the repeal of the Tenure of Offices Act in 1887. Passed in 1867 at the height of the Reconstruction controversy between Congress and Andrew Johnson, this act drastically limited the President's ability to remove recalcitrant executive officials without Senatorial consent. These limitations were denounced by Grant and Hayes, before Cleveland won their repeal during his first administration. See Myers v. United States, 272 U.S. 52, 176 (1924), for a useful description of the act and its posthumous condemnation.

6. For a useful summary, see James Sundquist, *Dynamics of the Party System* 134–169 (1983).

7. This kind of ideological instability is a systematic consequence of the system of Vice-Presidential selection bequeathed to us by the Twelfth Amendment. I shall be discussing this mechanism more fully in the next volume.

8. Perhaps Roosevelt's most significant triumph involved the passage of the Hepburn Act over conservative opposition. This victory prefigured a recurring twentieth-century scenario—in which a reluctant Congress follows a Presidential initiative on behalf of activist state intervention. A good account of these early experiments can be found in John Blum, *The Republican Roosevelt* (1967).

9. Woodrow Wilson, *Congressional Government* (1885).

10. Wilson's reform ideas changed over time but ultimately focused on a renewal of Presidential power. See his *Constitutional Government in the United States,* ch. 3 (1907); for a good discussion, see James Ceasar, *Presidential Selection: Theory and Development,* ch. 4 (1979).

11. For an appraisal of Wilson's techniques of plebescitarian Presidential leadership, see Arthur Link, *Wilson: The New Freedom* 145–175 (1956).

12. See Arthur Link, supra n. 11, 199–240, 423–44.

13. For a thoughtful effort to place the Wilsonian aspiration in world context, see N. Gordon Levin, Jr., *Woodrow Wilson and World Politics* (1968). For a brilliant

essay on Wilson's internal struggles, see Alexander George & Juliette George, *Woodrow Wilson and Colonel House: A Personality Study,* chs. 11–15 (1964).

14. The role of broad-based citizen movements has been questioned by Jerrold Waltman, "Origins of the Federal Income Tax," 62 *Mid-America* 147, 154 (1980), who emphasizes the way narrow tactical advantages motivated the proposal of an income tax amendment by Congress: "It was . . . only a peculiar combination of political events which saw the income tax emerge from backstage . . ."

But it is always true that considerations of short-term strategy explain why a constitutional initiative manages to succeed at one moment rather than another. The crucial question is whether the basic initiative also has the support of a broad-based movement. Despite his emphasis on short-term strategies, Waltman concedes that "[a]dvocacy of the income tax, as was the case with the Populists, was a central feature of most Progressive programs." Id.

So far as I can tell, no serious scholar has questioned the central role of popular movements in the enactment of the three other constitutional amendments of the early twentieth century.

15. See *We the People,* vol. 2: *Transformations* (forthcoming).

16. There is general agreement concerning the crucial significance of these two events, even amongst historians who disagree about almost everything else. Compare William Dunning, *Reconstruction: Political and Economic, 1867–1877* 220–331 (1907), with Eric Foner, *Reconstruction: America's Unfinished Revolution, 1863–1877,* 512–601 (1988).

17. The Slaughterhouse Cases, 83 U.S. (16 Wall.) 36, 67 (1873) (original Constitution, and the first twelve amendments, are now "historical and of another age," and must be synthesized with "three other articles of amendment of vast importance [that] have been added by the voice of the people to that now venerable instrument.").

18. See Adamson v. California, 332 U.S. 46, 68–123 (1947) (Black, J., dissenting).

19. Oregon v. Mitchell, 400 U.S. 112 (1970).

20. Raoul Berger, *Government by Judiciary: The Transformation of the Fourteenth Amendment,* ch. 2 (1977).

21. By "bad," I mean really bad. One example should be enough to encourage you to treat Berger's use of sources with extreme caution. Given Berger's premises, Justice Washington's famous opinion in Corfield v. Coryell, 6 F. Cas. 546 (C.C.E.D. Pa. 1823) (No. 3230) is a matter of great importance. As Berger recognizes, Washington's definition of "privileges and immunities" was quoted repeatedly by partisans to define the meaning of the Fourteenth Amendment. It is therefore understandable that Berger wishes to establish that Washington's opinion is consistent with his own view of the amendment as a superstatute, constitutionalizing only a fixed list of rights previously enacted in the Civil Rights Act. Unfortunately, Berger achieves this end by selective quotation and italicization so egregious that it shakes confidence in his basic reliability. Here is what Berger does with Washington's text (I place in brackets parts of

Washington's opinion that Berger conceals from the reader by the simple expedient of replacing Washington's words with ellipses):

We feel no hesitation in *confining* [italics not in original] these expressions to those privileges and immunities which are, in their nature, *fundamental* [italics not in original]. . . . They may, however, be all comprehended under the following general heads: Protection by the government; the enjoyment of life and liberty, with the right to acquire and possess property of every kind, and to pursue and obtain happiness and safety. . . . The right of a citizen of one state to pass through, or to reside in any other state, for purposes of trade, agriculture, professional pursuits, or otherwise; to claim the benefit of the writ of habeas corpus; to institute and maintain actions of any kind in the courts of the state; to take, hold and dispose of property, either real or personal; and an exemption from higher taxes or impositions than are paid by the other citizens of the state; may be mentioned as some of the particular privileges and immunities of citizens, which are clearly embraced by the general description of privileges deemed to be fundamental; to which may be added, the elective franchise, as regulated and established by the laws or constitution of the state in which it is to be exercised. [These, *and many others which might be mentioned* [my italics] are, strictly speaking privileges and immunities and the enjoyment of them by the citizens of each state, in every other state, was manifestly calculated (to use the expressions of the preamble of the corresponding provision in the old articles of confederation) "the better to secure and perpetuate mutual friendship and intercourse among the people of the different states of the Union."] But we cannot accede to the proposition . . . that . . . the citizens of the several states are permitted to participate *in all* [emphasis not in original] the rights which belong exclusively to the citizens of any other particular state.

Compare Raoul Berger, supra n. 20, at 31–32, with *Corfield,* supra, 6 F. Cas. 546, 551–52.

Now the great abstraction and sweep of Justice Washington's statement is itself not very hospitable to Berger's view of "privileges and immunities" as a superstatute. But I am not concerned here with matters of good-faith dispute. I am concerned with Berger's basic ethics as an historian: Why did he stop quoting just at the point where Justice Washington explicitly says that he is *not* presenting an exhaustive list of the rights protected by the concept of "privileges and immunities"? Including this sentence would have damaged Berger's case, for it would suggest that every time the participants quoted *Corfield* they repeated Justice Washington's express warning that "privileges and immunities" could not be reduced, as Berger suggests, to a closed list of rights codified in a superstatute. But this is hardly a reason that should persuade a responsible historian to mislead his readers by selective quotation.

I am also troubled by Berger's use of italics to suggest that Washington is emphasizing the limited character of his construction of "privileges and immunities"—when in the excised portion of the text he explicitly endorses a more expansive interpretation. This kind of shoddy work on a source as crucial as *Corfield* is inexcusable.

I make this point here only because I fear that the interest I take in Berger's methodological views might help enhance the influence of a book that, even by the standards of lawyers' history, seems exceptionally tendentious in its treatment of the sources. For correctives, see Chester Antieau, *The Original Understanding of the Fourteenth Amendment* (1981); Jacobus Ten Broeck, *Equal Under Law* (rev. ed. 1965); Michael Curtis, *No State Shall Abridge: The Fourteenth Amendment and the Bill of Rights* (1986); William Nelson, *The Fourteenth Amendment: From Political Principle to Judicial Doctrine* (1988).

22. A recent student of the debates summarizes the matter well: "The debates on the Fourteenth Amendment were, in essence, debates about high politics and fundamental principles—about the future course and meaning of the American nation. The debates by themselves did not reduce the vague, open-ended, and sometimes clashing principles used by the debaters to precise, carefully bounded legal doctrine. That would be the task of the courts . . . ." William Nelson, supra n. 21, at 63. For the classic, but too narrowly focused critique of Black's thesis, see Charles Fairman, "Does the Fourteenth Amendment Incorporate the Bill of Rights? The Original Understanding," 2 *Stan. L. Rev.* 5 (1949).

23. Michael Curtis has done a particularly fine job defending Black's views on "incorporation." See Michael Curtis, supra n. 21. Even he admits, however, that the Republicans of the time "devoted comparatively little direct attention" to the question. Id. at 16. For this reason, I do not believe that his book provides the kind of evidence a dualist should require before finding that a particular comprehensive synthesis was self-consciously endorsed by the *People*. Nonetheless, the materials he has brought to light—and especially his emphasis on the role of antislavery thought in the formulation of the Fourteenth Amendment—are of great importance for any judicial effort at comprehensive synthesis.

24. See n. 17, supra.

25. Especially in its Jacksonian variant. See Chapter 3, pp. 74–77.

26. *Slaughterhouse*, supra n. 17, at 71.

27. Id. at 78.

28. Id. at 71.

29. Many, but not all. The Slaughterhouse Cases were decided by a 5-to-4 vote, with the minority struggling to take a more comprehensive view of the synthetic problem before them.

30. See Chapter 3, p. 74.

31. I do not intend to limit the meaning of the amendment to the protection of property and contract rights, (see L. Vandervelde, "The Labor Vision of the Thirteenth Amendment," 138 *U. Pa. L. Rev* 437 [1989]), only to insist that these did play a central role.

32. See Buchanan v. Warley, 245 U.S. 60 (1917); Adkins v. Children's Hospital, 261 U.S. 525 (1923).

33. Which is not to say, it bears repeating, that the courts did a flawless job of synthesis. A critical assessment must, however, await the third volume in this series.

34. See Chapter 3, pp. 74–77.

35. See Pollock v. Farmers' Loan and Trust Company, 157 U.S. 429 (1895).

36. See U.S. Const. art. I, sec. 9: "No Capitation, or other direct, Tax shall be laid, unless in Proportion to the Census or Enumeration hereinbefore directed to be taken."

5. The Modern Republic

1. For a sensitive discussion, see James Ceasar, *Presidential Selection: Theory and Development,* chs. 5–6 (1979). While Ceasar sees the importance of the modern transformation, he fails to appreciate the ways in which the constitutional struggles of the New Deal have given constitutional legitimacy to the changes he describes.

2. See Samuel Kernell, *Going Public: New Strategies of Presidential Leadership* (1986); Theodore Lowi, *The Personal President: Power Invested, Promise Unfulfilled,* ch. 5 (1985).

3. These struggles, and their interrelationship, are remarkably underresearched. On court-packing, see William Leuchtenberg, "The Origins of Franklin D. Roosevelt's 'Court-packing Plan,'" *Sup. Ct. Rev.* 347 (1966), and "FDR's Court Packing Plan: A Second Life, A Second Death," *Duke L. J.* 673 (1985); for the basic story line, see Leonard Baker, *Back to Back: The Duel Between FDR and the Supreme Court* (1967). Roosevelt's effort to reorganize the executive branch is usefully discussed by Richard Polenberg, *Reorganizing Roosevelt's Government* (1966). More recently, Sidney M. Milkis has contributed some insightful essays. See, e.g., Sidney Milkis, "Franklin D. Roosevelt and the Transcendence of Partisan Politics," 100 *Pol. Sci. Q.* 479 (1985); Sidney Milkis, "The New Deal, Administrative Reform, and the Transcendence of Partisan Politics," 18 *Ad. & Soc'y* 433 (1987).

4. This is a recurring theme in contemporary political science. In addition to books by Ceasar, supra n. 1, Kernell, supra n. 2, and Lowi, supra n. 2, see William Leuchtenberg, *In the Shadow of FDR: From Harry Truman to Ronald Reagan* (1983); Richard Neustadt, *Presidential Power: The Politics of Leadership* (1976).

5. For a provocative study that raises many of the right questions—albeit within a framework that implicitly depends too heavily upon a constitutional myth of rediscovery, see Harold Koh, *The National Security Constitution* (1990).

6. See Fred Greenstein, *The Hidden-Hand Presidency: Eisenhower as Leader,* ch. 5 (1982).

7. At present, there is no single work that successfully integrates the populist, governmental, and judicial aspects of the Civil Rights Revolution. However, we do have many good books that focus on one or another crucial aspect of the process. For studies of (1) populist mobilization, see Taylor Branch, *Parting the Waters: America in the King Years, 1954–63* (1988); (2) governmental responses

by a succession of Presidential administrations, see Hugh Graham, *The Civil Rights Era: Origins and Development of National Policy, 1960–1972* (1990); (3) the role of the courts, see J. Harvie Wilkinson, *From Brown to Bakke* (1979). I draw on these, and many other useful works, in the sketch that follows.

8. Though the Civil Rights Act of 1957 was the first such enactment in the twentieth century, it was substantively inconsequential. Its most enduring contribution was institutional—authorizing the creation of a bipartisan Civil Rights Commission and a Civil Rights Division in the Department of Justice. Though these institutions would play important roles later on, they were toothless tigers at the time. Indeed, Richard Russell, the Senate leader of the Southern forces, considered his success in eviscerating the 1957 act as his "sweetest victory" in twenty-five years representing the state of Georgia. See Carl Brauer, *John F. Kennedy and Reconstruction* 10 (1977).

9. Compare James Sundquist's treatment of the Populists and the New Left in his *Dynamics of the Party System,* chs. 7 and 17 (rev. ed. 1983).

10. Perhaps the most remarkable success here was the enactment of a series of landmark statutes that revolutionized environmental policy in the late 1960's and early 1970's. For a preliminary study in a dualist vein, see E. Donald Elliott, Bruce Ackerman, John Millian, "Toward a Theory of Statutory Evolution: The Federalization of Environmental Law," 1 *J. Law Econ. & Org.* 313 (1985).

11. See John Ely, "Suppose Congress Wanted a War Powers Act That Worked," 88 *Colo. L. Rev.* 1379 (1988). On only one occasion since 1973 has a Presidential report to Congress included a reference to the Resolution's crucial provision that requires the President to "terminate any use of United States forces" within sixty days unless he receives explicit Congressional authorization. And even on this occasion, President Ford only said he was "taking note" of the provision, without explicitly conceding its binding character. See Subcommittee on International Security & Scientific Affairs of the House Committee on Foreign Affairs, 98th Cong., 1st Sess., *The War Powers Resolution: Relevant Documents* 45–6 (1988).

12. Jane Mansbridge contributes a thoughtful essay in *Why We Lost the E.R.A.* (1986), see esp. ch. 13 ("A Movement or a Sect?").

13. See Chapter 2, pp. 50–55.

14. See Chapter 4, pp. 86–103.

15. See Chapter 4, pp. 94–99.

16. See Chapter 4, pp. 99–102.

17. United States v. Carolene Products, 304 U.S. 144, 152 n. 4 (1938). This introductory sketch passes over other revealing essays in synthesis during the early New Deal period: Palko v. Connecticut, 302 U.S. 319 (1937); Erie Railroad v. Tompkins, 304 U.S. 64 (1937); West Virginia Board of Education v. Barnette, 319 U.S. 624 (1943); among others.

18. See J. M. Balkin, "The Footnote," 83 *Nw. L. Rev.* 275 (1989).

19. See, for example, West Coast Hotel v. Parrish, 300 U.S. 379 (1937); N.L.R.B. v. Jones & Laughlin Steel Corp., 301 U.S. 1 (1937); Steward Machine Co. v. Davis, 301 U.S. 548 (1937).

20. See *Carolene,* supra n. 17, at 152.

21. See *Carolene,* supra n. 17.

22. The word appears twice in the Fifth Amendment, which guarantees against deprivation of "life, liberty, or property, without due process of law; nor shall private property be taken for public use, without just compensation."

23. U.S. Const. art. I, sec. 10.

24. The Court also began experimenting with this more ambitious synthetic technique at about the same time in its landmark decision in Palko v. Connecticut, 302 U.S. 319 (1937). I shall discuss the relationship between *Palko* and this strand of *Carolene* more intensively in later work.

25. While the specialist literature dealing with the constitutionalization of criminal procedure is very plentiful, I have not found many efforts—like the one attempted in the text—to integrate this specialist study into more general patterns of doctrinal evolution. For a provocative discussion of this remarkable gap, see Howard Gutman, "Academic Determinism: The Division of the Bill of Rights," 54 *S. Cal. L. Rev.* 295 (1981).

26. For a recent libertarian use of this "clause-bound" strategy, see Michael McConnell, "The Origins and Historical Understanding of Free Exercise of Religion," 103 *Harv. L. Rev.* 1409 (1990).

27. For a usefully revisionist account, which enriches but does not—I think—finally undermine the conventional wisdom announced in the text, see David Rabban, "The First Amendment in Its Forgotten Years," 90 *Yale L.J.* 514 (1981); David Rabban, "The Emergence of Modern First Amendment Doctrine," 50 *U. Chi. L. Rev.* 1205 (1983).

28. See David Rabban, supra n. 27.

29. See, for example, Abrams v. United States, 250 U.S. 616, 624 (1919) (Holmes, J., dissenting); Whitney v. California, 274 U.S. 357, 372 (Brandeis, J., concurring).

30. The formula derives from Justice Holmes' famous dissent in Abrams v. United States, 250 U.S. 616, 630 (1919), though the extent to which it represents a deep Holmesian commitment to liberal principles is fairly arguable. Yosal Rogat & James O'Fallon, "Mr. Justice Holmes: A Dissenting Opinion—The Speech Cases," 36 *Stan. L. Rev.* 1349 (1984).

31. I am painting with a very broad brush here. Privatistic forms of expression have indeed been afforded First Amendment protection; only their status has always been seen as more problematic than those rights involving the exercise of citizenship. See Laurence Tribe, *American Constitutional Law,* sec. 12–15 ("The Assimilation of Commercial Speech into the First Amendment"), and sec. 12–16 ("The Continuing Suppression of Obscenity") (2d ed. 1988).

32. See p. 118, supra.

33. The most important text here is John Ely, *Democracy and Distrust* (1980).

34. I attempt a doctrinal critique in "Beyond Carolene Products," 98 *Harv. L. Rev.* 713 (1985).

35. See, for example, Adkins v. Children's Hospital, 261 U.S. 525 (1923).

36. Louis Lusky explains the historical circumstances that led the *Carolene* Court

to use a single footnote to introduce such disparate themes into modern constitutional law. See his "Footnote Redux: A Carolene Products Reminiscence," 82 *Colo. L. Rev* 1093 (1982).

37. For some preliminary discussion, see my "Beyond Carolene Products," supra n. 34.

6. The Possibility of Interpretation

1. William McFeely, *Grant: A Biography* 280–84 (1981).
2. Truman suggested a Truman-Eisenhower ticket to Eisenhower in 1948, and in 1952 Eisenhower delayed declaring himself a Republican in hopes of gaining the Democratic, as well as the Republican, nomination. See Elmo Richardson, *The Presidency of Dwight Eisenhower* 11–22 (1979).
3. On the circumstances surrounding Warren's nomination to the Supreme Court, see Richard Kluger, *Simple Justice* 657–65 (1979).
4. On Eisenhower's failure in 1952 to sweep large, anti–New Deal majorities into Congress, see Elmo Richardson, supra n. 2, at 21–22.
5. Most notably in the Dixiecrat defection during the Presidential election in 1948. See James Sundquist, *Dynamics of the Party System* 272–77 (1983).
6. A survey of voting patterns in the House from 1949 to 1954 reveals diminished support for new civil rights legislation, the result of a reduced number of Northern Democratic supporters of civil rights. Gerald Marwell, "Party, Region, and the Dimensions of Conflict in the House of Representatives, 1949–54," 61 *Am. Pol. Sci. Rev.* 380–99 (1967). The outlook for enacting civil rights legislation in the 1950's was further clouded by the domination of the key House and Senate committees by Southern Democrats, who actively used their influence to bottle up bills before they could reach the floor. James Sundquist, *The Decline and Resurgence of Congress* 182–87 (1981).
7. On the enormous influence of McCarthyism on Presidential and Congressional policymaking between 1952 and 1954, see Richard Rovere, *Senator Joe McCarthy* (1960), and Robert Griffith, *The Politics of Fear* (1970).
8. See Mark Tushnet, *The NAACP's Legal Strategy Against Segregated Education, 1925–1950* (1987).
9. For two outstanding discussions, see Gunnar Myrdal, *An American Dilemma* (1944), and William Wilson, *The Truly Disadvantaged* (1987).
10. See Mary Dudziak, "Desegregation as a Cold War Imperative," 41 *Stan. L. Rev.* 61 (1988).
11. Brown v. Board of Education (II), 349 U.S. 294 (1955).
12. A recent history summarizes the situation: "[w]hen the Civil Rights Act of 1964 was passed . . . ,American women were neither united, effectively organized, nor psychologically prepared to press effectively for its enforcement." Frank Graham, *The Civil Rights Era* 207 (1990). Chapter 16 of Graham's book usefully relates the rise of the modern women's movement with the changing character of Supreme Court jurisprudence.
13. See Alexander Bickel, *The Least Dangerous Branch* (1962); Robert Burt, "Con-

stitutional Law and the Teaching of the Parables," 93 *Yale L.J.* 455 (1984); Frank Michelman, "The Supreme Court, 1985 Term—Foreword: Traces of Self-Government," 100 *Harv. L. Rev.* 4 (1986); Michael Perry, *The Constitution, the Courts, and Human Rights* (1982).

14. Compare his relatively optimistic *The Least Dangerous Branch,* supra n. 13, with the anxieties of *The Supreme Court and the Idea of Progress* (1970) and the bleak pessimism of *The Morality of Consent* 1–30 (1975).

15. See Chapter 4, pp. 86–103; Chapter 5, pp. 113–130.

16. See Chapter 4, pp. 94–99.

17. For a suggestive analysis see Martin Shapiro, "Fathers and Sons: The Court, the Commentators, and the Search for Values," in *The Burger Court: The Counterrevolution That Wasn't* 218 (V. Blasi ed. 1983).

18. Brown v. Board of Education, 347 U.S. 483 (1954).

19. Plessy v. Ferguson, 163 U.S. 537 (1896).

20. *Brown,* supra n. 18, at 492.

21. Id. at 495.

22. See Muller v. Oregon, 208 U.S. 412, 420 and n. 1 (1908).

23. *Brown,* supra n. 18, at 494.

24. See, for example, *Federalist* No. 40, at 252–54 (J. Madison) (C. Rossiter ed. 1961), discussed in Chapter 7, pp. 173–175.

25. These documents will be discussed at length in volume 2: *Transformations.*

26. Herbert Wechsler, "Toward Neutral Principles of Constitutional Law," 73 *Harv. L. Rev.* 1, 34 (1959).

27. See, for example, the very different responses of Charles Black, "The Lawfulness of the Segregation Decisions," 69 *Yale L.J.* 421 (1960), and Louis Pollak, "Racial Discrimination and Judicial Integrity: A Reply to Professor Wechsler," 108 *U. Pa. L. Rev.* 1 (1959).

28. *Brown,* supra n. 18, at 492–93.

29. Dred Scott v. Sandford, 60 U.S. (19 How.) 393 (1857).

30. *Plessy,* supra n. 19, at 544 (1896).

31. Id. at 552 (Harlan, J., dissenting).

32. Id. at 551.

33. *Brown,* supra n. 18, at 489–90.

34. See Wrigley, "Compulsory School Laws: A Dilemma with a History," in *The Crusade Against Dropping Out* (J. Simon and D. Stipek eds. forthcoming 1991).

35. See, for example, Pierce v. Society of Sisters, 268 U.S. 510 (1925).

36. Even the most bitter modern opponents of compulsory education have not questioned the authority of the state to compel a minimal education. See Wisconsin v. Yoder, 406 U.S. 205, 224 (1972).

37. *Brown,* supra n. 18, at 493.

38. Id. at 490.

39. Id. at 494–95.

40. See, for example, Louis Henkin, "Privacy and Autonomy," 74 *Colum. L. Rev.* 1410, 1420–23 (1974) ("Whatever grade the professors might give to Justice Douglas . . . , the result is clear: . . . there is now a Constitutional Right of

Privacy."); Thomas Kauper, "Penumbras, Peripheries, Emanations, Things Fundamental and Things Forgotten: The Griswold Case," 64 *Mich. L. Rev.* 235, 252–54 (1965) ("accordion-like"); Ira Lupu, "Untangling the Strands of the Fourteenth Amendment," 77 *Mich. L. Rev.* 981, 994 (1979) ("magical mystery tour of the zones of privacy"). To Michael Perry, *Griswold*'s interpretive pretensions are so preposterous that he dismisses them in a footnote containing a single sentence. See Michael Perry, *The Constitution, the Courts, and Human Rights* 172 n. 18 (1982).

41. For a systematic development of this view, see Mark Tushnet, *Red, White, and Blue: A Critical Analysis of Constitutional Law* (1988).

42. The Founders' definition of government powers was also redefined by the New Deal. The legitimation of the activist state overwhelmed the decisional capacities of the three branches envisioned in 1787, leading to the elaboration of a host of new relationships between these branches and the burgeoning administrative apparatus. Compare, for example, the Court's focus on 1787 in INS v. Chadha, 462 U.S. 919, 946–59 (1983), with the dissent's focus on 1937, id. at 968–74 (White, J., dissenting). See also Note, "A Two-Tiered Theory of Consolidation and Separation of Powers," 99 *Yale L.J.* 431 (1989) (analyzing *Chadha* as response to New Deal constitutional transformation delegating power to administrative agencies). While this aspect of the synthetic problem has engaged increasing amounts of judicial energy over the last decade, the Justices seem to have despaired (temporarily?) at a second fundamental structural question left in the aftermath of the New Deal: the relationship between the states and the nation in an era of activist government. Compare Garcia v. San Antonio Metro. Transit Auth., 469 U.S. 995 (1985), with National League of Cities v. Usery, 426 U.S. 833 (1976).

43. See Dale Carpenter, "Revisiting *Griswold:* An Exploration of Its Political, Social, and Legal Origins" 5 (unpublished senior essay, Yale College, April 16, 1989).

44. See Brief on Demurrer to Information, State v. Nelson, at 47–48 (1939) (on file in Whitney Library of the New Haven Colony Historical Society, Box 2, Folder F). The brief for Planned Parenthood cited cases like Allgeyer v. Louisiana, 165 U.S. 578 (1897), and Liggett Co. v. Baldridge, 278 U.S. 105 (1928).

45. State v. Nelson, 11 A. 2d 856 (1940).

46. Brief for Appellants, at 22, Griswold v. Connecticut, 381 U.S. 479 (1965). The claim based on substantive due process is at pages 21–78 of a ninety-six-page brief.

47. Id. at 79–89.

48. Griswold v. Connecticut, 381 U.S. 479, 481–82 (1965) (citations omitted).

49. Id. at 486.

50. Id. at 482–83. The two cases the Court reaffirms are Pierce v. Society of Sisters, 268 U.S. 510 (1925), and Meyer v. Nebraska, 263 U.S. 390 (1923).

51. Boyd v. United States, 116 U.S. 616 (1886).

52. *Griswold,* supra n. 48, at 484.

53. Id.

54. Id. at 464.

55. See Chapter 5, pp. 122–127.

56. *Griswold,* supra n. 48, at 485.

57. For those arithmetically inclined, the fact that there were three concurrences and two dissents did not deprive the opinion of the Court of a majority—the Justices who joined the concurrence by Justice Goldberg also joined the opinion of the Court.

58. *Griswold,* supra n. 48, at 515.

59. Compare United States v. Carolene Products 304 U.S. 144, 152 n. 4 (1938), with *Griswold,* supra n. 48, at 508 (Black, J., dissenting).

60. See Chapter 4, pp. 90–92.

61. From this point of view, the common charge, see Robert McKay, "The Right of Privacy: Emanations and Intimations," 64 *Mich. L. Rev.* 259 (1965), that Douglas' use of the concept of privacy was light-years removed from the one contemplated by Warren and Brandeis in their great article on privacy could not be further from the truth. For the very point of this early essay is to use the concept of privacy to carve off values often protected by laissez-faire property doctrine—thereby enabling their preservation in a world in which other dimensions of property would be subjected to increasing regulation by activist government. See Charles Warren & Louis Brandeis, "The Right to Privacy," 4 *Harv. L. Rev.* 193 (1890).

7. Publius

1. *Federalist* No. 1, at 33 (A. Hamilton) (C. Rossiter ed. 1961).

2. *Federalist* No. 10, supra n. 1, at 84 (J. Madison).

3. See *The Legal Tender Cases,* 79 U.S. (12 Wall.) 457 (1871). For a good account of the remarkable constitutional politics required for this decision, see Charles Fairman, *History of the Supreme Court of the United States: Reconstruction and Reunion, 1864–88,* part 1, ch. 14 (1971).

4. See *Federalist* No. 54, supra n. 1, at 336–41 (J. Madison).

5. Article XIII stipulated that: "the Articles of this confederation shall be inviolably observed by every state, and the union shall be perpetual; nor shall any alteration at any time hereafter be made in any of them; unless such alteration be agreed to in a congress of the united states, and be afterwards confirmed by the legislatures of every state." Reprinted in Max Farrand, *The Framing of the Constitution of the United States* 223 (1913).

6. Article Seven of the original Constitution stipulates: "The Ratification of the Conventions of nine States, shall be sufficient for the Establishment of this Constitution between the States so ratifying the Same." I have discussed the legal status of this break with the Articles of Confederation at greater length in Chapter 2, n. 4.

7. See Chapter 8.

8. *Federalist* No. 10, supra n. 1, at 78 (J. Madison).

9. *Federalist* No. 40, supra n. 1, at 251 (J. Madison).

10. Id.

11. *Federalist* No. 40, supra n. 1, at 252–53 (quoting Declaration of Independence; emphasis in original). While the central argument on this point is made in No. 40, at 251–55, important ancillary texts include *Federalist* Nos. 39 and 43.

12. Are the italics significant? I do not know. Certainly if the *Federalist* were a twentieth-century text, the typographic emphasis (which I have verified in original editions) would have some significance. While I take note of the original italics in my discussion, nothing important turns on eighteenth-century typography. The italics merely emphasize meanings already evident.

13. The following paragraphs draw heavily from Gordon Wood, *The Creation of the American Republic, 1776–1787,* ch. 8 (1969), which in turn draws upon 1 R. R. Palmer, *The Age of the Democratic Revolutions: A Political History of Europe and America, 1760–1800,* ch. 7 (1959). Edmund Morgan has recently provided an illuminating discussion in *Inventing the People: The Rise of Popular Sovereignty in England and America,* ch. 4 (1988).

14. Recent work has assessed the extent to which the members of the convention/parliament were aware of, and struggled with, their legally anomalous status. John Miller, "The Glorious Revolution: 'Contract' and 'Abdication' Reconsidered," 25 *Hist. J.* 541 (1982); Thomas P. Slaughter, "'Abdicate' and 'Contract' in the Glorious Revolution", 24 *Hist. J.* 323 (1981). These uncertainties are reflected in the convention's debates, collected by David Jones, *A Parliamentary History of the Glorious Revolution* (1988).

15. The parliament of 1690 enacted "an act for recognizing King William and Queen Mary, and for avoiding all questions touching the acts made in the parliament assembled at Westminster, the thirteenth day of February, one thousand six hundred eighty eight," which explicitly declares "[t]hat all and singular the acts made and enacted in said parliament were and are laws and statutes of this kingdom, and such as ought to be reputed, taken and obeyed by all the people of this kingdom." 2 W. & M., ch. 1, para. II (1690), reprinted in Nevelli E. Williams, *The Eighteenth-Century Constitution, 1688–1815: Documents and Commentary* 46–47 (1960).

16. For an excellent essay treating the themes discussed in this paragraph, see J. P. Kenyon, *Revolution Principles: The Politics of Party, 1689–1729* (1977).

17. By 1778, the citizens of Massachusetts were rejecting a constitution proposed by their legislature on the ground that fundamental law could only be considered in "convention." The success of the subsequent Massachusetts convention in gaining the popular ratification of its proposal in 1780 set an important precedent for constitution-building during the next years. See Gordon Wood, supra n. 13, at 340–41.

18. *Federalist* 49, supra n. 1, at 315 (emphasis supplied) (J. Madison).

19. *Federalist* No. 50, supra n. 1, at 317–20 (J. Madison).

20. Id. at 320.

21. Id.

22. *Federalist* No. 40, supra n. 1, at 263 (Cooke ed. 1961) (J. Madison) (emphasis in original). This is not the way the text reads in the popular edition by Clinton Rossiter that is generally available in bookstores. Without explanation, Rossiter's

text omits the words within the brackets: "Instead of reporting a plan requiring the confirmation [*of the legislatures*] *of all the States,* they have reported a plan which is to be confirmed [by the *people*] and may be carried into effect by *nine States only.*" *Federalist* No. 40, supra n. 1, at 250. I follow the reading provided by Professor Cooke's critical edition, which is also confirmed by other editions. See, e.g., Henry Cabot Lodge's edition of 1891, at 245.

23. *Federalist* No. 45, supra n. 1, at 289 (J. Madison).

24. *Federalist* No. 49, supra n. 1, at 314 (J. Madison).

25. I speak of Publius because I do not think the obvious differences between Hamilton and Madison—see Alpheus Mason, "The Federalist—A Split Personality," 57 *Am. Hist. Rev.* 625 (1952)—implicate the bedrock principles of dualistic constitutionalism developed here. Thus, *Federalist* No. 9 (supra n. 1, at 72–73), written by Hamilton, asserts its intimate connection with the subject of Madison's No. 10, and seeks to locate the fear of factions within the larger commitments of Publian politics. While I will be relying mostly on Papers written by Madison, my reading parallels some of the larger dualisms others have detected in Hamilton's political aspirations. See Cecilia Kenyon, "Alexander Hamilton: Rousseau of the Right," 73 *Pol. Sci. Q.* 161 (1958).

26. See, for example, *Federalist* No. 8, supra n. 1, at 66 (A. Hamilton); *Federalist* No. 41, at 257–60 (J. Madison).

27. A particularly eloquent assertion may be found in *Federalist* No. 6, supra n. 1, at 59 (A. Hamilton). See also, *Federalist* No. 31, at 196–97; *Federalist* No. 36, at 218–19; *Federalist* No. 42, at 268 (J. Madison).

28. See *Federalist* No. 4, supra n. 1, at 49 (J. Jay); *Federalist* No. 18, at 122–23, 124–25 (J. Madison & A. Hamilton).

29. *Federalist* No. 18, supra n. 1, at 124 (J. Madison & A. Hamilton).

30. See the graphic description of the Greek failure in *Federalist* No. 9, supra n. 1, at 71–76 (A. Hamilton), which paves the way for Madison's famous analysis in *Federalist* No. 10, at 77–84.

31. See, for example, *Federalist* No. 5, supra n. 1, at 50–51 (J. Jay); *Federalist* No. 69, at 415–23 (A. Hamilton).

32. Baron de Montesquieu, *The Spirit of the Laws* 21 (R. Neumann ed. 1949) ("The politic Greeks, who lived under a popular government, knew no other support than virtue. . . ."), which the *Federalist* cleverly parries by citing Montesquieu in support of its very different project. *Federalist* No. 9, supra n. 1, at 73–72 (A. Hamilton).

33. See, for example, *Federalist* No. 9, supra n. 1, at 72–73 (A. Hamilton); *Federalist* No. 10, supra n. 1, at 77–84; *Federalist* No. 51, at 320–25 (J. Madison).

34. The dualist hope expressed in this sentence is developed most systematically in the six Papers beginning with No. 46 and ending with No. 51. Try to study these Papers together in a single sitting.

35. For express and repeated rejections of the polis as a model for American constitutional theory, see *Federalist* No. 9, supra n. 1, at 72–73 (A. Hamilton); *Federalist* No. 10, at 78–84; *Federalist* No. 14, at 100–01; *Federalist* No. 55, at 341–42; *Federalist* No. 63, at 384–85 (J. Madison).

36. *Federalist* No. 71, supra n. 1, at 433 (A. Hamilton). For another notable analysis of the problematic character of representation, see *Federalist* No. 58, at 357–61 (J. Madison).

37. *Federalist* No. 48, supra n. 1, at 310–11 (J. Madison quoting T. Jefferson with approval; italics in the original).

38. *Federalist* No. 63, supra n. 1, at 387 (J. Madison) (italics in the original).

39. Once again, the italics are in the original. See n. 12, supra.

40. This broad theme recurs in the second half of the *Federalist,* beginning with No. 52—which seeks to show how the different branches of government check the others' defects and thereby yield a whole more "representative" than any of its constituent parts.

41. *See Federalist* No. 39, supra n. 1, at 241–46 (J. Madison).

42. Id. at 243.

43. See Herbert Storing, *What the Anti-Federalists Were For,* ch. 4 (1981).

44. *Federalist* No. 39, supra n. 1, at 246 (J. Madison).

45. *Federalist* No. 10, supra n. 1, at 81 (definition of republic); *Federalist* No. 39, at 241–42 (J. Madison).

46. I am indebted here to the important work of Douglass Adair and Martin Diamond, discussed in Chapter 8, pp. 223–227.

47. *Federalist* No. 10, at supra n. 1, 79 (J. Madison).

48. Id. at 79.

49. See p. 194.

50. *Federalist* No. 10, supra n. 1, at 79 (J. Madison).

51. See Chapter 11, pp. 314–319.

52. A valuable elaboration of this theme may be found in Garry Wills, *Explaining America* 177–264 (1981).

53. *Federalist* No. 10, supra n. 1, at 83 (J. Madison).

54. Id. at 82.

55. Id. at 80.

56. Id. at 83.

57. See *Federalist* Nos. 52–82, supra n. 1.

58. *Federalist* No. 51, supra n. 1, at 325 (J. Madison).

59. Id. at 321–22.

60. This great dark passage comes toward the end of No. 51, which begins by denying that it can be treated as a self-contained unit. No. 52 begins, in turn, by bracketing the preceding four Papers as a single conceptual unity: "From the more general enquiries pursued in the last four papers, I pass on to a more particular examination of the several parts of the government." *Federalist* No. 52, supra n. 1, at 325 (J. Madison). Thus the passage in No. 51 is self-consciously linked to the argument, elaborated at pp. 181–182, supra, that begins with No. 48 and continues in No. 49 with an express acknowledgment of the necessity of keeping "a constitutional road to the people." *Federalist* No. 49, supra n. 1, at 314 (J. Madison).

61. See pp. 187–188, supra.

62. *Federalist* No. 78, supra n. 1, at 467–68 (A. Hamilton).

63. Id. at 465–66.

64. Id. at 465.

65. Id. at 469–70 (Publius's footnote to this text has been omitted).

66. The most influential interpretation of the *Federalist* that makes this mistake is by Robert Dahl, *Preface to Democratic Theory,* ch. 1, and especially n. 23 (1956).

67. See Chapter 1, pp. 7–10, supra, for a discussion of monism.

68. See pp. 173–174, supra.

69. See Chapter 2, supra, and the next volume: *Transformations*.

70. *Federalist* No. 49, supra n. 1, at 317 (J. Madison).

71. See Paul Kahn, "Community in Contemporary Constitutional Theory," 99 *Yale L.J.* 1 (1989).

72. *Federalist* No. 49, supra n. 1, at 314.

73. See Chapters 10 and 11, respectively.

74. Cass Sunstein, "Interest Groups in American Public Law," 38 *Stan. L. Rev.* 29, 45 (1985).

75. *Federalist* No. 10, supra n. 1, at 80.

76. See Chapter 9.

77. *Federalist* No. 76, supra n. 1, at 458 (A. Hamilton).

8. The Lost Revolution

1. For a useful guide to further reading, see the five-volume compilation by Philip Kurland & Ralph Lerner, *The Founders' Constitution* (1987).

2. See, for example, the materials considered by David Davis, *Revolutions: Reflections on American Equality and Foreign Liberation,* ch. 3 (1990).

3. Charles A. Beard, *An Economic Interpretation of the Constitution of the United States* (1913). Beard's work brought to a broader public a scholarly view already quite familiar in academic circles, most notably through the work of J. Allen Smith, *The Spirit of American Government* (1907).

4. See Robert Brown, *Charles Beard and the Constitution* (1956), and Forrest McDonald, *We the People* (1958). For a brilliant survey of the wreckage, see Richard Hofstadter, *The Progressive Historians* 167–348 (1969). For some recent econometric work casting doubt on the present historical wisdom that rejects Beard's empirical claims, see Robert A. McGuire and Robert L. Ohsfeldt, "Economic Interests and the American Constitution: A Quantitative Rehabilitation of Charles A. Beard," 44 *J. Econ. Hist.* 509 (1984). Since I am most interested here in recovering the political meaning of the American revolution, I do not think that anything very important turns on the precise mix of economic interests at play during the ratification struggle.

5. I am painting with a broad brush. There were scholars who resisted the Progressive tide, even at its height. Most notably, Douglass Adair was making enduring contributions as early as the early 1940's. See Robert Shalhope, "Douglass Adair and the Historiography of Republicanism," in *Fame and the Founding Fathers: Essays by Douglass Adair* xxv (Trevor Colborn ed. 1974). Later in this

chapter, I shall suggest that even Adair's vision was blinkered by the prevailing Beardian orthodoxy. See pp. 223–224, supra.

6. For a fine development of this theme, see Robert Wiebe, *The Opening of American Society* (1984).

7. Hannah Arendt, *On Revolution* (1963).

8. *Federalist* No. 1, at 33 (A. Hamilton) (C. Rossiter ed. 1961).

9. Hannah Arendt, supra n. 7, at 56.

10. See my discussion of parallel phenomena in the work of Louis Hartz in Chapter 1, pp. 25–27, and Douglass Adair in this chapter, pp. 223–224.

11. Arendt is a genuinely profound political thinker. She cannot be treated primarily as a critic of Marxism or any other -ism. It is, however, always a mistake to ignore the role of the immediate polemical context in shaping thought. While modern German and classical Greek philosophy served as the originating context for Arendt's affirmative vision, Marxism (and Nazism) undoubtedly served as the central object of critique; and critique and affirmation can never be fully separated in the dialectical play of thought.

12. For similar criticisms, see Richard Bernstein, *Philosophical Profiles* 248–56 (1986); Hannah Pitkin, "Justice: On Relating Private and Public," 9 *Pol. Theory* 327 (1981).

13. My recommended reading list: Douglass Adair, supra n. 5; Joyce Appleby, *Capitalism and a New Social Order: The Republican Vision of the 1790's* (1984); Bernard Bailyn, *The Ideological Origins of the American Revolution* (1967); Lance Banning, *The Jeffersonian Persuasion: Evolution of a Party Ideology* (1978); Martin Diamond, "Ethics and Politics: The American Way," in *The Moral Foundations of the American Republic* 75 (R. Horwitz ed. 1986); Robert Dahl, *A Preface to Democratic Theory,* ch. 1 (1956); John Diggins, *The Lost Soul of American Politics: Virtue, Self-Interest, and the Foundations of Liberalism* (1984) (this provocative book is certainly worth reading, despite its reductionist treatment of political culture); Forrest McDonald, *Novus Ordo Seclorum: The Intellectual Origins of the Constitution* (1985); Edmund Morgan, *Inventing the People: The Rise of Popular Sovereignty in England and America* (1988); J. G. A. Pocock, *The Machiavellian Moment: Florentine Political Thought and the Atlantic Republican Tradition* (1975); Caroline Robbins, *The Eighteenth Century Commonwealthman: Studies in the Transmission, Development and Circumstance of English Liberal Thought from the Restoration of Charles II until the War with the Thirteen Colonies* (1959); Robert Wiebe, supra n. 6; Garry Wills, *Explaining America: The Federalist* (1981); Morton White, *Philosophy, the Federalist, and the Constitution* (1987); Gordon Wood, *The Creation of the American Republic, 1776–1787* (1969). For thoughtful essays interpreting the historical debate from different angles, see Robert Shalhope, "Republicanism and Early American Historiography," 39 *Wm. & Mary Q.* 334 (1982), and Isaac Kramnick, "'The Great National Discussion': The Discourse of National Politics in 1787," 45 *Wm. & Mary Q.* 3 (1988). A discerning discussion of the historical scholarship from a legal point of view is provided by Frank Michelman, "The Supreme

Court, 1985 Term—Foreword: Traces of Self-Government," 100 *Harv. L. Rev.* 17–55 (1986).

14. Hannah Arendt, supra n. 7, at 55.

15. See Robert Brown, supra n. 4; Forrest McDonald, supra n. 4.

16. Stanley Elkins & Eric McKitrick, "The Founding Fathers: Young Men of the Revolution," 76 *Pol. Sci. Q.* 181 (1961). See also Pauline Maier, *The Old Revolutionaries: Political Lives in the Age of Samuel Adams* 280–94 (1980).

17. John Roche, "The Founding Fathers: A Reform Caucus in Action," 55 *Am. Pol. Sci. Rev.* 799 (1961).

18. For noteworthy exceptions to the generalization in the text, see Pauline Maier, supra n. 16; Ralph Lerner, *The Thinking Revolutionary: Principle and Practice in the New Republic* (1987).

19. Just as Beard's *Economic Interpretation* controlled the historical vision of the first half of the century, Wood's *Creation* has dominated the last generation. For example, when considering how best to celebrate the Constitution's Bicentennial in 1987, the leading journal of early American history could think of nothing better than sponsor a symposium on Wood's book. See "Forum—*The Creation of the American Republic, 1776–1787:* A Symposium of Views and Reviews," 44 *Wm. & Mary Q.* 549–640 (1987). This collection is very much worth reading.

20. For some suggestive links between Wood's work and my own, see Richard Bernstein, "Charting the Bicentennial," 87 *Colum. L. Rev.* 1565, 1599–1602 (1987).

21. For other efforts by legal scholars to profit from Wood's account, see Akhil Amar, "Of Sovereignty and Federalism," 96 *Yale L.J.* 1425, 1429–51 (1987); Frank Michelman, supra n. 13; Cass Sunstein, "Interest Groups in American Public Law," 38 *Stan. L. Rev.* 29, 35–55 (1985).

22. See Jerrilyn Marston, *King and Congress: The Transfer of Political Legitimacy, 1774–76,* pt. 2 (1987); Jack Rakove, *The Beginnings of National Politics: An Interpretive History of the Continental Congress,* pt. 1 (1979).

23. See Gordon Wood, supra n. 13, ch. 8; and see sources cited at nn. 13–16, Chapter 7, supra. For an important discussion of the "convention's" later history in America, see Daniel Rogers, *Contested Truths: Keywords in American Politics Since Independence,* ch. 3 (1987).

24. See Wood, supra n. 13, 310–19; and see sources cited at nn. 13–16, Chapter 7, supra.

25. A turning point came in Massachussetts in 1778, when a new constitution was rejected, partly on the grounds that it was not proposed by a convention of the People specially convened for the purpose. See Gordon Wood, supra n. 13, at 341. Other evidence of this evolution is collected by Akhil Amar, "Philadelphia Revisited: Amending the Constitution Outside of Article V," 55 *U. Chi. L. Rev.* 1043, 1056–60 (1988) (discussed more elaborately in Chapter 2, n. 4).

26. Gordon Wood, supra n. 13, at 363–90, 519–64.

27. For an exceptionally perceptive work in this genre, see Andrzej Rapaczynski,

"From Sovereignty to Process: The Jurisprudence of Federalism after *Garcia*," 1985 *Sup. Ct. Rev.* 341, 346–359.

28. Such a proposal was at the core of John Adams's remarkable *Defense of the Constitutions of Government of the United States of America* in 4 *The Works of John Adams* 391–401 (C. F. Adams ed. 1851).

29. See Gordon Wood, supra n. 13, chs. 8, 9, 13. For a discussion of this point in a more analytic mode, see Chapter 10, supra.

30. Since I believe that Wood's basic story is right, I do not think it worthwhile to extend my project further by writing up variations on his themes that have occurred to me in the course of my own research. I have thought it more profitable to concentrate my independent historical writing on Reconstruction and the New Deal. Since many of the crucial constitutional texts and debates in these periods are quite unknown or underappreciated, I will explore them at length in the next volume.

31. See supra n. 13.

32. Gordon Wood, supra n. 13, at 562 (emphasis supplied).

33. Compare Gordon Wood, "Interests and Disinterestedness in the Making of the Constitution," in Beeman, Botein, & Carter, *Beyond Confederation: Origins of the Constitution and American National Identity* 69 (1987) (Anti-Federalists as "men of the future"), with Cecilia Kenyon, "Men of Little Faith: The Anti-Federalists on the Nature of Representative Government," 12 *Wm. & Mary Q.* 3 (1955) (Anti-Federalists as backward-looking).

34. The political culture of Pennsylvania was far more democratic in spirit than those prevailing to the north and the south. Given their economic and social importance, the Pennsylvanians had surprisingly little influence on early politics (though it would be a mistake to ignore the contributions of particular individuals like Wilson and, later, Gallatin). The reasons for this relative weakness are worth puzzling over. See Henry Adams, *History of the United States of America During the First Administration of Thomas Jefferson 1801–1805*, ch. 4 (E. Harbart ed. 1986).

35. This theme is thoughtfully developed by Robert Wiebe, supra n. 6; see also Joyce Appleby, supra n. 13.

36. Wood himself emphasizes the distinctiveness and originality of Federalist thought. See, for example, Gordon Wood, supra n. 13, at 319, 342–43, 613–15. He only fails by questioning the Federalists' revolutionary good faith.

37. See Paul Kahn, *The End of Constitutional Theory*, ch. 3 (forthcoming, 1991).

38. Another important writer in this mode is Christopher Tiedemann, *The Unwritten Constitution of the United States* (1890).

39. See Chapter 4, pp. 84–85.

40. See, for example, Woodrow Wilson, *Congressional Government* (1885); Woodrow Wilson, *Constitutional Government in the United States* (1907).

41. Douglass Adair, "The Tenth Federalist Revisited," in Adair, supra n. 5, at 75.

42. In his *Economic Interpretation of the Constitution* (1913), Beard claimed that his economic view was "based upon the political science of James Madison . . . Those who are inclined to repudiate the hypothesis of economic determinism

as a European importation [i.e., Marxism] must therefore revise their views on learning that one of the earliest and certainly one of the clearest statements of it came from a profound student of politics who sat in the convention that framed our fundamental law." Id. at 14–16.

43. *Federalist* No. 10, at 84 (C. Rossiter ed. 1961).

44. See, for example, the passage quoted at n. 42, supra.

45. See Douglass Adair, "'That Politics May Be Reduced to a Science': David Hume, James Madison, and the Tenth Federalist," in Adair, supra n. 5, at 93.

46. See Chapter 7, pp. 187–188, 194.

47. So far as the revolutionaries were concerned, Hume the historian was at least as important as Hume the philosopher or political scientist. Increasingly, men like Jefferson and Adams came to view Hume's history of England as Tory "poison" that was corrupting a sound Whiggish understanding of the roots of the American Revolution. See Douglas Wilson, "Jefferson v. Hume," 46 *Wm. & Mary Q.* 27 (1989).

48. Adair, to his great credit, did not allow his enthusiasm for Hume to blind him to this side of the Founders. One of his most important papers reflects upon their extravagent pride in their revolutionary activity, their insatiable lust for fame: "the ruling passion of the noblest minds." Douglass Adair, "Fame and the Founding Fathers," in Adair, supra n. 5, at 3, 24. Taken by itself, the Founders' hubris is not precisely one of their most attractive characteristics—though Adair rightly suggests that their passion for fame does cast doubt upon Beard's picture of them as a bunch of hard-headed, tight-fisted folk on the lookout for Number One. Adair never got round to consider seriously the very un-Humean ideas of revolutionary virtue and legitimacy that redeemed—if anything did—the Founders' hubris.

49. Martin Diamond, "Democracy and *The Federalist:* A Reconsideration of the Framers' Intent," 53 *Am. Pol. Sci. Rev.* 52, 53 (1959). Like Adair, Diamond never managed to write the book that might have served to provide a comprehensive interpretation of the *Federalist.*

50. See his "The Revolution of Sober Expectations," in Irving Kristol, Martin Diamond, Warren Nutter, *The American Revolution: Three Views* 57 (1975). Diamond claims the Declaration of Independence "limited the dangerous passions of revolution only to the unmaking of a tyrannical government. It gave no license to new rulers to carry those revolutionary passions directly into the making of new government. That making of new government would have to find its way through still uncharted paths to be trod soberly and prudently." Id. at 70. Diamond would have us understand that the Federalists respected this remarkable limitation he finds in the Declaration—without, alas, confronting those *Federalist Papers* which explicitly speak in the Founders' revolutionary voice. See Chapter 7, pp. 173–175.

51. Martin Diamond, supra n. 13, contains the deepest statement of his views. A symposium on Diamond's thought may be found in "Dimensions of the Democratic Republic, A Memorial to Martin Diamond," 8 *Publius* 1 (Summer 1978).

52. See Chapter 7, pp. 188–190, supra.

53. Martin Diamond, supra n. 13. at 91.
54. Id. at 92.
55. Id. at 91.
56. See *Federalist* No. 10, supra n. 8, at 84.

9. Normal Politics

1. Garry Wills, *Cincinnatus: George Washington and the Enlightenment* (1984).
2. See Chapter 8, pp. 204–212.
3. This is the name adopted by a well-known organization founded by Nader.
4. Perhaps a note is in order concerning the derivation of this formula, which nowhere appears in the *Federalist Papers* in the manner precisely "quoted." I have derived it from Publius's definition of "faction" in *Federalist* No. 10: a group motivated by a passion or interest "adverse to the rights of other citizens, or to the permanent and aggregate interests of the community." *Federalist* No. 10, at 78 (J. Madison) (C. Rossiter ed. 1961). The formula in the text makes a positive out of this negative. I use the quotation marks (legitimately?) to suggest that this neo-Federalist definition has verbal roots in the *Federalist Papers* themselves.
5. Id.
6. Probably the most "philosophical" presentation of these views is to be found in James Buchanan, *The Limits of Liberty: Between Anarchy and Leviathan* (1975); James Buchanan & Gordon Tullock, *The Calculus of Consent* (1962); for an even cruder reductionism, see Gary Becker & George Stigler, "De Gustibus Non Est Disputandum," 67 *Am. Econ. Rev.* 76 (1977). This corrosive skepticism about citizenship is, predictably, beginning to have an impact upon legal scholarship. See, e.g., Frank Easterbrook, "Statutes Domains," 50 *U. Chi. L. Rev.* 533 (1983). For a useful corrective, see John Macey, "Promoting Public-Regarding Legislation Through Statutory Interpretation: An Interest Group Model," 86 *Colum. L. Rev.* 223 (1986).
7. For the classic statement, see Mancur Olson, Jr., *The Logic of Collective Action* (1962).
8. For a clear-eyed assessment of the failed efforts by clever modern scholars to explain to perfect privatists why they should vote, see Dennis Mueller, *Public Choice II* 351–53 (1989).
9. I am hardly the first to come to this conclusion. See, for example, Stanley Benn, "The Problematic Rationality of Political Participation," in Peter Laslett & James Fishkin, *Philosophy, Politics, & Society* 291 (1979); R. E. Goodin & K. W. S. Roberts, "The Ethical Voter," 69 *Am. Pol. Sci. Rev.* 926 (1975). There is, I think, a broadening appreciation of the need to move beyond the privatistic notion of the human subject generally presupposed by neo-classical economists. See Jon Elster, *Ulysses and the Sirens: Studies in Rationality and Irrationality* (1979); Amitai Etzioni, *The Moral Dimension: Toward a New Economics* (1988);

Albert Hirshman, *Shifting Involvements: Private Interest and Public Action* (1982); Howard Margolis, *Selfishness, Altruism, and Rationality* (1982); Amartya Sen, "Rational Fools: A Critique of the Behavioral Foundations of Economic Theory," 6 *J. Phil. & Pub. Af.* 324 (1977); Thomas Schelling, *Choice and Consequences* 52–112 (1984).

10. See Chapter 10, pp. 274–280, 285–288.

11. Turnout in Presidential elections might be increased by 15 percent if unnecessarily complex registration laws were eliminated. See Raymond Wolfinger & Steven Rosenstone, *Who Votes?* 88 (1980). Also, younger Americans vote significantly less than older ones. Ibid. at 105–108. Simply because the law allows people to vote at the age of eighteen, we should not be overly concerned if young people have trouble taking citizenship seriously—so long as they increasingly do so as they mature.

12. See Michael Kammen, *A Machine That Would Go of Itself: The Constitution in American Culture* (1986).

13. Candidates, in turn, will taken this failure in deliberation into account in defining their campaign strategies, leading to many of the pathologies discussed below. See R. Douglas Arnold, *The Logic of Congressional Action* (1990), for a thoughtful treatment.

14. For a seminal work representative of the "Michigan School," see Angus Campbell, Philip Converse, Warren Miller & Donald Stokes, *The American Voter* (1960); for a more philosophical discussion of studies in this genre, see Dennis Thompson, *The Democratic Citizen: Social Science and Democratic Theory in the Twentieth Century* (1970). Important studies emphasizing more rationalistic strains of voting behavior include: V. O. Key, Jr., *The Responsible Electorate* (1966); Morris Fiorina, *Retrospective Voting in American National Elections* (1981); Stanley Kelley, Jr., *Interpreting Elections* (1983); Arnold, supra n. 13.

15. This is a belated response to John Stuart Mill, who opposed the secret ballot because it would encourage each voter to believe that his vote was "for his own use and benefit to bestow simply as he feels inclined." John Stuart Mill, *Considerations on Representative Government* 195 (1861). Far better for each of us to cast his ballot in public, thereby requiring us to explain to our fellow citizens why our vote is in the public interest. See Andreas Teuber, *The Reformation of Public Life: The Case Against the Secret Ballot* (forthcoming).

I think Mill was right in warning about the dangers of privatization that follow upon the modern custom of secrecy in balloting. The only question is whether these dangers are outweighed by the dangers of coercion and corruption that open balloting makes possible. Since I believe the dangers of openness generally (but not universally) outweigh the dangers of secrecy, I do not advocate a change in our existing practices. Mill's point, however, serves to support my emphasis upon the "softness" of the normal secret ballot, and the need to design a dualist constitution which keeps this "softness" in mind.

16. *Federalist* No. 10, supra n. 4, at 80. For a recent essay in this spirit, see R. Douglas Arnold, supra. n. 13.

17. See Charles Lindblom, *Politics and Markets,* pt. 5 (1975).

18. While I favor campaign reform, I think that many "reform" proposals are counterproductive. I cannot do justice to this subject in a footnote, but hope to make some serious proposals sometime soon.

19. The classic work is David Mayhew, *Congress: The Electoral Connection* (1974).

20. See Chapter 7, pp. 186–188.

21. These pathologies are usefully dissected in recent works by political economists organized around the concept of "rent-seeking," intelligently surveyed by Dennis Mueller, supra n. 8, at ch. 13. Unfortunately, this literature suffers from a strong reductionist tendency to suppose that normal political action is exclusively motivated by the perfectly privatistic impulses that lead to pathological rent-seeking. This cynical view of politics unsurprisingly leads some to advocate the destruction of the modern activist state as the only hope for curing the pathology. See, for example, Geoffrey Brennan & James Buchanan, *The Power to Tax: Analytical Foundations of a Fiscal Constitution* (1980). Since I reject this black-and-white view of normal politics, I do not subscribe to such extreme solutions. Instead, the challenge (unmet by this chapter) is to design modern structures that will keep rent-seeking under control while allowing politician/statesmen reasonable leeway to legislate for the public good. See, e.g., Susan Rose-Ackerman, *Corruption: A Study in Political Economy* (1978).

22. Important works include those by Anthony Downs, *Inside Bureaucracy* (1967); William Niskanen, *Bureaucracy and Representative Government* (1971); Douglas Arnold, *Congress and the Bureaucracy: A Theory of Influence* (1979).

23. In addition to sources cited in n. 22, supra, see Morris Fiorina, *Congress: Keystone of the Washington Establishment* (1977); James Wilson, *The Politics of Regulation,* ch. 10 (1980). For an important comparative study, see Mancur Olson, *The Rise and Decline of Nations: Economic Growth, Stagflation, and Social Rigidities* (1982).

24. See Sidney Verba & Norman Nie, *Participation in America: Political Democracy and Social Equality* (1972).

25. For a fine treatment, see Murray Edelman, *The Symbolic Uses of Politics* (1964).

26. My distinction between the role of parties in normal and constitutional politics tracks the distinction between "great" and "small" parties developed by Alexis de Tocqueville, 1 *Democracy in America,* ch. 10 (Bradley ed. 1945). For a contemporary discussion emphasizing the "small" side, see Martin Wattenberg, *The Decline of American Political Parties, 1952–1984* (1986).

27. As Richard Fenno puts it:

> [What Congressmen] do is well known and straightforward. They allocate the tasks of their staffs in ways they think helpful in getting reelected. They choose committee assignments they think will bring identification with and benefit to their supportive constituencies. They vote in ways they think will be approved by their supportive constitutents. Or, better, they avoid voting in ways they believe will be intensely disapproved by their supportive constitutents. . . .

Richard Fenno, *Home Style* 224–25 (1978). See also Morris Fiorina & David Rohde, eds., *Home Style and Washington Work: Studies of Congressional Politics* (1989).

28. See Arthur Maass, *Congress and the Public Good* (1983); Steven Kelman, *Making Public Policy: A Hopeful View of American Government* (1987); R. Douglas Arnold, supra n. 13.

29. See Chapter 1, pp. 7–10; Chapter 2, pp. 35–36; Chapter 4, pp. 84–85.

30. For a classic statement, see American Political Science Association, Committee on Political Parties, "Toward a More Responsible Two-Party System," 44 *Am. Pol. Sci. Rev.* (Supplement 1950). The history of this school's central ideas is elaborated by Austin Ranney, *The Doctrine of Responsible Party Government* (1956).

31. While the text reports the received British theory, modern British practice is evolving in a direction that portends an emergent recognition of a two-level lawmaking system. Within the last generation, special referenda have been held on three occasions: in 1973, the residents of Northern Ireland were polled to determine whether they wished to remain part of the United Kingdom; in 1979, residents of Scotland and Wales rejected proposals for devolution of political authority; most importantly, in 1975 all residents of the United Kingdom voted to endorse Britain's continued membership in the European Economic Community.

   Although the results of these "advisory" referenda were not technically binding on Parliament, they were generally perceived as expressions of popular will that were more authoritative than normal parliamentary modes of lawmaking. Given the role of precedent in the British constitution, these referenda may well shape future practice. Indeed, in 1978 a Conservative Committee on the Referendum recommended the introduction of a Constitution (Fundamental Provisions) Bill "which would provide for a referendum before any fundamental change in the Constitution occurs." Philip Norton, *The Constitution in Flux* 215 (1982). So far this initiative has failed to gain parliamentary support. For a historical analysis of the introduction of the referendum into British politics, see Vernon Bogdanor, *The People and the Party System* 1–93 (1981).

32. See David Mayhew, supra n. 19; Morris Fiorina, supra n. 23.

33. For a recent essay relevant to this question, see Terry Moe, "Political Institutions: The Neglected Side of the Story," 6 *J. Law, Econ., & Org.* (forthcoming, 1990).

34. See, for example, James Sundquist, *Constitutional Reform and Effective Government* (1986). This is not the place, alas, to assess the particular reform proposals made by Sundquist and others.

35. I am focusing on the British system, which, like the American, creates great pressures for the formation of two, but only two, political parties. A comparison with Continental systems that encourage multiple parties, through proportional representation and similar devices, is quite different and will have to wait for another time.

36. See Chapter 7, pp. 183–186, supra.

37. See, for example, John Kingdon, *Agendas, Alternatives and Public Policies* (1984).
38. See James Buchanan & Gordon Tullock, *The Calculus of Consent* (1962).
39. See John Ely, *Democracy and Distrust,* ch. 6 (1980).
40. See Chapters 2–5.
41. See Chapter 3, pp. 68–69. Other important questions include the use of the legislative veto and executive orders. Beyond these particular issues lie deeper ones: the status of the bureaucracy as the "fourth branch" of government, the appropriate balance of power in the conduct of foreign relations . . .
42. See Chapter 1, pp. 7–10.
43. A. Bickel, *The Least Dangerous Branch* 17 (2d ed. 1986).

10. Higher Lawmaking

1. See Chapter 2, pp. 52–56.
2. See Chapter 9, pp. 236–243.
3. See Chapter 9, pp. 234–235.
4. Recall that Americans who are perfect privatists will not even find it worthwhile to go to the polls. See Chapter 9, pp. 236–237, supra. Consequently, we need not worry about how their (nonexistent) votes should be counted.
5. For a useful introduction to these puzzles, see Allan Feldman, *Welfare Economics and Social Choice Theory,* chs. 9–11 (1980). For a more advanced discussion and review of the burgeoning literature, see Dennis Mueller, *Public Choice II* (1989); Amartya Sen, *Collective Choice and Social Welfare* (1970) (very intelligent, but obsolescent).
6. See Allan Feldman, supra n. 5, ch. 9.
7. See Chapters 2–5.
8. For ease of exposition, I have spoken as if the thoughtful dualist would set a simple rule specifying the breadth and depth of popular support required for signaling. This is obviously an oversimplification, which should be corrected in a more elaborate analysis.
9. Or so I shall argue in the next volume.
10. See Chapters 4–6.
11. See my proposal in Chapter 2, pp. 52–56.
12. Up to the present, neither the classical nor the modern system has adopted the favorite higher lawmaking technique used in many American states and foreign countries: the formal referendum. To some extent, this reflects the fact that the referendum was in its infancy at the time of the Founding. So far as I can tell, only the Swiss were then using the device—see Benjamin Barber, *The Death of Communal Liberty* 180–94 (1974)—and I have not found any evidence that the Founders considered such a technique. For them, the People could be best consulted through specially elected constitutional conventions. See Chapter 7, pp. 174–175, supra. While Swiss-style higher lawmaking would sweep the world in the next two centuries, it has not led Americans to break with their Federalist

predecessors on this point. Although I think the time has come for the cautious assimilation of referenda into our higher lawmaking practice (see Chapetr 2, pp. 52–56), this is a large question deserving careful treatment at a later stage in the argument. See volume 2, *Transformations.*

13. In addition to requiring a movement to demonstrate legislative support on a number of occasions over time, the constitutional system may also test for decisiveness by insisting upon super-majority levels of legislative support: it is harder to win a two-thirds vote by strategic manipulation of Condorcet-style paradoxes than it is to win a simple majority vote.

　　Some recent formal work in social choice theory clarifies this basic intuition about super-majority rule. Andrew Caplin and Barry Nalebuff have proved that, under a wide variety of plausible configurations of voter preference, an option that wins 64 percent of the vote is sure to be a Condorcet-winner. See Andrew Caplin and Barry Nalebuff, "64% Majority Rule," 56 *Econometrica* 787 (1988); Andrew Caplin and Barry Nalebuff, "Aggregation and Social Choice: A Mean Voter Theorem," *Econometrica* (forthcoming, 1991).

14. See Chapter 4, pp. 94–103; Chapter 5, pp. 113–130; Chapter 6, pp. 140–162.

11. Why Dualism?

1. For further elaboration, see Chapter 9, pp. 232–235.
2. See Chapter 9, pp. 233–234, for further remarks on perfect privatism.
3. See Richard Stewart, "The Reformation of American Administrative Law," 88 *Harv. L. Rev.* 1667 (1975). In addition to this three-track system on the national level, an additional set of lawmaking tracks are established at the state level.
4. See Chapters 7–8.
5. See Frank Michelman, "Foreword: Traces of Self-Government," 100 *Harv. L. Rev.* 4, 36–55 (1986); J. G. A. Pocock, *The Machiavellian Moment: Florentine Political Thought and the Atlantic Republican Tradition,* pt. 3 (1975); Gordon Wood, *The Creation of the American Republic* (1969); and Chapters 7–8.
6. For example, I have seen President Bush claim that the People had given him a "mandate" to reduce the capital gains tax from 28 to 18 percent!
7. See Chapter 4, pp. 101–102; Chapter 5, pp. 129–130; Chapter 6, pp. 140–162.
8. See Chapter 9, pp. 240–251; Chapter 10, pp. 272–280.
9. I myself have never been enamored by the principle of consent, at least when it is used to serve as the bedrock of political life. See my *Social Justice in the Liberal State* 336–42 (1980). For present purposes, however, I am happy to put my reservations to one side if this helps make dualism seem sensible to some of my fellow citizens.
10. See, e.g., Anthony Kronman, *Living in the Law,* ch. 1 (forthcoming, 1992).
11. This tendency is pronounced amongst Straussians. See the discussion of Martin Diamond in Chapter 8, pp. 224–227.
12. See Joseph Schumpeter, *Capitalism, Socialism and Democracy,* chs. 21–22 (1942).
13. Schumpeter is cautious here, emphasizing only the role of regular elections in preserving freedom of speech:

> If, on principle at least, everyone is free to compete for political leadership by presenting himself to the electorate, this will in most cases though not in all mean a considerable amount of freedom of discussion *for all* . . . This relation between democracy and freedom is not absolutely stringent and can be tampered with. But, from the standpoint of the intellectual, it is nevertheless very important. At the same time, it is all there is to that relation.

Joseph Schumpeter, supra n. 12, at 271–72. For a contemporary argument in the Schumpeterian spirit, see William Riker, *Liberalism against Populism* (1982).

14. See Robert Dahl, *Who Governs? Democracy and Power in an American City* (1961); Robert Dahl, *Polyarchy: Participation and Opposition* (1971). Over time, a skeptical theme has became more prominent in Dahl's work. See, for example, Robert Dahl, "On Removing Certain Impediments to Democracy in the United States," 92 *Pol. Sci. Q.* 1 (1977); Robert Dahl, *Dilemmas of Pluralist Democracy* (1982).

15. For a fine essay in this genre, see John Gaventa, *Power and Powerlessness: Quiescence and Rebellion in an Appalachian Valley* (1980).

16. See Chapter 5, pp. 127–129, discussed at greater length in my "Beyond Carolene Products," 98 *Harv. L. Rev.* 713 (1985).

17. The journal *Public Choice* regularly displays a representative sample of this group's work. The intellectual leaders of this group include James Buchanan, Gary Becker, Gordon Tullock, and George Stigler. See, for example, Gary Becker, "A Theory of Competition Among Pressure Groups for Political Influence," 98 *Q. J. Econ.* 371 (1983); Geoffrey Brennan & James Buchanan, *The Power to Tax: Analytical Foundations of a Fiscal Constitution* (1980); James Buchanan & Gordon Tullock, *The Calculus of Consent* (1962); James Buchanan, Robert Tollison, & Gordon Tullock, *Toward a Theory of the Rent-Seeking Society* (1980); George Stigler, *The Citizen and the State: Essays on Regulation* (1975). For economistic explorations of the limits of self-interest in politics, see Joseph Kalt & Mark Zupan, "Capture and Ideology in the Economic Theory of Politics," 74 *Am. Econ. Rev.* 279 (1984).

18. For a sensitive discussion, see Charles Taylor, *Sources of the Self* (1989).

19. John Rawls, *A Theory of Justice* (1971).

20. This is the approach suggested by John Rawls, "Kantian Constructivism in Moral Theory," 77 *J. Phil.* 515 (1980).

21. Bruce Ackerman, *Social Justice in the Liberal State* (1980).

22. For my own approach, see Bruce Ackerman, supra n. 21, pt. 3.; Ackerman, supra n. 16.

23. See Chapter 1, pp. 15–16.

Index

Library of Congress Cataloging in Publication Data

Ackerman, Bruce A.
We the people / Bruce Ackerman.
p.   cm.
Includes bibliographical references and index.
Partial Contents: 1. Foundations.
ISBN 0-674-94840-8 (alk. paper)
1. United States—Constitutional history. 2. United States—
Constitutional law.   I. Title.
KF4541.A8   1991
342.73'029—dc20
[347.30229]

91-10725
CIP